Dedication

This book is for Patsy,
the Love of my Life

WATER UNDER THE KEEL

An autobiography of forty-one years at sea

Captain David Littlejohn Beveridge
Master Mariner

Glasgow
MMXII

WATER UNDER THE KEEL

First published in Great Britain in 2012

Copyright © David Littlejohn Beveridge MMXII

David Littlejohn Beveridge
59, West Coats Road
Cambuslang
Glasgow
Scotland

ACKNOWLEDGEMENTS

I would not have had much of a life without my parents.

I am deeply indebted, both to them, and to the benign Providence which, in the most unlikely circumstances brought them together, gave them a love for one another which lasted their entire lives, and ensured that my upbringing was firm, trustworthy, and enjoyable, grounded in hope, love and faith. They each contributed hugely to my understanding of these virtues in their own ways and laid the foundations for my life that was to be, but it was my mother who first taught me the meaning of unconditional love.

I must record my thanks to my first employers T&J Brocklebanks of Liverpool. They gave me a profession and by virtue of the nature of their business, took me to places both exotic and exciting. Above all I thank them for training me to be a seaman, for without that training I could never have been involved in protecting the fisheries of Scotland.

When I left deep sea sailing I was a Master Mariner and fully equipped to take on the demands of my next and last employer, the Department of Agriculture and Fisheries for Scotland. I am profoundly grateful to the Department and later the Scottish Fisheries Protection Agency for the opportunities which were offered to me and the trust which was placed in me by the leaders of these organisations. The work I was given enriched and informed much of my life.

I must record my indebtedness to the hundreds (perhaps thousands) of shipmates with whom it has been my privilege to serve, for all, in ways both large and small have also moulded me. As I review the years I can recall very few who were less than kindly disposed to me. I have related some names from the period when I was sailing with Brocklebanks, but I am not permitted to name any personnel from my time with the Fisheries. So I will just thank them all most sincerely for their camaraderie, support and friendship.

I will however specifically mention Captain Scott Horsburgh, Marine Superintendent of what is now Marine Scotland Compliance, who kindly read and checked the memoir as it pertained to the Scottish Fisheries. He shared with me in many adventures, both as my First Officer, and my partner captain. I will also name Allison Duncan of HR, who took the trouble to read the memoir and gave permission for its publication.

I have spoken about Michael Leek MA MPhil (RCA) FRSA who accompanied me on one of my last patrols. He has not only designed the cover of my book and provided the cover photograph (showing the *Jura* approaching St Kilda in 2007), but has helped and guided me in innumerable ways most generously. I now regard him as my friend indeed.

I must thank my son-in-law, Dominic Brown BA PGCE MEd, who proof read my memoir. He painstakingly repaired my flawed grammar, corrected my appalling spelling and generally kept me from running aground on the shoals of literary incompetence. He has also written me a synopsis for showing the book to a wider cadre of publishers for I found myself incapable of achieving an acceptable degree of detachment from the subject - namely me!

I salute my family who from ancient times, through the present and into the future, provide the beacons whereby I am able to plot my position in time and space.

My penultimate thanks go to Patsy my wife. She is the Pole Star of my life, the living hearth of my love. She holds the warm life of my hopes and aspirations in her care, and nourishes them with her love.

Lastly I bless Almighty God without whom none of this would have been possible.

CONTENTS

Chapter 1   1949 – 1954
Chapter 2   1954 – 1960
Chapter 3   1961 – 1966
Chapter 4   1966 – 1978 – *Mangla and Maturata*
Chapter 5   *Lucellum*
Chapter 6   *Lucigen*
Chapter 7   *Mahronda – Lucellum* Reprise 1
Chapter 8   *Luxor*
Chapter 9   I obtain my Second Mate's foreign Going Certificate
Chapter10   *Port Victor*
Chapter 11   *Lucigen* for a second time – I obtain my First Mates Foreign
                Going Certificate
Chapter 12   I return to *Luxor* as First Mate – *Lucellum* Reprise 2 – *Luxor*
                continued
Chapter 13   *Lustrous*
Chapter 14   *Lumen*
Chapter 15   *Lumiere*
Chapter 16   *Lustrous and Luminous*
Chapter 17   The new *Lucellum* – I obtain my Master's Foreign Going
                Certificate
Chapter 18   Container Ships
Chapter 19   Scottish Fisheries 1978 – 1983 – *Sw150ltha – Westra- Jura*
Chapter 20   *Scotia – Westra* 2nd *time*
Chapter 21   Domestic Aside 1
Chapter 22   *Westra* First trip in command
Chapter 23   *Scotia* 2nd *time* – St. Kilda recollections – Enforcement in 1983
Chapter 24   1983 – 1985 – *Morven* – Brief digression to *Westra* – Back to
                Morven – A bad storm at Lamlash in Arran – Illegal herring
                boats – Domestic Aside 2 – Back to *Morven*
Chapter 25   1985 – 1987 – *Jura* 3rd *time* – *Vigilant* (The fourth of that name)
Chapter 26   I become a Sea Captain
Chapter 27   *Jura 4th time* 1987 – 1988
Chapter 28   *Westra* 1988 – 1991 – The old Superintendent retires – EEC

	Inspectors – Emergency Landing – Rescue of *Protect Me* –
	FOGBOUND! – Sunday off in St. Kilda
Chapter 29	*Vigilant* 1991 – 2000 – *Port King* –The Caley Davit
Chapter 30	Domestic Aside 3 – My Father's Patrol
Chapter 31	*Lesivy*- New Year in Lerwick – *Swift*
Chapter 32	*Girl Maureen*
Chapter 33	*St. Carolus* – Mother and Daughter - *Skua*
Chapter 34	Customs Operation "Muckle Flugga"
Chapter 35	H.M.Customs Appraisal Patrol
Chapter 36	1998 – 2000 – Various Adventures – *Eclipse and Navigante*
	Magellenes – *Iroise* – *Boston Argosy* – *Du Couedic* – Three Men in
	a Boat – Assistance rendered to *Tenacious*
Chapter 37	Customs Operation "Yuletide" – Promotions Boards
Chapter 38	*Norna* 2000 – 2005 – Efficiency Gains and Cost Cutting
	Exercises – *Tahume* –Assistance rendered to *Harvest Reaper* –
	NORNA NEWS – The rescue of the crew of the *Aurelia* – The
	International Festival of the Sea 23-26 August 2001 – FIRE! –
	Croix Morand –2003 – Assistance rendered to yacht *Clione* –
	Skerryvore – *Bruix*
Chapter 39	A Mixture of Topics Recovering Junk – Digital Cameras,
	NEAFC – Island Hopping – Learning the Great Highland
	Bagpipe – Jo Borg, European Fisheries Commissioner –
	Assistance rendered to *Russa Taign*
Chapter 40	The new *Jura* 2005 – 2007 – A Mission to Denmark – Visitors
	and Junkets – Return to the Clyde – Last Patrol

FOREWORD

I am writing this account for my descendants, because children have lousy memories. I don't mean they remember bad things, which they do, I mean they remember badly.

You tell them things and they listen with half an ear. The information gets processed and then in time, regurgitated in a form which is barely recognisable. Somehow it gets altered in the family hard drive, and what comes out is not what went in. I suppose all parents experience this in some form or another. For example, I recall my wife had revealed she worked briefly as a post code checker in Tennant's Brewery in Glasgow, to make some spending money, during the summer holidays from university. After due process in the corporate cerebellum of our children, she had become a whiskey taster who consumed prodigious amounts of the product as she attempted to blend the perfect libation. We have an old tape, I think, of the children playing at news broadcasters, (this was a favourite game of theirs many years ago), in which she was reported in their news flash as a famous connoisseur of blended Scotch whisky. My wife has never taken any alcohol except communion wine, having sworn an oath of abstinence as a Pioneer through the good offices of the Catholic Church.

On another occasion she foolishly recalled that she had had a summer job working as a waitress in a highland hotel in Pitlochry. Whilst there, she and some of the staff (she tells me it was the female staff) had gone for a swim in the loch near the hotel, one night after work. I expect it was very exciting, swimming in the loch, in the dark, on a warm summer's evening, luxuriating in the cold water after a hard day running after tourists from the north of England. I am sure, knowing her, it was delightful, innocent fun, a happy prelude to what would become a life of unselfish and unremitting toil for her family. Our intrepid newscasters, however, on the same tape, had turned it into a night of whisky-induced, skinny dipping, and orgiastic Highland, debauchery. Am I being naïve here? Maybe the youngsters have a point.

Anyway I've made a start on this account to set the record straight as I see it, and so I begin...

To

Carl-Erik Carlsen

from

A
Captain David L. Beveridge.

3rd December 2019.

wishing you every blessing
in Christ Jesus.

CHAPTER ONE
1949 – 1954

I was born on Saint Patrick's Day, the seventeenth of March, 1949 in the fishing village of Rosehearty on the Moray Firth, in 23 Bruckley Street, in the front bedroom of my grandmother's house.

In those days children were, more often than not, born at home, especially in rural areas, and my mother told me that she was in labour for about 24 hours. My father, who was a marine engineer to trade, was at the fishing, on my Uncle George Ritchie's boat the *Maracaibo*, named after the lake of that name in South America. I believe they had adopted the name when they visited the place, serving together as engineers, during the war, on a tanker called the *Regent Panther*.

That's the Second World War.

I don't know why, but I have always been intensely proud of my birth certificate. It says I was born in Rosehearty in the district of Pitsligo, in the county of Aberdeen. To me it says you come from a sea place where people are intimately connected to the sea. A place of great antiquity where your roots go back to the Picts, where somehow you have in your genetic makeup an innate understanding of the land and the sea and that this, out of all the places you could have been born, is where you belong. The only other place I encountered a remotely similar feeling was Jutland, but I think I was just being fanciful.

My earliest memories are of feeling safe because I was surrounded by love and faith. My grandmother existed within an atmosphere of faith and carried on a running dialogue with God. She passed this awareness of God to all her children, including my mother and to me. Most of my cousins have the same tendency. In my grandmother's house when there was a shortage of money, or a crisis of any kind, we were always brought to prayer and I am glad to say I have carried on in that way and so I believe have my children, in their own ways.

When I look into that place in my mind where you look for visual memories, actual pictorial recollections, I see a house which was built for the sole purpose of yielding every minute particle of dust and dirt to the therapeutic power of Sunlight Soap, Mansion house polish and bleach. The smells still permeate the backwaters of my mind and the whiff of their modern equivalent conjures up warm recollections.

I remember home-made rag rugs which were constructed out of rags, (yes, rags) and old sugar bags. They were meant to be fireside rugs but, under the lubricating influence of the aforementioned polish on the linoleum, they invariably migrated in all directions until they fetched up on some domestic shore like a dead dog against a table leg or skirting board. You could belly flop on them and they slid for great distances, but that was later. I remember the smell of home-made soup, scones, potatoes and fish, usually salt herring, boiling in a pot – on the fire! Yes, my grandmother was very old school and you didn't light a fire without putting it to good use. Of course the fires were built for the task, being iron ranges. This memory goes deep inside me and it is still one of my great pleasures, to sit in front of a fire and cook something, or nothing.

On the other hand one of my earliest memories is of being burnt by a piece of eggshell which sparked from the same fire and occasioned much weeping and anguish on my part, until appropriately bribed and consoled. I have the mark to this day. And then there were the twin delights of Tytlers butteries, a species of what you might call a heavy duty croissant, but with much more body and better able to set you up for work, and Doddy Fytie's (George White's) ice cream. It seems to me that from the beginning they loomed large in my league of things most enjoyable in this world, and I cannot begin to describe either of them with any true sensory justice. Suffice it to say I have wandered the world in search of a proper replacement for both and found none.

You will notice that my father has not appeared much so far, and that is because he was at sea at the fishing and appeared sporadically, it seemed to me, although when he did come home it was a cause of great happiness and completeness. He was a hero figure for me but you will hear more about him later.

So far I have related notions gleaned from the first two years of my life, which for me would always reside in a quiet place in my mind to provide a yardstick for peace, I suppose. However things were about to undergo a radical change when poor results at the fishing forced my father to seek work in London.

Our migration to London in 1951, although not remembered in great detail, conjures up images of steam, the smell of coal smoke, a dimly lit sleeper carriage and a departure from everything that meant peace and security. I have no recollection of how they obtained lodgings, but my parents and I fetched up in the top flat of 76 Wandsworth Bridge Road, London. (I am tempted to end that with the words 'South West One'). Could that be true? It might be because my parents were quite keen that I should not be lost in the nation's capital and may well have indoctrinated me accordingly.

What shall we say about this time? The lodgings were formed out of a top floor flat comprising a kitchen/living room, a toilet and tiny box bedroom, and an attic at the top of a single flight of stairs. My parents slept in the attic and I in the box bedroom. Between the door of my bedroom and the first step of the attic stairs stood the dustbin. I recall one occasion when one of our fish from the small aquarium my father lovingly built, a catfish, as ugly a creature as ever drew breath through gills, died. My father unceremoniously dumped the carcass in an empty Heinz bean tin in the dustbin. I did not shed a tear for the deceased leviathan (it was big to me) but that night I woke with a bad dream and needed parental comfort. Of course I must pass the corpse of the ghastly catfish to get to the stair to my parents.

Picture the scene, a Victorian style house, a landing lit by a skylight which permitted only the glare of the street lights and the huge loom of London. It was the first time I had been challenged by a frightening situation and yet I can remember thinking the problem through. The fish was dead, or was it? Might it not be pretending, waiting to latch onto a tiny child? After all catfish have teeth which turn in towards the gullet and can only be released with great difficulty. And *I knew that!* I weighed all this up and can vividly remember making the decision to risk running past the horror and nip smartly up the stair, before the brute could snare me. I felt pride and elation when I reached the safety of my parents' bed and had learned something about myself which has remained with me to this day. Stay calm, evaluate the information and put the rest down to moral fibre. The catfish was not resurrected.

As I say, my father had come to London for work. He was a fine marine engineer and skilful craftsman and managed to obtain a place with the engineering firm Barrimars. They specialised in repairing the large broken components of big marine engines, but one of the jobs my father was involved in particularly interested me. It was a large and very old cannon and I recall him explaining to me the complexity of dealing with old metal. Of course I do not remember the technical stuff but the fact that my father was involved in the job made me proud. He must have been well thought of because when Barrimars produced an advertisement for the trade my father was on front of it.

London gradually became more acceptable, but it was never home, and every opportunity was taken to 'get back up north', usually on my father's 'Red Indian' motorcycle. These were enormous journeys to undertake with a young child, but they did it with the aid of a side car and a tarpaulin. I slept in the side car and they under the tarpaulin, so great was the yearning to get home. I suppose I became pretty spoiled because I was the only child, and I have happy memories of visits to the London parks, and museums, the 'funnies' (which was what we called the cartoon cinema), and caravan holidays in Hayling Island and day trips to Brighton.

On the other hand my mother was no push-over and to this day I remember having my backside smacked in the Northend Road for allegedly stealing a chestnut from a bag which was on display outside the fruit shop. The shopkeeper had complained about the three-year-old running his fingers through the chestnuts. My mother had responded by whisking me away complete with an unreleased nut, mouthing Doric curses upon the head of the unsuspecting Cockney. Only when we had gone some distance down the road was the offending nut discovered, and I can still see it spinning out on to the road as she shook my hand. I had unintentionally committed a crime of enormous proportions and would suffer accordingly. No child of hers would be a thief, hence the thrashing. It was only when she realised that the nut was not stolen but inadvertently removed that she calmed down. I assumed the role righteous martyr, to my great benefit. The lesson stuck and I have never stolen anything in my life.

I have a powerful memory of the death of Queen Mary 'the old queen' and saw her funeral cortège. The day was grey and black. There are three other things I can recall from my time in London. On one night we were all evacuated from the house by the police who were chasing a criminal across the roofs of the houses. All the residents of our area had to muster in the street and we could see the police running across the slates. It was very exciting and I was quite prepared to defend us with my toy cowboy gun.

The Queen, Elizabeth II, came to the throne in 1952 and we were all invited to a street party. It was huge and there are photographs to prove it. I think we had a happy time and my own contribution to the celebrations was to sing to the assembled crowd 'Home on the Range' wearing my cowboy outfit complete with the aforementioned gun.

Then there was the SMOG. In the winter of 1953, when I was four years old, a large area of high pressure lay over the south-east of England. For days there was hardly a breath of wind to stir the frosty air, with the result that the smoke which poured freely into the atmosphere remained swirling in the air above London with nothing to dissipate it. The density of the air thickened and thickened until the natural fog which formed in the anticyclone became laden with the noxious fumes from London's chimneys and the result was the thickest fog imaginable. It was so thick they coined a name for it – SMOG. I have a clear memory of going with my mother from the corner of the front garden of the house we lived in to the shop adjacent to it. The smog, like very thick smoke, prevented us seeing more than a couple of feet and breathing was difficult. On our return we missed the gate! It was very unsettling. This was before the Clean Air Act and everywhere was grimy and dark compared to now.

At last the yearning to return to Scotland became irresistible for my parents and my father was invited to work with my grandfather in his garage and hire drive business. I remember our return much more clearly than the journey to London three years before. Still, there was the smell of smoke and steam, the clatter of the wheels on the rails; but a brighter carriage and more detail. I particularly remember the fish I told you about before, being carried in a large green five gallon tin, and the water slopping up the sides when we braked or rumbled over the points.

CHAPTER TWO
1954 – 1960

I do not know what I was expecting from Glasgow, aged 5, but I never found it. Not even after all these years. I suppose it will always be for me a place of convenience on the way to my spiritual home, despite the fact that almost all of my happiest memories were experienced there.

Anyway, my parents obtained a flat in the top story of 43 Exeter Drive in Partick, thanks to my Great Uncle Dan, who was a lawyer. He owned a lot of property including this flat. The accommodation consisted of a 'Room and Kitchen'. That was how you described it. The 'Room' should have been a bed-sitting room, but it became my bedroom and I loved it because the windows were set into the very top tower of the tenement. For me it instantly became a castle keep. My father built a Captain's bunk bed in the bed recess and I was delighted. My poor parents slept in the kitchen in a bed settee called a 'Put you up'.

We had no hot water for quite some time; baths for me, which occurred once a week, were taken in front of the kitchen coal fire, with water heated on the stove. Only after my sister Pamela arrived in 1956 did we aspire to a papier mâché bath which was hers, but which we all used. On the other hand we had an inside toilet, unlike the two closes adjacent to us, and considered ourselves fortunate.

My parents between them made the flat very cosy and comfortable, my mother doing the wallpapering and my father the painting and woodwork. That was a division of labour which would last the rest of their lives.

When Pamela arrived I was delighted, and regarded her as very precious and someone to be protected. As she grew she would assert her own identity which was profoundly independent, so much so that when I was despatched to bring her in from play it always ended up with her clawing and scratching and kicking as she tried to escape the call to return home. I always found her, and brought her home, but it was always a bloody affair. For me!

I joined Thornwood Primary at the age of five and a half because I had missed the earlier intake. We lived very close to the school, in fact I don't suppose it was more than 200 yards away, and I cannot ever remember looking forward to going to school. I did not enjoy it. My first teacher was called Miss

Montgomery and she trim, well turned out, smelled of cigarette smoke and had a dearth of patience it seemed to me. I was not temperamentally inclined to be disobedient or to put in less than my best effort but I constantly performed below my best. I sometimes think that was how it was for me throughout primary school, always somewhere around the top third but never the best I could be. No excuses, that's just the way it was. I attended that school for seven years and as I recall the old feelings again it seems as if I dwelt under a cloud.

Several things I do remember, though.

Once, on one of the few occasions I remained in school during the lunch break, my pal Ian MacKeller and I were playing in the infants' playground. There was no one else there, and it started to snow. We had been wishing for snow for weeks and here it was, large as life. Of course we roared around the playground like lunatics revelling in this magical substance which transformed (and continues to transform) and elevate the winter for me, into something ethereal and mystical. Miss Bailey the Head Mistress however, was a woman of less imaginative mind set. The window of the staff room shot up like a well prepared guillotine and her strident call penetrated the erstwhile joyous atmosphere. We were summoned to her room. Our hearts instantly sank and fear unmanned us as we processed like condemned criminals to her lair. The door threw open to reveal a woman who clearly been successful in working herself into a frenzy of indignation and righteous fury. Had I known about them at the time I would have likened her to a Dominican priest of the Inquisition about to try some poor heretic by fire for water-divining or some other ludicrous charge.

There was no trial. We were guilty of the heinous sin of screaming at the snow and now we must pay for such a display of dangerous emotion. She belted us with the tawse several times. I got it first and eventually dissolved in tears of shame. It was not that it was so painful, it just degrading and dishonourable. Ian McKellar did not cry and I admired his courage in the face of unbridled anger, although I was able to rationalise this by the fact that I had stepped up first, taken the first blast of her spleen, and that he clearly had a less highly developed sense of honour. And I was softer.

They taught us how to write in Copperplate. 'Light up heavy down and do not take your pen off the page until the word is complete'. We had a subject named 'Dictation', which involved the teacher reading out some passage from a book which we had to copy in our best handwriting using an ink pen. Not a fountain pen; a piece of stick with a steel nib on the end. There was a whole liturgy to this lesson which began with getting out the tray of small porcelain inkwells. The inkwells were then filled using a bottle with a specialised pourer, prior to being distributed to each child's desk, to be placed in a perfectly fitting holder, like communion wine in a Presbyterian Church. Only the elect could carry out this task, most of us fell far short of the necessary degree of grace. I remember Anne Jackson and Julia MacDonald were superlative in this field, and indeed Anne went on to become a Church of Scotland minister. I don't know what happened to Julia; she came from the Highlands and had a truly lovely nature. Anyway we then all sat there doing our best to follow the formula, like neophyte monks copying the Book of Kells. I eventually became quite good at it in later life, and took great pride in writing up fair copy ship's logbooks in lovely copperplate, but not in Primary. 'Could do better, must try harder'.

They taught us very well in fact. By the time we left to go to the Secondary School we could all read, write, count and had a very good general knowledge of our own country (Great Britain) and the rest of the world. We were taught History and Geography in a very structured and thoroughly biased way but it did give good general overview, albeit a skewed one.

I was always pretty good at art, and I was always interested in the opposite sex. One afternoon, our class was joined to another for some reason, making the total number of children about 70. I and some of my pals ended up at the back of the class well away from the teacher's immediate field of vision. We were secretly discussing female anatomy and I was explaining my own anatomical findings with the aid of a sketch, to my pals. Unfortunately, whilst my friends had been suitably discreet, some clown from the other class looked over and let out a yelp when he saw my drawing. It was quite a good drawing in a childish way, and perfectly recognisable. Of course the teacher realised something was afoot and bore down on me with searchlight stare. I tried in vain to scribble across the image as she roared to me 'Come out here that boy [she did not know my name] and bring that piece of paper'.

There is a kind of fatalistic peace which comes over you when you realise that there nowhere to run and you are definitely going to be found out. I made the long walk to the front and the interrogation began, terminating in the final broadside 'Show me what you have drawn'. She was enjoying herself.

The silence was tangible, overwhelming, and pregnant. Seventy odd pairs of eyes looked on lusting for blood, especially the girls I thought, 'Naked ladies, Miss'. I remember wondering if she was a miss, such is the clarity of thought of the condemned; and the future looked very grim. Then, my teacher, Jack Benson came in. Jack had been a fighter pilot during the war and occasionally had a drink with my father in the Rosevale Bar in Partick. I was not supposed to know this but I did, and I reckoned Jack was one of the best. It was thanks to Jack that I ever got to the Senior Secondary. So now the drama was complete, as the female turned to Mr Benson for endorsement of what would be a suitable punishment I so richly deserved. They withdrew into chambers, as it were, for a consultation and legal debate. I do not know what passed between them, as I stood there still the depraved object of loathing, but I rather think Jack had taken up the office of advocate for the accused. In any event I was ordered to return to my seat, and not another word was heard about it, although I never drew naked ladies again in class. I did draw them elsewhere, however.

Then came the time of separating the sheep from the goats as it were; The Qually. This was an abbreviation for Qualifying Examination, which decided whether we should become academics or trades-people. No notion of continuous assessment here. You had one chance and one only to go to either Senior Secondary or Junior Secondary.

Writing the words today makes me cringe, the descriptions so loaded with judgement and pejorative, but it really was a watershed moment in our young lives and placed a child on one of two fundamentally divergent paths of life. Nor do I think there was much transmigration between the two in later life for our generation. On the other hand we learned there was such a thing as failure and everybody was not a winner.

I managed to get into Senior Secondary, as I say thanks in large measure to Jack Benson but it was a close run thing, since the preliminary exams were, as Jack put it, a 'Write off'. He used that term to great effect, because at that time my father was working as an automobile paint sprayer and panel-beater, rebuilding 'Write offs', and I was in no doubt what the term meant. Shortly after this, my father went into business for himself. Indeed I sometimes wonder if one of the reasons why things were not so good at school was my father's business. Mind you I remember writing out the first inventory of the business in my best writing on the back of wallpaper, and that document was around for years. For all I know it's still lying around in the attic. It was very exciting and we all went into the project full of hope and determination, and even Pamela, my little sister, would help out. I have a photograph to prove it. When I went to secondary school not only was I expected to help after school and at the weekend but the constant strain of making ends meet was very wearing for my parents and for me as the eldest son. Frankly, I hated working at my father's garage in Montague Terrace Lane, but I absorbed a huge amount of practical information there which stood me in great stead when I went to sea. It also taught me how to work hard and put up with challenging conditions, and in retrospect I gained much from the experience. If I wanted anything like a bike or camping equipment, I had to work for it, and that is no bad thing.

But I am running ahead of myself...

The years between 1954 and 1960, were in the main very happy. I had some good pals from school and we were uninhibited by any sort of restrictions imposed by danger from adults or computers. No one knew what a paedophile was and computers had not been invented. Our days were spent recreating wars of various sorts especially the war with Germany. Bear in mind that war had only finished a few years before and we dwelt in a post-war mind set. We had toy guns of all types and we constantly re-created the battles which we knew so much about. Our knowledge of the war was pretty comprehensive, probably gleaned by reading comic books like the *Lion*, the *Tiger*, and several others. Our role models were the heroes portrayed in the comics, and in the main I think it motivated us to aspire to manly virtues, albeit belligerent ones. In those days the seasons seemed to follow fairly well defined patterns although I suspect these memories become more idealised as time passes. There was always snow in Winter it seemed, Spring burst forth in April in a kind of rapturous green re-birth, Summer consisted of long warm yellow days free from the tyranny of school, and Autumn was indeed an orange, mellow time of harvest, fog and the beginnings of frost. Of course these are the dream memories of a man past his prime but that's the way it feels. We used to get into trouble from time to time but never with the police. Our trouble-making was a result of boyish, adventurous pranks not malicious vandalism, although I do remember one particular episode which went like this.

We had been collecting axes. Yes I know that sounds frightening but at that time we were being knights in armour or Vikings and of course battle axes were an essential part of our impedimenta. Somehow I had acquired an axe, then another had been found or *liberated* and pretty soon we had a collection of about four. We must have realised there were societal limitations placed on wee boys hefting axes, because we hid them at the top of a railway embankment adjacent to a road which acted as a bridge over a railway tunnel. This was very close to where I lived and in fact I walked over it every day on my 200 yard trek to school. One day as we played with the axes at the top of the embankment which overlooked the railway track coming from the now long disused Partick South Station, someone had the bright idea that if we put a penny on the line when the big steam engine ran over the penny it would come out flatter than normal. In those days steam trains regularly used the line, and indeed we had already established a rapport with some of the drivers by hanging over the wall which flanked the line and bombing them with mud bombs. It was all part of acting out the war again, you see. Anyway, we made our way down to the line and having placed a penny on the rail, duly withdrew to watch what would happen. Sure enough the locomotive appeared and passed over our penny without even noticing it. On inspection our penny had indeed expanded to about one and half times its normal diameter, which we reckoned was most satisfactory. So we decided to experiment, with something larger. We started small with cardboard boxes and the like and sure enough the next train simply disintegrated the pile. This was so like some of the exploits of the French resistance we had seen in the 'Pictures' (as we called the cinema) that we were very pleased with ourselves, and like all boys must go one step further. By the time the next train was due we had assembled several tea boxes and a couple of planks of timber, right on the corner of the track as it bent round to the tunnel.

The perfect place for an ambush.

With the benefit of hindsight, I suppose there must have been some dialogue between the drivers, because this time the train chuffed round the corner and slowed to halt, belching steam from the pistons and black smoke from the stack. The fireman got out, and cleared the line of the offending debris and shouted unrepeatable words at us, which we shouted back, in the same patois. I think the police must have been alerted because, having gone to ground for about a week, when we returned, our cache of axes had disappeared, and we had the good sense not to try to derail any more trains. Gradually even the sporadic bombing of the steam trains tailed off as well and the whole interlude, along with the much lamented steam locomotives, exists now only in the misty memory of an ancient mariner.

In the late 50's my father bought a boat from a man whose name I forget for £50. She was a 40 feet long ex ship's lifeboat, clinker built with teak planks on oak frames, and she became our pride and joy. She was called the *Kishmul*. She lay down at Balloch, on the River Leven which flows from Loch Lomond. She was on the stocks, in Keirs boatyard, out of the water, and had been for some time. She was a typical lifeboat of the time, the time being the 1920's or 1930's. After the Titanic debacle the Board of Trade took lifesaving more seriously and boats were beautifully built of the best materials. She was beamy, but with a fine entry at the bow and fine cutaway at the stern so you could say she was a 'double ender' like a Zulu or a Fifie. She had spent her life at sea on the deck of some passenger ship, dear knows which one, and she only did what she was built for when she became a pleasure boat. Every available moment was spent at the boat, and my father and mother really threw themselves into it. So did I; in my child's way. Father would work on the repairs, building a new superstructure and re-engining, and my mother on gutting the interior and making it truly delightful inside. I well recall the day we put the boat back into the water after who knows how long. She was transferred to Keir's big bogie (trailer) which was gradually inched down the slipway with the *Kishmul* sitting up there proud as can be. Slowly the bogie crept down the slip under the control of a big wire hawser which was wound onto a winch. Little by little the water level rose as she was tentatively lowered into the Leven. Then we realised that the water was continuing to rise and the *Kishmul* was showing no signs of floating off the bogie. Old Mr Keir was totally unfazed by this and indeed had been expecting it, which was why we had not put any furnishings into the boat. He continued to introduce her to the cold waters of the Leven until she was submerged up to her waterline then called a halt, and we secured the boat in the cradle, and the bogey in the slipway. 'She'll take up fine there' says old Mr. Keir and there she sat for the next couple of weeks. Sure enough she did 'take up' and then began the job of pumping her out. Incidentally, Mr. Keir actually built lovely angling boats for Loch Lomond and what he did not know about clinker built boats was not worth knowing. Pumping out was arduous and my Uncle Vincent (we call him Uncle Vinnie) was recruited to help. All day we bailed with every available receptacle and the semi-rotary bilge pump which was cranked by hand but at last, by the end of the day the *Kishmul* was afloat and ready to go to her mooring. The thing I recall most about that day was the fact that the ice on Loch Lomond was breaking up and large floes were careering down the river.

The *Kishmul*'s contribution to our family happiness was very great and there followed a period of a few years which were very formative for me and I daresay heavily influenced the path I would take in life. After fitting out to a standard which gave us a better lifestyle than the flat in Partick we had wonderful holidays on the Loch and I have not the space to tell it all. Loch Lomond is a magical place and its exploration is utterly delightful. Sometimes we met up with other boats and there would be a dance in Swing Bay on Inch Tavannach with a proper dance band, Tilley lamps to light the clearing on the beach and sufficient refreshment to ensure a happy time for all. I have to take my hat off to my parents here. When I recall these days I realise that my parents were profoundly different to any others I knew. They had the drive and courage to try just about anything and I am proud they were my parents.

The *Kishmul* gave us a lot but she demanded a lot of time, so much so that our Churchgoing had virtually ceased since most weekends were spent down at the boat. It must have been about 1959 or 1960, when we concluded that the Loch was too small for our adventures, and my father decided to take the boat down the Leven and into the Clyde. This was a major undertaking and required skilled planning, and timing. It could only be undertaken when the river was in spate and the crux of the voyage would be the negotiating of the broken weir, near Renton. I remember reconnoitring the river with my father and the break in the weir looked very malevolent, with the huge volume of dark Leven water barrelling through the narrow gap in the weir. I seem to have been with my father all the time on these excursions, but he would not allow me to come on the journey down the Leven, despite my disgusted protests. Instead he took my uncle Vinnie and my cousin Sandy Birnie, who was lodging with us while studying to become a Chartered Accountant. Well, they had the adventure of a lifetime I believe, with groundings, temporary loss of the rudder, and several other mishaps which matured them all greatly by the time they finally brought her to Port Glasgow on the river Clyde that night. It was a truly brave well executed mission and I salute them. They moored the boat where they were told by whoever was managing the berthing arrangements at the harbour and that night, because it was a very big tide the harbour virtually dried out and the *Kishmul* settled on the piles of an old pier or pier facings and sprung her planks. When the tide came back in she filled with water and foundered where she was moored. It was heart-breaking to see her on the bottom the next day and I remember my father weeping when he got home. We tried with might and main for the next six weeks to raise her, including getting divers down to put strops round her but the crane was not man enough for the job. Then at the next Spring tide my father and Uncle Vinnie tied a load of 45 gallon oil drums all round her gunwale and attached a hawser to the tow bar of the old Standard car they had, from the bitts on her focsle. The tide duly came in and sure enough the buoyancy from the drums was sufficient to break the suction which held her to the bottom and allow them to drag her across the harbour to the inner wall nearest the road. They went home that night exhausted. When they returned in the morning to continue the salvage some of the locals of Port Glasgow had come down overnight and cut the quarter out of her and removed the big Perkins Diesel engine! That was the last straw for she could never be rebuilt with the same strength and so my father arranged to have her broken up. I can still see her name plate floating in the filth of the corner of the dock like an MGM movie, and it still makes me sad. In time Port Glasgow would be filled in, the land reclaimed and I would pass it many times as master of my own ship, and I never missed an opportunity to bore the Officer of the Watch with that story.

I cannot remember the exact year, but around 1960 our family migrated from the top flat as previously described to one of the two bottom flats of 43 Exeter Drive. Ours was the one on the left of the close. This was a bigger flat by one room, and it had hot water on tap. I recall the first day we took occupation. In the kitchen, which looked out onto the back courts, wash-houses and the 'middens,' otherwise known in the vernacular as the 'midgies', and the Waash-hooses', was the most wonderful cooking range. It was huge to my child's eye and tiled all round with green tiles. I have already noted my affinity with this style of cooking and heating arrangement, and I cannot describe my disgust when my mother pronounced the diktat that the range and grate were to be removed. In later years we would lament this action, and we would remember fondly how useful and cosy they were, but at the time I suppose it made sense, as we were caught up in the movement to make everything in the home *contemporary*. This attitude to Edwardian and Victorian design and decoration, was born I think in a post war rejection of anything that was *old fashioned and dingy*. People wanted to brighten their horizons and who could blame them, but it resulted in the mass vandalism, encouraged by television, and other media, which saw virtually all interior decoration in most homes in Britain built in Edwardian times, being ripped out and cast away. One of the high priests of this particular sacrilege was one Barry Bucknell. In the early sixties he had a programme on television in which he 'educated' the nation on the best way to remove every trace of character from their homes. Picture rails, dados, moulded architraves, beautiful wood panelled display cabinets, ceiling plasterwork, panelled doors, Tudor wooden facings, indeed anything which later generations would yearn to have reinstated, this iconoclast drove us on to destroy with missionary zeal. I well remember him taking a plane to the mouldings of a lovely Victorian panelled door so that he could apply hardboard to the door and so render it bland and featureless. I often wondered if he had shares in hardboard, and when I came to attempt to re-instate my own home into some semblance of what it used to be, I roundly cursed him for the wanton destroyer he truly was.

I should explain about the *washhouse*. Each tenement had a back court in which were a midden, which held the refuse from all the homes in that tenement, and a wash-house, wherein each housewife did the weekly household washing, on a rota basis. The wash-house itself held two enormous porcelain sinks and a boiler (or as we called it, a 'biler') heated by a fire lit under a very large galvanised iron tub. The whole of this boiler assembly was built like a brick oven and looked a bit like a kiln. In the fullness of time the wash-houses fell into disuse and became obsolete due to the advent of the washing machine, and in so doing became the gang-huts of the children who lived in the tenements. Naturally I was the leader in our gang-hut and decided how it was to be embellished and fortified, and I can still remember buying a bolt for the door and painting the boiler with red paint. Attaching that bolt may well may been my first foray into the world of DIY. The gang-hut craze did not last all that long, because they were damp and smelly, the abode of wood lice and spiders.

CHAPTER THREE
1961 – 1966

It was around this time I went to the secondary school, but not before we had the primary school leavers' dance. For weeks before the dance we were taught 'Social dancing', in order to prepare us for this rite of passage. I personally enjoyed the whole process of enforced interaction with the opposite sex, and can still remember the thrill of asking a girl to dance and the less thrilling experience of sometimes being rejected. Catherine Prentice was one who rejected my overtures to accompany me to the dance. I remember making a point of playing on the disused plots overlooked by her top flat home, in order to impress her. Eventually, however, I realised that I would have to be less subtle and took it upon myself to go up to her house and ask her in front of her mother. It was a terrifying experience, not because her parents were unpleasant but because I became aware for the first time of the uniqueness and indeed the sanctity of a family home. To this day I can feel the excitement of knocking the door and being brought into the hall, to the smells of mince and a pie baking in the oven. (All houses seemed to smell like that in those days).Her mother was a good natured lady and very kindly informed me that Catherine would not go with me but would 'see me at the dance'. Frankly I was bitterly disappointed and in the end did not dance with her at all but paired up with Mary Shill who was a lovely girl and good fun.

It was a great night, marred only by my long trousers – my first pair. The problem was that they were just too wide and I knew it, and no amount of cajoling on my mother's part would change that. On the night of the dance I was constantly aware of the excessive drag caused by my outlandish pantaloons as I endeavoured to execute a light footed pas debar, and only Mary's kind reassurances allowed me to continue. As a matter of fact when the wind was from what I would later describe as 'astern' they would fill and belly out like two studding sails or as I thought at time, two Hoover bags. (In those days all vacuum cleaners were called Hoovers, and a feature of the older type was the air bag which bellied out when filled with air). In the end I habitually referred to these trousers as my Hoovers, and they were consigned to the rag bag at the first available opportunity. Dei Gratia. I reckoned they gave me an extra two knots when running before the wind down the street.

That was the end of primary school and in some ways the end of childish innocence. I must now attend Hyndland Senior Secondary School, and enter a whole new world of academic endeavour. I did this, however, without my Hoovers. New subjects were laid before us and we must make choices and declare preferences. I did not really comprehend the marvellous gift we were being offered with this free education. We would be taught by graduates who still wore their Geneva gowns and one or two still had mortar board hats. The communication of knowledge was, for some of them, I now realise, a life's mission and they held a very 'high' view of education, and took it very seriously; sadly some of us pupils did not. But I did.

In my first year, because of my choices of subjects, I was placed in the class 1C. This did not reflect some third level of rating, but the fact that I did not wish to study French and Latin simultaneously. I wanted only Latin. It blended better I thought, with my love of the past, and I reckoned I would 'just pick French up anyway'. That First Year was the most successful of my entire school career, and I actually ended up First in the class, and have the prize book, *The Master of Ballantrae*, to prove it. I was not able to collect my prize in person because as usual we had migrated north just before school closed for the summer. Winning this prize gave me a huge boost in both self esteem and commitment to my studies, and I have to say that although I never won another prize I managed to muddle through pretty well. Very recently when clearing out my parents' house on the death of my mother, I discovered my report card for secondary school, and I have to say that, in the main, I was a steady if uninspiring student.

Another choice we had to make was which sport we would take up, the options being either soccer or rugby. For me this was easy, as I reckoned football was pretty effete and much preferred the 'total commitment' of rugby. I reappraised my view in later life having met some pretty robust footballing types but at that time it was clear cut to me. I was picked for the team and continued to play for the rest of my school career, in the scrum at number seven or number five 'Lock'. Once or twice I played as Captain but my dedication to the game was not as great as it should have been and I could be unreliable some Saturdays. I really enjoyed playing though, and most of the teams we played were just like us, but I used to marvel at some of the well-heeled schools like Marr College where the rugby team actually attracted female support. I was profoundly envious of them. Mind you some of the fee-paying schools had very strict regimes and there was no sign of any damsels in that set up. Keil College on the banks of the Clyde was one such establishment as I recall, and their pitches were built on the side of a hill!

As I said I never really enjoyed school, but there was no choice so one made the best of it. I was there from 1961 to 1966 and I am now profoundly grateful for the education I received. In the first four years of secondary I walked about a mile and a half to and from the school twice every day to come home for lunch. It was only in my fifth and last year that I occasionally remained in school at lunchtime, having discovered school dinners. For a paltry sum you could buy a good-filling meal provided by the education authority. It was served in the YMCA building which was fairly close to the school by very cheerie 'Dinner Ladies'. Some of my fellow barbarians dubbed the arrangement 'Yesterday's Muck Cooked Again' but I never subscribed to that notion. I thought they were great meals and friendly women, and if you were nice to them and helped to carry the kits which held the meals you could get extras.

During these five years I did a lot of growing up. As I say, my father was now in business for himself and it was very challenging for him to establish a name for himself in the paint-spraying and panel beating trade and there was little financial help in those days. I went with him to the Bank of Scotland to get the first loan to start the business and he came away with £100. Even in those days it was not enough to get going properly but he did it and by sheer hard work and determination managed to provide for us for seven years.

From early morning till sometimes very late at night he toiled away rebuilding damaged and scrappy old cars, with very primitive and basic tools. I remember when he bought a new compressor to power his paint spraying equipment. It was welcomed like a new baby. Its predecessor must have escaped from a museum and the sense of uncertainty when you kicked the flywheel into life on a cold morning will remain with me forever. In time my father built up a good reputation for producing excellent workmanship and jobs came in sufficient quantities to keep the family going. But it was never certain, and there were sometimes very slack periods which engendered great anxiety in my parents and me. We could never really be relaxed about money, and eventually the situation began to take its toll. My father, in an attempt to escape from worry and endless toil started to visit the pub on his way home and his arrival at home got later and later, until it coincided with closing time, which in those days was around ten o'clock. This caused huge tension between my mother and father, and I used to dread the sound of the handbrake going on as the car stopped outside the house, knowing that within a short space of time the voices would begin to rise and I would have to get up to perform the role of mediator and pacifier. Sometimes, in my middle teenage years I did not get to bed till very late and this must have affected my school work. Even in the fifth year I remember appearing before the depute headmaster for persistent late coming one week, and was given the choice of the belt or essay writing. I chose the belt. To this day I loathe the sound of raised voices particularly when drink is involved.

You should not assume from all this gloom and doom I am telling you, that our family's life was unhappy. That is not the case. We had a loving and stable upbringing with many truly happy times, and thanks to my mother our home was cosy and clean and homely. And remember this, she was putting a huge amount of work in the garage as well, standing shoulder to shoulder with my father and sharing much of the physical effort of preparing the cars.

During these years I developed a love of the outdoors which persists to this day. My head was full of expeditions to remote places particularly the Poles and I read everything I could about polar exploration in the Partick Library. In order to satisfy this craving I began camping, climbing and hill walking, partially through the Scouting movement. I had joined the 26th Glasgow Boy Scouts as a Cub in the late 50s then left after a couple of years only to rejoin as a scout around 1963. This Scout Troop was associated with Newton Place Parish Church near Partick Cross, which I joined of my own volition around the same time. I suspect my motives were not entirely religious because a couple of my pals had already joined via the Youth Club, and there were some very nice girls in the Youth Club. On the other hand Donald MacDonald from the Isle of Skye was the minister during this period and his preaching at that time could be described as 'conservative evangelical'. It was he who ran the First Communicants Class and I was impressed by his zeal and ability. In later years, long after he left Newton Place, I think he became frustrated by the intellectual, indeed cerebral nature of the theological camp he found himself in and embraced a more gutsy social gospel. He used to contribute to Life and Work, the Church of Scotland's monthly magazine, and I felt I could detect the change.

I returned to Newton Place in 2009, to find it razed to the ground, and a new purpose-built and much smaller church called Partick South, standing on its foundations. Our old Church Halls, which also served as Scout Hall, Youth Club, and indeed any other Church Family gathering place, had survived the rebuilding programme, and I happened to meet one of the parishioners. She would have been about the same age as me and I asked about Donald MacDonald. She informed me that drink had got the better of him and he was separated from his wife. I really did not want to hear that and I left feeling quite low, and very sorry for him.

To return to the Great Outdoors, I threw myself into this with a whole heart and set about accumulating the equipment I would need to begin my adventures. This would have been about 1962 because I have a photograph from that year of Ian Tannahill, Ian Ferguson and me away in Aberfoyle, scrambling up Craigmore. At first I had to put up with any gear I could cobble together but in time I studied every camping catalogue I could get my hands on and worked hard at the garage to make the money to buy the gear. My father was very generous in making up my shortfalls and I eventually gathered together all I needed. Tent, rucksack, sleeping bag stove etc. mostly purchased from Black's of Greenock, who had fitted out more expeditions than I could number. So I began camping and going on little expeditions from around 1962, shortly before I joined the Scouts. Usually I went with the other two but as time went on and they became more interested in playing in a rock band, I would just go alone. I was supposed to be the bass guitar player in this band but I never got the length of buying a guitar because my heart was not in it.

Our band was called the 'Trojans' and 'Fergy' and 'Tanny' as I called my friends, to give them their due, actually got the length of playing at some dances and they sounded fine. We called them dances in those days before 'discos' and the like, and they were most enjoyable, and usually fairly civilised although there were always idiots there to cause trouble. Maybe they were compensating for something?

In the Scouts you are required to attempt to obtain Proficiency Badges. Many of them are fairly straightforward 'Life Skill' topics but some require a bit more planning and effort. The one I wanted more than any other was the 'Explorers' badge. Part of it required a thirty mile hike and a week-long boat journey, both of which had to be 'written up' with reports on the preparations, logistics and execution. It was quite a challenge for fourteen year-old boys. The first part was relatively straightforward, and I elected to hike from Balloch to Glen Douglas and back. This hike was in the main carried out on the paths which ran along the side of Loch Lomond then took a more westerly route up Glen Douglas. It involved only one overnight in Glen Douglas then all the way back. My biggest mistake was wearing the brand new Kastinger climbing boots I had recently purchased. The boots had a very stiff welt and were actually made for use with crampons, so they were totally unsuited to this low level path walking. By the time I reached Luss, seven miles up Loch Lomondside, large blisters were forming on my heels, and by the time I reached Glen Douglas my feet were in poor condition. Anyway, I managed to find an exquisite camp-site on a farm well up the Glen and half an hour of steeping my feet in the burn went a long way to improving the situation. Another mistake was carrying a big Brown Best rucksack (I still have it) in which I had packed food for 3 days, - including tins! On the other hand the surroundings were glorious, my new tent was just the job and with a full stomach I was very cheerful. I think it was around this time that I began toying with the idea of joining the Marines.

Next morning was another lovely day and I broke camp and started retracing my steps back down the Glen. Part of the path runs very close to the burn, and I had not gone very far when I heard a plaintive bleating among the rocks near the burn side. I investigated, following the wails and sure enough, wedged in among the rocks was a very young lamb with a broken hind leg. I managed to extricate it from the rocks and carried it in my arms down to the foot of the Glen where I was able to hand over my responsibility to the owner of the camp-site at Ardbeg. All the way down the Glen I kept thinking about the Good Shepherd and the Ninety and Nine sheep which were safely in the fold and the one that was lost, and many years later told the story to the Sunday school, for a Children's Address. My feet did not improve on the way down the Loch side, but I kept thinking about the great explorers who had really had a hard time and pressed on. By the time I reached Slate Bay, outside Luss, I was beginning to limp a lot, when who should appear but my family in the car. They said they were out for a run but I knew they had come to see how I was doing. They offered to pick me up but they knew better than to argue when I refused. So I carried on and eventually arrived at Balloch where I caught the train for home. Next day I went to school and could not take part in the PE class because I had blisters like half-crowns on the soles of my feet. Mr Cooper was our PE teacher and a man not easily impressed but when he saw the feet and heard how I had obtained the blisters he let me off PE, and I think he viewed me in a different light after that.

The next part of the badge was to go away for about a week in a boat. I cannot remember the exact amount of time you had to do this for but I think it was about a week. The first thing you need for a boat journey is a boat, and remember we had lost all things nautical when the *Kishmul* sank. However my Uncle Vinnie still had his wee boat the Puffin which he and my father had built and the Puffin had a dingy. Uncle Vinnie was duly approached and arrangements made to collect the dingy, from good old Mr Keir's slip. Now you will recall that when we launched the *Kishmul* she would have gone straight to the bottom had it not been for the bogie holding her up. That was because her planks had dried up on account of being out of the water, and so also the oakum between the seams of the planks. Well the same thing had happened to Uncle Vinnie's dingy which had lain upturned for a good while on the beach round at the caravan park at Balloch, which is no longer there. There is a shopping Centre there now called Lomond View, but it used to be a caravan park. The arrangement was that my father and I would wait for him at Keir's slip while he brought the dingy, driven by his outboard engine, round, down the Leven to the slip. It was turning to the gloaming on a March evening when we finally sighted the silhouette of the boat, or I should say its bow wave passing the island upstream from where we stood. As we watched it was clear that all was not well, for Uncle Vinnie's actions became more and more animated as he neared the slip. He was simultaneously steering and bailing the boat which by now had barely her gunwale above water. It was a close run thing as he finally drove the boat up the slip, full of water with not a second to spare. We dragged the boat up and consoled a shaken Uncle Vin. At no point did it occur to me that this might not be the best craft for the expedition. There was no other.

Anyway we put the boat which was about ten feet long on the back of the trailer and conveyed her to the Garage where I worked on her for the next couple of weeks. First I filled her with water so she would 'take up', then set about filling any remaining leaks with Sealastic, a kind of gunk which allegedly sealed leaks. Ian Tannahill would accompany me on this trip and he made his own preparations.

We were ready for the Easter holidays, which must have been late that year, because I am pretty sure it was April 1964, when we arrived in the late afternoon at the caravan park at Balloch. The light was beginning to fade and there was a brisk northerly breeze blowing down the loch. My father and Uncle Vin had driven us down with the trailer and we loaded the boat, which was leaking not too badly. Our only lifesaving appliance was an inflated inner tube from a large tyre which we stowed in the bows under the breast-hook. When I look back I am not entirely sure that my father had exercised due parental care in this case, what with the leaky boat and the inflated inner tube. I asked him about it many years later and he said he was so fed up with me going on about the expedition that he just gave in and let me go. Anyway, we set off into the breeze, one rowing and one bailing and began one the best experiences I ever had. I made my first command decision after about a couple of hours rowing into the wind and decided to come under the lee of Inchmurrin where we spent the night. We bivouacked on the beach under a plastic tarpaulin and cooked the soup which Tannahill's mother had made. Lying there, under the stars, supping that delicious soup, we could not think of anywhere we would rather be. Next day we woke early and it was a joy to cook over the fire for there was loads of tinder dry wood. We breakfasted well and then set about the exploration of Loch Lomond. Over the next few days we rowed from island to island, bivouacking where we would, and my memory is of very benign weather conditions which did not challenge us until we tried to get past Rowardennan. The Loch narrows there and acts like a funnel accelerating what wind there is. We must have been under the influence of an anticyclone for the entire trip, and that would account for the predominantly northerly breezes.

Whatever the climatological set-up, it was just too tough for us to get past Inversnaid and so we put about and ran down for the lee of the shore, where we camped. Over the last couple of days of the trip we experimented with using the tarpaulin as a sail, and we discovered how gloriously indolent it was to run before the wind, (that is all we could do) and recover the ground which we had laboured to make in the early part of the trip. We returned home with mission accomplished having grown up a bit too. When I look back I realise that benign Providence had guarded over us and knowing what I know now, we had no business being so successful.

All this camping, trekking and boating had fired my imagination, and as I mentioned the notion of joining the Marines began to form in my mind. It seemed to me that the only profession which could possibly fulfil my needs would be a commission in the Royal Marines, but I was much too young to go to a recruiting office so I did the next best thing and put my name down to go to the Ullswater Outward Bound School. I cannot remember how I came to know about this place, perhaps it was through the school. In any event I could not wait to go and all my spare time was filled preparing for it. I reckoned I was pretty fit anyway with circuit training and rugby training and swimming so did not think there would be any problem with the medical. I was wrong. They sent out a medical declaration which you were required to fill in truthfully and I was honour bound to report that I had a congenital varicose vein in my left leg and suffered from hay fever. I duly sent it and waited. I was then called to go down to the office they had in Glasgow to pick up some final information and on presenting myself at the counter was told that I had been rejected on both counts. It was the greatest disappointment of my life to that point and it set me back on my heels for a minute or two. On the other hand I seem to have been built with a kind of resilience that says 'Stuff your Outward Bound, I'll make my own outward bound', and so I did. In my life I suppose I have done far more arduous things than I ever would have at Ullswater, but I must say it still leaves a bitter taste in my mouth that they did not even have a doctor look at me. I still have the varicose vein. It's been operated on four times but the hay fever disappeared in my late forties. I now realise that was not the way I was to go, but I am getting ahead of myself again.

From this time till I was sixteen was a period of trying to study for and pass first O Grades and then the Highers, liberally seasoned with a lot of scouting and private excursions. I think I sat and obtained seven O Grades and found out I had been successful whilst attending a Scout Jamboree in Germany. That was a marvellous holiday as well, and I remember a lot about it. Our Troop Leaders Gordon Brown and Tommy Weir were tremendous fellows and they organised everything. Gordon took six of us who were all patrol leaders and seconds all aged between 15 and 17. We wore kilts all the time and it set us apart from everyone else. We travelled down to London by coach then on down to Dover and on to Calais by ferry. We camped out on deck that night, which was a serious test of stamina, because it was foul weather but we built a kind of shelter out of our Bergens and stuck it out. Inside the accommodation was unthinkable really, because people were being sick and there was a bit of drinking going on too. From Calais, which was a blur, we took the train to Germany passing through Aachen, a journey made truly memorable by bone hard seats and the stench of foreign tobacco. We arrived at Hamburg Hauptbahnof in the morning some time, feeling pretty washed out, but we were met by the two German Scout leaders, Hiewe and Capelle, and they conveyed us in a Volkswagen van, over the autobahn to our camp-site in Schaalsee, in Sleswig Holstein in Upper Saxony. I don't know how to spell the places properly but I can tell you when we got to the camp after a couple of miles hike, we were starving! I will never forget the taste of the cheese, German black bread, jam, and cold tea with milk! I have to say that was a step too far for us, and we made it clear that from then on the Jocks would have hot tea.

The Germans had all the tents pitched already, and their tents were revolutionary to us, since they were black and consisted of many pieces of tent laced together. In other words, each man carried his own bit of tent which was big enough to provide shelter for him but they could all be laced together to form a tent any size you wanted. It was a brilliant, typically German, idea. There then followed ten days of tremendous fun for young men with pioneering, orienteering (we did not call it that in those days), swimming, sports of all kind and we even had a parents' day. There was one bit we were not so keen on where we had to act out a sketch in which a courting couple sat down in front of a statue which came to life and started tickling the girl. I was the bloke and I think Rikki MacDonald, who had fashionable long hair, acted the girl with his kilt on. Of course we sat down in front of this statue and pretended to be a couple tastefully, and embarrassingly, doing what couples do. I had to put my arm round Rikki's shoulders and then this blasted statue started coming to life and touching her/him in inappropriate places. The Germans loved it! They are not famous for their sense of humour. I have photographs to show this – pretty funny in retrospect. Thankfully that was followed by a chariot race on 'chariots' made from quarter staffs. We had one charioteer and four 'horses'. It was quite robust and I have photographs of that as well.

Towards the end of our time under canvas we foreigners, made up of Belgians, French, Swiss, Austrians, an Englishman and us Scots, had to pair up with a German to stay with their family for week. The chap I paired up with was Rainer Sauervine. A really nice fellow with lovely parents and a stunning sister, called Hannalowe. I thought I had died and gone to heaven.

Mr. and Mrs Sauervine were older than my parents by some way and I reckoned they must have married later in life. They were really nice to me and we went away one day to the Baltic village of Kappeln where some of their relatives stayed. This will abide in my memory as a salutary lesson in not showing off to girls. We had gone down to the beach for a swim. The Baltic being very shallow, heats up during the German summer and it really is quite pleasant. Anyway Hannalowe and I had to go for a swim together so we struck out for the middle of the Baltic somewhere, and of course pride forbade that I should be less able than this girl so I stuck with her wondering how long this madness could continue as I watched the shoreline disappear. I began to realise that I was getting to that place where I should have turned back 5 minutes ago, when suddenly she stood up in front of me! In my panic-stricken pride I had failed to notice the bottom shelving, and have never been so glad of anything in my life. I inwardly rejoiced in my salvation and the view of Hannelowe standing there glistening in the sun was pretty good too. We returned to shore ready for lunch at the relatives'. They had a big table with a lot of people round it and I thought this is kind of nice. I put the thought of the big table in my mind's back pocket for much later, and began to engage the head of the house in conversation. He spoke perfect English with just a slight accent which I could not place. I commented on his English and he informed me he had refined it for four years in a prisoner of war camp in Yorkshire and that accounted for the accent, and I wished I could float quietly out of the window through which drifted the coastal sounds of the hot German summer.

All in all it had been a humbling day, but we were soon to set off for Berlin, West and East, and that meant going through the Iron Curtain. It was 1965.

You do not realise how big Germany is until you try to cross it by bus. As I write that, I am thinking about the men who fought over that ground in the last war on both sides on foot, and I realise what an unbelievable waste war is. We had said our fond farewells to our adopted families after what was for me a truly delightful time. Rainer's family could not have been kinder and the lovely village of Rheinbeck will always occupy a special place in my memory. I believe there is Luftwaffe base there now and I found that out when I spoke to a big blond Saxon F16 pilot at the Lossiemouth Air Show, back in the 80's. He said the village had not changed much and was still virtually hidden from the air by the trees. That's the way I remember it.

To get back to the bus journey, young men in buses invariably start singing at some point, and as the German countryside rolled past and we effortlessly ate up the concrete miles of the autobahn, we were all obliged to do a turn. Normally when on the rugby bus we started off with 'Three German Officers Crossed the Rhine' and went downhill from there, but it seemed, even to barbarians like us, a bit insensitive so I suppose we cobbled together what we could remember of our Scottish repertoire. "The Bonnie Banks of Loch Lomond" and that sort of thing. Actually as a Scout troop we sang quite a lot together so we did not do so badly. When it came to the German lads having a go, they burst into what I now believe was the 'Horst Wessel'. If it was not that, it was like it. All hands sang with great gusto, and as the song went on I gained an insight into the German psyche. The feet started tramping and there was a sort of glazed look in their eyes, and I thought, remembering their flags, which each patrol possessed and of which they were so proud: 'Things have not changed so much after all'. I wonder if it is just that, as a nation, they have great solidarity and belief in their nationhood and they do not have our ability to not take ourselves seriously. I wonder if that comes from the strong Celtic roots we have and they don't. Maybe that's why you don't see a lot of German comedians?

The Zonnengrenze, or border, hove into site and it really had to be seen to be believed. A two hundred metre wide ploughed field running north to south across the whole of Germany with barbed wire, big wooden searchlight towers and machine-gun posts, patrolled night and day by armed guards. It was like a latter-day Antonine's Wall, and was called the Iron Curtain. And you need to remember that the city of Berlin which we were still a long way from was actually on the east side of that border. That city itself was divided by Die Mauer, or 'Wall'. When you think about it, it was a pretty ludicrous situation but that's what happens when you give big laddies dangerous weapons.

It took a long time to get into the East, passing through the Kontrol and they were extremely thorough which is what you would expect. But then this was 'Divided Germany' This was really why Hiewe the leader and organiser of the Jamboree had wanted to bring these young men together, to show how daft and deeply wounding to the people of Germany the whole set up was. He certainly made the point to me, and when I recall his sensitive, kind, intelligent, features I remember a highly principled man who was determined to do something to prevent it happening again. I would not be surprised if he went on to become one of the principal architects of the removal of the 'Wall' in the 80's because he loathed it with a vengeance. Or maybe he didn't.

Berlin in the 60's was Day and Night. Life and hope and energy, on the one side; twilight, drudgery and depression on the other. We were lodged in a Youth Hostel from which you could see a big 'Radio Telefunken' sign on the top of the factory bearing that name. The accommodation was basic and adequate, and divided into Male and Female Blocks. You could look across from our side of the inner courtyard (a bit like Colditz, because I am in German mode) and see the females on their side. Having received encouraging signals one evening across the great divide, some of us mounted a midnight excursion to the 'Forbidden Land'. This involved sneaking past a guard station where the night watchmen kept their vigil to ensure there would be no co-mingling of the sexes. They were armed and alert and it was quite difficult to time the sortie, so in the absence of any drawings to find an alternative route past them we had to admit defeat on that occasion and turn in early. Incidentally that was a multi-national cadre, so some of us were clearly beginning to act as a team of like-minded individuals. I do not remember any Germans being there though. Germans are good with rules.

The Kurfürstendamm was a jolly place as I recall, with loads of cafés with outdoor canopied table areas. It was full of colour and cheerfulness and human interaction and I for one could have sat there all evening just watching the parade of life. Somehow it was redolent of Chaucer's Canterbury Tales, or maybe nearer to Bunyan's Vanity Fair, so diverse and interesting were the characters. When we came to leave one of our crowd had omitted to pay for whatever they had. I am not convinced they did not do it intentionally; in any event we were prevented from leaving by a waist-coated waiter, who had eye contact with a policeman, until the appropriate sum had been paid, and to this day the occurrence puts a dampener on the memory of the evening. They obviously had not been subjected to the North End Road treatment as dispensed by Helen Beveridge.

The next day we were allowed through 'Checkpoint Charlie', which was the main control point through the Wall. Don't forget the East Germans were not allowed into the West and people were being shot for attempting to leave the East to be reunited with their families, or just to get away from communism. I am fairly sure no one was ever shot trying to get into East Berlin so to me that speaks volumes about the attractiveness of life under the all-powerful influence of Stalin and later Khrushchev.

There was a museum which we visited, very close to the wall, cataloguing the exploits of those who had perished trying to escape that iniquitous regime, and even to young lads like us it struck a sympathetic note. We travelled on the U-bahn, or underground, with the big English Scout we had teamed up with, because he spoke German and was a good guy anyway. So I think we were four Brits in our group. The subway seemed to have been unchanged since the war, locked in a time warp. It was profoundly depressing and we were glad to surface somewhere in East Berlin. As we were about to exit the doorway of the underground a guy sidled up to big Tony the Englishman, and asked him to buy him some American cigarettes, for which he would pay. East Berliners were not permitted to buy Western cigarettes. Tony translated for us and we had a debate there at the mouth of the subway. The tobacconist shop formed part of the exit so it was close enough. We agreed, and devised a plan whereby Tony would buy the cigarettes and a news paper then slip the illegal cigarettes to the German as simply a newspaper. It all went pretty well, the transaction was flawless, then we noticed the East German guard with a sub-machine gun keeping an eye on things, and he was clearly aware something had taken place. That was the point at which we four Brits began to make ourselves scarce.

When you think about it all we had done was to allow a guy a basic human right to go into a shop and buy what he wanted as a free man, but this regime was making criminals of us all.

And the guard was still following us.

We walked briskly without making it too obvious towards a big beer garden which was full of people, and mingled. I suppose the guard lost interest and went back to his post. Now I said that the East was dull and depressing but the human spirit is fairly indomitable and even here where you could not buy what you wanted in a shop, folk would manage to make themselves cheerful. And the beer and the sun helped. Tony, who was just about to enter university, insisted we visit a bookshop before leaving East Berlin. Looking back, I am glad we joined up with Tony, because not only could he speak German but he was willing to discuss things and we had some good talks. You can learn a lot about a place by the very existence of bookshops and the books they sell. Never stay in a country which curtails bookshops or censors what they sell. Tony showed us book after book written about Britain and America which were so obviously political propaganda that even without German one could get the gist. To be frank there is a lot to be said for living on an island on the edge of the Atlantic, and keeping a close eye on the people in power.

We got safely back to the West and next day visited the Reichstadt. The bullet holes from the war were still visible and we were given a tour of the nether regions where we were shown where they hung people from big hooks in the ceiling. It was a solemn and sobering place and made you realise what can happen when ruthless men get hold of the corporate mind of a nation. I have not told you about our visit to Hamburg where we saw 'Jungfrau Strasse' and its dubious delights, and St Pauli Church with its vertiginous tower, nor have I told you about how we went to the Rathaus or Town hall in Reinbeck where we were photographed with our kilts because Germans seemed to like the kilt and bagpipes, oddly enough. But that will have to wait for another time. This visit was coming to an end. There would be several other trips to Germany in the future but for now we had to make the long trek home.

I am glad I did not have to do it on foot!

Around this time, my little brother (he is bigger than me now), Derek was born. He was blond where we were dark and as healthy and happy a little chap as ever lived. But there was no mistaking which stable he came from across the eyes. He was and is the most peace-loving soul you could imagine and I loved him then and still love him now. I had a lot to do with his nurture in his early years before I went to sea because there were fifteen years between us, but of course he does not remember that.

At sixteen I began to seriously consider what I would do for a living, and as I said I was becoming more and more attracted to the Royal Marine Commandos. They seemed to have everything I could want, and so I set about getting the paperwork for a short service commission. I filled it in and then the old chestnut of the varicose vein and hay-fever raised its ugly head again. When I watch the young men coming home from Afghanistan now, with bits missing, my vein and hay-fever pale into insignificance, but I suppose they have to set standards, and I was below par. So with my usual response to shut doors I went next door, literally, to the Royal Highland Fusiliers, which in those days had a recruiting shop next door to the Marines in Sauchiehall Street. Actually I always thought of them as the HLI (Highland Light Infantry) but I later found they had amalgamated to become the Fusiliers some time before. Again after filling in the paperwork I was rejected and it never occurred to me to lie. All that was left was the Navy and I remember coming home pretty disconsolate and talking it over with my father. He listened for a while and then said 'What do want to join the Services for anyway? All your ancestors on both sides have been at sea since the Vikings and anyway you're far too much an individualist to join the bloody Navy' (his words). Several things went through my head when he said that; that my father understood me far better than I thought, that I had never considered my forebears much, but he was right, and that despite my regular fallings out with him over his drinking, I had a really wise Old Man. From that day on I had a new sense of purpose and direction.

Something else happened around the same time, when, during one of my forays to Partick Library to look for books on exploration, I came upon a book called 'It's a Sailor's Life' by Jan De Hartog. I well remember reading out passages from the book to my parents at night, and the gales of laughter it brought about. De Hartog worked his way through all the ranks and the stereotypical characters they possessed, and for me, at that time; it was enough to draw me in further to the notion of making the sea a career for life. Almost fifty years later, forty one of which were spent at sea, I still admire his huge talent for encapsulating the essence of these characters.

In 2010 my wife bought me my own copy of the book, and the writing is as fresh as the day I first read it, although I now have my own visions of the alchemy that somehow created these types. In any event I now began making Sunday sorties down to the docks in Glasgow, which at that time were very busy with every type of cargo ship. I was often accompanied by my father and we would rove around just talking about the ships and where they were bound, the cargoes they carried, and of course he was very knowledgeable having been at sea himself. You see, my father and I were great friends; it was only the drink which caused friction between us. One of De Hartog's descriptions of a certain type of cargo ship particularly took my fancy. An old fashioned 'Three Islander', so called because of the fact that her accommodation was built in three blocks, one forward, one amidships and one aft. And of course the most significant feature of these old ships was the long 'Woodbine' funnel, so built as to maximise the updraught to remove the smoke and exhaust gasses from the boilers and engines. In fact in seaman's terms, when referring to the build of the female form, we called slim women 'natural draught' and more tubby types 'forced draught'. This was by no means a comment on the desirability, or relative merits, of one type over the other, you understand, merely sailorly observation. Anyway, one Sunday we were ambling about the Queen's Dock which was a two-legged dock built on the north side of the river, gone now with most of the other Glasgow docks, when we came upon this huge, old cargo ship with an enormous black funnel painted with a blue stripe and a white stripe. At the bottom of the accommodation ladder was an officer wearing his doeskin navy blue uniform, intent on reading the draught as I recall. He was probably the Third Mate and it was Sunday morning and it was a nice job for a quiet day alongside in Glasgow. I looked at my father and said 'Will I talk to him?' 'Definitely' says he, and so I did.

I asked how one could become an apprentice seaman to train to be a Sea Captain. I remember he was a cheery soul and he cast a mirthful look over me in my school uniform, (I did not have a good suit at that time) and said 'Come aboard and I'll give you some details'. It was my first exposure to a Scouse accent and I was exuberant as I mounted the accommodation ladder behind him, with my father following on. I glanced back and noted the delight on my father's face as he revelled in the remembered ambience of the deep sea cargo liner. He went no further than the entrance of the accommodation and was content to engage the Quartermaster in conversation, whilst I ascended higher through the various decks of her ample accommodation, to the Third Officer's cabin. To this day I can conjure up the different strata of the ship by the changing smells lodged in my memory. From the thousand cargo smells which drifted around the deck mixed with bunker fuel issuing from the engine-room, up through the lower decks where petty officers and Junior Officers resided, replete with Brylcream, Eau de Cologne (no after shave yet) tobacco and sweat, past the polished linoleum decks of the Senior Officers, with the smell of Gin and Tonic blended with the unmistakable fragrance of Flit insecticide. I would later become well acquainted with Flit, because these old ships were overrun with cockroaches and weevils, and it was the Sunday routine for the Deck apprentices to spray the whole ship, her alleyways, and stores – everywhere, to try to combat these pests. Frankly, we fought a losing battle, and I later found out those cockroaches, and probably weevils as well, had been around since the beginning and could even survive a nuclear blast. What chance for the Flit gun then? That's how we applied it, you see, with a little tin pump action spray unit. This had all to be carried out before 1030 hrs. on Sunday, when the Master would inspect the ship. I also would become acquainted with Gin and Tonic.

We reached the Third Mate's cabin and he set about writing down the name and address of the person I should contact in the firm of T&J Brocklebank, of Liverpool, to whom the ship belonged. This name was, Captain Brand, Marine Superintendent in charge of recruitment and training for Deck Officers. He and I would later exchange letters due to a minor disagreement over how I should undergo my training, but we have not arrived there yet, and I was still bedazzled by this new experience. In time I would discover that Brocklebanks, was one of, if not *the*, oldest shipping companies in the world and still proudly bore the broad white line around their massive topsides to show that they operated under 'Letters of Marque' which more or less allowed one to legally indulge in a little lucrative piracy, should the occasion present itself. Sadly I joined too late to become involved in this trade but I still tell my pupils, in the Chanter Class I run, that I used to be a pirate!

As I looked round the Third Mate's cabin I felt intoxicated by strangeness of it all. His bunk, with a big lee-board to prevent you falling out of bed in bad weather. The Thermos water jug; which would become so important when trading in the Tropics, without air conditioning. The 'Punkah Louvres' which attempted to stir the air in the cabin and would be next to useless when temperature really climbed and the relative humidity rose to one hundred percent. On his desk I noted the cargo plan he was working on, the books on his book rack, a few novels and 'Ship Stability for Masters and Mates' and the discarded copy of Playboy at the bottom of his immaculately laundered bed. I took it all in and loved it. I thanked him from the bottom of my youthful and naïve heart, and having taken my leave, recovered my father who was still yarning with the QM and went home that night to compose my letter to the Company which would become simultaneously my benefactors and exploiters for the next twelve years.

I was pretty well qualified to become a Deck Apprentice since one only needed four 'O' grades, and I had seven of those and three 'Highers', however the spectre of the vein and the hay-fever continued to haunt me at this time. Nevertheless, after a short time I was sent a letter inviting me to attend an interview in Liverpool, at Cunard Buildings in April I think it was. I had just turned seventeen.

I suppose it is the same for all young people going for a first job, but I did not view this as a job. For me it was more of a vocation; I felt called to go to sea and I was not embarking on some light undertaking, but the way I would live and make my living for the rest of my days, and I have to say I never altered my view of sea-going.

I travelled down from Glasgow on a 'Sleeper' so I could make the interview time without difficulty, and that in itself was a delight although I am not sure that the sleeper carriage was much improved from the ones I had travelled north in twelve years before. In those days I still regarded England as much a part of my birthright as any other part of the UK and I was not conscious of any difference beyond the way I spoke, between me and the English. After all, my surname was Anglo-Saxon and I felt part of the whole of Britain. Part of me still does, remembering that we British fought together, and lived together, for so long, but things changed after Thatcher and I for one am sad about it. Anyway, Lime Street Station hove into view around six in the morning and after a cup of British Rail tea and a Digestive biscuit I was ready to sortie forth and find breakfast. Not so easy in those days, issuing like a moth from the chrysalis of the gloomy station into the just as gloomy streets of an awakening Liverpool. It took a good hour for me to find an establishment willing to serve a young ravenous Scot, or anyone else for that matter, with a hot breakfast, at seven thirty in the morning. Thankfully such places exist, like oases in the barren desert of the urban sprawl, and in the main I have found them run and operated by cheerful souls who are kind and well disposed to hungry folk. Therefore, replete with bacon, eggs, beans and all the rest including a big mug of tea I set off to be interviewed.

Even today Cunard Buildings are impressive. Of course it was built that way. To impress!

Now I constantly refer to it as Cunard Buildings but of course it was just one gigantic building standing beside the equally impressive Liver

Building. They were built on the profits of trade, and trade meant ships, and ships meant seamen, and so we all had a profession. There were marble floors, beautiful huge, varnished wooden doors, lofty ceilings and cases and cases of model ships. Some of them were Brocklebank ships and some were Cunarders, because Cunard had bought over Brocklebanks some time before although they traded as separate entities.

I eventually found the floor I was supposed to be on and a kind girl behind an enormous mahogany counter pointed me in the direction of the office I was report to. I have to say it was quite intimidating waiting for the secretary to usher me in but eventually I was escorted in to the pleasant ambience of an office of a man who was content with his lot. Do I remember the smell of pipe tobacco? I think I do. Captain Brand was an archetypal ship master tending to expand amidships but still retaining a strong force of character and personality, and like so many I would meet in the future, he possessed a penetrating gaze which, whilst apparently looking deep into ones cerebral cortex, was still able to convey humour and mirth. It's a gift and you learn it after a lifetime of dealing with men. We began, and I have no recollection of the details of what was said by either party, such was my desire to be what I thought I was supposed to be. Suffice it to say that I left the office after about an hour in the certain knowledge that I was to be an Apprentice Ships Officer, and no mention of varicose veins or hay-fever. I was invited to go to the nice girl behind the huge mahogany counter to reclaim my expenses and the day began to improve immeasurably. I had the hope of a profession, money in my pocket, and when I issued forth from the portals of Cunard Buildings, where my Company, T&J Brocklebanks, had their business, I could not have been happier. The Mersey ferries busily went about their ferrying business the sun shone, people looked happy and busy and I set off north with strong feelings of achievement and manliness bubbling around inside me.

During the next couple of months I made preparations for going to sea with complete assistance from my mother and father. We did not have any spare money, but thankfully they had an insurance policy with the Co-op which they cashed in and I later found out that my father had obtained a loan to supplement the short fall. On instructions from the Company we repaired to Malcolm's, Naval Outfitters, under the Hielanman's Umbrella in Glasgow where I was kitted out with the necessary uniform for my trade. To this day I remember the total cost coming to over £200, which was a colossal sum for us. In fact as I look at my Indentures, now suitably framed to remind me of how it all started, I note that my first year's salary is £240 or £20 per month. Incidentally, the real family name of the people who owned Malcolm's, was Mallinson, they were a Jewish family, and I mention it purely to recall, how anti-Semitism, which I abhor, was still prevalent.

In the month of May I bumped into Ann Allan coming out of Sloan's Dairy which stood in Exeter Drive, about a hundred yards from where I lived. She lived in the next close to the Dairy and was a lovely girl. I remember her eyes clear and honest and bright and her face surrounded in a halo of golden curls. It was one of those moments. In my mind, as an aspiring mariner it was important that I should be able to write to a girl back home and so I went to her home after our meeting, and asked her out to the pictures.

The Allans were a good family of Methodists, and it was important that proper protocols be observed, on both sides; after all I came from a good family of Presbyterians. I took her to the pictures and we had a nice time and I saw her home, and we wrote to each other for a while, but when I came home on my first leave I had changed a lot and I am ashamed to say that I did not do the right thing and explain that to her. I played the coward and just avoided her which I think is despicable, and still grieves me.

Around the beginning of June I was assigned my first ship the *Mangla*. I was to join her in the Prince's Dock in Glasgow, which was no stranger to us, and I remember my father carrying my sea chest for a spell on the way down to the ship. I wore my uniform, which was quite normal in those days, and I felt a bit like young Hornblower, always the romantic. She was a big six hatch ship the *Mangla*, as indeed were all Brock's ships. And they all had names which began with MA. My father accompanied me aboard and, after he had seen me settled in the two berth cabin, and met my fellow apprentice Dave Byrne, a wiry, pleasant Scouser, who was senior to me by a couple of years and took the job very seriously, he handed me a new watch as a parting gift. I was very touched then, but am much more touched now, when I realise what it took for them to rig me for sea then bid farewell to their eldest son. And that was it. I must now become a seaman.

Now we stand on the shore of the rest of my life. I was about to embark on a life at sea which would span forty one years without a break except for leave. So I will have to be ruthless about the way I relate it. I will not tell you all that happened or that I can remember, for you would have to live my life again. But I will give you a flavour of it and try to let you feel it, and recall some of the more exciting parts. Remember, most of life is pretty mundane, thankfully, although there were never two days the same at sea; therefore the plan is to recount the next forty-one years in two parts, the first twelve whilst sailing with T&J Brocklebanks and their subsidiaries and associated companies, and twenty nine years whilst sailing with the Scottish Fisheries under the Blue Ensign. Against the background and contained within these large chunks of time will be the story of my family. But I will tell you about my first trip in some detail.

CHAPTER FOUR
1966 – 1978
MANGLA and MATURATA

We sailed from Prince's Dock in daylight in June 1966 and the passage was uneventful for everyone, I think, except me. You recall I had not come across the Scouse accent before and most of my shipmates were from Liverpool, except the crew, who were mostly Indians. I think in the early days, I had better communications with the Indians than the Liverpudlians and I really had to study to understand the peculiarities of their speech. Of course to make matters worse my station when we were manoeuvring the ship was to man the telephones. Now today we are used to superb sound quality in telephones, but these phones on the bridge of the *Mangla* had been built to survive a direct hit from the *Bismarck* and were made out of massive forgings like small dumb bells. The mechanism for connecting from one station to another was a brass lever which one had to throw when making a call and similarly when receiving one. When calling, you cranked a rotating lever which energised the circuit. When a call came in, a window showing a white marker flagged up and again you flipped the brass lever. This performance, added to the fact that I could not understand either the accent or the jargon, was to become my bête noire until I finally cracked the linguistic code some time later. At this point I hated these phones with a vengeance because they made me look stupid, having to have the officers repeat the messages I was supposed to be relaying. I wished I had gone with a Scots company at this point. Nevertheless we managed to get away from the Clyde and I did not return to what was left of Prince's Dock, (the Canting Basin), for forty-one years, until 2007, in command of my own ship the *Jura*

Next day we arrived off the Mersey and went to anchor until the tide turned and we could head up river with the last two hours of the flood. I was on the focsle (forecastle) for stations this time with the Mate, Derek O'Byrne, who to me looked every inch the British Merchant Seaman. He was kind and patient and scary, and taught me some of the commands and messages I was having so much trouble understanding on the phone and some of the mysteries of weighing anchor with the windlass. It was very cold on the focsle that night and I had only worn my doeskin uniform and a shirt and tie. The Mate had dressed more appropriately and once we hove up the anchor, and were on passage up the river, he eventually let me go aft to get on more gear, because I think my chattering teeth were annoying him. That was a lesson I never forgot; always dress appropriately. At one point on the passage upriver, we embarked Brocklebanks own pilot, who I think was called Mr. Collins or was it Thompson? Now we were coming up with a strong tide, and the idea was to try to get to the lock gates into Vittoria Dock, Birkenhead, with the last of the flood turning to slack water. Well, I think we must have been a bit ahead of time, and Mr Collins must have been a fine ship handler because it looked to me as if there was still a good tide running and he had to earn his fee to stop the *Mangla* from taking charge and hitting the lock entrance, but he did it with the help of the tugs. You see, I was no stranger to ship handling and the movement of ships, albeit on a smaller scale, and the feelings for the ship came naturally. I would do the same manoeuvre myself many times in later years but I always remember that first time with the Brocklebank pilot. As I say, we were to berth in Vittoria Dock, Birkenhead, which we did in time for breakfast, and I began the business of learning my ship intimately. I had hardly begun this task when word came through that I was to change ships and go to sea in the *Maturata*, which was berthed further up the dock. I must say this was not particularly welcome news as I had already begun to form those ties and associations which turn us into shipmates. However there was no debate about it so I packed my gear again and set off down the quay, as instructed.

All ships are different in their own way and you can sense the different atmosphere as soon as you board. For some reason I felt 'comfier' as I made my way onto the *Maturata*'s deck; she felt less 'intense '. Maybe it was just me but I reckon it all stems from the man at the top and his approach to life, and while she was every bit as ship-shape as the *Mangla,* she seemed to be more at peace. I again reported to the Mate, Hugh Evans, a big Welshman with black curly hair, who would have graced any front row in the scrum, and he introduced me to my new Senior Apprentice, Hugh MacMaster.

Now before I tell you about my mate Hughie (apprentices always referred to each other as 'my mate' or 'my oppo') I need to explain that the Chief Officer, Second in Command of the ship, was always referred to as 'The Mate'. He virtually ran the ship apart from the Engine Room, and we would sometimes refer to him, as Harry Tate. This was common parlance at sea on merchant ships. The mate received other names as well, but we need not go into that in detail.

Hugh MacMaster had been blessed with a face and body that seemed to send women into rapturous paroxysms, and he knew it. He looked like a Greek statue and was as strong as an ox. He could easily have made it as a leading man in swashbuckling movies and of course, since he was about four years my elder, and just about out of his time, I thought he was just great and tried to copy some of his characteristics. A tall order for someone with varicose veins and hay-fever. Hughie's big faults were that he could get himself into awful trouble very quickly just through lack of foresight and not taking things seriously enough. It had actually prevented him moving up the ranks as quickly as he should and he had a name as a 'bit of a lad'. But I thought he was admirable and he 'showed me the ropes' both aboard and ashore.

Shortly after I joined the *Maturata* we had a run ashore and went across to Liverpool and fetched up in a bar near the old cathedral. Hugh would introduce me to strong drink in the company of some giggling females. He attracted them, you see. Well I suppose I could only have been into my third pint of beer when the room started to roll and pitch quite a bit and we seemed to running into some really bad weather. The faces of the giggling girls were assuming more ghoulish forms and for some reason their heads were moving in circular orbits. I think Hughie realised that I was beginning to founder and sensibly arranged our exit. I will never forget the loss of control of my tongue and legs as we made our way back to the ship and in the morning I was a living corpse. It took me several days to recover and several years to learn that I had a low tolerance for alcohol and that if I went past my natural limit I would suffer – a lot. I now regard it as a blessing but then I was a bit disappointed in myself.

Our cargo consisted of everything that the ingenuity of the British workforce could produce, from safety pins to anchors. We literally had everything, including frozen food and Centurion tanks for our troops in the scattered outposts of what remained of the Empire, and railway engines and steel for India, which they would use to build their own ships and put our shipyards out of business. It was absolutely fascinating, and of course there was a technique for stowing and carrying everything so that it would arrive in good condition. I loved this part of the work because it was so practical and I would lament the day when Container Ships would come and we would carry everything in boxes. Yes, I sailed in container ships as well but it was a soulless affair by comparison to the general cargo ship. One of my great joys in Birkenhead was to tally ammunition aboard and listen to the Scouse stevedores bantering with each other. They were hilariously funny, and they knew it. They used to work the 'welt' whereby half were in the pub whilst the other half were down the hold. Scallywags to a man, but they could make you laugh. Eventually we were laden and sailed and I do not remember much more till we raised Gibraltar on the horizon. This was the beginning of my foreign travels and of a voyage which would take me from Gibraltar to Malta, Tripoli, Benghazi, Suez, Aden, Bombay, Bedi Bundar, Bavnagar in India and Karachi in West Pakistan, then back home to Avonmouth where we paid off. Here are some things I remember.

Valetta harbour in Malta dazzles the new arrival with its sun-coloured stone, so bright that for my northern eyes it was intolerable at first. I did not yet have the wherewithal to buy a pair of sunglasses so on my first run ashore I just squinted a lot. It was habit which continues to this day and I have ended up with heavily incised crow's feet round my eyes, but I still have the sight of a water closeted rodent. The next day I went ashore at night with Hughie, Chippy the carpenter, who had a dearth of fingers due to his close familiarity with a rotary saw, and a couple of others, one of whom was Sparkie, the Radio Officer.

To explain, at sea the Sparks is the Radio Officer whilst the Electrician is the Lecky. We ended up in a bar, as seamen do, but this time I was on my guard with no intention of repeating the Liverpool experience. Because of this I was able to observe my shipmates more closely and one memory I have is of Chippy, who was bald headed and diminutive in stature, apparently imparting great cheerfulness to one of the locals girls with what remained of his fingers. The other thing I remember is that England won the World Cup that night and the joy of the local garrison knew no bounds, which state of euphoria appears to have remained undiminished for the last fifty or so years.

Tripoli and Benghazi were much more interesting for me; it seems hardly credible, but I remember wandering around the streets and alleys at night with never a thought for safety, drinking in the sights and sounds of the Arab world, the language, the smell of herbs and spices and the ordure from the drains. I had read T E Lawrence's *Seven Pillars of Wisdom* and his *Letters*, and I was ready to be intoxicated by the sheer exotic unfamiliarity of it all. They always say you remember your first trip with greatest clarity and as I dredge up these images from the past there may be some truth in that notion. We eventually arrived in Suez and it really is one of the wonders of the modern world. A great cut through the earth which allows you to miss out Africa! Ships which gather there form up into a great convoy in the anchorage then make the transit south in one long line of multifarious shipping. It is a truly impressive sight.

There are several preparations for making the transit. First the Suez Canal searchlight must be rigged. This is usually mounted on a set of rails in the focsle head and then pulled forward to shine through a large circular watertight opening in the bow to allow the pilot to see at night. Then derricks are prepared and swung out to pick up the several 'bumboats' which accompany the vessel during her transit. Some of these have legitimate marine functions whilst others exist to bolster the trading economy of the street vendors. These will sell you anything from a 'lovely leather camel doll' to a 'lovely English School teacher' *Cave Emptor!* They will also sell you some dubious photographic artwork depicting impressive gymnastics on the part of the subjects, and stimuli to enhance the performance of the most lacklustre couple. It all goes to expand the knowledge of the young mariner, and supplement the nautical training which by now was beginning to amass some significance.

Brocklebank ships and indeed many cargo liner companies carried three or more Quartermasters. They were usually men of middle to late middle age, frequently hailing from the Highlands and Islands of Scotland, who were seeking a less energetic life than that of an Able Bodied Seaman. They had great practical experience in seamanship and for the most part were expert in imparting it. Among their duties were steering the ship, keeping look-out, seeing to the upkeep of the bridge and wheelhouse area (especially the 'bright-work' like brass, varnish and rope-work) and generally be around to assist the Officer of the Watch. They kept a gangway watch in port and tended the accommodation ladder. They also helped with the practical training of the Apprentices, and I am indebted to them for their patient, kind and often fatherly advice.

From Suez we made our way through the Red Sea to Aden, which at that time was an important military base with the requisite garrison and naval facilities. By now we were sailing into 'flying fish' weather and it was an opportunity for the Mate to continue to inspect and overhaul the derrick and lifting gear, which had begun when we entered the Mediterranean. Everything had to be checked and overhauled, from the humblest shackle to the mighty six-fold purchase of the jumbo derrick. Brocklebank ships were all six hatch vessels with four derricks per hatch plus a 'Jumbo' 80 tonner between number two and three hatches, and a twenty tonner between five and six. The big jumbo was for Centurion tanks and locomotives, whilst the 20 tonner was for smaller 'heavy lifts'. As I say, everything was checked and even with the large crews which we had at the time it was an enormous task and all the deck crew including the Apprentices were involved. It was wonderful training, however, and by the time we finished the overhaul, I had a good idea of the cargo gear for a merchant ship, and how to use it. This experience allied to what I was learning from the 'old' Quartermasters would provide the bedrock of my knowledge which I continued to build on until I retired. Always learning, you see?

Aden was a great place to buy duty free radios and cameras and was very busy with the garrison and the naval dockyard. Soon after this, following the rebels' fight for independence, Colonel 'Mad Mitch' Mitchell would gain fame and notoriety as he led the Argylls to recapture the colony, but it was merely an interlude before the British pulled out for good. In these days though, it was warm, and bright and busy.

The next leg of our voyage took us across the Arabian Sea in the south-west monsoon, and the steel (which you may recall was loaded in Birkenhead in the bottom of number two and three holds for stability purposes) began to make its presence felt. The effect of having so much weight so low down in the bottom of the vessel made her very 'stiff'. What happens is, the centre of gravity of the vessel is very low with the result that the distance between the centre of gravity and the metacentre of the ship is very large. This results in large righting levers which seek to return the ship very quickly to the upright. It's technical. The outcome of that is that the ship will roll on wet grass, let alone with the effect of the south-west Monsoon on the beam. So we rolled and rolled all the way to the Maldive Islands! We had cargo for the port of Malé.

One event lodges in my memory from around this part of the voyage. The Mate had set us apprentices to checking the lifeboats, which involved stripping the gear out of them, checking it against the lifeboat stores list, renewing any cordage on the sails and becketted lines and painters so on, and painting the insides with Stockholm tar. This is a tar derived from steaming the wood of fir trees in the northern wastes of Scandinavia and is outrageously expensive nowadays. It is very good for preserving wood.

So Hughie had said to me as we stripped this boat out, 'Don't try to shift the oars, mast and lugsails yourself in case she rolls and you go over the side. I'm going down to see Chippy about something'. 'Fair enough' says I and carried on with the bits I could do. Hughie took an unconscionable long time at what he was doing so I decided to surprise him by shifting first the oars, which were no problem then the sails and finally the mast. Now the mast whilst not enormous was still a significant weight plus the fact it was rigged with wire stays, halyards and downhauls.

In readiness for painting the inside of the boat we had rather foolishly it appears now in retrospect, hung the pot of Stockholm tar from one of the awning spars which were as yet *sans* awnings. They were white awning spars and the pot swung over the beautiful pitch pine deck outside the Mates accommodation on the Boat Deck. I started out pretty well lifting the mast from the outboard side of the boat, then the next move involved me rotating in azimuth one hundred and eighty degrees to place the mast on the awning spar near the inboard side of the boat. And that is really where things started to go slightly awry. You recall the monsoon had been blowing and although the wind had eased that day to allow the sun out, there still remained a residual swell. It was the swell which disturbed my rotation and for a moment as I pirouetted on the outboard side bench of the lifeboat I actually thought I might end up in the Indian Ocean clinging to this wretched mast.

However, I managed to recover my balance but in so doing created accelerating, centrifugal forces on the end of the mast, which, connecting with the pot of Stockholm Tar rendered the paint airborne until it connected with the pristine pitch pine deck. And Hughie appeared. A hideous slick of thick black tar was migrating across the deck and Hughie, who had hitherto been getting on well with the Mate could see his hopes for a Fourth Mate's job evaporating. He was pretty angry but did not resort to physical violence, which when I look back seems strange. We immediately set about clear up operations which were carried out in a tense atmosphere, then as we scooped and scraped and scrubbed we realised we would have to tell big Hugh Evans. Once again I felt the loneliness of the condemned man as I made my way up to Harry Tate's room. He had his wife him that trip and they had been turned in for an afternoon siesta after the curry at lunchtime.

I knocked the door and waited. I could hear sounds of life inside and eventually the Mate appeared complete with spouse. I recall she was a thinnish lady. I explained my sin to them both in the doorway and observed the tempest form on the brow of our Brythonic Chief. I also noticed just a hint of humour in the eyes of his wife who, while striving to support her husband through this tragedy, could nevertheless detect the humour in my discomfiture. Hughie in the meantime had drawn up alongside me and it is not impossible that it was his presence which tipped the scales of Mrs. Evans' mirth in my favour. Hughie had that effect on women of all ages. Next they must view the scene of the crime along with Mr. and Mrs Sparks and every other Mr. and Mrs. who occupied the Senior Officers' accommodation. Then, after the Mate had issued some unnecessary orders about the cleanup operation they must take photographs as we toiled to remove the offending stain. Those photos exist somewhere as a memorial to a young seaman's folly. Eventually even the Mate began to see the humour of the situation and a type of calm returned to the *Maturata's* boat deck

The Maldive Island men are excellent seamen and we always carried a few for overhauling the topping lifts of the Jumbo derrick, amongst other things. They seemed to relish dangling aloft, more so than the average Indian seaman, and having seen the Maldives I think they get it from climbing the coconut palms which grew in abundance. They were small in stature and always cheerful, a bit like marine, tropical Ghurkhas. I liked them. I do not remember much more about that visit to Male, but I returned on a later voyage and I will relate that when I get to it. We now had the wind more astern and ran before it, more comfortably, to the port of Cochin in south west India which I remember for two things.

Firstly, I bought two watercolours from a local artist called A P Joseph, which depict stylised scenes from the river on which Cochin stands, and which until recently hung in my parents' house in Gardenstown. Secondly, I made a complete fool of myself ashore having been led astray by some of my senior officers who should have known better. What I see is a night journey through the lush jungle of the environs of Cochin and the glow of Tilly lamps and rudimentary electric lighting issuing from shacks and lean-to dwellings, all tinged with the green glow of the tropical forest. What I can feel are the blushes of a young man exploring life and the sighs of an old man recalling it.

And that is all you need to know about that.

From Cochin we set a course for Bombay which for some reason they have started to call Mumbai without even consulting me. When you land there, as we did by boat, threading a route through the crowding traffic of the seafront, you come upon the 'Gateway of India'. It is a kind of triumphal arch welcoming arriving travellers, and, through the good offices of Google Chrome, I find that it was only completed in 1924. This surprises me because I was under the impression it was older, say Victorian. I have no memory of that visit to Bombay beyond buying some trinkets in a market.

But I have other tales on later visits.

The rest of our voyage would occupy us with loading the vessel for home, in Bedi Bundar and Bhavnagar. I thought we went to Karachi but I am not sure now. In any event our cargo would comprise a concoction of various local products including oil cake, rice bran, shellac, and bagged latex. Now you have to be careful with both oil cake and rice bran, because they are both susceptible to 'spontaneous combustion', brought about by overheating of the contents deep inside the gunny sacks. In order to circumvent this problem, the cargo has to be ventilated by building temporary wooden ventilation shafts throughout the whole stow, which was a huge job employing several local carpenters. In addition to that, we apprentices had to be constantly vigilant, armed with a stab thermometer which we took great pleasure in thrusting into the guts of unsuspecting sacks. In the main as I recall, the temperatures were acceptable, but on one occasion I had to repair ashore with the Mate to condemn a consignment of oil cake, and it gave me an opportunity to see a part of India which up to that time was as yet unspoilt. In this place, I think it was Bhavnagar; there were few motorised vehicles and plenty of carts drawn by cattle. The pace of the town was very slow compared to Bombay and I remember being grateful that I had witnessed it. The other thing we had to look out for were weevils, and believe me if there was something we did not need aboard the *Maturata* it was weevils. To this day I habitually knock out a piece of bread before I eat it, and I recall one night down a hold tallying bags of rice bran and suddenly becoming aware that the surface of some of the bags was heaving with the these little brown insects. Of course, we shipped the offending bags back ashore, but there was no way we had prevented them coming aboard.

One last thing I need to tell you about while I was in Indian waters. I was on bridge watchkeeping the twelve to four in the morning with the Second Mate, when we came upon a phenomenon called a 'milk sea'. The water in Rann of Kutch was full of plankton, the sky was overcast with stratocumulus, and it seemed as if sky and sea merged into one so that there was no sense of distance. There was no horizon and it felt like being inside a ping pong ball. So disturbing was it that the Second Mate called the Master and we put on the radar, which was a true measure of how unsettling it was, since in those days it almost required an Act of Parliament before either action could be permitted.

We had now completed our work of loading and began to steam for home. In the meantime the South West Monsoon had eased off and we were pretty comfortable and all hands were put to painting round and smartening up the ship for going home. This was traditional for ships coming home after a voyage and all ships' companies tried to make her look good for arrival in the UK. Back through the Suez Canal and through the Mediterranean, the Bay of Biscay and up the Bristol Channel to Avonmouth, where we tied up on a grey, miserable day to complete my first voyage.

CHAPTER FIVE
LUCELLUM

It had been an enjoyable experience, but to be frank it was not all I had expected. For one thing there were a lot unnecessary protocols and taboos and traditions which I found tedious, and an attitude of resistance to change which even I could see was out of place in a world where the pace of change was accelerating. I seriously wondered if I had made the right career choice. When I returned I was coming back to a new family home since my parents had left Partick and bought a house in Yoker. It was a lovely big sandstone villa called 'Smithfield' and much grander than anything I had known before. It was built on three storeys and we owned them all. It was truly liberating for each one of the children now had a room of their own, and mine was huge. My father had been very busy while I was at sea and built a set of built-in cupboards and a desk for me, and my mother had papered and decorated with great gusto.

While I was home we built a kind of raised dais where my bed area was. Luxury! I was glad to be able to help a little financially because whilst at sea I had not only saved some money, but we apprentices had received a significant rise in our wages and improved working conditions. I had not been home long however, perhaps a fortnight, when a letter arrived instructing me to proceed to Smith's Dock in North Shields to join my next ship, an oil tanker, owned by H E Moss and Company, a subsidiary of Brocklebanks and therefore also of Cunard. She was called the *Lucellum*. If Brocklebanks ships all began with MA then Moss Tankers all began with LU and were something to do with light. Whilst home I had danced around my misgivings about my future at sea but my father was able to reassure me that it was always like that, and my mother, who was never one for weakness, more robustly reminded me that once you put your hand to the plough there was no turning back. So that was that. I repaired aboard the *Lucellum* in Smith's Drydock, North Shields. I would serve on her for the next eleven months.

Tankers are nothing like cargo ships, beyond the fact they float and move goods from one part of the world to another. Their entire ethos is different. There is a greater sense of urgency, an awareness of the need for great vigilance and a generally more upbeat atmosphere. There was much less hidebound convention and a genuine feeling amongst the officers that they were a kind of cut above the rest because they had to be quick and accurate in what they did. With some pride they referred to themselves as 'Tankermen'. I felt much more at home in this environment. Product-carrying tankers would be my favourite ships for the next eleven years. Of course, this new trade involved learning new skills and I had now to learn about valves, pumps, pipelines, tank cleaning, gas freeing, cargo sampling and many other things besides. This trip, my senior apprentice was a chap called Dave Stillwell and we became good pals, although we never met up again after the voyage. Dave was another Scouser, very wiry with shoulders like a boxer and very capable and keen on the job, and I was happy to learn from him.

As I say, we were in dry-dock and it is only in dry-dock that you really begin to understand a ship and gain an impression of how she is constructed and how big she is. One always remembers the massive propeller and rudder and the lovely form of the plating round the bow which, even in a workhorse like a tanker, was clearly skilfully constructed.

Apprentices were very important in tankers because they were able to take on so many of the duties that would otherwise fall on the Chief Officer. They were in charge of tank cleaning, working with the Bosun and the Pump-man and we very soon became very skilful at organising the men through the Bosun, and arranging the cleaning of each tank in the ship through the Pump-man. We had heavy but portable Butterworth machines which had three slowly rotating nozzles in the vertical axis whilst the whole machine rotated in azimuth. Theoretically then, the liquid which was pumped through the machine via heavy rubber hoses at high pressure would cover every part of the tank they were in. To ensure we hit as much of the tank as possible we dropped the machines in three ten foot drops with varying lengths of time at each drop depending on how dirty the tank was. We could also pump hot water and chemicals or even gas-oil (diesel) through them if the circumstances required it.

We had white crew on this ship and most of them came from the Tyne, and so were 'Geordies', but the Bosun was one Joe Block who hailed from Malta. Hughie MacMaster who I had sailed with last trip told me about Joe having sailed with him on tankers before, and I remembered that Joe had done time for manslaughter having dispatched a near relative with a knife. The descriptive terms 'face chiselled out of mahogany' and 'hands like hams' began to mean something. But I got on great with him and so did Dave and we had the good sense always to work through the Bosun. Joe Block was a real character and I would sail with him again when I became Third Officer of the *Luxor*; he always called me 'Mr. Davie' then, and I continued to give him genuine respect. Another memorable character of the *Lucellum* was the Pump-man and I am sorry to say his name has gone from memory, if I ever knew it. To us he was 'Pumps', and that was that. But 'Pumps' taught us a huge amount about cargo handling and getting the best out the steam driven centrifugal pumps. Look at me; I can remember the cargo pumps were Drysdales but not the name of the dear man who taught us so much about them. I say 'Dear man'; he was a rough old diamond and capable of some pretty lamentable behaviour, but his heart was in the right place and he always called me 'Waur haggish'. This means 'Our Haggis' in Geordie. Most of the folk on the ship though, from the Mate down called me 'Jock', which I was very happy about, and used to play up to by wearing my old Scout Balmoral hat when working out on deck. Apprentices were 'dogsbodies' who were expected to be able to take and carry out anything given by the Mate, or anyone else senior to us, for that matter. We had to be prepared to do any job no matter how menial, because the day would come when we would command ships and would need to know what men were capable of, and how to do any task on the ship. What I found was, if you rose to the challenge and really got stuck in without whining you gained a lot of respect, in the eyes of the whole crew, and it was a wonderful feeling when you realised that that you were really becoming a leader whom men would be comfortable trusting. The whole process which had developed from the time men started going to sea, was designed to be character forming and in the main I think it was successful. We were supposed to be 'Characters' as apprentices.

We sailed from the Tyne with enough ship's stores to last us a year and the general remit to go and make money. The *Lucellum* was a tramp tanker working on the spot market, and we could literally be sent anywhere in the world. This was my kind of seafaring and I relished the thought that we might end up anywhere. My memory is a bit hazy on this but I think we set off for the Mediterranean and loaded a cargo of gas-oil (diesel) in Gela in Sicily for somewhere which might have been the continent. Then we went back through the Mediterranean via Suez to the Persian Gulf. Nowadays they call it the Arabian Gulf, where we loaded in Ras Tanura for Jeddah. These were the days before Aramco built the pipeline across the desert; and our company won, and retained, the charter to ship oil from the Gulf to Jeddah for many years to come.

We were the first ship, I think, on that run and I am afraid we were very good at it, because we were stuck on that self-same run for the next seven months. Always the same two ports. The routine was de-ballast, load four grades of product, Mogas (petrol), Avgas (aviation fuel), gas-oil (diesel) and Kerosene (paraffin), in Ras Tanura. That took about twenty-four hours in total. Then we carried it round to Jeddah, where we discharged, which took about three days, then we sailed and tank cleaned for four days all the way back to the Gulf. The steaming time from the Gulf to Jeddah was about seven days and of course the same back, so the round trip was about three weeks. The only thing which changed was the amounts of the different grades of product and the weather, which varied from hot to exceedingly hot. Of course the *Lucellum* was not built with air conditioning so when I say that she was hot, you can have no conception of what that is like, particularly up the Gulf.

When we got back to sea and rounded the Quoins to exit the Gulf after loading, it was like rebirth for we could open the doors in the fore part of the accommodation and allow the sea air to drive out the heat. Don't forget tankers had to be battened down while working cargo, so no ports were allowed to be open and we had to rely of air blowers and fans. Down the pump-room was a nightmare because not only was it breathtakingly hot but the bilges were awash with product which had leaked from the glands on the drive shafts of the pumps, so not only were we in danger of suffering dehydration, but we could also be gassed by petroleum fumes, not to mention being blown into a million tiny pieces. When I think how things are now at sea and compare it to those days, there is no comparison. Safety is now of paramount importance and one simply does not allow dangerous situations to occur. Mind you, tankers still blow up, although not so frequently. Frankly I never felt afraid on tankers while I served on them and it was only in later years that I thought about it and realised that we took a lot of chances. The most dangerous time for a tanker is when she is in ballast and before she has been gas freed. At that time the explosive mixture of gasses is at its most volatile and a spark can cause an explosion.

So the routine was; clean the tanks as I told you before, then gas free them as you moved from one tank to the next and finally line wash the cargo lines. And where did all these tank-cleanings and line-washings go? Over the side! I blush about it now, but then that was the way everyone did it. Gas freeing the tanks was carried out by either rigging sail chutes over the tank lids and down into the tank or driving air into the tank by employing a Gotaverken venturi tank blower. These were big brass (to avoid sparks) trumpet-like devices, which were the same diameter as the Butterworth openings on the deck, through which you drove steam through a narrow nozzle. As the steam entered the tank it sucked in fresh air and filled the tank with air displacing the gas. They were noisy brutes and if you had a few going on deck it was intolerable with them all roaring like dragons. In later years we were supplied with water driven Vent Axia fans which were less noisy and more efficient.

Tankers in those days were hard physical work for all the mates and particularly the apprentices because the valve wheels were large and often stiff, so we sometimes had to use wheel spanners or wheel keys to 'Break them off the seat 'if they were jammed. One tried not to use a wheel key too often as it was possible to bend the valve spindle which ran from the valve wheel to the valve some forty odd feet below. I think there were about one hundred and twenty valves on deck and a similar number down below in the pump-room, and they would all be 'swung' open and shut several times during the cycle of a cargo. Carry these actions out in the searing heat of the Gulf and the Red Sea and you will appreciate that we were very strong and fit. I remember once having to get a cholera injection in some port or other, and the young female Indian doctor was astonished when the needle bent as she tried to force it into my upper arm. I felt pretty good about that and gave her a wink when she finally managed with a heavier gauge needle. She blushed. And I smiled. Jolly Jack at every turn.

Now, Saudi Arabia is of course the spiritual heartland of the Islamic faith, centred on Mecca, and as such alcohol is strictly forbidden anywhere ashore. We had a dispensation to carry some alcohol because we were keeping the place going with fuel, but it was very strictly controlled and even on board it was rationed; not that it bothered me very much, but I can tell you that human beings being what they are will always kick against the goads, and I can remember the old Arab pilot going ashore with his ditty bag full of booze and cigarettes. I will not tell you his name in case somebody raises a fatwah against him but he was a very good pilot and he needed to be, because the entrance to Jeddah harbour is impressive, and I for one did not grudge him a tipple after his work. One enters by two so-called Gateways, which are gaps in an otherwise impenetrable ring of coral reefs to seaward of the harbour. On a bright morning, which most mornings are there, one can see the coral with brilliant and beautiful clarity, but to the mariner, concentrating on the swing of his ship as she passes through these gateways, they were a sobering and frightening threat, which could open the hull of your ship like a can opener. Once inside the Inner Harbour the pilot would guide her towards the oil platform, then at the right point, drop the starboard anchor and let the cable run. After we had veered about five shackles (450 feet) which had the effect of slowing her up and turning her head seaward, we would drop the port anchor then come astern, always paying out more cable on both anchors until we were able to run mooring ropes by boat to each of three buoys which lay astern and on each side of the stern of the ship. It is called a Mediterranean Moor, and we did it every three weeks.

Once we were tied up, it was the job of the Deck Officers and the Apprentices to discharge the products, without any admixture, which was affectionately called in the trade a 'cocktail'. Cocktails were to be avoided at all costs, and one's reputation now and forever more hung on one's ability to get the 'line up' of the valves on deck and in the Pump-room correct every time. There was no room for error here, and that is why I say we had to be alert at all times. It used to take us about three days to discharge due to pressure restrictions on the cargo hoses which were fished up from the sea and bolted onto the manifold amidships. These were three fairly easy going days and that is why I mention the alcohol, because we did not miss it. Instead, when we were allowed shore leave, which Dave and I could never take together as there always had to be one of us aboard (working six hours on, six hours off) we used to get up to either the 'Souk' (market place) or to the Swimming Club, of which we had honorary membership.

The Souk was a fascinating place, more or less unchanged from the time of Lawrence of Arabia, and you could buy just about anything there. I bought a pair of Ray Ban sunglasses there long before they became popular, for ten pounds or the equivalent in Riyals. I suppose that was about half a month's wages so they were quite expensive even then. Rugs, carpets, radios and cameras and every species of duty free goods, but as always, it was the smell of the place which evokes the most intense memories. Spices, kebab shops, hookahs giving off the smell of Turkish tobacco, heavy thick coffee and ten thousand things besides…

I would like to say that our visits to the swimming club were opportunities to meet the fair sex, but I would be lying. Opportunities for intersecting with them were limited because they were fairly cliquish even if they were expats like us. But the view was nice and you could get a cold soft drink there.

One happy day occurred when, having completed the overhaul of one of the lifeboats we decided to take it away under sail and under the command of the Second Mate. We secreted a case of beer aboard unbeknown to the Saudi guard, then launched her from the davits and set off at a great clip under the standing lug and jib sails. Now, anyone will tell you that, while the older type of ships lifeboat (like the *Kishmul*) was very stable and strong, they made poor sailors into the wind, and the best you could hope for was about 6 points off the wind, in other words about 67 degrees on either side of the course you actually wanted to steer. So while we made great progress before the North-east Monsoon (that's the best time of year in that part of the world), when we came to turn back *sans* beer and a few miles downwind, it was not such a laughing matter. Or rather it was. Of course she would not sail into the stiff breeze so we had to furl the sails and proceed under oars, since even the Third engineer could not get the engine going. We had a pretty scratch crew comprising the Second Mate, Third Mate, Stillwell, Beveridge, the Third Engineer, Sparkie, the galley boy, the pantry boy and a few others besides, now forgotten. I think the Mate must have taken pity on us that afternoon and let his Mates and Apprentices off for some R&R which is why we were all together. You have never seen such a performance trying to get this mob to row in time, and of course the beer was not helping. She made progress like a drunken water beetle with her sails down and this motley bunch who could not row for toffee. Eventually, after about an hour of this performance, the beer began to wear off under the dual effects of the sun and the exercise, and they began to shape up as crew, but it took us up to dinner time to come back alongside the old *Lucellum* when we hove the boat up into the chocks of the davits. On the strength of this I think the Mate issued the two catering boys with a lifeboat ticket!

On a more sober note one day the alarm bells started ringing when we were in Jeddah. I had detected a lot of running about in the vicinity of the entrance to the Engine-room. I quizzed someone about what was happening and he said the Third Engineer had had an accident down below. I went down into the Engine room and sure enough there was a huddle near the entablature doors of the big Doxford opposed piston main engine. I made my way down to see what had happened, to find the Chief Engineer and a few others in a state of shock, and Mick the Third (who had been with us on the life boat) with his foot half off. The bottom piston which they had been lowering onto the studs of the liner had jammed in the liner, slipped out of the hook of the chain block, then started to move with a rush. The poor Third Engineer's foot was on one of the studs. Well, it was a pretty gruesome sight, but something had to be done so in consultation with the Chief Steward I shot up and got some Morphine ampoules from the medical locker then tore back down and got the job of administering the injection.

Funny how squeamish folk can be about that sort of thing.

The Second Mate and the Mate by this time had arrived and they started to organise moving him on the Robertson stretcher. The Robertson is a flexible stretcher designed for manoeuvring a casualty round tight spaces. It was desperate work getting him up all the steps with his foot hanging off, and then trying to get him into the boat which the Captain had organised. We lowered him over the side on the end of the runner of the manifold derrick, having braced up the dismembered foot as best we could in the hope it could be saved, but it really was mangled. That was as much as I knew about it. The Mate and the Second Mate went ashore with him and apparently were stopped by the guard at the landing because they did not have some bit of paper; however he saw sense when the Second Mate, despite the language difficulties, threatened to shove his gun where there was no chance of ultra violet rays. Mick came back to see us the next time we were in Jeddah and he looked fine, but they had been forced to remove his leg below the knee. We all felt for Mick, but I think the Company compensated him in the end, and it certainly concentrated our minds on safety for a while. You see, it was different at sea in those days and we were very carefree as we went about the deck. We all stripped to the waist, wore shorts and turned as black as the ace of spades, and on our feet we wore flip flops. When I think about it now I get a knot in my stomach but then it was just the way it was. You adapted and survived or got out.

In Ras Tanura there was no town or harbour or market or swimming club, just a 'T' shaped jetty at the end of which was a seamen's club house which was just a big shack. But it did have air conditioning and showed a movie at night. You could also buy American candy bars and Coca Cola but that was it. So the highlight of the loading port was the movie in the air conditioning. Also, being an American installation they had iced water machines and chocolate covered salt tablets on the loading jetty which were much easier to swallow than ours which were like blocks of salt. We had no such devices on board, and of course water and salt are vitally important in the Arabian desert, which is in fact where we were. We did have movies, however, provided by the Company through a distributor called Walport. We had three movies supplied in a tin box which we could swap with other ships which we met up with. The movie at the week-end was the highlight of the week at sea, and they were shown on a projector by the faithful old Apprentices. Every Saturday night we would rig up the gear in the Crew's Mess and everyone who was not on watch would attend with few exceptions, to sup their two beers and relax. The films were a tremendous escape for us and I for one am profoundly indebted to the film industry for providing these interludes when we could enter another place and time and vicariously live other lives, however briefly. Also there was a whip round at the end of the trip on Pay-off day, by the men for the 'Boys' - that was us, and we both earned more out the generosity of these seamen than we did in two months hard labour. They were always lavish in their praise of us and would say 'Whay aye, two good lads yi nah' when we put round the hat.

At last after about seven months on this run we received orders to proceed to Bombay to load for Thailand. To say this news was received with ecstatic joy is to seriously understate the case. Whilst much of the last seven months had seen us operating in the North-East Monsoon, much had not, and the very high temperatures and humidity of the South-West Monsoon in an old fashioned tanker without air conditioning had a very debilitating effect on the crew, including us, not to mention a dearth of most of the comforts which the majority of mankind takes for granted. India and Siam therefore, particularly for the youth on board, beckoned like two exotic beacons of pleasure and fantasy, and we endlessly discussed and daydreamed and speculated about the conquests and amorous adventures which surely awaited us in the tropical wonderland that was the Far East. The older hands just listened, said something prosaic or wise or foul, and winked to each other. Some of them agreed it would be nice to see some trees.

We tank-cleaned most of the way from the Gulf to Bombay and, polluted the beautiful Arabian Sea with our four grades of petroleum products. Of course, I was an old hand in Bombay having been there the previous year, but to be honest, although I had not even scratched the surface of the place, I had no particular desire to go ashore. The time we had off watch was very limited because we were berthed out at Butcher Island, Bombay's loading terminal, and you might as well have been in Swansea for all we saw of the city. Remember, loading only took a couple of days at most, even in India, so by the time you were showered, caught the liberty boat, started sweating, climbed ashore at The Gateway of India, sweated some more, had a look around and bought some trinkets, it was time to get back for your next six hour watch. Certainly there was no time for dusky maidens, unless you were exceptional or undiscerning. So Bombay or (if you will) Mumbai, was pretty much a non-event for the Deck Officers and Apprentices.

It occurs to me, as I write this, that the Naval term 'midshipmen' is a good term, because we were between the Mates and the crew, in our own ambivalent world, a twilight zone of blurred demarcations, and in my opinion, it is good place to be when you are learning how to run a ship. I did have one run ashore to Butcher island itself, and a few of us were wandering about when one of the AB's (Able Bodied Seamen), one Paddy Boyle from Belfast, who would later pass into the Beveridge family memory banks as the fellow who coined the phrase *'Do you promise to take this fire brigade to its local station? Do you promise to take this fire brigade to its local station? And do you further promise to take this fire brigade? 'All* of this rubbish followed by a foul invective to remove oneself from the immediate vicinity... (yes, he was nuts)... Where was I? Ah yes. Paddy discovered an old naval graveyard from around the early 1800s and it was quite sad for several of its inmates were chaps about our ages who had succumbed to 'fever'. The other thing I remember from that sortie was visiting a tiny Hindu temple. I think it was dedicated to Vishnu and was clearly well tended and cared for, because incense was burning and it was lit by candles. The floor was laid with linoleum and there were stone side benches. Of all my memories of India that is the most iconic.

I think the whole crew was saving itself for Thailand, and the passage from Bombay down the coast of Mangalore round Dondra Head in Ceylon and the across the Bay of Bengal was soon accomplished, and during that time we got on with maintenance. Being laden in a tanker is when you can push ahead with painting ship and so on, so time went by pleasantly as we carried out the chores which never stop on a ship.

We could not go straight up the Bangkok River but had to lighten ship at a place called Siracha, because we were too deep in draught. We anchored there and discharged into small coastal tankers, and the agents arranged to send out fresh fruit and vegetables and general stores, which were accompanied by large numbers of the most delightful Sirens that deprived mariners could hope to clap eyes on. We called the boats the 'Meat Boats'. I think the girls were all beautiful and had names like Kim Yu, Pak Li, and so on. For many of our crew the temptation was too much, and many succumbed that day and in the days to follow, as the *Lucellum* got lighter along with their pockets. I for one did not fall, not out of any altruistic reason, but because I had become terrified of catching something incurable, having read an article in Reader's Digest, shortly before arriving in Siracha.

Funny the way things turn out.

And I can assure you I was sorely tempted because it turned out I was the double of one of the current Thai heart throbs. Whether on watch or off watch there was no peace and I was importuned at every turn, so much so that I invented two stories; one, that I had a hernia due to too much valve swinging and two; that I was saving myself for some imaginary beauty at home. Pure fantasy of course, but within six weeks of finally departing Bangkok we were administering antibiotics like an aid station in a disaster zone, to stem the epidemic of STDs.

Eventually we were light enough, in more ways than one, to proceed up the Bangkok River and I well remember the houses built out of teak, on stilts, very basic, but every one of which had a television going. That image, added to the predilection of the river boats, for exhibiting neon or ultraviolet lights on their boats which zoomed around everywhere with long extensions on the propeller shafts of their engines, cast a surreal atmosphere over the whole night river passage. As always, these images were made more intense by the powerful odours of the Far East.

The discharge in Bangkok, as I recall, was leisurely and it permitted the opportunity for a couple of sorties up town. One night I went ashore with the

Second Mate and ended up, yes you guessed it, in a bar. The place was very spacious and would put you in mind of the Jewish restaurant in 'Once Upon a Time in America', but with gaudier paintwork. There was a girl there doing a strip tease which ended up with her being completely naked, and try as I might to relax and revel in my baser instincts, I kept thinking she was someone's daughter or sister. This really was not for me, and although I said it had been a great night, I felt pretty cheap. The next day I went ashore myself and wandered around just enjoying the strangeness of the place, and came to the conclusion that the Thai people must be amongst the most beautiful in the world. I was looking for postcards and ended up in the General Post Office, which was an enormous Colonial type of building built in an outrageously grand style. On the postcard stand which stood on the counter, they were selling postcards of some of the many temples, each more exotic than the last. I remember one was called Wat Po (I think Wat meant temple) and another was the temple of the reclining Buddha. This was a statue over one hundred feet long, covered in gold. As I pondered which cards I would buy, an absolutely stunning girl came over from behind the counter to assist me and started to tell me about these temples. She spoke excellent English, and her descriptions were fascinating; and so was she. To this day I can see this beautiful, petite young woman in a saffron mini dress with luxuriant black hair and almond eyes, taking the time to talk to me. This went on for quite some time and I think we were beginning to draw stares from some of folk round about when she asked me if I would like to go to one of the temples. I could not believe it! This lovely creature was offering to show me round the temples. I think it was all down to this lookalike thing with the actor, but in any case I was not complaining, and made an arrangement to see her the next day. I went back to the ship with light step and a lighter heart. This was the sort of romance for me, and my fantasies knew no bounds. I had no sooner flown up the gangway with the prospect of the morrow stretching ahead to be greeted by the gangway watchman who told me with great relish that we would be sailing that night! I was utterly crestfallen.

We ballasted, disconsolately on my part, during my watch, and the crew began to stagger back from ashore, everyone them as drunk as lords. We had to intercept them coming aboard with booze, and relieved them of it with the promise they would get it during the voyage. Just as well we were a good natured crowd or it could have been ugly. When we went on stations for departure, my mate Dave had to steer the ship and there was only the Mate, myself and the Bosun Joe Block, on the focsle, and he was not exactly a picture of sobriety. Joe that is; the Mate was fine. In those days we had multi-plait manila hawsers and they weighed a ton, especially when wet, so it was a very slow process to 'single up' (that means to reduce the number of moorings to a safe minimum) and then 'let go'. In the end we got all the moorings aboard and managed to make our way safely out of the river, past the boats and little houses with orders to return to... Ras Tanura!

But time was wearing on, and as we rolled our way back across the Bay of Bengal, polluting the sea as efficiently as we could, and rolled our way across the Arabian Sea, gas freeing and getting on with maintenance of the old *Lucellum*, the Master received a signal from one Captain Brand whom you may remember from long ago when I joined the Company. During my service on the *Lucellum*, the training of Apprentices was undergoing a huge re-organisation, part of which was that we were now to undergo a Mid Apprenticeship Release (MAR) course at Warsash near Southampton, thereby deserting our old association with Liverpool Nautical College. Part of this reappraisal of what every aspiring young mariner should know was a complete overhaul of the Physics and Mathematics syllabi. Several new species of subject had appeared in the menagerie of learning, which seemed to me to have little to do with seafaring. Probability and Statistics, Differential Calculus, Analytical Geometry and much besides. Of course, in order to learn these new topics at a distance by correspondence course, a whole posse of new books was required, which I simply could not get my hands on. I tried honestly, in Jeddah and Bombay and Bangkok to no avail. And it was from Bangkok I had written to Captain Brand, informing him that, through no fault of mine, this seismic upheaval of the time-honoured path by which mariners progressed in their studies had caused me to fall so far behind in my studies that I had decided to take a more 'traditional' route. My plan was simply to learn from old *Nicholls Concise Guide*, *Nicholls Seamanship*, *Ship Stability for Masters and Mates* and so on.

I think, in retrospect, that I could have worded it more tactfully.

I was on deck, tank cleaning, when the Master, Captain Gordon Ward, appeared loping up the flying bridge like a barrister turned flamingo. To me he exactly fitted how I imagined Nelson to have looked, with an intelligent brow, aquiline features and sandy hair all mounted on a gangly skinny frame. I admired him as a ship-master and a man immensely. He spoke very precisely and genteelly; and I was acutely embarrassed when I realised by Dave Stillwell's surprised upward glance that Captain Ward was above us on the flying bridge with his signal all hot from the Kremlin, and me mouthing off to Dave in focslehead language of the very basest sort. He had clearly been unsettled by this communiqué and demanded in a most civilised way what I thought I was playing at writing the script for my training. We slowly migrated down the flying bridge into the accommodation and up to his cabin where he placed himself behind his desk, joined his figure tips together like a nautical Sherlock Holmes, and began to interview me 'ex cathedra', while I remained firmly on the carpet. It did not take long to relate my tale, for it was nothing but the truth, and as I continued, I could detect a softening of the pale grey eyes, and a kindred spirit, albeit a lofty one. The fact is, I was regarded on board, along with Dave, as the other half of the two best apprentices the Mate had ever sailed with, and I am pretty sure the Master endorsed that point of view. Suffice it to say that Captain Ward wrote back to Captain Brand and I eventually received a letter informing me that I would not be participating in the new training system, would not be going to Warsash, would not be referred to as a 'Cadet' which pleased me no end as I regarded it an appalling term for aspirants to the high office of Ship Master, and lastly, I jolly well better make sure I got my ticket when I went for it! That suited me just fine and I got on with the business of becoming a seaman.

The tanks of the old *Lucellum* were not painted. No tankers of that vintage had painted tanks, and as soon as the tank was gas free, which we apprentices confirmed with an explosimeter, we had to go down into the tank with the crew and start 'tank diving'. This involved shovelling up all the rust which had fallen from the steel of the tank, in sheets, and hoisting it up on deck for disposal. In the sea! You just have to accept it, that's how it was done. Anyway this was hot miserable work in the Indian Ocean, and not only that, but with the best will in the world, we could not guarantee that there were no traces of product, under the piles of rust shale. Sure enough, particularly in tanks which had carried Avgas or Mogas, after half an hour of shovelling the gas would start to get the better of us and we would have to vacate. Loud, exuberant singing was a good sign that it was time to take a blow. At the end of these days we would be issued with a tot of rum from a big raffia-covered carboy, which held dear knows how much rum, and let me say it was good stuff, because it broke up the gas a treat, and made all hands feel pretty mellow. Of course it was taken neat, and I don't think many watered it down.

At last the Quoins hove into view again and we knew we were almost back in our old stomping ground ready to load another cargo with clean tanks and an overwhelming desire to find out what our orders were. Sure enough, the news which we had all been hoping for came through that we were to load for Jeddah where we would all be relieved from the Master down. Never was ballast discharged or cargo loaded with lighter hearts than that last visit to Ras Tanura, and before twenty four hours had passed we were on our way to Jeddah. Somehow the passage along the coast was more enjoyable and yet for me tinged with a degree of nostalgia, for I was beginning to enjoy the barrenness of Arabia and the vast, empty sterility of the land. It had its own kind of beauty which appealed to the aesthete in me, and to this day I can see the moon, huge over the silhouette of the Frankincense Mountains and a sprinkling of Bedouin camp-fires on the blackness of the plains. I did not know that I would return there many times during my career as Third Mate and Chief Mate, and in total spend three years sea time on that run.

Cunard/Brocklebanks/H E Moss & Cos. had not done much repatriation by aeroplane up to that time, being more in favour of a 'Go on and stop on, and bring her home for refit' type of policy. Come the day for leaving the ship, our reliefs came aboard on one boat, and we went off on the next, having handed over as much as we could of what had become our lives for the last eleven months. All our chores and tasks had become second nature and we were all, as it were, hard wired to the fabric of the *Lucellum*. We knew every bolt, weld and rivet in her. (She was both riveted and welded as I recall) and we had become a crew in the best meaning of the word.

They had chartered a whole aeroplane for us from Transavia Airlines, a Dutch company. The aircraft was a DC6, big brother to the old DC3 Dakota. I think it was more or less identical, but bigger, more salubrious, and had four engines instead of two. We had to remain at the airport hours ahead of flight time while we were individually checked to see that we were not carrying inflammatory literature, or anything that might offend the Islamic code operating at the airport. Bear in mind in these days Jeddah airport was very rudimentary and constructed in what I would describe as 'Early Penitential' style, and of course it was as dry as an Aussie summer. By the time the men boarded the aircraft they were gasping and the bar on the aircraft was complimentary. Well, they emptied the bar by the time we had over flown Suez, which we could see because they flew at around eighteen thousand feet, and we had to put into an airport in Italy to take on more liquid stores. I loved being able to see the land rolling past. Of course the stewardesses did not get much peace with this mob and were probably black and blue by the time they paid off in London, with the unsolicited fumbling that was taking place as they went up and down the alleyway, but they took it in good part and there was no trouble. The men were just happy to see European women again. So was I.

In London the Company had hired a room and arranged for the Shipping master to come down and see the men as they paid off. 'Any complaints?' he would ask, 'Whay no man, it wer a canny trip ye nah' 'Good crowd ye nah, and she was a greet feeder'. All the above conveyed with slurred vocals and maladroit optics. At this point, when the men had been paid, the Apprentices traditionally put round the hat for showing the films during the trip, and as I say Dave and I made about two months' wages in as long as it takes to say it. Then we all went home, and most of us never met again. Board of Trade acquaintances.

According to my Discharge Book, they left me at home for two months after that trip, and during that leave, because I had not had enough of the sea, I signed on with Clyde Shipping Company which along with Steel and Bennie provided towage on the Clyde for all vessels from coasters to super tankers. My father was Chief Engineer with this company at the time and I obtained a berth on the *Flying Mist* which was skippered by John Stewart, who was friendly with my father. It was fascinating work and John Stewart was a good man to learn from. Of course I was signed on as an AB (Able Bodied Seaman) but Captain Stewart knew I was an apprentice and was willing to show me everything he could. It was from him that I learned how to gauge the strain on the towing wires when to put on and take off power and when to work the 'junk' which is a kind of tensioning bridle allowing the tug skipper to transfer the pull of the ship from the midship's towing position to the stern, to prevent turning the tug over. This was a system perfected on the Clyde in combination with the 'Clyde' towing hook, which could be released instantaneously if the tug was in danger. Even fitted with these devices, boats could still be pulled over and I think it happened to the *Flying Dipper* and the *Flying Wizard*, with loss of life. It was all about 'feel' and I never forgot these lessons. Anyway I was on the *Flying Mist* for about a month and I think I made as much as I had done on the previous eleven months. This was because we worked a lot of overtime, berthing and sailing huge tankers up Loch Long, at Finnart Terminal, at any time day or night.

On one memorable day while I was on the *Flying Mist*, the *Queen Elizabeth the Second* was launched from John Brown's Yard. We were not actually on her launch but were given the job of holding one of the early 'jack-up' rigs which was being fabricated at the same yard, in mid stream; away and downstream from the mighty QE2. I was on the wheel, but Captain Stewart sent me up the mast to get a good view. I never forgot that and invited him to our wedding, and he came with his wife, Margaret.

CHAPTER SIX
LUCIGEN

Seamen are never left at home long and inevitably my orders came to join the *Lucigen*, another tanker, again in Smith's Dock in South Shields; however this time there would be a subtle difference as I would be sailing as Senior Apprentice. I cannot tell you how that altered my perspective on life for whereas, hitherto, I had been learning and not expected to take a lead, now I was and would be responsible for my neophyte 'mate'. I met his father the night he placed him on board and he asked me very solemnly to look after him, and I vowed that I would. Gregory Wills Pool was sixteen, came from the West Country, Dorset or Devon or maybe even Cornwall, and was undergoing the metamorphosis from boy to man. His voice could range over several octaves in one sentence, and all imparted within the vehicle of his warm, homely accent. He instantly became a favourite with everyone, and folk looked out for him as you would for any young person.

The *Lucigen* was built at a time when they could not make up their minds whether or not to build a midship's accommodation block for the Deck Officers (like the *Lucellum* had), and so they went half way by building a 'centre castle' for storerooms but leaving off the accommodation block. To me she always looked half finished. One day, whilst still in Smith's Dock at the lay-by berth, I was searching for the Mate to get jobs off him. Gregory was in convoy astern of me and we had just gone through the forward watertight door onto the fore deck, when the tanker which was tied up alongside us exploded at number three centre tank. The flames shot up like a blow torch about eighty feet in the air, and I know this because they burned the triatic stay above the tank. The Mate was on the fore deck and I shouted to him 'I'll phone the fire brigade'. I went down the flying bridge like a whippet and noticed the Catering Staff, under the command of the Second Steward, making a sedate but speedy exit onto the shore down the gangway. Word travels fast on a ship, but these chaps were incredible. I arrived at our telephone in breathless condition and got through to the Fire Brigade as fast as the electrical impulses would let me, only to find that someone had beaten me to it. I immediately returned to the fore deck to find that the situation was resolving itself, and two welders were exiting the tank – unharmed! She had not been properly gas-freed and their hot work had ignited a cloud of gas at the higher level of the tank. They were fortunate to be alive. The ship was the *Elora* and she was owned by Trident Tankers. Come to think of it, Trident had a lot of accidents in those days, and that may have been because P&O, who owned them, were employing cargo-ship men to do a tanker-man's job.

The *Lucigen* will forever remain in my mind as the ship on which I spent the most prolonged period of tank cleaning in my life. It started in the Tyne in November 1967, where we cleaned every tank with a chemical injected into hot cleaning water designed to remove the heavy black oil which she had carried the trip before we joined her. That process took about a week and my new responsibilities weighed heavily on me until I had mastered the pipeline system and the pumping arrangements. We then sailed in ballast to go out into the North Sea to change ballast and returned to the Tyne to complete the cleaning. I will never forget clearing the Tyne piers and meeting a beam swell which rolled her as far as I had seen a ship roll up to that time. I was sitting in the crew's mess having a cup of tea when she took one which set the athwart-ship tables on end. We all fetched up on the lee scuppers under the tables, and the tea. After putting in clean ballast and pumping out the dirty ballast we returned to the Tyne, and continued cleaning for the next week. Eventually the chemists from Dasic (that was the name of the chemical we used) declared the tanks fit for loading the next cargo, and away we went for Romania.

But the Mate was not happy.

He had found traces of the previous cargo under the heating oils which kept black oil cargoes and crude oil fluid enough to be pumped, and now we had to go through every tank and scrape under every coil and remove every trace of black oil. This was tedious work because there were miles of heating coils, and as we progressed further into the Mediterranean, the temperature rose rapidly. There were twenty seven tanks in our ship and we became intimately acquainted with every one of them. On the plus side, the tanks were painted with epoxy paint and that made a big difference. Of course the Mate relied heavily on his apprentices to make sure this work was done correctly and that meant I had to be on my game and get Greg trained up as quickly as possible. Day after day it went on until finally the Mate called a halt to the tank diving about the time we rounded the Peloponnese and turned into the Aegean. As I say, we were bound for Romania, specifically the Black Sea port of

Constanza. I remember, as we passed through the Dardanelles I happened to be on the bridge, perhaps I was steering when, in the vicinity of ancient Troy, we were struck by lightning. The noise was deafening, and I thought we had blown up like the *Elora*, but it was forked lightning and the ship rang like a bell for many seconds after the strike. The temperature rapidly fell as we made our way through the Back Sea and by the time we got to Constanza it was cold.

After de-ballasting, the Tank Inspector, wandering around and pursing his lips and wiping the heating coils with a white rag, condemned all our beautiful tanks. We were to load two hundred tons of gas-oil in number nine centre tank and clean all the tanks again by pumping the gas-oil through our Butterworth machines, and back into nine centre tank. I mentioned it was cold, but now the temperature really began to plummet, as we undertook one of the most miserable jobs I have had the misfortune to be involved in. The Mate put the whole crew on six hours on and six hours off and for the next ten days we sailed about in the Black Sea in miserable, freezing weather. For us apprentices it was particularly unpleasant as we had to make sure that not only were the machines moved around and deployed correctly, but we also needed to make sure the Butterworth openings were opened and closed as required. There were twelve nuts on every Butterworth plate and usually two or three different sized nuts amongst them. So instead of carrying one spanner you had three and a set of Stillsons. I remember being so cold that I covered my hands in grease and wrapped them in burlap. The sheer physical work was not the worst of it for the gas-oil (diesel) seeped into our clothes and started to bring us out in boils round our wrists and forearms, and if we did not end up with some kind of cancer it was not for the want of trying. After a week of this cleaning with gas-oil, we cleaned them again with hot water and finally after ten days went back alongside.

This time the tanks were passed and we later found out that they had been rejected because the cargo was not ready!

Mind you for this work the Company were truly appreciative and we Apprentices received sixty pounds or three months wages as a bonus. At that point I would have gladly jumped over the side for the Company.

I do not remember much about Constanza except that Christmas was coming and I ended up coming back from my run ashore in the back of a lorry at night. Someone had bought an enormous cake ashore and as he passed it down from the tail-gate of the lorry it fell apart. All of us who were passengers on the back of the lorry turned to in order to save the cake, and having salvaged as much as we could, got it on board the ship. We ended up in someone's cabin and scoffed as much as we could before turning in. I think it continued to appear at 'Smoko' (tea-break) for the next week or so.

If memory serves me correctly, we went back round to Antwerp after that, because I recall purchasing my first pipe in a pipe shop, the walls of which were completely covered with every shape and colour of pipe imaginable. I chose a discreet little briar with a black distressed body, and slight curve in the stem, but my big mistake was buying Holland House tobacco to smoke in it. It is a very light tobacco and it burned very hot with a scented aroma. Whilst ashore I had visited a hostelry and sampled a few Oranjeboom Beers, which came in big brandy-shaped glasses. It was strong stuff and it did not take much for one to work up a good head of steam. I made my way back to the ship and foolishly tried out the pipe before I turned in. When I woke, the smell of the tobacco and the after effects of the beer were sufficient to ensure that I spent some time hanging over the ship's side shouting for 'Hughie'. I was undeterred however, I think because I was very lonely, and my pipe and the many others which would be acquired over the years became a source of solace and a great way of passing the time. I continued to smoke the pipe for the next ten years until I was up for my Masters Certificate in 1977 when I suddenly stopped, which I will explain later.

I do not know where we went after Antwerp but we ended up on the other side of the Atlantic in Aruba loading three grades for Okinawa, to fuel the giant B52s and all the other aircraft the Americans were throwing at Vietnam at the time. Aruba in those days was exactly like the set for a Spaghetti Western and there were a couple of bars which were designed for sea-going clientele and of course our Geordie crew made good use of them. You recall I told you about the *Lucigen's* centre-castle? Well, by not building an accommodation block on top of it they had formed a large flat area about the size of a tennis court, which was used if ever you needed space, or for just lying around if the mood took you. I relate this tale to demonstrate that there is a strange Providence which looks after drunken seamen. We had finished cargo and were lying singled up waiting to let go when the Bosun reported that one of the men was missing. This did not please the Captain as you can imagine, because time was money on the tankers, and it was baking hot as the afternoon wore on. Scouts were dispatched to find this fellow and the whistle was blown until there was hardly any steam left in the boiler; the Old Man was about ready to have a stroke when the lost sheep appeared on the dusty ridge above the loading jetty. He wove a wondrous and circuitous route down the road to the berth, occasionally falling over and sometimes stopping to check his bearings by the transit of the sun across the heavens, all watched with some mirth by everyone including the pilot and excluding the Master. Now the *Lucigen* was tied up against rubber fenders which were supported at the end of narrow girders about a foot wide. The gangway had been taken in long before and the Captain had no intention of putting it out again, so Jolly Jack was obliged to come aboard via one of these girders. Smart as a rat he mounted a girder up near the fore-castle and without anymore ado crossed the gulf betwixt the ship and the shore over this narrow bridge, with not a care in the world. He climbed over the ship's rail like an ibex, then started to bounce his way down the flying bridge in between the handrails which ran the length of the fore deck, to the centre-castle. It was only when he came to the huge, empty, expanse of the centre-castle itself, that the true degree of his inebriation could be appreciated, because as soon as he cleared away from the guidance of the handrails his gait took on a meandering quality and he was clearly having difficulty lining himself up with the exit from the centre-castle. At this point even the Master began to see the funny side of it and allowed himself a wry grin, whilst making a mental note to log the man a day's pay when he sobered up, for delaying the ship.

We proceeded from Aruba through the Panama Canal into the mighty Pacific which name represents the least accurate nomenclature for any ocean in the world. True there are vast areas where there is hardly a breath of wind at certain times of the year but the Pacific is so enormous that it can brew up the most terrifying gales and TRSs, otherwise known as Tropical Revolving Storms. The prudent mariner will do his best to avoid these monsters of the deep for they can send even the most seaworthy ships to the bottom. Thankfully we did not run into any particularly violent weather on this passage and for the most part one just got on with the work, each day waking to be overwhelmed yet again by the sheer immensity of that Ocean. I remember very little about the rest of this voyage and without my Discharge Book I could not tell you that having joined in South Shields on the 10November 1967, I signed off in London on the 30 May 1968. This must have been another occasion when we flew home and settled up in London airport, because we did not take the *Lucigen* to London.

CHAPTER SEVEN
MAHRONDA

I had now been at sea for just under two years, and having had twelve days leave after my seven months on the *Lucigen* I was sent to join the old Brocklebank cargo liner *Mahronda* as Acting Third Officer. I have a photograph of her which I obtained when I was on her and she looks very old. She was built in William Hamilton's yard in Glasgow in 1947, but I was not complaining because after only two short years, I was to be Third Officer. In these days it was not normal for un-certificated officers to sail in charge of a watch, but the Company must have reckoned I was up for it because here I was. I was nineteen years of age, and very pleased with myself, because at last I would no longer be paid slave wages. It was not that I resented poor wages it was simply that I aspired to better things, remembering my old school motto *'Spero Meliora'*.

Mind you I had a lot to learn on the *Mahronda*, because whilst I was well thought of amongst the tanker-men, I was now back amongst the old hidebound regime of Brocklebanks; not only that, but I really had not spent much time on the bridge at all. Thankfully I was sailing with some really good fellow officers particularly Norman (Boots) Dudman, the Second Officer, one of the most decent men that ever trod shoe leather, and Graham Beaton who taught me what it was to be an efficient Chief Mate. They had infinite patience with me, and pretty soon I was able to take sun sights with the best of them. I had managed to buy my own sextant during my leave having posted an advertisement in the Glasgow Herald as it used to be.

'Wanted – Mate's Three Circle Sextant'.

I was down visiting my grandfather in Port Bannatyne on the Isle of Bute, when my mother informed me that a man had phoned to say he had a Plathe, Kreigsmarine sextant and was I interested? A Plathe being the Holy Grail of sextants, I rushed home and bought it for £30. It is a beautiful instrument completely without errors and still bearing the swastika of the German Navy. It is my pride and joy and I would never sell it. To this day, thanks to my mother's hoarding instincts I have the sight book I used around this time, and it records the *Mahronda's* voyage down to Mauritius then on to the Indian Ocean.

We ended up in Colombo in Ceylon (Sri Lanka) and for the one and only time in my life I saw a swinging derrick and a 'dead man' being used. This is a very rapid way to use a single derrick as the dead man acts as a counterweight to bring the derrick back over the hold. We used it to discharge coke; black, hot and dusty. The poor fellows who had to fill the swinging basket worked in awful conditions and had to be hosed down every now and then to contain the dust and cool them down.

I loved Colombo and we were there a comparatively long time, so there were opportunities to see things. This was so different to tanker life. We were invited up to Kandy by the stevedore to see the Perahera, which is one of the highlights of the religious year in that part of the world. In addition to the liturgy of Buddhism, it involves decking elephants out in the most colourful costumes imaginable complete with fairy lights and flowers. The parade takes place at night to the accompaniment of giddy and ecstatic sub-continental music. It is a truly wonderful sight.

Getting to Kandy is an experience in itself involving a long train journey on rolling stock which was old when the Raj was in power. At one point they have to shackle on two trains to best the steep gradient and this achieved by running backwards down the mountain to a siding in the jungle. It is a thrill not to be missed. I was with Norman, whom we shall call Boots, because the Mate must have taken pity on us and allowed us off the ship together, which was jolly decent of him. We had to spend the night in a bungalow in the mountains in the same bed. I will never forget that night. Boots was given his name for good reason; being in possession of the largest pair of feet I have ever seen in my life. Nor were they the same size, there being at least half a litre of capacity difference between one shoe and the other. One unkind person quipped that they should have had Plimsoll lines and draught marks painted on them to fulfil the requirements of the Board of Trade, but I always reckoned that was a step too far. Anyway, we ended up in the same bed that night with only a sheet to cover us. We both positioned ourselves on the extreme longitudinal sides of the bed and mutually took up the slack of the sheet, which came under such tension you could have bounced pennies off it. In addition to that, there was a Gecko lizard on the ceiling which cut about all night capturing unsuspecting mosquitoes with its long tongue.

It was not a restful night and we were glad when morning arrived and we were able to wash in the burn, surrounded by the cool mountain air, and caressed by the leeches which dwelt there. One of the wretched things attached itself to my foot and I only noticed it when I dried myself in the bungalow. I can assure you he never sucked anyone else's blood. Strangely they were not attracted to Norman's feet, gigantic though they were, and I unkindly suggested that it might be something to do with Athlete's Foot, although this was unlikely as he took good care of them; featuring, as they did, so prominently in his life.

Other delights to be enjoyed in Colombo were The Swimming Club, in those days barred to the Ceylonese, and populated by grumpy old Englishmen and delightful water nymphs from the various Government Offices or in transit to and from the tea plantations. The barber's shop where one could have a haircut, and neck massage, occasionally interrupted by a sip of cold beer, and The Grand Oriental Hotel or GOH, later known as the Taprobane. This was a superb old colonial hotel which served exquisite devilled prawns and Rockland's gin and fresh lime. In my view there was no better way to spend a couple of hours off watch.

One day I was given the job of taking one of the wives, of whom there were several on board, up to Mount Lavinia beach which was overlooked by the hotel of the same name. It was a remnant of a bygone age, made all the more attractive by its fading grandeur. Swimming in the surf there was quite without comparison to anything I had experienced up to that time, and my companion was clearly thrilled by the experience, as much as I was. Warm surf and sun will do that to you, creating a very romantic experience with overtones redolent in my mind with the exploits of James Bond.

And the devilled crab claws were a *tour de force* as well.

I was nineteen years of age and up for anything. The moral piles which supported the fabric of the structure of my Presbyterian upbringing were being shaken by a veritable tsunami of liberal (not to mention libertine) thinking, and I found the freedom intoxicating. I would later live to regret my 'liberated' living but for the time being I revelled in it.

We must have sailed round to Calcutta after that, ending up in Kidderpore Dock to begin loading jute and jute products for Dundee. I cannot do justice to the wonder of the dawn in Kidderpore Dock when the bargemen from dozens of barges, came to life and began their morning ablutions. Each one meticulously going through the ritual cleansing in more or less identical procedures *in the dock water!* How they did not contract every bacteriological disease known to man I have no idea, for the water was putrid, but there it is.

I had to read the draught every morning and there was a boat supplied for that purpose. It was just a sculling punt, but to me it glided like an elfish skiff in Lothlórien, quietly through the morning air which pulsed and scintillated with the promise of the heat to come, and bore in its ether the mouth-watering aroma of chapattis cooking on a griddle on an open fire on the after end of the barges.

We completed loading the jute products in Chalna and Chittagong where the gangs of tiny stevedores , always singing their chants, could pack the jute bales and gunnies into a stow so tight that no matter what weather we encountered it would never shift. In fact, I have seen stevedores in the USA having to bring in fork lift trucks to break out the bales, so consolidated were they. Eventually we were fully laden and began the long voyage back home via the Cape of Good Hope, because the Suez Canal was shut.

LUCELLUM REPRISE

I should have told you about this because I have just remembered; I was there, in Suez Bay, lying at anchor on the Lucellum waiting for a cargo, when the Six Day War started. We were due to load at the Suez oil refinery, and that evening, just after tea when the crew started to meet on deck for a blow and a chat, (no smoking), from Port Tewfik to Suez, the bay lit up with trails of tracer bullets and a couple of rockets. Shrapnel landed on the deck, and the noise of big guns in far distance could be heard like doors banging. The harbour authority imposed a blackout on all shipping and navigation lights and in the morning they towed an old T2 tanker from the Second World War into the canal and sank her at the south end thereby blocking the Canal. And that was it, shut till it opened, whenever that would be.

We bailed out the next night under cover of darkness, and went on the Jeddah to Ras Tanura run.

It took a long time to get back to Europe via the Cape and I think our first port was Boulogne, where I had the great pleasure of sampling Fillet of Sole Mignon and a nice carafe of white wine in a little restaurant in the shadow of the ancient city walls. As usual I was alone because I was becoming less interested in bars and sailors' haunts and more interested in the culture and atmosphere of the places I managed to go ashore in. From there we went to Dundee and were relieved by the coasting crew who would load her for her next voyage.

Now, if I did not still have a Discharge Book with the details of which ships I joined and when I left them, I would have completely forgotten that I rejoined the *Mahronda* after leave and sailed on her in what would be her last voyage for Brocklebanks. I joined in Tilbury on 21 November 1968 and left her in Colombo in Ceylon on 17 February 1969. Most of the voyage is forgotten with the exception of one memorable night on Gan Island when we entertained the Sergeants' Mess from the Airfield. In fact as I write that, I recall why this event took place. We were making for Gan with the usual stores for the troops when the Burra Tindal (third in line in the rank structure of Indian deck crew) fell over on the spare propeller which was mounted on deck and secured by large clamps and bolts, damaging his kidney. He became very ill and our Chief Officer, Graham Beaton, spent a great deal of time nursing him. We were heading for Gan at best speed when his condition deteriorated even further. The Master, Peter Margeson, sent a signal to Gan, and they dispatched one of the air-sea rescue launches to meet us with a doctor. We rendezvoused in the middle of the Indian Ocean, took the doctor on board, and he stayed with the Tindal till we got to Gan. That launch crew did really well to get out to us because we were about two hundred miles from Gan when they set off.

Anyway because of this service, it was felt that a party was in order and so preparations were put in train to hold a Race Night. These always took place on Number Four hatch lid as I recall and of course we had fairy lights and loads of beer in forty five gallon drums which had been halved and filled with ice. All the service men came out in uniform like us and it was really a great night for all concerned except me because I was duty officer. The whole crowd were well lubricated by the time it came for them to go back to base and nothing would persuade the Mate that he should let me take the servicemen back. He had felt a tremendous sense of relief after the Tindal had started to recover, and now nothing could curb his enthusiasm. So he took up station in the stern sheets of the lifeboat and directed the servicemen to deploy along the thwarts and side benches. There must have been about thirty of them. He cast off and came up the port side of the ship, under the anchor cables which were both ranged and down the starboard side. Of course, it was pitch dark outside the loom of the ship's lighting, and as 'Trog' (that's what we called Mate behind his back in a kindly way) passed under the ship's stern moorings, he miscalculated the clearance under them and knocked every one of the Queen's servicemen down like ninepins. Just like a scythe going through corn. Of course they were pretty well anaesthetised but even so it was a shock for them. I have to admit Boots and I laughed out loud when we realised they were unhurt. He got them back to the jetty alright and when he came back alongside the accommodation ladder on his return, with his hand on the tiller looking like something out of the Cruel Sea, he just fell backwards into the sea, and all that could be seen were bubbles and his white-topped cap floating forlornly in his dissipating bubble-stream. Boots and I were really quite worried for a few seconds till he surfaced and the crew got him out. Then we laughed again.

And as I finish that recollection, on the topic of parties, I am remembering another tremendous party that voyage, in the Seychelles. Nowadays everyone is going to the Seychelles but in those days it really was a French Colonial paradise. One of our cadets (we are calling them cadets now) was the son of the President of the Seychelles and as such had connections with everyone that who was anyone on the island. His name was Eddie Houaraux. I have the spelling wrong I know but it is phonetically correct, and this will probably never reach outside the family.

The Seychelles, which of course British seamen call the 'Seashells', were truly beautiful. Imagine the most delightful picture you can of an island paradise, multiply it by two and that is the Seychelles, and in the Sixties it was virtually unspoilt. Some of the officers, including me, were taken by someone, it might have been Eddie, to see Beau-Vallon beach and it was like the real-life version of National Geographic, with palms growing down to near the water's edge, set at just the right angle to provide the perfect photographic frame for a turquoise water's edge blending into the aquamarine of the deeper lagoon.

There was not, and perhaps there still is not, a pier for big ships in Port Victoria, and so all cargo handling took place at anchor, with the goods being discharged into enormous rowing boats. Consequently Eddie's party had to be held at the anchorage. As usual the event would take the form of a Race Night, which for this occasion would be prepared for, in true *Mahronda* style with new racehorses and track being fabricated. New bigger and better dice, special programmes which the Chief Engineer prepared with his own enormous hands and not inconsiderable wit, and all the other paraphernalia which went to host a successful event. The Chief invariably assumed the role of Master of Ceremonies on these occasions and was most impressive as an impresario. He was very tall and possessed a large, two-stage equatorial region above and below his naval. I say two-stage, because it had been formed mostly by beer in his early years as he climbed the ranks from Junior Engineer to Second, and had then been consolidated by gin and tonic when he reached the pinnacle of his career. Many of our senior officers had a comparable personal topography formed by similar processes. Our Chief had sweptback thinning, dark, wavy locks and a ring-master's moustache, which the dewlaps below his chin only enhanced. So he was perfectly equipped to play the part to the letter. He was also a splendid engineer who, like many senior officers on these ships, felt the time weighing heavily because their subordinates knew the job inside out, and they trusted them to get on with it.

Come the night of the party, there was an air of expectancy gently throbbing through the vessel, and the fairy lights, tropical aromas, gentle undulating wavelets, given serpentine life by the ships lights; music provided by an antiquated record player, and all the pieces were in play for a special evening.

The guests were borne out to us on shore launches, (no ship's lifeboats, the Mate had learned his lesson in Gan) and just as well because they conveyed the most exquisite flock of island birds of paradise I had ever seen up to that time. Of course most of them were spoken for, and were accompanied by chaperones and partners, but even at a distance of a couple of cables you could see there were some refined, demure, unattached, lovelies.

I do not know how it always turned out like this, but whenever these soirées were arranged I seemed to be Duty Officer, which office carried with it the two-edged sword of allowing one to be the first to greet (inspect) the guests as they coped with the accommodation ladder, providing manly, capable and professional assistance to damsels in high heels, and the last, and least likely, to be able to engage same in meaningful conversation! I recall, as the night progressed and the Chief whipped up the racegoers to ever higher levels of frenzied excitement, increasing the frequency of my patrols round the decks in the hope that I might bump into some disaffected female punter in need of advice and comfort, but no such crumb fell from the Master's table as it were. In fact the only person I did bump in to was the inimitable Trog, who seemed to be under the impression that I, Duty Officer and therefore the one sworn to sobriety and celibacy by the strictures of my charge, was making an ass of myself. This was rich coming from a fellow who was having great difficulty keeping both eyes on the same horizontal and vertical focal alignment. I was very annoyed, in fact I was incensed, and suggested he go and look in a mirror where he would behold an ass of the most asinine sort. Things were never quite the same between us after that.

In the fullness of time even the most assiduous doyens of the track must retire and our guests took their leave on the water-borne charabancs with rather less polish than their arrival, but that was only to be expected and I think that some meaningful, not to mention 'dangerous', liaisons of a temporary sort were formed. I in the meantime had learned that the Mate was two faced as Janus, and that, 'All that glitters is not gold.'

It was a fairly short hop from The Seychelles to dear old Colombo (I was becoming familiar, you see) where we were duty bound to sell the old *Mahronda*. She had been a fine ship in her day but with the cost of bunkers rising year on year, and the freight rates dwindling due to undercutting by India's own mercantile Marine, which Brocklebanks and others had carried the steel to Visakhapatnam where they built their new fleets, she could no longer compete. So she was to be sold to Singaporean interests, re-registered in Cyprus, and renamed something ridiculous like the *Lucky*. Pretty disgusting for a fine old lady. In those days all ship's navigating officers who were serious about their profession carried their own sextants and we were no exception. When the buyers came down to negotiate the fine detail of the inventory they accused us of taking away the ship's sextants, if you will! Of course we were outraged and I in particular would have shed the blood of anyone who laid a finger on my beautiful Plathe. On the other hand they needed at least one sextant to get around (no GPS in those days) so Boots, who had only recently bought one from Cookes of Kingston in Hull when he was promoted to Second Mate offered to sell them it- at twice the price! We reckoned it fair in the light of their scandalous assertions. Now, I know I said I never stole anything in my life, after the North End Road incident, but of course in absolute terms, that is impossible, so I will confess here and now that when I saw, in the couple of days she remained alongside before sailing when we were handing over, the appalling way the new crew were treating our lovely old ship I had not the slightest compunction in 'liberating' two oil binnacle lamps from the huge steering compass binnacle. This was truly a work of the finest craftsmanship, lovingly cleaned and tended by generations of Highland quartermasters, and far too fine an article to be brutalised by these pirates. So I did the only thing that any man of sensibility could do, and removed the two little oil lamps which illuminated the binnacle to preserve them for posterity and they remain in my possession to this day.

And I am utterly unrepentant, for on the 14May 1970, a little over a year after she was sold, she was severely damaged by fire in Rotterdam and ended up being towed to Split in Yugoslavia where she was broken up in December of that year.

Now I realise I have made a bit of a meal of it getting to this place in the story, but the trouble is that when you start to relate the tale, like getting together with old shipmates, you start remembering and then the difficulty is stopping.

CHAPTER EIGHT
LUXOR

I see from the Discharge Book that I next joined the *Luxor* on 9 April 1969 and left her in Hong Kong eight months and eight days later. As I study the handwriting in the 'Engagement' entry, I see old Hugh Mason the Master, who was one of the neatest writers I ever met and as nice a gentleman and as fine a ship-master as you could wish to meet. He had been through the war, in command, and had many tales for us who sat at his feet as it were, like the apostle Paul at the feet of Gamaliel. Of the voyage I remember little, but I remember Big Hughie's kindness. Actually the call sign of the *Luxor* was GHBL and I remember that because Captain Mason called her 'Great Hughie's Beautiful the *Luxor*'. We ended up on the South African coast for a while running products from Lorenço Marques down to East London, Durban and Cape Town. It was hard work in fact because we were in and out of port a lot and never seemed to stop.

I think we were in Cape Town one night, and Hughie came back from a run ashore with Mrs. Mason who was with him that trip. They had had a nice time and arrived on board at the turn of the watch at midnight when I was handing over to the Second Mate, Trevor Frankish. We were in the cargo office discussing the discharge and Captain and Mrs. Mason came in with armfuls of langoustines butterfly grilled, with chips and a bottle of Lagosta wine. I can still taste them and I would have died for the man that night quite happily. Mind you, he could be pretty strict. We were coming out past the Quoins which you now know stand at the entrance to the Persian Gulf, having sailed from Bahrain at the start of my trip, and I had taken off my shirt because it was a hot as the Earl of Hell's kitchen when Hughie appeared at the door of the wheelhouse. He worked away at the chart table long enough for me to drop my guard then said in a cultured Geordie accent 'Do you not wear shirts in Brocklebanks, Mr Beveridge'? So I felt thoroughly chastened and remembered that although I was sailing on a tramp tanker, proper protocols would be observed.

He taught me a lot about ship handling and staying calm under all circumstances. One day we were going to anchor in Kawasaki Roads in Japan and Big Hughie had the con. The anchorage was heaving with ships and we had to find a spot to plonk the *Luxor*'s hook on the bottom to wait for a pilot.

Captain Mason was as cool as a cucumber and seemed to have the *Luxor* wrapped round him, for even when some of the ships around us started making unexpected manoeuvres and wasting our approach, as soon as we reached the spot he wanted to be in, away went the anchor on his command, and us still carrying way of three or four knots. Out ran the cable to about four shackles and in the meantime he had put the engine astern and taken the way off her. That was the first time I had seen that done although I had read about it, and I would use it hundreds of times in my own ships in the future, but it was good to gain the confidence from this fine old seaman.

When we sailed from Kawasaki I was on watch leaving the Sea of Japan, it was black dark and the place was like Piccadilly Circus. I was seriously concentrating on everything in the universe to make sure there were no mistakes when I suddenly noticed a blip on the radar, which was covered in targets, much closer that I had appreciated by my eye. I checked and double checked then realised that I had been deceived by the disposition of the mast-head lights which made her look like a big ship far away rather than a small ship near at hand. My heart did a couple of somersaults and I decided discretion was the better part of valour and went hard to port to avoid this vessel so close on my starboard side. As the *Luxor* started to swing and the swing increased in rapidity, the blind arc caused by her big forced draught funnel cleared to reveal a large vessel's lights very close astern of us in what had been our wake, clearly about to overtake us. For a second time that night my heart rotated in axis as I mentally calculated the relative approach of this new and very present danger and watched my manoeuvre achieve the required outcome. At that point Old Man appeared on the bridge. He had been taking the air on the deck below and keeping an eye on the 'Boy'.

There is something magical about the Master appearing on the bridge. Suddenly the weight falls off one's shoulders and anything is possible and everything is going to be all right. I have sensed it many times in my own commands, especially with the young and inexperienced, and tonight was no different.

He said very quietly almost in a whisper, 'What happened there? I described the situation and my appraisal of it and said 'I panicked, sir.'

'No, no Mr Beveridge, that's fine.'

And then after a short pause, 'You don't panic.'

For the second time that voyage I would have followed that man to Hell's Gate itself and back, and for the second time that trip I felt trusted, valued and in the right place in time and space.

That is leadership, and I had learned several valuable lessons.

Not long after that Captain Mason retired from the sea and had not been ashore long when he died of lung cancer. I for one, though young, felt I had lost a great teacher and example and Hughie's memory would often accompany me in the long years at sea which would follow. That is the nature of sea-going, we pass on to those who follow the lore of the sea and the leading of men, and all our experience is there to guide and give courage to those who follow. That is why I missed not knowing my grandfather for he was my direct connection to hundreds of years of lore through many generations of fishermen and seamen. When I look at my family tree on my mother's side there is only one following – that of the sea.

CHAPTER NINE
I OBTAIN MY SECOND MATE'S FOREIGN-GOING CERTIFICATE

I notice that I spent the next six months ashore, for now was the time to obtain my Certificate of Competency as Second Mate. Brocklebanks, true to the word of my Indentures, undertook to pay for my time at college and Captain Brand was not wrong to let me prescribe my own 'old fashioned' training, for I obtained the certificate at the first sitting, which must have been one of last times it could be undertaken under the old syllabus. You see, there was a book called the 'Self Examiner for Masters and Mates'. I think Brown, Son & Ferguson of Glasgow produced it and it contained every question which ever would, or ever could, be asked of a ship's officer to see if he knew his trade, for all levels: Second Mate, Mate, Master and Extra Master all suffixed (Foreign Going). (The description Foreign Going on a certificate of competency means that the holder is able to serve in that capacity anywhere in the world as opposed only to the Coast of the UK/Continent). The Board of Trade unashamedly used it to set the questions for the exams and so if you could answer every question on every topic in the book, for the certificate you were going for, you would pass. Before you shout 'Easy' or 'Shame' we had to obtain seventy percent in each of, I think it was, seven subjects, and if you failed in one you lost the lot and had to sit them all again. I do not remember much about the period except the wonderful Glasgow rolls at 1030 in the morning with bacon and eggs in the canteen and curry and chips in the Laurieston pub for lunch with appropriate liquid lubrication and feeling deliciously soporific in the afternoon, especially when we did celestial navigation in the planetarium. This might sound a bit cavalier but you need to remember that most of us were coming from virtually three years at sea at least, with only short breaks and very hard, responsible work. We were not rolling up to university for the odd lecture, enjoying normal life ashore, so you might want to cut us a bit of slack.

CHAPTER TEN
PORT VICTOR

I was back at sea by 9 June 1970 on an old Port Line ship called the *Port Victor*, no longer an 'Acting Third Officer' but a fully qualified Third Mate, sailing with a superior certificate. Incidentally, seamen almost always refer to their certificates as 'Tickets'.

She had been commandeered during the war when being built, entering Naval service as *HMS Nairana,* and made into what was known as a Woolworth carrier. She then transferred to the Dutch Navy and became their first aircraft carrier named the *Karl Doorman.* These were fleet aircraft carriers, cobbled together to protect the convoys which were assembled to supply the country during the Second World War. One feature which was interesting was the armour plating they possessed. It ran along the waterline of the ship, allegedly six inches thick, to protect her from torpedo attack. Whether it would have worked or not, I do not know, but it made her very heavy, and that, combined with her twin screws and single rudder set between the propellers made her a sow to steer. None of this was in any way ameliorated by the automatic steering which I have never seen the like of since (thank goodness) which required about ten separate functions to change from manual to automatic.

She was commanded by a Liverpool Scotsman, Duncan Campbell, and had been seconded to the Brocklebank Line as part of a consortium pact which Brocklebanks had with Port Line. This was not a sensible arrangement, because the trade to India was very hard on the ships and their gear, and the *Port Victor* had been on the meat run to Australia and New Zealand, so her refrigerated holds were beautifully sheathed with marine plywood covering cork insulation which could not stand up to the heavy machinery and goods we were used to carrying. Anyway, that was not my problem and as I flew down to Cape Town to join her clutching my trusty sextant and with my brand new Ticket in my pocket, life could not get much better. When I repaired on board, I reported to the Mate, who was a Scotsman, then met the Second Mate (another Scotsman) and of course we were all sailing under Duncan Campbell, whose Scottish genes were just jumping out of him; so I felt very much at home. The crew were mostly English lads with the exception of the Bosun who was Polish had served in the modern equivalent of the Polish Lancers. He was tough and capable and he and I got on just fine.

I had not been aboard long, maybe a couple of days, when one day a jack-up oil rig was being towed into the harbour by four very powerful and beautifully built Japanese tugs. They were clearly skilful tug-men and knew their business, but there are times when the forces of nature take charge, as happened this day. There was a strong, gusty wind blowing across Cape Town harbour; the basin in which we lay, while wide and spacious, rapidly shrank when visited by an enormous rig and four hefty tugs. The tugs did well to pull the rig into more or less the right aspect for going alongside when, as so often happens, the elements conspire to humble and chasten us. So the wind blew strongly in a squall and the big rig with its legs sticking high up in the sky took charge, and nothing would stop her. Faster and faster she accelerated across the intervening space between itself and us; despite the best efforts of the tugs, a child of two could see she was going to hit us. And she did! With an almighty crunching clang, the structure connected with the old *Port Victor* and proceeded to crumple at every point of contact. There was no contest. The *Port Victor* had been built to survive torpedoes and this was small beer by comparison. After a brief period of the rig lying alongside us whilst the squall blew itself out, the tugs were able to lift it off again and lay it alongside the allocated berth. The *Port Victor* suffered no damage beyond scraped paint; the rig on the other hand would need a couple of weeks of repair. After that, I felt pretty good about our old ship and was prepared like her, more than I thought I might.

My cabin was like something from the Jurassic, with no sink, and a hole cut in the wardrobe at the foot of the daybed to allow one to stretch to full length, so when having a siesta one's feet were caressed by whatever hung down from the rail in the wardrobe. All the Deck Officers shared the washing and toilet facilities and the ambiance made me think of old Jan De Hartog's book. I was inclined to like it. I also liked my fellow officers who were now supplemented by a Fourth Mate because we had no apprentices. He was a likeable big tall English lad with a shock of brown curly hair, long sideburns, and ways that would put you in mind of a young Harry Flashman. He lived for listening to hard rock bands like Led Zeppelin, Santana and Deep Purple, and eventually bought the biggest record player most of us had ever seen. Some nights we would gather in his tiny cabin and 'enjoy' one of his recitals.

The Second Mate was a bundle of fun and it was not long before he and Sparks, another live wire (aided and abetted by the Fourth Mate) would organise a party with the nurses from Groote Schuur hospital in Cape Town. I could not believe this social whirlpool I had dropped into but was quite content to go with flow, as it were. We arranged taxis for the ladies to come down from the hospital and I do not remember how many came but they were a welcome and lovely sight, all dressed like royalty. We had a lovely time and Paul's record collection (he had not yet bought the player) got a good thrashing along with our bar-bills. But it was worth it because it was great fun, and there was one girl there whose look and demeanour would inform what I found attractive in women ever after. I talked to her and danced a fair bit but I did not have the skill or experience to impress her for more than a short while, so she remained aloof in her ivory tower while I increased the store of things I did not know about the fair sex. They all went home together that night in yet more taxis and as far as I know we all behaved in an exemplary fashion.

I think we went up the Red Sea after that and ended up in Massawa in Eritrea, but to be honest there is no clear memory of how the voyage route took us, except that we did definitely go there, because it was there I discovered a fire in the Contactor Room for the windlass motor, one night. What had happened was that when we had tied up, someone had left turns of mooring rope on the drum end of the windlass then backed the mooring up on the bitts. This was perfectly acceptable, but no-one had checked that the control for the power to the windlass was switched off properly. It had not been and the first I knew of it was a report from the watchman that he had detected smoke coming from the access hatch on deck (called a booby hatch). I checked the control wheel and realised what had happened and shut it off. I sent him to rouse the Bosun and the crew, and I called the Mate and Second Mate, then whipped smartly back up on deck to organise the crew. By the time the Mate arrived, I had them playing water on the deck to cool it down and had a gang pulling cargo back from the Contactor Room bulkhead in Number One Hold in case the heat transferred to the cargo in there. When the Mate came on the scene we realised we would have to hit the fire by the only access, which was the booby hatch, and that meant someone going down with breathing apparatus and a fire extinguisher. We had the Duty Engineer pull the circuit breakers on windlass to make it electrically inert, so when all was ready we gingerly opened the hatch lid to be met by a lot of heat and the pungent odour of burning cables. There was no flame and by gradually opening the lid little by little we got it fully open and the Mate, who was suited up and wearing breathing gear was able to descend and put out the fire with a carbon dioxide fire extinguisher without damaging the rest of the equipment. He did a good job because it was as hot as the hobs of hell in there.

After another couple of hours with the hoses cooling the plates down, the heat was literally out of the situation and we all stood down. The Second Mate, who should have jumped at the first call and at the two later calls I gave him, had turned in 'as full as a whelk' and never surfaced yet, but that was Jim for you. The Mate and I ended up in the Old Man's cabin for a dram at about three in the morning and he was pretty pleased with us. Because of the fire we had to send the motor ashore for rewinding which took about a fortnight so there was nothing to do but spend large amounts of time in the Swimming Club which had a lovely air conditioned lounge and a swimming pool and Italian ladies. I actually hurt my back there doing a swallow dive off the high board when showing off to same females, but of course pride forbore that I admit it.

With a fully functioning windlass (you cannot sail without one, incidentally) we made our way to Mal'e in the Maldives again, where we discharged the usual general cargo then stood south-easterly in the south-west monsoon which was blowing very strongly. Now, the people of the Maldives are very poor and they value simple things like rope and fabrics, goods you might not attach too much importance to. It so happened that when the stevedores cast their eyes over the cargo we had in number five and six orlop deck (this is a deck which runs continuously between two holds) they were overwhelmed with temptation, not for the dozens of very expensive automobiles, including Rolls Royce, Jaguars, and all the other trinkets modern man craves, but for the lovely manila rope which the expensive cars were lashed down with, secured with loving care by their brother stevedores in London. Thus they set about removing as much rope as they could without detection. Now, I was not involved with that hold and had I been, what was to follow might not have happened but the Second Mate had been on duty when five and six were worked and he should have checked them before departure, as, for that matter, should the Mate.

Of course when we sortied out, into the Indian Ocean again on the leg down to Ceylon, the old *Port Victor* started to roll and pitch as only she could with a full gale on the starboard beam. It was very boisterous, and at one point in the passage the masthead light went out and needed a new bulb. I offered the job to my watch-keeper but I could see he was not up for the challenge since she was rolling about thirty odd degrees on either side of the vertical. So I did it myself and was thrilled to be at the top of the mast in such weather describing an arc of sixty degrees in a grey driven sky, sometimes overlooking the sea on the starboard side and sometimes the port. Just like shortening sail in an old wind jammer, and I wished for a moment I had been born a hundred years earlier. But such nonsense wore off quickly when the steward brought morning coffee and I concentrated on trying to get a sight of the sun, to find out where we were. Eventually we reached Colombo and opened the hatches. Number five and six orlop was like a scene from a disaster movie, with piles of colourful junk lying everywhere, barely recognisable as the objects of desire they should have been. This was not a small thing and I felt very bad for the Mate and very annoyed at the Second Mate who should have been vigilant and seen to his duty. It was a rum do and the Mate was not asked back when we paid off in London.

I hated being associated with failure born out of negligence, and that has persisted with me throughout my career. I never condemned a man for lack of native ability but I was ruthless if I suspected carelessness.

In the fullness of time we made our way up to Calcutta and would have to moor in the Hooglie River, which is cursed with a phenomenon called a 'bore'. This is a mini, sometimes not so mini, tsunami brought about by the rapid narrowing of the river banks causing the flood tide to rise up into a wave which proceeds at some pace upstream carrying all before it which is not properly secured. I think our mooring was around Garden Reach.

It is a big job to prepare a ship for the bore coming, and here is a brief description of what needs to be done. The vessel makes fast temporarily, head upstream, to buoys fore and aft with the ebb tide starting to run down stream. Both anchors are then 'hung off 'on slip wires, and are disconnected from the cables. Two shackles of cable are then paid out into two *'heava boats'* (bathtub-like boats made of steel about thirty feet long) which are then manoeuvred by tugs and wires and taken down aft to the stern. They have no propulsion of their own. The cables are then hove up onto the stern of the ship and used as the after moorings, being connected to the buoy astern. In order to absorb the huge sudden tensioning of the chains as the bore passes, relieving tackles are set up, comprised of a set of six fold coir purchases for each chain, which when hove tight relieve the strain on the chains and provide a 'buffer' or 'cushion'. The forward anchor cables are then each shackled to the forward buoy. Bear in mind, the anchors weighed about six tons and each link of chain was about a foot long. In order to pass lines and so on between the various craft, sculling punts are used like the one I told you about in Kidderpore Dock. It is a really antediluvian system.

On the day we were carrying out these evolutions, I was down aft and all was going according to plan when a young boy fell over the side of one of the sculling punts. He was probably a son of the boat owner. The ebb tide runs out at about three or four knots and is very powerful, the mud brown water churning and swirling in eddies and overfalls. It is a horrible river. The boy surfaced and managed to lay hold of our mooring hawser which was trailing slack in the flowing water. He held on manfully as his elders on the stupid punt (I could not imagine a more inept craft for this kind of work) tried to manoeuvre round to him but they were so slow. So strong was the ebb that the child was making a big bow wave with his body as his elders battled so clumsily, it seemed to me, to get to him. I have never felt such frustration in my life and could think of nothing to assist the boy. We could not throw him a life buoy for he would surely miss it. We could not heave up the mooring and put more strain on his tiring arms, and we could not summon help despite informing the pilot on the bridge. Eventually the child let go and disappeared, his family following after him. I was angry and outraged by the whole affair and later punished myself for not thinking of donning a life-jacket and swarming down the mooring to him. It may have been the jacket would have kept the two of us up. We will never know. I know that on that day I vowed that if I was called on to save a life in the future whilst still at sea I would do all in my power to help, and you will find if you read on, that I did and the Good Lord never tried me further than I could bear. But that is away in the future.

The bore came and went and was quite spectacular in its way, and when we had completed cargo at the buoys, we went into Kidderpore Dock again. At least we tried to. We entered the lock and as our crew threw a heaving line from the focsle, the weighted monkey's fist at the end of the line to make it carry in the wind, arced through the air and bounced off the head of one of the linesmen. Of course the crew found this very amusing, and laughed. In an instant the shore labour had formed into huddle, and migrated like a testudo to the dock office door, some distance from the lock. And so we sat, with the tropical afternoon advancing, stuck like a cork in the bottle of the dock, while the labour ranted and raved ashore. This went on for quite some time, and one hour was turning into two when I said to Duncan Campbell 'Let me go over and speak to them'. He looked at me through his tortoiseshell glasses with the blue smoke of his cheroot swirling in the light of the chart table lamp, 'Do you think you can do anything?' 'I don't know, sir,' says I, 'but dinner time is approaching and this is tedious'. 'Well' he says 'You better have a go but don't lose your temper'. Now I have no idea why he said that because even then I was not all that fiery, but there it is.

Five minutes later I was down the pilot ladder, onto the lock wall and striding towards to mob which had grown considerably in the encircling gloom. I briefly thought what I might say and asked God to help me, which was quite strange since I was in a humanist mindset at that time. As I approached the throng, one white-uniformed soul amid so many others, they parted like a bow wave and I zeroed in the offended man. There had clearly been much anger and emotion already vented and I looked around for someone who looked like a spokesman. I found him easily enough and asked him in quiet tones what the problem was. He told with indignation in every syllable that the white crew had laughed at his colleague who had sustained this damage to his head and dignity. I mentally noted that when you do not possess much, dignity is important. I tenderly and carefully looked at his head with genuine concern for I was still smarting from the loss of the child, then I said to the spokesman that I considered the men on my ship to be less than 'gundas' which in Hindi means less than the scum between your toes, and there was general assent among the mob and wonder that the 'Sahib' knew the word in the first place. I put my arm round the offended man, looked every worker who surrounded me in the eye and said that on behalf of the Captain and myself and the Company (and every well intentioned soul in the universe) I was sorry and asked his forgiveness. That was it; the kind answer did indeed turn away wrath and we all went back to work and got tied up before dinner time!

Needless to say, when I had made my way back to the ship and ascended the pilot ladder from the lock wall, I did so with the wings of Mercury at my heels and was aware of a new status in relation to the men. Old Duncan was absolutely delighted, and when we tied up I was offered another dram. It felt good. The regard within which a man is held by his superiors and subordinates is the very breath of life to his self esteem.

We made our way from the sub-continent, via the Cape of Good Hope, to the United States of America and from that amazing country I remember two things. No, three.

We were going up the coast of the southern states from Texas, to Mississippi to Georgia, and places like that, dropping off parcels of jute products to supply the mills which produced whatever they did, perhaps carpets and linoleum like Dundee.

Anyway, we had to navigate through the multitudinous oil rigs which proliferate in the Mexican Gulf. I think we had cargo for Galveston and Houston, and you would think I would remember because I was the one who drew up the cargo plans in great detail. I still have one up in the loft of my time on the *Mahronda* and it makes me cheerful to recall the hours spent on it. Access to these ports requires the negotiation of the Houston Ship Canal which, while an impressive work of man, is very narrow in places; passing other ships going in the opposite direction always concentrated the corporate mind of the Bridge Team. (We did not call the folk in the wheelhouse a 'team' in those days; it was just the Old Man, the Pilot and the Officer of the watch and the helmsman). It was a bright sunny day as I recall when we made our way up to Houston, and as I mentioned before, the *Port Victor* was an awful ship to steer, especially in relatively shallow water. The pilot was getting on in years, maybe in his fifties, which of course to me meant he was close to the Sweet Bye and Bye, and he kept going on and on about our ship's steering. The helmsman was beginning to get twitchy because he felt it was his fault and that is a bad thing, for when you undermine a man's confidence he will tend to make mistakes. It was a hot day and this drawling Texan went on and on. In the end I turned on him and said 'Listen pilot, she's a lousy ship to steer. I've tried her myself in all conditions and I can get no better than three degrees either side of the lubber line. This helmsman is doing an outstanding job and we'll get no better man this day. So you'll just have to put up with it, or if you want I'll take her up'. So he shut up and did his job and that was that. I think that's what old Duncan was referring to when he told me not to lose my temper in Calcutta.

When we got to Houston, the Second mate and Sparks were away as quick as a flash to find some females up in the city and sure as night follows day, back they came with a brace each, for a 'party'. Of course I was invited and I put in an appearance from time to time, but I was beginning to take stock of where I was in the great scheme of things and I was not sure the 'party' scene was my favourite genre. One of the women, who was quite a looker, seemed to take a shine to me and we chatted about this and that, and it turned out her husband was in Vietnam, so I suppose she was fed up, but I could not help thinking it was pretty low of her consorting with ship's officers and her husband dodging bullets up the Mekong River. Came the time for them to leave to go dear knows where, she says to me 'You have come-to-bed eyes ,' whereupon she kissed me in an exuberant fashion, to which I suppose I must have responded in like manner, being made of weak flesh and blood and far from home. So away they went, and I think the Second mate and Sparks met up with them later.

I did not, and instead, as I passed through the Officers' Lounge, noticed on one of the tables a pile of books which had been left by the Port Missionary. I lifted one up and the title read Good News for Modern Man. Of course I knew instantly what it was, the New Testament in Modern English. So I reckoned they had been left to be read and I took one. And it co-habited with the books on navigation and ship stability, cheap novels and the Playboy magazines for quite some time before I started to read it. Incidentally I have never bought a Playboy or any other kind of similar magazine in my life, they just existed as part of the fabric of the ship, and appeared who knows how?

Our next port was New Orleans, where the Mate and I and a few others went up one night to listen to the jazz. Who could forget the atmosphere of the place, with its narrow streets which all seemed to be called 'Calle de,' something or other, the colourful shop fronts, the liveliness of the people and the sense of fun everywhere. They seemed to dwell in a perpetual Mardi Gras, and from every available shop the sound of the most exquisite jazz playing could be heard for free! I was overwhelmed by the accessibility of it all. Needless to say, we ended up in 'Your Fathers Mustache' which was a chain of beer houses all over the States. I do not know if they still exist. They sold American beer in huge jugs with as many smaller glasses as you needed for the number of people at the table, and the idea was you just dipped in as required. As I said I was never much of a drinker but this was novel and so was the headache next day. They put far too many chemicals in their beer and it was just like drinking poison.

And so on to Savannah, where in order to turn the ship round in the river you run her bow up on the soft mud in a little cove on the riverbank, and let the flood tide carry her stern round. Then you just give her a kick astern, square her up in the stream and proceed to the berth heading seawards ready for sailing. I think this was our terminal port and a fascinating place it was, possessing as it does some very old clapperboard houses set in beautiful little streets. I bought some chewing tobacco there after speaking to some 'good ol' boys' in the barber shop, but I could not take to it, I am glad to say, and dumped it and stuck to my pipes of which I now had a substantial collection. I reckoned Petersons made the best pipes, and one of them, with a fill of 'Bogey Roll' was difficult to beat.

The nuclear-powered ship *Savanah* was berthed up the Savannah River at that time and they tell me they developed much of their expertise on how to build the nuclear submarines from what they learned from her. Anyway, we could see her from our berth and we could also see a lovely three-masted barque just downstream from us. I decided to visit the barque and it turned out she was built to about two-thirds size for a movie that was made. I found this out from a tartan-clad girl in the foyer of the ship, who was just as nice as could be to me. She was so easy to talk to and so appreciative of everything I said, and kept getting me to repeat things because she liked the accent so much, I thought 'This is really nice Davy, you could be fine here'. And as I recall she was quite keen for us to take a spin round the 'ancient' bits of Savannah, but as always there was some reason I had to be elsewhere.

That night I was on watch thinking about this female I suppose, but mindful of the debacle with the cars in the Indian Ocean, and resolved to never let that happen again on any ship I was associated with. Cargo had ceased being worked around ten o'clock that night and I decided to go through every hold to check all was well. I started forward in Number one hold and worked aft. I was alone with my torch and I knew every nook and cranny in her, so it was no problem. I got down as far as Number four hatch I think, and all was well in the forward three Holds; for some reason I entered Number four hold via the booby hatch where it was black dark inside and still contained a fair bit of jute in various forms. Jute bales and gunnies, which are enormous bales of Hessian, and jute rolls for carpet manufacture. I just used my torch to have a look round and my eye caught sight of a cargo light (we called them cargo clusters and they were dome-shaped enamelled steel lights containing a big bulb and a flex which could be plugged into any convenient socket). My eye followed the cable to the socket and it was still plugged in. The cluster just looked malevolent in the darkness and I climbed down to check it. I gingerly lifted the edge of the light and to my horror the wooden deck and cork insulation under the light were glowing like a barbecue. Now you might wonder 'so what?' but you see in these jute carrying ships fire was a constant danger and the air was literally saturated with tiny, fine particles of jute. In fact I could see them thickly clustering round the beam of my torch. I replaced the light, disconnected the power, and beat a hasty retreat up on deck.

In quick time I called the Bosun and his men and got the Mate up in as long as it takes to tell the tale then straight up to raise Old Man whose ship could be afire in the very near future. I mustered the crew under the Bosun and then with them standing by re-entered the hold with a bucket of water. Again I exposed the coals and applied the water. It had an instantaneous effect and that was followed by several other buckets. In no time the fire was dealt with and the Mate had the crew dig up about a square yard of wooden sheathing to make sure there was no more fire. Next salute, I was back up with Old Duncan and the Mate in the Captain's cabin having a dram, and the Old Man thanking me for saving his ship from a disaster, which it would have been. I felt as good as gold. The Mate moaned at me for telling him about the fire 'Too calmly!' But he did it with a smile and a wink at the Master. When I paid off, in London, Captain Campbell wrote in my Watch-keeping Certificate that I was a man of 'Exceptional ability with Exemplary behaviour and of Unquestioned Sobriety', so that was fine.

I never did go back to see the girl on the 'Hollywood Barque'.

CHAPTER ELEVEN
LUCIGEN FOR A SECOND TIME

I had a couple of months leave after that then went back on the *Lucigen* as a fully fledged Third Mate and spent another six months on the Jeddah to Ras Tanura run., and frankly, I cannot remember anything about it. I was sailing with a skipper that I was great pals with but I will not mention his name because a time would come when we would no longer be friends and that is quite sad. But at this time, it was good fun and we officers were all on top of our game so the ship was efficient and well run; there were no incidents, and on completion of that trip I had enough sea-time in to go for my First Mate's Ticket.

I OBTAIN MY FIRST MATE'S FOREIGN GOING CERTIFICATE

The prospect of a prolonged spell ashore, even if it was to study, was delightful because it offered a chance to interact with people at home in a more natural way. I had met a girl called Gaynor Allen when I came off the *Port Victor* and had written to her while on the *Lucigen* but it was not a romance as such and I was probably as friendly with her older sister Vivien as I was with her. In fact we used to hang around together, go out for meals and generally socialise. The girls were both nurses but Gaynor was an Auxiliary while Vivian was fully qualified, and Gaynor was preparing to go into university. In the fullness of time Gaynor went to Dundee University and I visited her in her lodgings. She shared it with several other young women and I had never seen such a disgusting mess of a place in my life. There was not space on any surface to put down a sixpence so cluttered was it. Her wee room was alright but I spent the night on a sofa in the lounge and that was enough for me. Anyway while I was away she had been seeing someone who was not a gentleman like me so that is all I can say about it. I continued to be pals with Vivien for some time but something was about to happen which would change everything.

Every now and then on a Friday night some fellows and I would go to the dancing in the Locarno in Sauchiehall Street in Glasgow after we finished at the college. The First Mate's Ticket was taken much more seriously by us, and the afternoon sessions at the Laurieston had disappeared as we came to terms with the new syllabus, so it was good to relax at the end of the week before continuing to work over the weekend. One night, I cannot remember if it was a Friday or a Saturday we met up at the dance-hall and were discussing a project we had been thinking about after we left college. The idea was to buy a yacht and charter her down in the Mediterranean and make pots of money by sailing tourists around the Greek Islands. I had taken a glass of whiskey or two during our discussions and decided I would 'take the floor,' I surveyed the scene and noticed some girls sitting down stairs from us. They were obviously friends and there were no males about so I sallied forth and asked one with long red hair to dance. I noted that she was literally twiddling her thumbs. She agreed and we went onto the floor and danced whatever latest form of shuffling and arm flailing passed for dancing at the time. It was difficult to talk for the noise, and I found myself wanting to know what she was replying to my questions. Usually that level of verbal interaction is not memorable. But I found it quite frustrating, that I could not hear her. You recall the girl in Cape Town had provided a kind of marker for what I regarded as attractive in women and here moving very attractively in front of me was the archetype. I say she had long red hair set up from the sides of her head and clasped at the back. She had grey eyes with flecks of green, a delightful figure and that look which some Irish women have. A kind of self-contained essence which speaks of self-reliance and yet beckons you try to break in. This is not fanciful; I have had a lifetime to think about it. After the dance I escorted her back to her seat and we all chatted away, but I was listening only to her. Come the end of the night I was offered a run home to Yoker in her friend's car and by the time they dropped me off in Yoker I had arranged to meet her to go out, on a date. In those days that just meant going to the pictures or something, not the connotations it now has through the American movies. Also for the first time in my life I was worried that she would say no.

We arranged to meet under the big clock in Central Station at a certain time, and for some reason, which I cannot recall, I was running late. I was seriously concerned about this because the last thing I wanted to do was disappoint her. Anyway I got to the station and bolted for the clock to find her gone! I was distraught and ran to the steps down to Renfield Street and there at the bottom of the steps just about to exit was Patsy. I shouted and she turned, and that was the beginning of the rest of my life really.

We started going out together a lot and I lived to finish at the college in the evening and meet her in town. She had to come all the way up from Kilmarnock after work at the Dick Institute where she was the curator of the museum. I never thought about it but it was a huge effort to do that day after day. I resented the other interests she had such as the Operatic Society, but I realise now that I was profoundly immature in those days, and yet these were the happiest days of my life up to that point. We continued to go out very frequently while I was at college, and Patsy Anne McCluskey, first generation Irish on her mother's side and second generation on her father's and as Catholic as the Vatican, was also studying for a diploma in Museum Curator-ship. She already had a Bachelor of Science Degree and was, and is, very clever.

Our 'keeping company' took the form of going for meals, seeing movies, sitting in a lounge or café; anywhere to sit and talk and find out about each other. We would also just walk, and I recall one night walking in Kelvingrove Park, talking about her Judo classes (she had a yellow belt at the time) and she was extolling the merits of this martial art. I was a bit sceptical to tell the truth, and had no sooner voiced my scepticism than she took me by the arm which was lovingly draped around her shoulders and proceeded to hoist me over her shoulder and lay me gently on the deck! She told me later that when we met at first she thought I was much older than my twenty two years, probably divorced or 'had something wrong with me'. Which I think is a euphemism for being queer!

One of our great treats on a Sunday was to meet up and go to the Central Station Hotel in Glasgow and have afternoon tea. It cost a pittance and they provided a lovely tray of scones and cakes, a pot of tea and comfy Westminster chairs. There, we could just sit and talk, and it was there we planned our ascent of Ben More. It was exciting talking through all the gear we would need and thrilling for me to be doing it with someone who complemented me so well. Frankly I was interested to see how she would do, because I knew she had been on the hills before, but going up Ben More at the tail end of winter was always a challenge. I cannot remember how we got up there but I think Patsy drove her mother's car. Anyway we set out, straight up! No gradual approach up by the bealach.

Now it was blowing a bit even at the lower levels, but as we gained altitude it really started to howl with the cloud scudding across the still distant top framed in the cobalt sky. And it was cold as a Polar Bear's backside. We plodded on, the ground becoming more and more frozen, the grass tussocks now collared in powder snow. But still my plucky wee companion was up for it and no sign of backing off. As we drew near to the summit it was clear that it was covered in ice which had been polished by incessant wind throughout the winter. So in the absence of an ice axe or crampons I cut rudimentary steps in the ice and we pulled ourselves up to the top. It was thrilling to be up there in icy wind with this lovely girl whom I was beginning to value more and more and whose being so complemented mine. To this day she denies she has red hair but if you look at the photographs taken at the summit that day you will see that I am right. It now behove us to retrace our steps and I set off downwards first. I could not have gone more than a couple of steps when my Kastinger boots slid off the step and I rattled down on my backside at an alarming rate, fetching up at the bottom with my knife in the ice to brake my descent. The knife, by the way, was one I habitually carried at sea as an apprentice. It was a butcher's knife adapted to marine use by having the back of the blade tooled with a saw cut serration, which made cutting through hawsers very easy. Now it was Patsy's turn, and she was doing just fine, better than me, when 'Woosh', away she went and started to hurtle down at a rapid and accelerating pace. I braced myself and grabbed her round the waist which hit my arm like a train. But I had her safe and I thanked God most energetically for it. As I held her and looked over her back I saw the knife I had been holding in my left hand, with its lethal blade, blue-black and threatening and razor sharp! I made a mental note that if I ever went up that mountain with her in winter again I would do it with crampons and ice axes.

Funnily enough, we never did, in winter, but we did about five years ago around the equinoxes and again it was blowing a gale. This time discretion proved the better part of valour and we bailed out at the bealach, maybe just as well for someone was blown off An Casteil the same day. Anyway, she had more than passed the test. When we got down we went to the pub where I would have a beer a she an orange juice (I told you she never took alcohol).I started to make up a pipe and went for my Swan Vestas matches. Every single one of the heads had ignited. I was astonished, then realised that my backside bouncing down the ice slide must have set them off and I had known nothing about it. It put a whole new connotation on the phrase 'I'll warm your backside for you!'

Our biggest, indeed our only problem, was religion. As I say, she was a Catholic and meant it, and I was a Protestant and knew very well why I was. I can remember my father actually saying to me 'Never marry a Catholic, son.' Of course I vowed to follow his vehement imprecation, but the word of a twelve year-old is subject to adjustment and I had no qualms in respect of my father. My objections were, and are, entirely theological. In fact meeting Patsy drove me out of my mental lethargy in respect of my faith and caused me to study and read the scriptures and commentaries to this day. The dalliance I had indulged in with far eastern religions and indeed all and any faiths now evaporated in the crucible of my re-visitation of the ancient arguments of the past. We broke up three times over religion and three times I had to get her back. It was clear that if I was to be complete as a man then I must have her, and that meant my children must be brought up as Catholics. She simply does not possess the ability to compromise on this issue. And that is the situation to this day. In the main it has been a most happy outcome and I have no cavil with the human beings of the Catholic Church. My problem is the inability of that church system to convey the simple gospel of Jesus Christ in an evangelical way. But we are running ahead of ourselves.

I was getting on fine at college, and at the end of my six months sat and passed my First Mate's Foreign Going Certificate of Competency at the first sitting, for which I was deeply grateful. I now had to get back to sea and make up the three years sea-time for my Master's certificate. I had now re-established my childhood relationship with God at least on a reading and praying level and daily brought my anguish over my love for Patsy to Him. I recall one day after I had obtained my certificate, being on my knees in my room in Hawick Street, in Yoker, asking for guidance when the phone rang and Maggie Waugh's London accent assailed me. Maggie was a gem who handled all the personnel movements of the officers. She arranged our certificate leave, our leave, our travel arrangements- everything. Whatever they paid her it was not enough. Anyway she came on the phone, and asked if that was Mr Beveridge. I confirmed it was and she said that they wanted me to join the *Luxor* in Barry Dry-Dock in Wales -as Chief Officer! I replied that I thought she had the wrong David Beveridge but she insisted. I reminded her that the ink was hardly dry on my First Mate's Certificate and she assured me that the Master on the *Luxor* had asked for me specifically. When she said his name that explained it, and as I say

I cannot tell you who it was because we fell out years later and that is that.

So I had my marching orders and my Discharge Book is there to prove that I never sailed as Second Mate, having gone straight from Third Mate to Mate. Actually this was very unusual, and I began to consider more deeply my relationship to God and this answer to prayer so speedy and extraordinary. In addition to that I started to quake as I realised how unready I was for the task.

CHAPTER TWELVE
I RETURN TO THE *LUXOR* AS FIRST MATE

Leaving Patsy was difficult. I had fallen in love with her and I now saw her as potentially being my wife. The thought of leaving her for months was hard. On the other hand my going to sea again would be an acid test to see if this relationship was made of the right stuff and anyway I had no choice. This was my life. So that was that. She saw me off at the station and I began to mentally prepare for what would be the hardest baptism by fire I would ever endure. When I arrived on board I was glad to see my Captain again and instantly I knew that he would guide me through this settling in period. What we both knew was that while I had not had much experience working out the cargo figures on the old fashioned adding machines, I knew the *Luxor*'s deck and pipeline system like the back of my hand and could run the crew without any trouble. I was one month into my twenty third year.

What they did not mention was that the Mate who had been deep-sea with her had died of a heart attack on the way home, and that the fellow they sent to take over from him, fully qualified with a master's ticket, and able to write salty articles in the maritime magazines, only lasted a week before he wanted off. She had turned into wreck, you see, in the two years since I had left her in Hong Kong, Old Hughie had died in the meantime, and her age was really catching up with her. We were undergoing refit prior to going on charter to British Petroleum and everything had to be tested and proven and brought up to specification. All the big oil companies were like that. They would charter ships which they knew would toil to keep up to their charter requirements, and then evoke penalty clauses to claw money back. It had been going on since Noah signed up with the Good Lord. They also placed on board volumes of these instructions which we hardly had shelf room for let alone time to read, and required us to keep pumping records and loading records on big sheets which squirrels in BP's head office would scrutinise and bring to the attention of the claims office. On the other hand they were employing us, so we had to make the best of it.

Everyday in dry dock there would be another disaster, from leaking cargo lines, to leaking valves, to valves which blew up under pressure test to pumps that would not produce the correct pressure. The list was endless and lesser men would have buckled, but not us. We had a decent enough crew which if memory serves me correctly were Indians, but I might have got that wrong. After a couple of weeks we were declared ready in all respects to go and make money whereupon we shifted to Swansea where we loaded three grades for Gefle in Sweden. The loading went without a hitch until the very end when the Old Man realised that we had come onto our marks too quickly because the *Luxor* was 'sagged' like a banana. Ships either hog or sag. That means they bend up or down amidships. Because she sagged the Plimsoll line touched the water too quickly so loading had to be stopped to obey the law. Now this was very bad because if she could not lift her dead-weight she would constantly incur a penalty called 'dead-freight'. There was only one solution this night and that was 'Sink the marks'. Now I knew fine this was not allowed but we had no choice. It was her first cargo to BP and we had to be seen to perform adequately so that is what we did. We sunk the marks four inches and put it down to Fresh Water Allowance, which although present did not account for four hundred tons! I could see that this was going to be a problem for the whole trip and we realised that the problem had been brought about at her building when they had given her extra thick plating on the bottom. It is running in my mind that H E Moss bought her when she was being built as the *Haukefjells* and she was strengthened for ice being a Scandinavian ship. We got away with it and made our way up the Channel, into the North Sea and so to the Baltic, where the temperature started to fall rapidly. We had to punch northerlies all the way to our destination and it was so cold we started to build up a lot of ice on the focsle and had to run the deck machinery which was steam driven continuously, to stop it freezing up. We smashed the ice off with hammers.

The rest of that voyage is a blur. It was seven months of hard labour and worry and one could never relax. I cannot even remember where we sailed to after Sweden although I think we went back to Swansea and dear knows where after that. The sort of thing that would happen would be like the day the Serang (Indian Bosun) came on the bridge in the morning and told me that the Fore Hold was flooded. That is quite alarming because we could have been sinking. So I investigated and sure enough the hold was awash and oil drums and paint tins and stores were wallowing around like the leftovers of a tsunami. What had happened was that a crack had formed in the bulkhead between the forward coffer-dam and the fore hold. We had to always fill the forward and after coffer-dams, which each held two hundred tons, with fresh water to feed the boiler which provided steam for the auxiliary machinery. This actually had the effect of reducing the sag, but of course it took four hundred tons to do it so there was no real gain. We just had to keep on bending the law. We never had enough fresh water on the *Luxor* because, in addition to all her other problems, the safety valves at the top of the funnel leaked steam constantly. So I had the problem now of getting about one hundred tons of fresh water out of the fore hold. We could not pump it because the suctions were blocked with debris and baling out one hundred tons with a smallish crew is quite a task. Now it so happened that I had already had difficulty with pumping out the after coffer-dam on another occasion when the engineers were unable to pump it due to a collapsed valve. (See what I mean she was falling to bits.). On that occasion I had been at my wits ends with no one to turn to and I brought my problem to God. I was roving about the centre castle when I did this and I suddenly spied the biggest educator I had ever seen lying under some junk. An educator is a portable device for sucking water which receives its ability to suck by utilising the venturi effect of high pressure water passing over an orifice. The trouble was it was un-rigged without hoses and couplings so it was useless. So I laid the problem before God and continued to search. As the day progressed I began to put together the parts I needed, and before long was able to get the Serang to rig my 'miraculous' educator down the coffer-dam and pump it out at twelve tons per hour! So also in the fore hold. When I found the problem it was indeed a crack, I managed to repair it with a cement box which went with her to the breakers yard.

On another occasion the main sea water cooling line to the main engine developed a crack. It was a casting and could not be welded. The Chief came to me to see if I could build another cement box, like the one in the fore hold which had assumed saga-like notoriety. It so happened that I had brought literally tons of sand and cement aboard for just such an exigency and so was able to construct a stall which I filled with cement, in the bilges of the engine-room around the pipe. That also went to the breakers with her, for when the surveyor sighted it he reckoned it was as good a repair as was needed. They painted it and it became part of the ship.

We changed Captains at some point and my new skipper who will also remain nameless for different reasons was a thoroughly decent man with whom

I got on really well. I cannot name him because I heard thirty odd years after we sailed together, from my Second Officer on the *Jura*, that he had committed suicide while employed as Superintendent of the ferry company in Shetland. It's a small world.

We loaded in old Butcher Island again this time for Calcutta. As we were leaving Butcher on that occasion I looked up at the tall, concrete fire monitor towers which overshadowed the ship. There sure enough, was the Moss flag which I had painted on years ago on the *Lucellum*.

LUCELLUM REPRISE 2

Actually that is worth relating, so I will wind the spool back a bit. We loaded at Butcher several times and on my second visit there I noticed the jetty was covered with graffiti from the many ships which visited the terminal. In fact the jetty was so covered that the only place it was not were the concrete towers. Now I had done a fair bit of rock climbing and was quite comfortable with heights so I resolved to make our mark where it would never be bested and that was under the overhang of the pill box at the top of the tower. As a matter of fact the towers were very similar to the ones dividing Germany only they fired water not bullets.

So I laid my plans and one day accumulated all I would need, a bosun's chair and gantline, a lizard (a length of two and a half inch rope with a hard eye in one end) pots of red, blue and white paint, three brushes and a line to tie on and off the pots of paint. I only needed help with the change of one colour to the next and co-opted the Third Mate for that. He was pretty windy about it but I won him round, after all it was my neck. That night the south-west monsoon was blowing quite strongly but I decided to go ahead, so I nipped ashore taking care to avoid the armed guard who was patrolling at the end of the approach road to the jetty. That was easy enough for there was plenty of shadow. I swarmed up the iron ladder in no time with my Bosun's chair, gantline and lizard, made the lizard fast round one of the stanchions which supported the roof of the pill box and fleeted out the gantline and set the chair. This was just what we did on board when painting masts and so it was second nature. I climbed out, settled myself in the chair and lowered myself down to below the overhang. I then got the Third Mate to bend on the first tin and brush and started to haul it up. It had no sooner cleared the concrete of the jetty when the wind took it and it started pendulating back and forth like a grandfather clock. I shortened it up as quickly as I could and started the first colour.

Blue for the back-ground.

That completed, I changed to red and so on until my work of art was finished. Each time I hove up and lowered the tins I had the same problem with the wind and tried to time it with the guard's perambulations. I must have been successful because he never twigged. When that was done I simply hauled myself back up over the overhang using the sheet bend on the chair like a prussic loop and de-rigged the whole set up as quick as it takes to tell. The next day I was on the bridge for stations with John Murray, the master, and said 'Aye, sir, they've made a right mess of this jetty with all that graffiti.' and he grunted 'Aye it's a mess.' keeping an eye on what the pilot was doing. 'I persisted 'And look at that, is that not our flag there right at the top of the tower? Some scoundrel must have done that.' JM looked up at the tower and over to me, shook his head and turned away smiling. Maybe the flag is still there.

LUXOR CONTINUED

So we loaded for Calcutta and had to moor up again for the Hooglie bore. There were no horrors this time although I thought about the wee boy a lot as we drifted the chains down aft. This time I was not a young lad learning to be a mate I was the Mate. It was just as well that I knew the drill and had everything ready. It went like clockwork, not only that, I had two sets of six fold purchases of my own which I had the Serang reeve with four and a half inch manila rope so we did not have to rely on the dubious coir purchases of the rigging crews. That night as we waited for the bore to come the old *Luxor* decided to blackout and we were dead ship as the time approached. The Old Man and I could do nothing more for her so we opened a couple of cold beers and waited. Sure enough, in the dying light we sighted it wheeling round the bend. It was a big one, certainly bigger than the ones I had seen before. On it came, with a growing sense of excitement rising in us. Then it hit us, big and strong, the stern rising instantaneously to the upsurge of the wave. The bore tackles sprang to a singing tension then the cables grunted to their work of preventing the *Luxor* from carrying all the way to the Howra Bridge. As that wave passed it was followed by another which again set the tackles singing. We could see the ship pitching as if at sea; then she settled down, all fell quiet, the birds resumed their evening love songs, and we finished our beers.

Apparently I paid off in Little Aden which is the loading terminal for

Aden on 4 November 1972, but the only impression I gained of the place was that it had deteriorated so much as to be virtually unrecognisable with little or no commerce and trade and not many smiling faces. There were no servicemen or their wives, no life, no colour. But they were independent.

Frankly I could not have cared less because I was going home to my girl, lean and fit after a hard trip in which I had cut my Mate's teeth. The office would have been perfectly within their rights to put me back to Second Mate but they never did, and I would remain in that rank for the next five years. On that flight home I decided to ask Patsy to marry me. Her letters had sustained me while on that trip and she became the focus of all my aspirations. I could only think of my career now as a means to an end which was to marry her and spend the rest of our lives facing whatever would come, together. I was twenty three and all the man I would ever be. This is why I become annoyed when I see young men today twittering around like virgins in a brothel about making commitments. It is pathetic.

I left the *Luxor* at the beginning of November 1972 and having spoken to Patsy's parents, and received their blessing we were married in St. Columba's Roman Catholic Church in Viewpark near Uddingston, on 27 December of the same year. The speed with which this was achieved was entirely due to Patsy's mother who, not believing in long engagements made all the preparations in as fast time as could be imagined. She was a veritable whirlwind of energy and organisation and I got on well with her. Patsy's father James was the obverse of Mary Agnes and was a quiet, lovely man with a winning smile and a twinkle in his eye. To me he was an archetypal tall, slow Irishman and I liked him very much. It said a lot for both of them that they would trust their lovely daughter to a ship's mate, but they did, and if I could live it all again I would take more time to love them for who they were, just to let them know I appreciated their worth.

I have already admitted I was desperately immature in my understanding of the mores of ordinary folk. The conventions and traditions of ordinary living seemed to have passed me by and I was almost inured to people's feelings, about simple things like how long one should stay at their own wedding. I whisked Patsy away far too quickly from our wedding and it is only in recent years that the deeply wounding nature of my behaviour and expectations has come home to me. Not only that, I was extremely jealous of any other male near Patsy with no justification whatsoever, and if I could alter anything it would be that.

Apart from that I am perfect! *(I JEST)*.

Anyway that is the way I was and we caught the sleeper to Boat of Garten where we had a wonderful honeymoon. And that is all you need to know about that.

We migrated from there to Rosehearty where we had a second reception for all my folk in that area and I do not remember much about that. Our next problem was to find somewhere to live. We were blessed immediately with a child from our honeymoon, and for me it was imperative I find them somewhere appropriate to live, for when the baby arrived in September. Patsy had been staying with a lady called Mrs Chalmers, in Kilmarnock, in a tiny single room which served all purposes, I can see it now in my mind's eye and that was our first married quarters. It had a bed, a sink and a wardrobe, which was a recess covered by a curtain. We made arrangements to stay in a flat owned by a woman who lived in a bungalow, but that fell through. So we thumbed our noses at that and went to see Wimpy who was building the Wellpark estate at that time. We selected a detached house which was under construction for six thousand pounds, in Scalpie Place, and I went back to sea on 14 February 1973 on a fairly new ship called the *Lustrous*.

1. 23 Bruckley Street, Rosehearty (Patsy Beveridge)

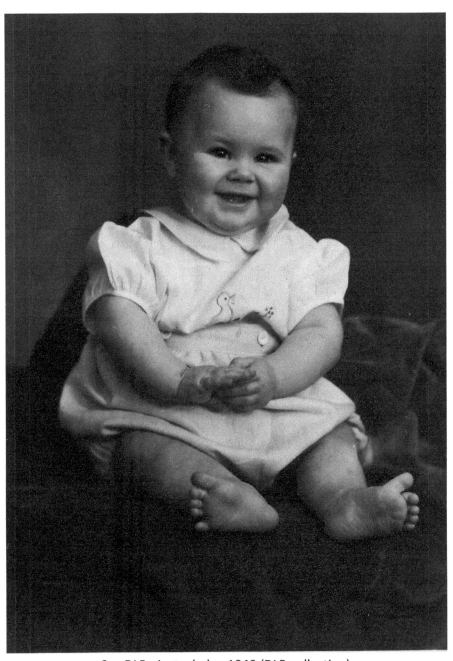

2. DLB - just a baby, 1949 (DLB collection)

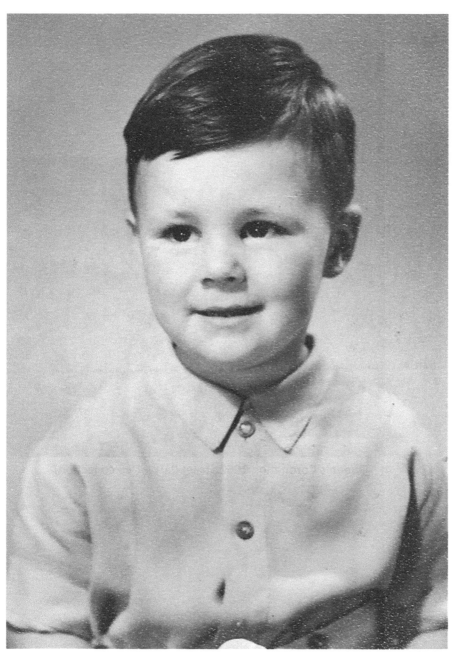

3.   DLB - 3 years old (DLB collection)

4. Queen's Coronation 1952 Street Party (DLB collection)

5. DLB - wee Highlander (DLB collection)

6.   DLB - with 'Cuillin' (DLB collection)

7. Thornwood 1957 or 1958

8. Thornwood 1959 or 1960 with Jack Benson

9. DLB - about 10 years old (school photographer)

10. Mum, Dad, Pammy and DLB on Kishmul late 50's (DLB Collection)

11. 'Fergy', 'Tanny' and 'Bevy' Luss 1962 (DLB collection)

12. DLB - scrambling on Craigmore Aberfoyle 1962 (DLB collection)

13. DLB - First Year Hyndland

Die Schotten sind es gewohnt im Blickfeld des Interesses zu stehen. Wohin immer sie kommen, sie fallen mit ihren kunstvoll gefältelten Kilts auf. Und jeder Clan (Stamm) hat sein eigenes Karomuster. Die Schotten wollen sogar noch untereinander verschieden sein. foto: klebe

14. Reinbeck Town Hall 1964 Germany Jamboree (newspaper photographer)

15. Germany Jamboree chariot racing 1964 (Rainer Sauerwein)

16. Checkpoint Charlie Berlin 1964 (Rainer Sauerwein)

17. Hyndland Class 5C circa1965 or 1966

18. DLB and Dad arriving at Rothsay 1965 (Pier photographer)

s. *MATURATA*

THOS. & JOHN BROCKLEBANK LTD. —Launched 17th June, 1955 (7365 gross tons)

19. Maturata first deep sea voyage 1966 (pen drawing by unknown artist)

20. Lucellum (www.fotoflite.com)

21. DLB on Lucellum – Jeddah 1966 (David Stillwell)

22. Lucigen 1967 (photographer unknown)

23. DLB - aged 19 (DLB collection)

24. Mahronda 1968 – 1969 (Skyfotos)

25. Luxor (www.fotoflite.com)

26. DLB - on Luxor 1971 (photographer unknown)

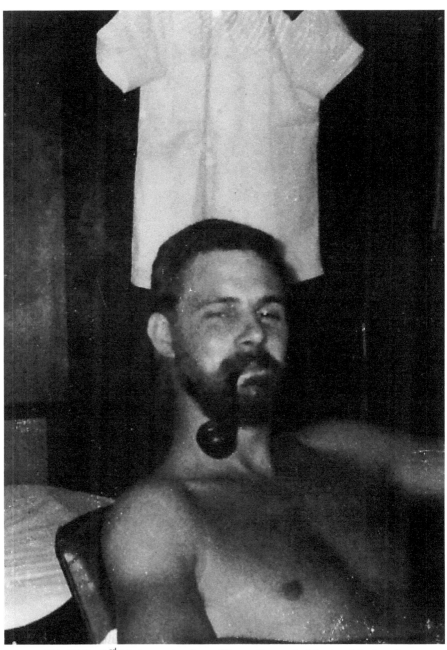

27. DLB - 3rd Mate on Lucigen (Terry Scarret, Master Mariner)

28. Port Victor (www.fotoflite.com)

29. DLB -1972 just obtained Mates Foreign Going Certificate (photographer unknown)

30. DLB and Patsy married in St. Columba' s Church 1972 (Sharps of Hamilton)

31. Lumiere (River Class Product Carrier) (www.fotoflite.com)

32. New Lucellum (DLB)

33. ACT 3 (www.fotoflite.com)

34. ACT 6 (www.fotoflite.com)

35. Switha (RAF Nimrod Aircraft Crew)

36. Jura (RAF Nimrod Aircraft Crew)

37. Jura as a Naval Vessel (Royal Navy photographer)

38. Morven (SFPA personnel)

39. Vigilant before SFPA (DLB)

40. The Old Norna – first command (RAF Nimrod Aircraft Crew)

41. Westra (RAF Nimrod Aircraft Crew)

42. Embarking Extra personnel on Vigilant 1997 (DLB)

43. New Norna (SFPA Aircraft Crew)

44. Norna in a breeze west of Shetland (SFPA Aircraft Crew)

CHAPTER THIRTEEN
LUSTROUS

It broke my heart to leave Patsy on the platform of Kilmarnock station on a freezing foggy night. The image is still as clear as a bell, her slim lovely figure, as yet showing no signs of our baby, sheathed in a black maxi coat with the yellow ringed light of the platform lighting shining through her red hair. As a matter of fact all lighting at night for me was ringed with a halo at that time because I was suffering from astigmatism. Thankfully it disappeared when my arteries hardened up in my forties. I remember very little of the voyage except that, instead of the old gut wrenching valves I was used to, she had hydraulically operated valves on deck which worked with a lever. Easy to operate and easy to make a mistake. So I had to be on the ball at all times when the lines had to be set. I just would not trust anyone else to do it. I did not mind them opening and shutting valves within the parcels of cargo which were protected by double valve separation, with their handles lashed, but I would not let the other mates set the lines without my supervision. I kept that rule throughout the rest of my time on tankers and never had a cocktail. The pump-room was still manual. For six months I served on the *Lustrous* and from what I remember I liked her fine. The Master Walter Flett came from Findochty, so we were from the same area. Many years later my parents met him after he retired, when they were exploring along the coastal villages including Findochty, and he said that I was the best mate he had ever had. So I must have been doing something right.

I see from the trusty Discharge Book that I joined her in Ras Tanura for a change, and paid off in Mombasa. And that brings back one or two pleasant recollection The *Lustrous* was on charter to Mobile Oil and they had wonderful runs out to the Pacific Islands via Singapore and Hong Kong , out through the Timor and Arafura Seas to places like Tahiti, Fiji, East and west Samoa, New Caledonia, Espiritu Santo, and many, many other places. The down side of multiple port discharges for the Chief Mate of a product carrier was that you had to pre-compute the discharge programme for the entire voyage to make sure it was feasible, bearing in mind that there were draught restrictions in many of the places. Sometimes we only received the amounts we had to load as we entered the Persian Gulf and it was a lot of work to plan, not only how the cargo was to be loaded, but also how it would be discharged with so many variables. Thankfully the first portable electronic calculators had come on the scene and I bought one in Glasgow accompanied by Patsy. It cost sixty pounds including an adaptor, but it was worth its weight in gold. You can buy them now for next to nothing.

You know they talk about 'jet lag', but I remember, as I tell you about it, that I came from a frozen Glasgow into the dry heat of the north-east monsoon in Saudi Arabia, was driven down to the ship in a taxi and met by the mate who was leaving. Because I was a 'tankerman' they did not reckon I needed much of a hand over, which was just as well because I did not get one. We were to load ten grades for a multi-port discharge in the Pacific and no one thought anything about it. Get off the plane, into a boiler suit and on deck. Learn the pipeline system as I went on, and try not to make a mess of it. But I was conscious of a Power greater than me or anyone else working in me and I laid my worries before Him and managed fine. I did not get to bed till she was laden about twenty four hours later, when the Old Man chased me off to bed and let me sleep my head off! As I say I cannot remember much about the voyage, but Walter and I got on fine and he was very supportive when he realised I was 'old school'. We sailed together for the whole trip but I think I went home before him from Mombasa, because I was alone when I fetched up at the door of 'The Beachcombers Club' in that town. It had been a hard voyage again, but with the difference that the pressure was mental rather than physical. I really had to pay attention to my sums when working in the Pacific and in addition to that Patsy had begun to realise that living in Kilmarnock alone with the baby coming was not such a good idea. So we had a lot of sending telegrams back and forth , some of which I am told were less than sympathetic on my part, as we decided what to do, and in the end we decided to sell Scalpie Place before it was finished and get a council house in Viewpark. Of course Patsy would be a prime candidate for this because her parents had been tenants for a very long time. Well, she applied for a house but before she went on the list one came vacant across the road from her mother and father, and her mother asked for and got it.

As I look back now after a lifetime, I see the hand of God in that as well, although at the time I was not so keen on the idea of living across from my in-laws. That was crassly immature when I think about, it and now when my own children talk about moving home I say 'Come and live near us. There is strength in numbers', and I can feel my sons and daughters in law, wilting in silence.

The Beachcomber Club was just the place to wind down and wait for a flight and I just stayed in the hotel, ate the lovely food, relaxed in the pool, and thought about my 'family' waiting for me in Viewpark. By the time I arrived home Patsy had hired a painter and decorator to completely decorate our home. When I walked through the door I can still remember the thrill of it, the smell of paint and new carpets and the joy of seeing my wife bearing our child. I had never known such happiness, and I now realise that these moments of pure undiluted joy are few and far between and should be treasured in the quiet place of your mind and taken out from time to time to remind you what can be. Mind you I have had more than my fair share of these experiences I suspect, and count myself truly blessed.

I arrived home around 20 August and immediately set about selling the place we were signed up for in Kilmarnock. My cousin Sandy Birnie had a business at the time in Hope Street in Glasgow and owned his own Chartered Accountants and insurance firm, Scottish Fiduciary. I asked him to sell it and he put someone on it and in jig time it was sold for a thousand pounds more than we paid for it. So we were a thousand pounds to the good without even lifting a spade. Remember in 1973 a thousand pounds was a lot of money. In the meantime Patsy was busy making everything ready for the baby coming and the knitting needles hardly stopped. I set about working on the garden and building fences and gates and it was a time when we set the benchmarks of how we would live our lives in the future. We make a great team. My parents came down from Gardenstown half-way through September and to be honest, although glad to see them, the extra strain of looking after them bore heavily on Patsy, and almost certainly brought the birth of the baby forward. Be that as it may her waters broke on the sixteenth and she went into Bellshill Maternity that night. The baby, a girl whom we called Lucy Helen, was born on the seventeenth. She was the most beautiful baby I could imagine with red hair and brown eyes, and my cup was running over. Patsy wanted to feed the baby herself and it was then we realised that the baby was not feeding properly. She was taken to intensive care and I remember the worry on my lovely girl's face and felt the gut wrenching anguish inside myself. I felt utterly helpless and simply begged God to let the baby be alright. I stayed at the hospital and they found a bed for me but sleep was fitful and without refreshment. Eventually they diagnosed streptococcal meningitis and I can still see my little girl struggling to fight the spasms of the disease that was killing her. We had her baptised in the intensive care room by a Father Foley, the hospital chaplain, and on the 19th she died. My heart was broken and something inside died which never regenerated. All I wanted to do now was comfort my wife and make everything 'all better'. Whatever differences had existed in our worship and appreciation of God were swept away in our shared grief and I learned a tenderness for Patsy which has grown with the years. At no point did I blame God or turn my back on Him, I simply fell at His feet and asked forgiveness and peace with a heart that was empty and riven with grief. In a way I felt I deserved what had happened when I considered how I had shunned Him for that period after I went to sea and I remembered the time when King David of old wept for his dead child, and there was a kind of comfort in that shared experience which spanned three thousand years.

We gave permission for an autopsy to be carried out and they discovered that Patsy was a carrier of the Streptococcus B virus and she was put into isolation. In fact after this she was always put into isolation for her pregnancies. I then made arrangements for Lucy's funeral and found a lovely place in the graveyard at Tannochside where I purchased a lair. Accompanied by my father in law James McCluskey brother in law Jim Rodgers, Patsy's Uncle Pat Coyle, and the parish priest, we buried her in a little white coffin under a beautiful rowan tree. I cannot remember who else was there but as I committed her body to the ground and stood back enveloped in a misty numbness it was as though all my male relations going back to ancient time were gathered round the grave with me to support me, acknowledging that I had now become like them, and known the intense pain of loss. You may call it fanciful but I left the graveside considerably stronger than I went in.

Patsy was soon discharged from hospital and we decided to take a brief foreign holiday, to get away from everything, and chose Tenerife. Our hotel was the Grand Tenerife a four star establishment in the Playa de los Americas and if that was four stars I do not know what you would require for five stars. It was palatial in the 'Spanish' style with white walls and dark furniture. Actually it is a style I am very fond of, and if I was not married to Patsy would probably employ it more. Of course we were not really used to hotels and the first couple of nights we went out for a meal instead of staying in the hotel, because we did not realise that we had already paid for it! It was only when we met an older couple that they put us straight. It was just what we needed and between swimming in the sea off the black sandy beach and swimming in the pool and generally loafing around we were able to rest and gather together our resources. I had already said I wanted Patsy to come back to sea on my next trip so that is what we resolved to do. It was a good decision because the experience was unlike anything she had encountered before and just what was needed to blur the memories of the past few months.

CHAPTER FOURTEEN
LUMEN

We flew out to Hong Kong on 20 November 1973 to join the *Lumen* and immediately Patsy was catapulted into the exotic world of the Far East. It was just such a cultural upheaval for her that there was no room for looking back, and if she did it was not obvious. I think however, that her abiding memory of Hong Kong is of being given a boiled egg which was not cooked properly. She almost gagged and her memory of Hong Kong will always be coloured by that event. The ship had been discharging bunker fuel there which is black, and thick in cold weather, and not very volatile until heated. When we sailed I had to clean her for dry-dock in Singapore and it was a rushed affair. I had to work continuously on the passage down as we were cleaning with hot Butterworth machines. After the initial pass with the machines the tanks had to be hosed down with a hand, high pressure hot lance to pick off any 'holidays'. The Serang and I did a lot of this until the men got the hang of what I was after and then I could let them get on with it. I did not get to my bed for ninety six hours and one afternoon after taking a breather under the flying bridge I stood up and broke my nose on a Butterworth valve. I took a rest for an hour after this then got back out on deck to complete line washing. I went up to the doctor in Singapore and he scared Patsy witless when he came out for a consultation to find out if I wanted a Roman or a Greek nose. We told him to leave the way it was and the scar is still there. Singapore was a favourite place of mine and once the job had settled down we were able to take a run ashore together. I took her to the Bamboo Hut restaurant which was a favourite of mine on the Orange Road. I had been there several times and I told Patsy the tale of Margaret Hung Ho Yin, whom I went out with once while in dry-dock on the *Luxor*. I had met her when shopping in the People's Park shopping mall, which comprised lots of little shops under one roof. The shop was owned by her father and sold lovely trinkets of which I may still have a couple. As one does I asked her out next day, but as it always seemed to happen to me we got a new Mate that day and he needed me to ballast the ship for him because he did not yet know her. Of course I had no option, (although I did because I had already done a day's work) but I told him I would but would have to get away in time for my date. I got most it done and left him to finish off. As usual it made me late and I was just arriving at the Orange Road Cinema as she was about to leave. There were tears running down her face and I felt bad about putting her through the mill as it were, but anyway we had a nice night and I escorted her home safely to her father after the cinema and the meal. And that was that. Margaret Hung Ho Yin.

We have photographs of Patsy under the ship in dry-dock with her wee boiler-suit and helmet on and there is one of me with a plaster over my nose. Come to think of it at that time I shaved off my beard but not my moustache so I must have yielded to Patsy's incessant moan that she hates beards. She picked the wrong guy when she married me because I have had a beard since I could grow one.

Another wonderful night out was when the dry-dock owner took us out for a meal. The Captain, George Wilson and all the senior officers and some wives including of course, Patsy, were there and the meal was gargantuan in the number of courses and quality of food. There was a Chinese floor show as well and I think it was a truly memorable night.

All too soon we completed dry-dock and had to sail for dear old Ras Tanura to go on the 'Run'. And that was the routine until we paid off in Jeddah on 4 April 1974. We managed to get ashore once or twice but of course the Mate was seldom able to leave the ship, and I was too jealous to let my wife go up the road with just anyone, so I think it was an arid time for her. I do remember however, that on 27 December we were ashore in the Souk and we realised it was our anniversary! It has been like that ever since and we simply acknowledge the passage of the years without much fuss. We are in our fortieth year as I write this. Also during this time Patsy's father died and her mother told her not to come home which I was glad about. We sent some money home, and her mother was able to take a holiday after the funeral, but as always I was unable to grasp the complexity of feelings she must have endured. I think some bits have been missed out of me.

When we paid off in Jeddah I recall being on tender-hooks as Patsy came down the accommodation ladder, and I am certain that we knew that our eldest son David was on the way, the only one of our children conceived at sea in Arabia.

They left me at home until the end of May when I was sent to join the *Lumiere*. During that leave we consolidated our home-making and life was blissful, although I could no longer relax into the joyous expectation of a new baby coming. For me, from now on, I would await our children's arrivals with a benign numbness which I suppose was my mind's way of preparing me for future heartbreak. It was also a function of lack of faith, I realise now, but you have to live through doubt and worry, like nursing a ship through a storm of wind, to emerge on the other side stronger in the inner man.

CHAPTER FIFTEEN
LUMIERE

My next posting took me to Apia in Western Samoa as it used to be called. As the pictures begin to form in my mind, conjured up by the names of places, impressions not accessed for long years, flashbacks and images melding to create memories, I recall it was quite a mission getting there. I flew to Los Angeles to begin with, where, along with over three hundred other, weary travellers I stood in one of three queues to be processed through immigration, and border control. It took a long time for them to get through all these folk and I remember noting how incongruous, and surreal it was that in this vast hub of an air terminal they could only come up with half a dozen officials to welcome us into the Land of the Free. I watched helplessly as they called my flight and then me, personally, as the Polynesian logo on the tail of my aircraft taxied away into the night. That night I ended up in LA in some motel with brashy neon signs and cheap fittings and   furniture, and as I settled down for the night, my imagination wandered off to construct a scene from a Micky Spillane story. I was awakened by the desk in time for my flight and whisked away to board the aeroplane for Honolulu, which will forever dwell in my memory as the place I was quizzed about whether or not I was carrying Rhinoceros Beetles. Apparently these creatures figure high in the Polynesian psyche due to their destructive tendencies in respect of pineapples, but it turned out I was fine, having only been shipmates with cockroaches and weevils, so they allowed me into the terminal while they sprayed the plane with insecticide just in case we were lying and had secreted some of the monsters on board.

You go to Pago Pago first, from Honolulu, and you pronounce it Pango Pango. In those days it was in Eastern Samoa, but I believe they now call it American Samoa. We arrived there at dawn and I think there were only a couple of other people disembarking with me. They were borne away by some benign agency, and I was left alone, on the tarmac as it were, with no sign of life anywhere and an enormous cumulonimbus cloud hovering on the near horizon. I was enthralled by the majestic progress of the cloud as it processed towards me framed in the early beams of the new sun. Eventually it took up position over my head and deposited it's not inconsiderable contents on me, my only shelter being a palm covered walkway which was remarkably waterproof.

Things were looking pretty glum at this point until I became aware of the unmistakable roar, forming far away, of an American B57 Stratofortress. I knew this noise from when we had taken fuel out to Okinawa where there were literally hundreds of these gigantic aircraft, at the height of the War in Vietnam, mounting an almost continuous rain of horror down on the heads of the communists and anyone else that got in the way. Sure enough it made its approach and lazily circled the airstrip, then, having weighed it up as it were, set itself down like a mighty, black pterodactyl. I watched with great interest as the door swung open and a ladder appeared followed by legs and bodies as the crew disembarked like visitors from another galaxy. Now, the up side of all this activity from my point of view was, that, as soon as the wheels of the B57 touched the tarmac, lights began to appear in the tearoom which had hitherto been as black and quiet as the grave, and as the astronauts migrated towards the café outpost, the aroma of coffee began to mingle with the post-deluge scents of mimosa and bougainvillea and life took on a more cheerful aspect. I say these plant types as if I knew what I was talking about, but in fact they are probably the only tropical species I know. Suffice it to say that ere long I too had availed myself of hot coffee and victuals and settled down to listen to the twangy drawl of the Americans and await the next and last leg of my journey.

Flights between East and West Samoa are fairly regular and undertaken by jolly little aircraft with very flexible wings and engines, the throb of which, varies playfully with alterations in height and air density, so that one is never sure if all is well or if one should be preparing to vacate at some point into the vast wastes of the maldescribed Pacific. I well remember the grey-turquoise white topped waves as we speed to our final destination, Apia, at two hundred and forty miles per hour, some three thousand feet above them.

Aggie Gray's in Western Samoa has been around since the 1930s. When I was there it had retained most if not all of its original features and instantaneously transported the imaginative tourist to a time now long past. I was thrilled to sit in the bar, open to the warm Pacific breeze, with the large wooden, ceiling mounted fan twirling nostalgically, the radio giving out its Hawaiian, lullaby and the beads of moisture forming rivulets on the brown glistening side of a bottle of beer. It was a delightful ambience spoiled only by the certain knowledge that my ship would arrive next day and I would again be catapulted into the reality of hard demanding work which would require my complete attention until my tour of duty was fulfilled.

Captain Jackie Waters was famous in Moss Tankers, having been promoted shortly after the Pleistocene ended. He was large and florid, strong in presence and character, with greying curly hair and a strong Geordie accent. He completely filled his command in all respects and would in time, teach me much about leadership and the running of ships. At this point, on our first meeting however, he was distinctly overwhelming. We served together as Master and Mate, until 5 October 1974 and during that time we cruised between Singapore and the Pacific Islands and eventually ended up in dear old Ras Tanura. He always liked to be on the bridge when making alterations of course at night, and would sit in his cabin quietly tippling on Gin and Tonic until alteration time. Then he would arrive on the bridge large, imposing and trustworthy, oversee the alteration, then retire with the words 'Back on the GSCs, Dave.' which meant Good Sleeping Courses. I liked and respected him tremendously and learned much from him. He taught me that you only need certain essentials to keep a ship going: bunkers, water, flour, meat, potatoes. The rest is non-essential. Whilst the above constitutes a decidedly monastic diet it demonstrates the point that when the Chief Steward rushes up to you to report that the Chandler did not supply the ice-cream, you can smile at him benignly and tell him that we will still be sailing on time and without it!

There were a couple of times when I had the pleasure of achieving things for the ship, and I suppose, for him, which set me in a good light. Once when at anchor somewhere up the Gulf I went forward to weigh anchor only to find we had picked up an old cable at least as big as our own. This old chain was badly wrapped round our anchor with what seemed to be a couple of half hitches. I reported this and the Captain who reminded me that if we did not get clear we would miss our turn for berthing, which would have meant penalties. Of course my time on the Indian coast had given me a lot of experience with big cables so after some private praying on my part and organising the Serang to prepare the necessary equipment we began passing the loops of the offending cable over our anchor flukes using a wire hawser. Bear in mind these were seven tonne anchors and links made from forty millimetre thick steel. We managed to disentangle most of it except the last hitch. We needed to manoeuvre the wire we were using to lift the chain off our anchor into a very specific position, and I was stumped. The Old Man came on the radio again and

I begged for another couple of minutes. I racked my brains, and then it came to me. I could float an anchor buoy under the foreign cable, which was now carrying a lot of weight, with a gantline attached ,heave up the gantline with our wire hawser made fast to it, then haul it up on the drum end. We did this and suddenly with a rattling rumble which caused me to roar at the crew to stand clear, the cable slipped off and we were clear. Jackie was like a dog with two tails and my star was in the ascendant.

On another occasion we had a damaged cargo valve right at the fore end of Number seven starboard cargo tank. We could replace it if we could get it out but therein hung the rub. To manoeuvre the valve from forward to aft to the tank lid, involved moving it over four sets of what we called 'deep floors'. These were part of the ship's structure which lay athwart-ships and were deeper than the height of a man, so you can imagine the difficulty of hoisting a valve weighing half a ton over these floors, even if we did have something to attach a hoist to, which we did not. It was at this point that I remembered I had ordered two sets of six fold purchases (like the ones we used up the Hooglie) in the last storing, just because I liked having gear aboard which was useful. The Office never questioned such requisitions because it fell into that mysterious category of 'Seamanship'. They would question the number of toilet rolls because they understood that, but not six fold purchases costing hundreds of pounds. Any way I must have had some kind of inspiration because I suddenly realised that we could rig a purchase directly over the valve by slinging the lifting point between two Butterworth openings, then rig the other purchase from the tank lid at the aft end of the tank. Thus in theory, we could lift the valve out of the pipeline with the tackle rigged over it, then connect up the tackle from the tank lid to the valve and by slackening off on the ford tackle and heaving in on the aft tackle sway the valve across the tank with ease. Once I had explained what I wanted, the Serang and his men set about the job with a will. They enjoyed practical seamanship as much as I did and this was clearly a bit of fun. Do I have to say that it worked perfectly? With an ease which was a delight to watch we had that valve on deck in no time at all and the other one back down and in place before we knocked off that night. I was delighted with my men and Jackie was delighted as well so all in all, we were all delighted. And that is all I remember about the *Lumiere* which I left on the fifth of October in Ras Tanura.

CHAPTER SIXTEEN
LUSTROUS AND *LUMINOUS*

Our son David was born on 14 October 1974 and I thanked God quietly, unable ever after to indulge in exuberant feelings. I was profoundly grateful that Patsy was in such capable hands as the good medical staff of Bellshill Maternity Hospital. Our child was immediately taken to intensive care to have antibiotics administered and that would be the routine for all our children from then on. It was a strategy which worked, for they have all survived thus far. During the next two months we had a wonderful leave and wee Davy thrived. He grew in time to become the natural leader of our children both in order and in fact, and provided a splendid example for them to follow. He is now the owner of his own law firm employing several lawyers. I am very proud of him.

We were now a family and I especially began to think about where we should live. On the Eve of Christmas Eve 1974 my leave came to an end and I had to proceed to Singapore carrying the Bill of Sale for the *Luxor* which had been sold to far eastern concerns. I was then to transfer to the *Lustrous* for the next four months. Walter Burdon the Managing Director of Brocklebanks and Moss Tankers came to hand over the Bill of Sale at London Airport with his wife, and had the decency to say it was a crummy time of year to be joining a ship. I said 'You will never know, sir, but it is just part of the job'. It was Christmas when I arrived on board the *Luxor* and she looked like a disaster area. Morale was rock bottom and there was a bad feeling aboard. I was delighted when the *Lustrous* hove into sight and I could get on with running her, joining her on Boxing Day 1974.

I have more or less excised that trip from my memory because it was one the most uncomfortable times I ever spent at sea. I had sailed on her you will recall a couple of years before with Walter Flett, and it had been a most enjoyable experience but on my return, different personalities and crews had transformed the 'feel' of the ship. The master, who will remain nameless, had been a friend since he was Second Mate and I was an apprentice. Now he was Master and I was Mate. In fact we had sailed in the same respective ranks on the *Lumen* but I detected a change in him. Or maybe it was I who had changed. There was a strong 'party' atmosphere existing in the ship which involved not only some officers and their wives but also certain members of the crew, in particular the Indian fitters. I mentioned this to the master one day that I felt the discipline of the ship could be compromised and his response was to announce to his circle that 'The Mate says there is too much partying and it has to stop'. Of course I immediately became 'public enemy number one' universally hated by just about everyone except the Indian deck crew.

In due time that master was relieved by John Watson, whom I had known from the time he came into tankers as a Second Mate from cargo ships. He was a as sound a fellow as you could ever hope to meet with a stolid North of England approach to life. It is running in my mind he came from Bradford and we had a good working relationship. The resentment which had been festering since I had made my observation to the previous master had tended to pull the crew into two camps, and this allied to the fact that the crew were not being relieved on time created a volatile atmosphere. It eventually erupted one night when the Serang burst into my cabin at about two in the morning announcing 'Sahib, Sahib, I have killed the fitter!' I was instantly awake and on my way out of bed demanding clarification from the Serang. I then noticed he was clutching a long square file which had blood on it. I asked him what he had done and he told me he had hit the fitter over the head. I made a mental note that that was slightly better news because I had feared he had driven it into the fitter's body. I called the Master and the Chief Steward then rushed down to the crew's accommodation. When I arrived there the fitter was on the deck bleeding from the head, surrounded by his fellow fitters. As I approached they gave way and I was met by the full fury of the downed man who clearly blamed me for his condition. In no uncertain terms I was told I was the worst kind of man and to be frank I was quite happy about that, because this fellow was clearly not about to enter the afterlife. I focussed on his head which was bleeding profusely like all scalp wounds and set about trying to staunch the flow whilst he made the examination as difficult as possible by roaring at me through his rage and thrashing about on the deck. I tried placating him but it had gone far beyond that. By this time the Master and Chief Steward had arrived, and they were able to help me restrain the fitter. Now the Chief Steward was as gay as a chorus girl but I tell you, that night he rose mightily in my estimation. He was a big fellow and could use his weight and I for one was ever so glad to have him on my side. We got the fitter to his feet but he was still behaving like a crazy fiend. The Old Man decided to try and knock him out with a couple of swings at his chin but all it achieved was to daze him and set him on his heels for a second or two. Eventually we managed to wrestle him into a Roberson stretcher which could double as a straight jacket and pump some Morphine into him. I then dressed his head and we set a watch on him all night.

By morning he had calmed down a good bit and a kind of fragile, eggshell peace descended on the ship which was very wearing. I for one, being the object of so much loathing took to locking and disabling my lock at night for fear of being attacked in my sleep and so it continued until I, the last of the original officers was relieved in Ras Tanura at the end of April 1975 The Chief Steward said to me one day in conversation 'You are a tower of strength.' I thought at first he was having a go at me but he actually meant it. Maybe he could see something I could not. When I got home I was called into the office and I met with Noel Bower the Managing Director. Now Noel had been Mate on the old *Lucellum* when I was an Apprentice and had taught me much of what I knew about tankers. It was he who had referred to Dave Stillwell and me as the best apprentices he had ever sailed with. Now he was a Managing Director. I thought I was on the carpet for a rocket, but instead he said, 'We just want you to know, that we think the situation was handled perfectly and you did everything right.' I was not at all sure that was the case; however it was very kind of him (them) because I was feeling a bit like a pariah at that point in time. It had the effect of restoring my confidence and I went home in a better frame of mind to resume my role of husband and father again.

I cannot remember what Patsy and I did during that leave but I think I dug our garden and we set it with potatoes, onions and every kind of green vegetable. The ground had not been worked for decades and was full of huge tussocks which I buried in a deep pit. But the results from that virgin ground were amazing, and we still have photographs of that first bumper crop. I think I built Patsy's mother a large window box about the size of a coffin and we had a lot of fun transporting it over to Bellshill on the baby's pram wheels. Around this time we purchased a car, and I joined the church in Burnhead in Viewpark, and in moments of repose, which were not many I studied theology.
It was also around this time that we decided to buy a home of our own.

All too soon it was time to go back to sea and 3 July 1975 saw me back in Ras Tanura again this time as Mate of the *Luminous*. I had met up with the Captain, whose name was Stan Paterson, in the airport and we travelled out together. Changing both master and mate at the same time, was not a good idea, but they did things like that when both master and mate were tanker-men. Only when one of the pair was a cargo ship man were they exercised about continuity. Ras Tanura was as hot as the hobs of hell at this time of year and it was always a challenge to step out of an aeroplane and start working on deck. My new captain seemed to be alright but he had weird sense of humour and had a strong streak of the cynic in him. Anyway he probably thought I was a bit weird as well, so we just made the best of it, like all seamen.

That voyage we were chartered to Mobile Oil so we would eventually get out to the Pacific, but we had a few hoops to jump through before we got there. The *Luminous* like all our 'River Class' ships so named because the design was first produced by British Petroleum and all their ships were named after rivers, had very small fresh water tanks. One tank was for human consumption and the other for engine-room use. Because the tanks were so small the fresh water supply was augmented by two evaporators which could produce about two and a half tonnes of evaporated water per day each. When they worked! And that was the problem; our engineers had huge trouble keeping them going with the result that we could find ourselves on water rationing very easily. In addition to this the crew were due to be relieved, and the company were dragging their heels. The Articles, under which the crew sailed, were quite clear that when the crew had put in a certain amount of time, if the ship came into Indian Territorial waters they could pay off. This was the situation, when one night as we made our way up the Indian coast on our way back to the Gulf, our evaporators both gave up the ghost and we desperately needed spares to be flown out. The only thing we could do was have them sent to Bombay then brought out by the pilot. Of course the crew knew perfectly well that we were off their home port and were in no mood to be co-operative. I well remember the pilot coming up the pilot ladder clutching the spare part and looking decidedly sheepish as the crew glowered at him. They were distinctly hostile to him and shouted at him in Hindi. He made the transfer as quickly as he could and beat a hasty retreat. The crew would not assist and in fact were not responding to my orders either. They asked me 'Sahib, where is this place?' I said 'That is Bombay'. 'But Sahib, men want to go home.' 'Yes, but actually we are not within territorial limits,' I lied, 'and so we cannot pay men off'. To be fair we were well off that night but the men were not happy and it was just as well they paid off up the Gulf when we got there, and we received a new crew.

The spares which we had received turned out to be the wrong thing and the Master was starting to become very impatient with the Chief. Frankly the old Chief was out of his depth with a modern ship like the *Luminous* but it did no good for the Master to keep on his back. In the meantime I had to put all hands on rationing just to get to the Gulf and rigged up a system of issuing water from a Binks Bellows pump rigged down in the water tank through which each man received a bucket of water for all purposes in the morning and in the evening. It was antediluvian and a serious pain in the neck to be forced into a position like that in 1975. Mind you some of the crew took it in good part and referred to going for water as going to the well, as they did at home, and called the well the 'Boudey'. In retrospect they were a good bunch and I had a lot of time for them. But the problems with fresh water continued throughout that voyage until one day, during the afternoon watch, after a particularly frustrating time, I moaned to the captain that I was fed up transferring water around the ship and rationing it out, adding that in ships with evaporators it was not my job anyway. He scuttled off the bridge and came back after about half an hour with the ship's Official Logbook under his arm. He opened the page with a flourish and there, with today's date, was an entry to the effect that I had complained to him that I was handling the transfer and issue of fresh water and had quite correctly pointed out that in ships with evaporators this was not the Chief Officer's job. Consequently he had instructed me to no longer carry out this task and to leave it to the engineers whose job it was. I was then invited to sign. You might think this is pretty trivial, but what it amounted to was the Master logging the Chief Mate. I looked at him and said 'I thought we were supposed to be a team? Master and Mate! Am I not allowed to blow off steam to the only man in the ship I am able to moan to?' I was sickened, because he knew perfectly well that there was no one on the ship in the engineering department capable or in a position to take on that task so I said 'Give me your logbook. I'll sign it but I don't agree with it'. I signed it. The Mate had to witness all entries including entries against himself. We staggered on up to the Gulf and had to load in Bandar Mashur which is miles up the Khor Musa. It is deep in the dessert and the banks of the river are littered with chunks of tankers which had blown up in the past. There is nothing there but heat, rock sand and oil. I forget what we loaded but it might have been naphthalene. Now the thing about naphthalene is that it is loaded at such a high temperature in places like Bandar Mashur that the only thing it can do is shrink as one heads into colder water. So, one can bring the cargo right into the coaming of the tank lid in the certain knowledge that the level will go down. It is also very volatile and smells awful. It is an easy cargo for the Mate you just get it on board and virtually forget about it. We loaded up pretty quickly and were lying singled up, with the pilot aboard. I was on the controls having been up for the last twenty four hours when the captain shouted through to me 'Let go forward and aft'. We are conditioned to pass on orders immediately which I did over the VHF when I suddenly realised the engines were not clutched in. This was the Captain's duty and he had forgotten. The ropes were being let go and I bellowed out to him we had no engines. The flood tide began to carry the *Luminous* up the quay towards a Greek tanker astern of us also loading Naphthalene. With increasing velocity our stern crumpled into the bow of the Olympic ship and I could see her moorings taking the strain. Just then the tugs which were lying in attendance saw what was happening and pinioned us hard against the quay to stop any more movement till we got our engines clutched in. We were all quite glad we had not disappeared in a ball of flame as we gathered way into the flowing stream away from the Greek, who was also reeling from the shock of the contact.

There is a spell of quietness comes over men when they have just survived a near catastrophe and as we made our way down the dark river paying attention to the navigation lights and seeking to return to normality we started to make a turn to port at a big bend in the river when the steering gear failed. I could not believe it. Again we went to action stations and the Second Mate who was still up forward was told to let go both anchors. In the meantime I had put the engines to zero pitch then astern to take the speed off her. We watched as the beacon we were careering towards drew closer and the anchor chains flew out of the lockers in a shower of sparks and rust which flared in the inky darkness. I watched as the speed fell away on the electronic log and the cables began to do their work of slowing her up. We did not run aground for some reason and once the steering gear was repaired we got the anchors up and continued downstream to Bandar Shapur anchorage. By now Stan Paterson had had enough and refused to get under-weigh until the engineering of the vessel was more reliable. We also had to effect repairs on the stern and so we spent a hot couple of days at anchor. At last we got away and made our way out of the gulf.

I do not remember much more about the voyage, except that we continued to be dogged by problems with fresh water, until we reached Suva in Fiji, where I paid off, on the 18 November 1975. With a couple of days to kill there, I ended up in the biggest church gathering I have ever witnessed. There were probably a couple of thousand people in this church and there was a visiting 'healer' from the States. He did not do much preaching as I recall but there was plenty of singing by the choir and people with different ailments were going forward to be healed. All of them seemed to come away better than when they arrived, and I am not saying they were not healed it just made me a bit uncomfortable and put me in mind of movies I had seen about 'healers' in the American Bible Belt. I later met this healer on the runway at the airport and he was sporting a big wooden cross round his neck. I looked him in the eye and to tell the truth I would not have given you tuppence for him. I shook his hand and it was pretty limp. Maybe I am wrong but that is the way I felt, anyway I was not caring for I was homeward bound to see my lovely wife and son to study for and sit my Master's Certificate of Competency.

I did not pass it.

I failed in Ship-master's Business and Stability, and they told me to back to sea for six months. To be honest it was quite a blow because thus far I had done well at exams but the syllabus had been radically changed and I obviously had not risen to the challenge. On the other hand I now had a daughter Patricia, born on 26 March 1976 and whilst I was away on the *Luminous* Patsy had organised and orchestrated our removal from Viewpark to Hamilton into a new home which we owned. She did this incidentally when she was seven months pregnant!

We would spend the next eleven years there and make many happy memories. I remember holding our new baby in my arms and thinking about all the travail which would be hers and asking God to especially gift her to deal with it all. My prayer was more than answered for she has plenty to cope with between one thing and another but through it all she is still the one who can light up a room and make us all laugh, with her outrageous humour.

I joined Avon Street Church of Scotland around this time, in which I would eventually run a bible study class, preach from time to time, try to become a Reader, and become an Elder.

CHAPTER SEVENTEEN
THE NEW *LUCELLUM*

After my failed attempt to obtain my Masters Certificate I returned to sea on 13 July 1976 to take the new *Lucellum* to sea from Falmouth where she had been laid up for a year. I was still Mate of course, but I was going back with my old friend who had sent for me to go with him on the *Luxor*. This was to be a sad voyage for me because I really liked this captain but we had both changed, I probably more than him. I was no longer foul mouthed and lusty and we had much less in common than before. It was not a happy set up and ere long we were disagreeing about how to go about the maintenance of the ship. Of course he wanted her to be perfect because she was theoretically brand new, but lying up the Fal for a year had done her no favours, and as soon as she met salt water she began to bleed rust everywhere. I wanted to get paint on as quickly as possible to give her a skin but he wanted everything prepared according to the book with grinding and intense surface preparation. Of course it was his call but it got us off to a bad start. Things generally deteriorated after that because I no longer took part in socialising and ribald humour, so I could understand why he felt as he did towards me. I had no option my allegiance now lay with a Higher Authority and I would just have to do my best. Which is what I did, but I was not happy. Added to this was the fact that the *Lucellum* had built into her some early modern innovations like remote tank readings and valve controls which were operated from a control room instead of out on deck. I hated this stuff because you could not trust it, and as I write it down here on the page the memory of the uncertainty and constant tension come flooding back. Tension, not only over the equipment but also between myself and the Captain.

I recall we loaded crude in Bonny in Nigeria at a crazy rate where you could see the ship sinking before your eyes. I think it was more than two thousand tonnes per hour and we finished loading in less than twelve hours. I cannot remember exactly but it was frightening. When we sailed we made our way across the Atlantic and ran into bad weather. As she pitched in the heavy seas I noticed one of the fancy new Butterworth lids had not been secured properly and was leaking crude oil on deck. I asked the captain to put her on a safe course to let us work on deck to fix it, so he hove her to text book style with the sea a couple of points on the bow so that every now and then she scooped up big green seas over her port side. It was really a dangerous thing to do but he was unwilling to let her run before it for a while when we could have worked away in safety. Anyway I turned to with the Serang and secured the offending lid. As we were coming back up onto the flying bridge she shipped a big green sea which ripped the accommodation ladder off its mountings and sent it hurtling down the deck. Now we had problems and would have to secure the ladder. The Serang got some lashings and more men and we sortied out to secure the ladder. Bear in mind the ladder here referred to was about forty feet long and weighed about a ton. We were just getting to terms with it when another green one boarded and drove the ladder against the structure of the flying bridge pinning and breaking one of the men's ankles. With that the Serang left the deck with all the deck crew carrying the injured man, with the words 'All men die Sahib' and left me on deck with the two apprentices. One of the lads was called Jim Atkins and I forget the other one's name. I think it was Phil. I sent one of the lads for a couple of wire strops and some bottle screws then we jumped down again. Most of our work had been done for us by the big wave which had ripped the ladder off its mountings so we hid behind the pipelines, then when the moment arrived swarmed out and lashed the ladder to the pipelines and made it fast. From that moment on I no longer trusted this captain for he saw our predicament and we could have ended up smashed to bits or overboard in the Atlantic. This was entirely brought about by his intransigence and in my view lack of seamanship. I had to deal with far worse situations in later years in smaller ships and worse weather but I never blatantly put my men in harm's way like that.

In the fullness of time we ended up in Houston Texas. Remember, that is where I had picked up 'Good News for Modern Man' years before. I was at my post down in the control room for the cargo valves and pumps, with a heavy heart and deep in prayer. Now you should know, those of you who do not pray, you can do your job and still pray. That is what the Apostle Paul means when he says 'Pray without ceasing'. So anyway, I was praying and the door opened and a smallish man with a beard walked in. He said 'Hello, I am the port chaplain, Tom Malone; I hear you are a Christian'. I said 'Who told you that?' and he told me that some of the crew had said it. 'Well, Tom,' I said 'I am trying to be a Christian but I am not doing so well right now'. So he asked me what was the problem and I gave him a canned history of my experience thus far. We conversed for a while and then he said 'You know Dave, what you have to do is actually believe that Jesus has done the work. He has already paid the price of your sin and mine and you need to believe that.' With that he embraced me and said 'Receive the Holy Spirit'. Then he left.

My life was never the same after that. I had a new dynamic which filled me and controlled me and transformed the way I viewed my life and its purpose. From now on I would reference everything to the Will of God and my will would be subsumed in His. And now, thirty six years after that moment, nothing has caused me to alter my view. Like Paul, I have learned 'in whatsoever condition I am, therewith to be content'.

When I made my way back up through the Officers' Mess later that day, I found another 'Good News for Modern Man'. It had a different cover so I again took it to my cabin. Of course, I was now carrying my own King James Version of the Bible but it was handy to dip into the modern translation. I must be very slow sometimes, because it was not till years later when I was looking at the two Good News books that the thought crossed my mind that they had been left by the same man. I checked and sure enough there it was 'Tom Malone- Port Chaplain 'on a stamp on the fly of both books. You could have knocked me over with a feather when the significance of this hit me, and I was broken by the sheer kindness and love of God to a wretch like me. To seek me out in my misery and send a good man to call me home. Now every time I sing that great hymn of Charles Wesley *'And can it be that I should gain an interest in the Saviour's love'* I am broken again. Why, I have not managed to finish singing the words for years!

Also during that voyage, we went up the Penobscot River to Bucksport and Searsport with furnace oil which pleased me because it felt good to supply people with fuel for the winter. Then we went to Westport near Boston, again with bunker fuel. In Westport I managed to get ashore to church and met some lovely folk in the Congregational Church there. We continued to Cuba and I finally got off in Tampa in Florida where I parted with the Captain who had been my friend and now had no time for me. So I worshipped in the First Presbyterian Church there and it was just like being home only much, much hotter. As I write these words I am remembering that I worshipped in New Zealand, Australia and many other places on earlier voyages and I still have some Orders of Service from these places. The trouble is, I cannot put them into correct correlation because the memory is not there.

I got home in time for Christmas 1976 having paid off on the eighteenth of December of that year, in Tampa.

I OBTAIN MY MASTER'S FOREIGN GOING CERTIFICATE

I returned to my family and Patsy always made it such a special time. It is entirely due to her that the children love me so much because she kept me alive in their memories while I was away. She would talk to my picture and read my letters to them, and in some ways I am only beginning to understand the true value of this mighty bond which is our marriage. But I had to go back to college for I had still not passed my Master's Certificate. I studied hard and probably was pretty intolerable, in fact I know I was because Patsy said she was profoundly thankful when I eventually passed, fearing that the vows which bound us might not be up to the test of another spell in college. Also during that time, I gave up the pipe when I realised that I was relying more on that than on God for peace. I just stopped one night.

While I was at home studying, Maggie Waugh phoned me up to offer me the supertanker *Oloibiri* as my next job. She was two hundred and seventy thousand tonnes if memory serves but whatever she was, I declined. In fact I was a bit annoyed that she had called when I was trying to get my ticket. I never sailed on another tanker after the *Lucellum*. I told Maggie I had had enough of tankers and needed a change, so having obtained my Master's Foreign Going Certificate at the second attempt on 13 June 1977, joined the *ACT3* in Wellington, New Zealand, four days later.

CHAPTER EIGHTEEN
CONTAINER SHIPS

This was completely foreign ground for me. The *ACT3* was a container ship or, as we called them, a 'box boat'. She was run mostly by ex-Port Line men and as I said before, they were good men for routines. I had a lot to learn very quickly, and somehow the need was more pressing because I was now sailing with a superior certificate. Mind you, the pressures were nothing like as intense as tankers, because after all one cannot co-mingle aluminium boxes. The worst that can happen is you have to discharge and reload. Not only that but the cargo was calculated and planned ashore and that was a huge weight off one's shoulders. So all in all this was a more gentlemanly approach to sea-going than I was used to and I was prepared to enjoy the job. The accommodation on these ships was palatial even compared to the new *Lucellum* and they ran very efficiently. They had British crew in my time and were propelled by steam turbines which consumed fuel voraciously. In fact, I think they burned about four hundred and something tonnes a day and carried about eight and a half thousand tonnes of bunkers, steaming at a service speed of about twenty knots.

Little wonder then, that they were re-engined later on and converted to diesels. What I was less keen on were the 'self-tensioning' winches which were needed to automatically compensate for the rapid fluctuations in draught due to the short loading and discharging times brought about by the inherent efficiency of the system. I suppose they worked well enough, but they could actually cause the ship to 'creep' along the quay if they were not set correctly. The other thing I had to get used to was the lashing system, which was very detailed and specific to each type of box stack. It took time but once I understood the principles it was straightforward enough. The lashings were solid steel galvanised rods which slotted into the corners of the containers and were tightened by 'turn-buckles'. These were large bottle-screws which incorporated a wheel to allow tightening and slackening. They also had 'twist-locks' and these were used to fix the corners of boxes stacked on top of each other. The other thing I liked about our box boats was the forty ton forward crane. It plumbed number one and two hatches and was a great piece of equipment.

Having joined the *ACT3* in Wellington, we went from there across the

Pacific to Panama then up the Eastern Seaboard of the United States, visiting Charleston, Norfolk, Philadelphia, Boston, New York (northbound), St John, New Brunswick, then back down the coast again. That was quite hard work because there were so many ports, but the stress levels were much less. I even got ashore to church a couple of times. We had the job of transporting, over several voyages, an entire power station out to New Zealand from St. John and that involved heavy lifts, so I was in my element stowing that cargo. It all had to be really well secured and that was something I reckoned I was pretty good at. For all the weird shapes of the components, nothing ever moved on my watch, which could not be said for every box boat that sailed out of the Bay of Fundy and south by Cape Hatteras.

Frankly, the only thing that spoiled my time on the *ACT3* was the two captains I sailed with. For different reasons I just could not get on well with them. It was tolerable but never enjoyable. Maybe they were too English and I was too Scottish. Towards the end my time with the second skipper I raised the subject with him and he reckoned I did not understand his sense of humour. No quibble there on my part. He did not have one! But he did say that I was an excellent Mate, or Chief Officer as they called them. That was good enough for me. I paid off back in Wellington on 12 November 1977, and that was the *ACT3*.

I do not remember the next leave in detail, but it was spent preparing for the birth of our second son who arrived on 13 January 1978. We called him Joseph Ritchie, after his great uncle Joe who was lost at sea with my grandfather in 1927, on their yawl called the *Lark*. Like all our children he was immediately taken into intensive care and given antibiotics and he survived just fine. As I write he is helping to build a power station in Manitoba in Canada. He has a Ph.D. in electrical and mechanical engineering.

Three weeks later I was back in St. John, New Brunswick, to join the *ACT6*, in minus twenty three degrees centigrade. Patsy had knitted me a woollen jumper to my own design which I still have and was delighted to have it. It is too warm for ordinary weather. The *ACT6* was similar in all respects to the *ACT3*, although newer, and we would be on a virtually identical run to my last voyage. Again we were loading parts of the power station which was destined for New Zealand and again we had to pay attention to securing arrangements for the heavy lifts, particularly at this time of year, when very violent storms occur on the eastern seaboard of North America. I once saw the results of one of these storms on a box boat in Newark Container Terminal and the sea had simply pulverised some of the boxes. I did not intend to let that happen to my ship.

Our new Captain would be joining in St. John as well. His name was Michael Twomey RNR, and he had a reputation among the Port Line men, of being a hard and demanding man. I intended to make sure I made a good job of sailing with him and arranged to be at the top of the gangway with a full report of our status as he boarded. As he mounted the accommodation ladder I could see a face wrapped in what had been a fiery red beard now greying, with thinning curly red hair also showing grey round the temples and the weathered complexion of the Celtic seafarer. His eyes were penetrating blue and there was mirth etched in the crow's feet at the corners. I liked him immediately and knew instantly that we would be good shipmates. The voyage was uneventful all the way down the Eastern Seaboard through Panama and across the Pacific to Australia and New Zealand, except to mention that the biggest wave I have ever seen hit us one afternoon in the Bass Strait, on our way to Australia.

I will never forget, it was twenty past four in the afternoon and I had just taken over the watch. It had been blowing strongly for some time from the west, and of course there is nothing to stop the wind in these latitudes; it just blows and blows and the seas reach tremendous heights. When all that energy is funnelled into a relatively narrow stretch of water, the billows tend to rear up even bigger and steeper. We were going along at a good clip, maybe eighteen knots, when I sighted this ridge of water forming on the port bow about half a mile away. I knew it would rear up as a huge wall by the time it got to us so I took a bit of speed off her. Now big steam turbine ships take a while to react and slow down but even so I did not want her ploughing into thousands of tonnes of sea with all that heavy lift cargo in number one and two holds. The way slackened quickly and she began to rise quite sweetly to the advance guard of the oncoming monster; then just as I had feared, I felt the gigantic power of the wave suck her down into the trough.

Ahead, now very close, reared a wall of malevolent grey, green water, shot through with spume streaks, and capped with a foaming angry crest, about eighty or a hundred feet above the height of the wheelhouse windows. Now, our wheelhouse was seventy five feet above sea level, and I was looking up to at least the same again. She dug her bow in and the Bass Strait tried to climb aboard us, but all the time her huge reserve buoyancy in the flare of her bow was seeking to drive up through the over-towering billow. Slowly, slowly, she powered up towards the crest then sensing the clear air on the other side, she broke through, felt the crest roar under her, then hurtled down the back slope of the mighty wave. Faster and faster down the hill of sea green, to burrow her bow into the guts of the next gathering ridge of ocean. More green sea attempted to board as she again buried her snout, and again the great flare of her bow did its work and bore her focsle skywards. Eventually, after another couple of sickening, headlong plummets, the train of the swell lengthened and normal pitching was resumed. By now, the Old Man had managed to clamber up to the wheelhouse and I asked him to relieve me so I could check our cargo. I made my way forward and, starting at number one hold, I worked aft. Nothing had moved, not even a forty ton transformer stowed in number two, which the apprentices and I had worked hard to secure on leaving the Bay of Fundy. I was very surprised that all was well, but the lesson learned in Malé in the Maldives had clearly served me well, and we arrived in Melbourne with no damage to report.

On sailing from Sydney, we had a nasty experience. I was up on the focsle with my crew and we were letting go the forward tug which had been made fast with our combination towing hawser. This is a hawser which is made up of wire for the most part, with a length of nylon hawser of similar breaking strain to absorb shock, for towing a big ship in harbour. We had been given the order to let go the tug and, having slackened off the wire, the tug came in under the bow and let go the nylon end. Normal practice in tugs is to prevent the end going into the water by paying it out slowly, thereby allowing the men on the ship time to heave it in. Our tugboat men must have been absent the day they taught that at tug school, because they let it go without a thought and the nylon end sank like a stone and went straight into the bow thruster, which was spinning at dear knows how many revolutions. Of course, the hawser went straight into the thruster and then started ripping wire off the drum end. I was up in the eyes of the ship with the wire between my legs! I looked round and saw my men going down like ninepins, with the wire whipping round completely out of control. I jumped over the wire as it exited through the forward towing lead and made a tally of injuries. Thankfully, it amounted to a broken arm, broken wrist, some broken ribs, some lacerations and loads of shock. We had come off lightly, for it could have been much worse. We sent the men ashore in the pilot boat for medical treatment and they all eventually fetched up back on board.

We were demonstrated against in Melbourne for carrying radioactive waste away from Australia, and I could never make up my mind if they were angry about sending the waste to another country or losing it out of their own. Such is the mindset of the merchantman. I could not have cared less as long as it made good freight. I changed in later years, but at that time I was happy enough as a simple ship's Mate. Anyway, they formed cordons and prevented the lorries coming in through the main gate, so the port arranged for another access point and got the boxes aboard that way, in the dead of night, whereupon we sailed. We coasted round Australia to Brisbane then sailed to New Zealand, where we loaded in Auckland and Wellington. From there we made for Panama.

Now the Captain had decided, in cahoots with the Second Mate, to sail on a Great Circle Track from New Zealand to Rapa Island then run a rhumb line to Panama. A Great Circle is the shortest distance between two places on the globe but it requires daily or sometimes twice daily course adjustment. In order to follow the Great Circle track to Rapa, we would need to go well south and it is running in my mind that we would go as far south as fifty six degrees. This is an area of uninhibited wind south of the Roaring Forties and it was winter in the Southern Hemisphere. When we sailed from New Zealand, I recall the weather was not so bad with big swells and moderate westerly winds ushering us along at a rare lick, and we were able to get on with maintenance on deck. When we had been out over a week and were about as far south as we would go, it was during the morning watch when the Third Mate, whom I had not much time for since he was fat, indolent and as much use as a hip pocket in a singlet, was working out his sight. Of course, his head was down in his sight book and he failed to notice that we were passing a yacht on the port side. Thankfully, Sparkie's wife was looking out of the port in their cabin and was a bit more alert than the man on watch! She raced up to the Wheelhouse and thankfully the fat third mate had the wit to call me. He had tried the Master but he was at his 'constitutionals'. I went down to the Old Man's cabin and spoke to him through the door and we reckoned it would be wise to turn round and have a look since we were so far south. I went back to the Bridge, started turning her round and prepared to slow down. As soon as the Master arrived on the Bridge, I went forward with the Bosun and the men to the focsle. Soon, the way came off the *ACT6* and we approached the yacht sedately. The Captain laid her close to the yacht and I was able to converse with the occupant of the single masted sloop. It went like this:

'How many are you?'
'Just me'
'Are you all right'
'No'
'Do you want to be rescued?'
'Yes!'
'OK'.

So we set about bringing the yacht alongside and put a ladder over the side. We took the man on board and he looked all in, emaciated and worn out. He was taken up to the hospital by the Chief Steward to be put in a bath while we set about transferring everything out of the yacht. When this was complete we got the Bosun, who had gone onto the yacht, back aboard and, having decided not to try to lift her on board due to the swell, we set about running her down.

We could not sink her. The Captain and I thought we would have no more ado than to plough into her with the ship's bow, but no matter which speed we hit her at, we could not sink that little boat. We could not even damage her. So the *Rogue*, for that was her name, was cast adrift in the mighty Southern Ocean, and for all I know she is still afloat!

It turned out this man's name was 'Starkey', like Ringo Starr. He had set out from Sal Saleta in California weeks before, with a plan to sail to Easter Island, to view the big heads which are carved there. He had run into a storm which had blown him away to leeward, during which he had suffered a heart attack. On recovering from his heart attack and the storm, he had decided the best idea would be to point his yacht towards the thousands of islands in the Pacific and hope for the best. Then we happened along.

He had three baths that day before he was clean, and then he began to eat. He refused nothing over the ensuing days, and went through every course on the menu, scooping up as many leftovers as were available. He soon began to recover as we forged on up to Rapa and then on to Panama, and by the time a week had passed he was a changed man. Changed in more ways than one. He knew that the chances of being rescued down in these latitudes depended on odds which were nothing short of astronomical, and as we chatted away he began to realise that he had been spared under the most extraordinary circumstances. When we found him he had no food, very little water and some vitamin pills. I was not slow to point this out to him and I think that our talks gave him a new direction for the rest of his life. Who knows? The Captain radioed in that we had picked this man up and when we arrived in Panama the American press corps was there to meet him. For a brief moment he enjoyed a celebrity status, then I suppose he simply blended into his role in time and space. As did we.

I have been a member of our 'Union' or 'Association' for some forty six years as I write this. It has gone through a couple of manifestations in that time, changing its name from 'Merchant Navy Officers' and Airline Pilots' Association' to 'Nautilus' as it is now. They have always produced a newspaper, called the *'Telegraph'* which is well received by officers at sea. It is informative and keeps one up to date with changes in the world of shipping. In recent years the problem of piracy has been very much to the forefront of seamen's minds. I mention this newspaper because on one occasion they featured an article on the latest vessel built by the Department of Agriculture and Fisheries for Scotland. Her name was the *Jura* and when I saw her photograph I thought she was the best looking ship I had ever seen. She was much smaller than anything I had sailed on during the past twelve years, but it was her size and sturdy lines which appealed to me. The image went into my mind and remained there.

I paid off the *ACT6* on 25 June 1978 back in St John, New Brunswick, and flew home. Captain Twomey wanted me to come back for another trip after leave, but I was not sure what lay ahead of me and could not promise anything. When I arrived home and saw my lovely family I was aware that I was coming to one of those times when things are changing. My new son Joseph was lying in his cot when I came in and of course I wanted to pick him up. He was six and a half months old and he dissolved in tears! I had left when he was three weeks old.

At that moment I resolved to find another way to provide for our family, because these long voyages were too painful. In addition to that, Maggie Waugh had phoned me up after six weeks at home and asked me to coast the

ACT2 from Tilbury to Bremerhaven and back to Liverpool. I talked it over with Patsy and she advised me to do the job then call it a day. I had no idea what I would do at this point but I knew it would have to be at sea.

So I coasted the *ACT2* under the command of yet another Port Line man, who will remain forever in my memory as a man who was a most reluctant mariner. On the night I arrived in Bremerhaven we had to warp the ship six hundred feet up the quay, but that did not stop him walking off with his wife and leaving it to me. Again, when I asked him in front of the other officers what his orders were with regard to fog, he said that we had all spent a long time getting our tickets so we should just carry on. Either he was the most trusting fellow afloat or he really did not want to be there. I am guessing the latter.

Anyway it all worked out fine, but when we got to Liverpool, a chap came down from head office to have a chat with me. It was evening time as I recall, and I had just come off deck, when he came into the cabin. I was very civil to him and we sat down. He said that complaints had been received from the parents of the two deck apprentices we had carried on the *ACT6* that I had worked them too hard. He said that Captain Twomey and I were understood in the office to be 'old school' seafarers and that I needed to understand that these young men were very qualified nowadays and had to be treated accordingly since things had changed. I absorbed this then asked him if he was acquainted with the training books the 'cadets' now had. He said he was. I invited him to look at what had been achieved this voyage and to note that the advances made by these young men on their voyage with me far outstripped any previous voyages they had done so far. I also said to him that someday these young, allegedly highly qualified men, would be asked to navigate ships through storms and dense traffic for long periods, and did he realise that the stamina to do that was developed as a young man. I said the sea had not changed, it still killed people every day and we had to be able to cope with it. That is what Captain Twomey and I had taught them. I went on, 'But you need have no worry about me overworking any more 'cadets' because I have decided to resign from Trafalgar House [as the company was now called] and seek employment elsewhere. And incidentally neither of these fellows is as qualified as I was when I joined.'

So that was that. I resigned from my old employers without any regrets or any idea of what I would do next. And that was the end of my deep sea voyaging. It was 18 August 1978.

CHAPTER NINETEEN
SCOTTISH FISHERIES 1978-1983

I was out of a job, with a wife and three children and a mortgage. Strangely, however, I was completely unafraid and certain I was doing the right thing. Patsy and I discussed it this way and that, and it was she who suggested that I contact the Union. Always listen to your wife; she is your helpmate, if you have a good one. So the next day we packed the bairns up and went into Glasgow to the Union offices. I was seen by a very kind man who asked me if I had any notion of what I might want to do, and it was at that moment I remembered the picture of the *Jura*. I told him I had a notion for fishery protection, and he replied that that was peculiar, because only that day a friend of his, who was Marine Superintendent of the Department of Agriculture and Fisheries for Scotland had been in touch about whether or not there were any bright young men with Masters' tickets in the offing. He asked if I would like him to get in touch with the Marine Superintendent and I did, and he did, there and then. They chatted for a bit and before I knew anything else I was being invited to a 'Board' which would be convened in the next couple of weeks.

We went home feeling much better and in the fullness of time I was sent a bundle of paperwork to fill in, which I completed and returned blithely. They wanted to know everything about me and my antecedents, I supposed because this was a government concern. Before long I was called up to the 'Board' and sat before three mature fellows including the Marine Superintendent, a Captain from the Board of Trade, and a Personnel Manager of the Scottish Civil Service. They gave me a good grilling which I thoroughly enjoyed, for I had done my homework in the Hamilton Library, and apart from that I kept coming up with inspired ideas. For instance, they asked me about why I thought fishery protection was necessary, and it seemed axiomatic to me that if the law was to mean anything it had to be enforced. Not only that, it appeared to me that if a country took itself seriously, there was a clear connection between its sovereignty and its determination to protect its fishing rights. I said that we had our own law, our own Church and a long history of self-determination, so we should also see to our own seas. I think they liked this nationalistic tendency in my thinking. There was plenty more in this vein, and I realise now that the words which came so easily were being provided by a better brain than mine. I was destined to go into the Fisheries, and again I felt the power of answered prayer.

I was given a contract immediately as Second Officer, which would be ratified on completion of a year's satisfactory service. In addition to this I would in time be issued with a warrant as a British Sea Fisheries Officer. The price of leaving deep sea sailing and having more time at home would be about two thousand pounds a year, which in 1978 eight was a lot of money, equating to about a quarter of the salary we were used to. But the benefits far outweighed money. The patrol time was only sixteen days, with five days alongside in the home ports of either Greenock or Leith.

My first ship was the *Vigilant*, the fourth vessel to bear that name, and I well remember seeing this tiny craft, only one hundred and fifty feet long, lying in the James Watt Dock in Greenock. It required a colossal readjustment on my part to come to terms with her. Having been built between the wars, she had the hull and general configuration of a middle water trawler of that period, and indeed when commissioned she had all the gear and winches of a real trawler made out of wood! She was a fisheries 'Q' ship, and the idea was that she could pretend to be a regular trawler till she came close to an illegal fleet of fishing vessels, then drop her disguise and set the cat among the pigeons, as it were. Of course, such a ruse could only be sprung a limited number of times before the fishing community would be wise to it, so before too long she underwent a refit to remove her phoney winches and gear, and became a bona fide fishery cruiser. That was her condition when I first saw her and when I met the Captain, who would become a mentor, trusted colleague and friend. He came from Campbeltown, spoke with a broad Kintyre accent, and ran the little *Vigilant* as his 'Wee Battleship' with glottal stop on the 'T's of battleship.

I liked him immediately, but was not to sail with him just yet, for having spent only one night on this vessel, I was transferred to the *Switha* lying in Leith. She had been built the *Ernest Holt* as a distant water research vessel, then bought by the Department as an interim response following the findings of the Cameron Report which recommended, among other things, the renewal of Scotland's Fishery Protection Fleet, to enable it to patrol the recent extension of fishery limits to 200 miles.

SWITHA

At one hundred and seventy eight feet in length, she was in all respects similar to all wartime distant water trawlers with beautiful lines and a look that instils confidence. Engined with a triple expansion steam engine and fitted out internally with wood panelling, moquette upholstery, railway carriage windows in the wheelhouse, no automatic steering and thirty odd years of sea service under her belt, I felt I was again experiencing something of the magic that Jan De Hartog had woven all those years before. My new Captain was a corpulent giant of a man whose robust blustering appearance masked a kind and sensitive soul inside. He was always willing to pass on wisdom and lore and I would discover that he was apparently utterly unmoved by the severity of the weather, referring to big angry seas as 'Gentle undulations'. The First Officer of the ship came from the Orkney Islands, and he too was willing and able to pass on a great deal of expertise and knowledge about the coast of Scotland. Both of these men were excellent ship handlers and I learned a lot from them.

I joined her in October of 1978, serving on her till February or March of 1979, during which time my knowledge of the coast of Scotland and the Fisheries Law of Scotland expanded exponentially.

I also discovered seasickness.

There is no comparison between the motion of a big vessel and a small one in a big ocean, and whilst I was enthralled with the ambiance of the *Switha*, revelling in her connection with the past, her antics at sea invariably sent me to the sink in the Captain's sea cabin, which was attached to the wheelhouse. This condition persisted for the entire time I served on the *Switha* and at one point I really thought I would not be able to carry on. I cannot describe the relief I felt when we came to anchor in some bay or loch in the Orkneys or on the North Coast; strangely, all I could consume after these bouts of seasickness was orange juice, blue cheese and cold fish with vinegar. Explain that, if you will.

That winter was not a benign one, and in fact I do not remember any of the winters being benign for the next twenty nine years! In some way or another they were always hard, but of course the most important feature by far was the wind, and the Shipping Forecast was listened to, written down, and studied by every watch. I developed an abiding interest in the weather around this time and started sending in synoptic reports regularly to the Meteorological Office from the *Switha*, which continued on all my other ships for the rest of my career. The Captain was delighted when he received a prize for sending these reports which of course he had not initiated. I received one as well and went on receiving them till I retired. It was always an 'improving' type of book one received, starting with a dictionary then continuing through an Atlas; a 'Book of Facts' and so on until eventually, when they had given you about fourteen of them as Master you received a barograph. Unfortunately, by the time I was due a barograph the Met Office had run out of funds for that level of reward but I still have my books, of which I am very proud, although the children have used some of them to a state of disrepair.

During that winter while 'dodging' in the North Sound, which is a huge bight, almost an archipelago at the north end of Orkney, we were joined by a fleet of Faroese fishing vessels seeking shelter from the unremitting gales which were strafing us at the time. It was then that I carried out my first 'boarding'. This meant that I would go on board one of these fishing vessels and carry out an inspection of the vessel's paperwork, her catch and fishing gear. The difference between then and now was that we had to make a report out to the Fisheries Secretary detailing exactly what had taken place, and it was sent to his office for scrutiny. To be frank it was pain in the neck, but at that time I knew no better and took it extremely seriously, and would continue to do so till I retired; however, in the not too distant future the procedure would be completely overhauled and streamlined. I think it was because of the cumbersome nature of the paperwork that few inspections were undertaken, and I remember that the notional number of boardings which should be carried out in a year was about twelve. In the light of later developments this is an absurdly low number, but you need to remember that this was at the very beginning of offshore patrolling and none of the parameters had been set in stone. In later years it would be frowned upon if a ship did not clear three hundred inspections at sea in a year!

The name of the first vessel I boarded was the *Jupiter* FD.150. FD stands for Fuglefjord in Faroe Islands. You always remember your first. The part I enjoyed most was the transfer from the *Switha* to the *Jupiter* and back, which was carried out in an RFD inflatable rubber boat with an outboard engine. When I think of how things progressed over the years that followed and the marvellous boats and gear we ended up with, we had to have a lot of heart using these craft in the hostile North Atlantic. We were not even supplied with oilskins in these days and one procured one's own from any source, so we looked more like pirates than fishery officers. My own oilskins had been purchased in New Zealand and were real black cotton oilskins, which were fine except that they leaked due to abrasion when sitting on the rubber sponson of the RFD boat. The *Jupiter* was legal in all respects and was permitted to go about her lawful occasions, but the event kindled in me a love of skimming over the sea in a fast boat, climbing on board hugely differing vessels, and enforcing the laws of my country. I know that sounds jingoistic, but that's me.

Halfway through our patrol we would go into Kirkwall if we were working in the North or Stornoway if we were in the West, for what we called a 'half-landing'. This term was coined from the fishing industry but it was very appropriate for us. I loved these periods because we were in for two nights and it allowed time for routine jobs like chart correction and maintenance, and also for a run ashore to phone home; this was really living! In the early years I made a point of visiting all the ancient sites I could or going to the pictures at night when these ports still had cinemas. I was not interested in pubs or drinking by this time. In fact, shortly after Davy was born I stopped drinking altogether for twenty five years until I resumed having a glass of red wine at night 'for medicinal purposes'. Incidentally I still can only manage a glass of beer or wine because I still get a blinding headache if I take any more. It amounts to a kind of enforced moderation and I thank God for it.

It is difficult for me to convey just how liberating this new way of life was for me. I had begun to realise that I had always wanted to sail on small ships, on the frontier as it were, doing something which I actually believed, and still believe, made a difference to the wellbeing of my country. Even although the weather was abominable most of the time, I knew I would adapt and eventually beat the sea sickness and so, I think for the first time in my life, I was happy at sea. The *Switha* was a magnificent sea boat and could handle anything the elements could throw at her; in fact when she was punching into a big head sea, her triple expansion engine would apparently slow itself down so that she did not damage herself. Mind you, she was very wet on the main deck due to her low freeboard, but so are all distant water trawlers of that vintage and you just have to bear it in mind.

So life staggered on through that winter with us sailing from Leith running up the coast to Orkney then working variously out from there towards the Western Isles, depending on where the fleets were fishing Often we were driven to seek shelter and I was glad that I sailed with men who were well acquainted with the coast and the places where you could safely anchor and wait out a heavy gale. In later years I would use all these bolt holes when I had my own ships, but I gained the confidence to do so from these men. When we had worked out in the West or North for a spell we took our half-landing then would watch the weather for a chance to go home.

I recall on one of these occasions running along the North Coast before a westerly gale. Actually the gale was blowing from the south-west and we should have had some lee from the coast but as so often happened on that coast, the wind veered a couple of points due to the effect of the land and blew more westerly. We were also running slightly behind where we wanted to be to catch the last of the east-going stream at the Pentland Firth. We passed Strathy Point doing a good speed but the tide was slackening off and by the time we came to the west of Scrabster things were not looking good. I could see the sea beginning to form big combers, made bigger and steeper by the turning tide, and I called the master. When he saw the conditions he decided to make for Dunnet Bay, so now we had the sea running under us on the starboard quarter. They were big vicious seas as well and I will never forget the sheer malevolence of it as it corkscrewed the old *Switha* and made her roll sickeningly. We all breathed a sigh of relief when we came into the bay and lost that ghastly sea, finally dropping the anchor as full darkness came on. We remained there for a couple of tides then we had to move to get home in time. By this time the wind had backed southerly and was still blowing strongly so we arranged to be at Duncansby Head around slack water. Again we ran into very heavy seas made worse by the turning tide but eventually we bore through, past Wick and into the more benign Moray Firth. In all of this, I never felt sea sick. Just scared.

And that is all I remember of the *Switha*.

I left her soon after and was transferred to the *Westra*, and was at sea on her when I heard that the *Switha* had run aground on the Herwit Rock off Inchkeith, outside Leith, due to a navigational error. The rescue services got all the crew off and indeed, after the weather improved, the crew were able to go back and forth to salvage bits of equipment and spares, but she was a total loss. The Navy placed explosives to remove her fuel oil, and despite this she remained a navigation mark for most of the rest of my career. She only disappeared a few years ago, a sad end to a brave little ship.

WESTRA

During my time on the *Switha* I had started to collect and read theological books, mostly bought in the Evangelical Bookshop in Stornoway, and because there are no secrets on a ship it was not long before my Christianity was known about. This is inevitable when men are thrown together in the confines of a small ship and it was not long before I discovered that I had a nickname 'The Rev Bev'. I do not know how it happens but there is always some wit who can find a name which gets to the heart of a person's character. You notice how the Plains Indians or indeed any of the first nations of the United States are able to name a person in a way which exactly encapsulates that person's character. It is a gift. I never had it. Patsy has it, I think, because after some discussion we were able to call our next wee girl Jennifer Rachel, when she was born on 29 December 1979. (Jennifer is a Welsh name meaning 'fair' or 'white water' as in a storm of wind both very appropriate to Jenny). I have a diary entry for this period, which conveys feelings of peace, gentleness and love. And we now had four surviving children. Jenny was a beautiful baby, in fact they all were, but when she was little I thought she had the bonniest face. I always thought she looked a bit like me! She is now married to Dominic, the man who proofread this book, and they have a lovely wee girl of their own – Annie.

Before I left the *Switha* I had started making toys for Christmas; I made three hobby horses for Davy, Tisha (That is what Davy called Patricia and it stuck for life), and a small one for Joe. This was to become a practice of mine for many years to come, working away in our garage especially at Christmas time in all weathers, constructing a carousel, a castle, a garage, a doll's house a fire engine, and many other toys. It was called 'Doing Santa's Work'. Funnily enough we still have the doll's house which I have been forbidden to throw out and our grandchildren play with it still. Patsy always appreciated my work more than I did and I am glad she kept the house.

During that period we always seemed to get a spell of snow, so sledges were required and these were also built in the garage. Some of our happiest times have been spent sledging. Along with sledges came bikes, never purchased new, always reconditioned and made to look like new. And of course all children should have a bogie, which I constructed from the rear wheels of an old tricycle, a piece of wardrobe and the front wheels from an old pram. The steering was managed by the handle of another old pram and I was able to build in a braking system as well. It did sterling service for many years. On reflection, that was a special time. Strangely, we seldom recognise these times as we live through them; it is only when we look back, as I am doing now, that their true value becomes apparent.

But I have digressed a bit. I only served on the *Westra* for a few patrols, but in that time I again met people whose comradeship I would value in years to come. I would sail with these chaps, who were all senior to me in the Service, on several further occasions in later years, but we have time for a moment to note in passing that the Junior First Officer and I together was a hilarious combination, and handing over the watch took a long time. He enjoyed painting pictures as I did, and we would talk about art, as well as solve all the fishery problems in the universe. He was very tall and would put you in mind of Long John Baldry whilst the Senior First Officer was short and round and lived in Auchtermuchty in Fife. I always thought of him as a beaver or a gerbil, especially when he was eating which he did quite a lot. But he was an excellent fishery officer and knew his job. Years later, when he sailed with me as First Officer on my first command, the old *Norna*, (he had difficulty passing his Master's Ticket) he wrote out for me the Lord's Prayer which he had copied in a Fife graveyard, written in old Scots. His calligraphy was excellent and I mounted it in a little frame, and attached it to the wheelhouse bulkhead of every ship I commanded. It now has an important place on my wall of memorabilia. Sadly he died at a young age, of liver cancer. We all went to his funeral.

The Officer in Charge was ex-Navy and had served in destroyers and cruisers during the Second World War. He spoke with a typical 'posh naval' accent of that time and sported a monocle. For all that, he was a good fellow and had a plethora of good stories and repartee. I recall one night we were on the way home when we came on a few boats trawling just inside the three mile limit south of Aberdeen. He got on the VHF radio and called up one of the vessels after we had identified him with the searchlight. 'Good evening skipper!' says the Captain, in thick navalese, which is as far as you could get from the Doric of the fishing skipper, "What are you fishing for tonight? (dramatic pause)....Rabbits?" Laughter all-round the *Westra*'s wheelhouse and on the fishing boat. The skipper came up with some cock and bull story but we let him go because we were going home.

JURA

My next posting after this short sojourn on the *Westra* was the *Jura*, which I joined in James Watt Dock, Greenock, sometime in 1979 I think. At last I would be serving on my dream vessel, and although she and the *Westra* were identical there was something about the *Jura*.

The *Jura* was the first of what would become a class of vessel called the 'Island' class. Her hull was based on that of a deep sea trawler, the most notable feature of which was her 'Tulip' bow. Our Department designed and built her and the Royal Navy negotiated a lease of the vessel shortly after she was completed, to try her out to see if she would suit their requirements. She must have done just that, because they went on to build another seven of their own, I think, and returned our boat like a wreck. It took our engineers about eighteen months to bring her up to our standards, for they had given her a sound thrashing. The *Jura* could take it though, and she bounced back better than ever.

I now regarded her as 'My ship' in my mind although I was still only a Second Officer, but I ploughed into my work with gusto. Her charts were about eighteen months out of date and I used every available moment to bring them up to scratch. I reckoned that if the government ships were not right, who would be? This made a very good impression on the Commander who, having gone through forty one Second Officers before I arrived, was getting a name for being hard to please. Second Officer number forty two, who was a few months senior to me, also managed to survive, and eventually became a good friend. At that time a ship had a Captain, a Senior First Officer, Junior First Officer and two Second Officers allocated to her. When the Captain went on leave the Senior First Officer took her out as 'Officer in Charge' and everyone else acted up. I think we only had four trips off at that time during the year so the rest of us tried to divide up the leave slots as equitably as possible. I missed a lot of Christmas holidays, Patsy tells me.

As I look back now in the light of how things developed, I realise that this was a transition stage in Fisheries and the rules were still being made up. The Common Fisheries Policy had still to be written and we were still working with the Three Mile Limit and By-laws. Although we had a two-hundred mile limit, no-one really knew what to do with it. The thought of running out to Rockall spooked a lot of the older skippers and for a long time was regarded as going to the Moon. Because of this, detections of breaches of Regulations were few and far between at this time, and we had still to build a *modus operandi* which would yield results. I for one was desperate to capture any fishing vessel but it was almost as though there was reluctance on the part of the administration to prosecute offenders. I do not think we detected anyone while I was on the *Jura* during this period. Mind you, we were still using little rubber boats to carry out inspections and our launching equipment was primitive, to say the least. Add to that the fact that expectations were low anyway, and you have a combination for inertia. I simply enjoyed sailing around on my beloved *Jura*, and improving the bits I had charge of.

The one event I recall which is worthy of recording was the occasion when we were asked to assist an Icelandic fishing vessel called the *Eldhammer*, which had broken down about 300 miles west of the Butt of Lewis. It was a long way off but the weather was benign and we were not doing much anyway, as I recall. The Officer in Charge that trip was a bit chary about running out there, but we set off anyway and prepared for towing. This was interesting for me because I had never towed in the ocean before and was keen to see how it was done. We had to join together several mooring ropes to make up a tow length sufficiently long to create a catenary which would allow the strain to be borne without parting the tow. This we coiled in a large circle on the poop. Really, it was uneventful; with fair weather we made good passage and the only bit of excitement was when we were making fast the tow line. Our Officer in Charge took the *Jura* extremely close to the *Eldhammer* and I for one had never been in such close proximity to another vessel at sea. The thing was, he was as blind as a bat and did not realise the distance he was closing to until it had come and gone. When I mentioned it to him it took about three cigarettes to calm him down! We towed her to East Loch Roag in Lewis.

Our Officer in Charge was one of those guys who was unconsciously funny. Whenever we came in to our home port, the Assistant Marine Superintendent would visit the ship. He was a tough character and would

159

brook no nonsense. After our Officer in Charge had undergone a private interrogation with him about how the patrol had gone, and the Assistant Marine Superintendent had left, our commander would come down to the Ship's Office for a coffee and a couple of cigarettes to wind down and 'debrief', as it were. Invariably, as his dander rose, he would regale us with how he had 'Just told him that so and so was the case, and he would just have to accept it!' All of this was delivered with eyes pointing to somewhere outside the port hole in the Crab Nebula, and the index finger of his right hand cocked up in a defiant, authoritative gesture. All of this would be accompanied at some point by the refrain *'It'll be Puff the Magic Dragon and Good Night Irene'*. This is now indelibly etched onto the psyche of the Beveridge family and been imported into the language. I liked sailing with him, and thankfully it was he I sailed with most of the time, only sailing with the substantive Captain on a few occasions, which I have to say were quite stressful. One never knew which character was going to arrive on the bridge. Sometimes I suspected he was bi-polar.

I recall being told that, shortly before I had joined, they had been punching into a gale for a couple of days and had driven the anchors into the hull plating. So the engineers were called to effect a repair. The best they could do was to fix on a fibre-glass patch, to get them to port for repair. The Captain asked how long it would take to cure and was told twenty four hours. So he ran before the gale for twenty four hours to the minute then promptly put her head into the weather again and re-opened the holes in the hull! Obstinate and very impractical. I think he would have made a good head clerk in a workhouse! He ended up blotting his copy book by deploying the *Jura* to the North Sea when he had been specifically ordered to remain on the West Coast. This happened one year, when the Danes were threatening to 'fish up to the beaches' with a huge fleet of industrial trawlers. The Department did not take kindly to that and he was demoted to command the old *Brenda* for a while. He was eventually reinstated to the *Jura* for a spell before he retired, and sadly he did not last long after his retiral.

I served on the *Jura* for about eighteen months over this period and was very happy. The job was not challenging, there being very little pressure; whatever there was coming from the weather which was either bad or abominable. I think one has to have a particular type of mental attitude to survive months of hostile conditions wherein the predominant colours are grey,

grey-green, grey blue and grey white, occasionally highlighted by inky blue-black. Of course it is not like that all the time but I can assure you that good days are at a premium. We changed Commanding Officers twice more during this period and it is not clear in my memory who came at which time. The first was tall, finely featured with sandy hair and a refined accent. He looked and behaved like a barrister and saw himself as a dilettante in the old Scottish style. He was a dyed in the wool Nationalist and even went to the trouble of learning a bit of Gaelic. He still writes to the Scotsman and they frequently publish his contributions. We used to have good discussions about politics and religion, both of which subjects are usually taboo on a ship, and we were not so far apart, except that he had come out of a liberal theological stable whereas I was firmly in the conservative evangelical camp. He could speak French pretty well, for his father had been an ambassador to Cairo I think, and for some reason that made him good at French. At any rate, I learned a lot of his handy phrases which were extremely useful when interviewing French trawlers. *'Chalutier Français, Drake, Drake, c'est le navire garde de pêche Jura, Jura, bonjour patron, combien de jours êtes-vous à la pêche dans cette zone?'* Of course, one had to be ready to translate the reply, but that came with time as well. After a while I could prattle away with them and get the gist of what they were saying, and I think my accent was passable.

When this Captain came, he wanted to stir things up a bit and started to do more inspections than had ever been done before offshore. I remember him throwing out a challenge to the Senior Captain, who commanded the *Westra*, when we had passed the twenty mark for the year. It sounds a paltry sum now, but then, we were really setting the heather on fire. He was a pretty good skipper and I quite enjoyed his style. He used to say 'I cease to function in anything over a force 8!' This was very nice if you could get it, and most of the time he did!

One day, whilst he was in command, we came away from the lay-by berth of Govan dry-dock where we had undergone refit for some time. We were due to sail down to Greenock to resume patrolling. Anyway, he started his manoeuvre and backed out of the lay-by berth into the Clyde. I was down aft at my station when I noticed that, when we arrived at the point where he should have been taking speed off, she was actually accelerating! Faster and faster she went, pointing directly at the Meadowside Granary, the quayside of which was faced with huge granite coping stones. I realised something was radically wrong and shouted to my men to 'Bale out lads.' Some of the men later claimed that I uttered foul invective but I do not think so. Maybe in the heat of the moment, who knows? The *Jura* just kept on picking up speed, then I heard the anchors being dropped. She drove her port quarter hard onto the coping stones then, not satisfied with that, did it again! Well, you can imagine what came off best between the granite and her ten millimetre plating. Eventually the engines stopped and I arranged for the men to rig hoses in case of fire in the Steering Flat. Her port quarter was badly distorted and crumpled and several frames were bent. We managed to get her back alongside, then we heard what had happened on the bridge. They had realised early on that she was not responding to the pitch control lever, putting on astern pitch instead of taking it off. The Captain ordered the Senior First Officer to emergency stop the engines, which he tried to do again and again until he pushed the buttons through the console! Immediately after that she hit and the First Officer was catapulted over the Pilot's chair with the force of impact. After we heard the stories, the Captain went away home and left us to it for the next fortnight! That was his style.

The Second Officer who had arrived shortly before me became a good pal on that ship and we used to spend hours discussing how we would reform the Fisheries. You see, things were starting to crystallise and we were beginning to understand what would be required under the Common Fisheries Policy when it finally came in. One of our ideas was that the Department should build two fast patrol boats for inshore work based on the Aran lifeboat, and it is quite sobering to realise how prophetic these notions were in the light of what subsequently took place. But at this time we were just enjoying ourselves.

I recall one night when we sailed from Greenock, for some reason with the Junior First Officer in charge. We came round the Mull of Kintyre and ran straight into a north westerly gale. He decided to keep her going into it, and by the time we got the Rhinns of Islay she was really performing, diving headlong into steep, tidal-induced seas. At midnight my pal came up to relieve me and I went below to do my rounds before turning in. After the *Port Victor* I never failed to do that as Officer of the Watch. When I got down to the Steering Flat I detected the unmistakable odour of petrol, very thick and strong. I opened the door to the Steering Flat, which housed the machinery that powered the rudder, and it was like a tanker's pump-room, the air shimmering with petroleum gas. I immediately thought that if a random spark should be struck from one of the motors, we would blow up. I told the watch to go round and tell any late bedders to stop smoking, ran upstairs and told my relief then called the Officer in Charge. His response, in his London accent, was 'Oh no, I've only just got over to sleep!'

I thought, if you do not get up now, my friend, you might be sleeping a lot longer than you want to. But I just said 'You better come up'. So he did, and the other Second Officer and I put on our survival suits and life-jackets (the gear was getting much better by this time) and sortied out onto the poop. It was a filthy night and we worked our way aft with heaving lines to stop us going over the side. I made an investigation and sure enough it did not take long to discover that one of the tins of petrol which we kept for the boarding boat had burst its top off and was leaking petrol, the fumes of which were being sucked into the Steering Flat vent. We threw the offending tin over the side and gingerly vented the Steering Flat and that was that.

The fact is, you can never relax at sea for if you do she will conspire to kill you, by one means or another.

Before I left the *Jura*, the Captain I had first met on the old *the Vigilant* took over as C.O. And the 'Battle of the Atlantic' started in earnest. He was determined to ramp up the number of boardings and by the time the year had drawn to a close we had clocked up one hundred boardings! This was unheard of, and of course it threw down the gauntlet to all the other skippers. Some of them picked it up.

My time on the *Jura* was coming to an end. Sometime during my tour on her, we were joined by another First Officer who had been a pilot in East Africa with my fellow Second Officer. They were colleagues of old and I got on well enough with him. He was corpulent, florid, and jocular on his own terms, and blasphemed a lot. Mind you, he was a good ship-handler and we were amiable enough. The new Marine Superintendent must have thought highly of him because he was promoted very quickly.

CHAPTER TWENTY
SCOTIA

As far as I can remember, I was sent to the research vessel *Scotia* next, as First Officer, somewhat disconsolate at having to leave the *Jura*. On the other hand, this was a completely new field of work for me and I set about trying to learn as much as I could.

The *Scotia* was a big stern trawler, which went out for six weeks as opposed to sixteen days and that in itself took some adjustment. It is extraordinary how quickly one becomes accustomed to good things. Most of the crew, including the Fishing Mates, came from the Buchan area which made me feel very at home. We loaded gear in Aberdeen from the Department's Laboratory and the nature of this equipment would depend on the type of trip we were undertaking. Some trips involved trawling, some buoy work, some sampling work and some a combination of all. There can be little doubt that this was a fascinating type of ship to sail on and I became very enthusiastic and keen to assist the scientists in their investigations. It was a whole new world for me with new challenges coming with each new piece of equipment.

My first voyage on her took us to the Faroe Islands and involved towing a piece of equipment called a 'bomb' (I forget its official name) which did indeed look like a bomb about eight feet long, a parallel-sided cylinder with a conical end, in which was fixed a removable fine mesh net. This was a survey to sample the density of herring larvae in the water, and was backed up by an extremely specialised type of echo sounder called an 'Integrator'. This device had been designed and built by one of the laboratory's own scientists who, being close to genius, eschewed the simple practices of lesser mortals, like washing and changing clothes, being too absorbed in his investigations into the world of sonic image analysis. No question about it, this man was world class, as were many of his colleagues. Should one be interested, I am sure that the Laboratory's web-site would be justifiably replete with their achievements.

The *Scotia* stood in direct line of descent from the *Scotia* of Dr. F.F.Bruce's expedition to Antarctica, an unsung Scottish achievement at the beginning of the twentieth century, which was initiated and driven by pure science with hardly any elements of the 'flag waving' of later expeditions, although they did carry a piper!. They went down to Antarctica, spent a couple of years down there, built a laboratory, were trapped in the ice over the winter, amassed galactic amounts of information, and came home with their ship intact. No one died. The true story of their achievement is only now being given proper recognition. In between the funnels of the *Scotia* I served on, was an enclosed space which was not used for much, but which later had photographs mounted on the bulkheads, of the original *Scotia*. I felt proud when I returned to command her briefly in 1988, to be following in their footsteps, albeit less spectacularly, since part of our remit was to monitor the dispersal rate of the effluent of Glasgow discharged by the sludge boat *Dalmarnock*! In fact command of a research ship did not really suit my character, for it required a great deal of discussion and compromise with the scientists and in a way was a command without command. Indeed I was so bored; I painted a rather nice watercolour whilst working in the Clyde on the above survey. It is called 'Arran-calms'. There is a new *Scotia* now, built early in the new millennium to a Norwegian design.

WESTRA (SECOND TIME)

I did not serve long on the *Scotia* and ended up back on the *Westra*. She was the flagship at the time, being the newest, but she was not the same as the *Jura* for some reason. Shortly after my transfer, my Scottish Nationalist Captain transferred from the *Jura* to the *Westra* as well, and our Senior First Officer was a man whose antecedents came from Orkney. He had served in Salvasens in command for quite a long time, and told great stories of his time in that company. I enjoyed sailing with him. He was one of the first to appreciate the value of computers and had a Sinclair ZX long before anyone else. He used to produce a newsletter on it which was invariably peppered with insightful comments about crew members. He was a good shipmate.

The Island Class of which the Jura was the first whilst good sea boats, were prone to roll heavily and were very unpredictable when manoeuvring in wind. They had suffered a very bad press from some of the staff when they came out, but I could not agree. I remember the Marine Superintendent who, having inherited them from his predecessor, considered them out of date when they were built, asked what I thought of them. I said I could take them to the ends of the world, and meant it. The tendency to be unpredictable was due to the variable pitch propeller which created a volume of 'dead' water in front of the rudder when the pitch was set to zero. Of course, the pitch must pass through zero if the ship is to be stopped and the propulsion directed accordingly, so there were many nail-biting moments until it was decided to fit a bow thruster to both the *Jura* and the *Westra*.

The heavy rolling was overcome by the fitting of stability tanks at the aft end of the ships' boat-decks. These tanks, designed by Ulstein, worked supremely well in my opinion and the two modifications made both Island Class vessels very handy and sea-kindly. The only down-side was the thruster tunnel which caused shuddering when pitching in heavy seas. On dirty nights when we were pitching heavily, it felt like being a kipper in box being shaken vigorously. I am not sure why this particular image comes to my mind but it describes the feeling accurately for me.

Sometime during this period I was promoted to First Officer, after about two and a half years in the Service. It was actually 15 January 1981. This put some people's noses out of joint but it did not trouble me in the least for I had a large and growing family to support.

CHAPTER TWENTY-ONE

On 10 May 1981 Rebecca Louise was born, and again thanks to the skill of the staff at Bellshill Maternity she survived and thrives to this day. She was always a wee girl to catch one's attention with her bonny face. Difficult to believe she is married now to Peter with three children of their own and is a superb nurse specialising in coronary care. They have recently emigrated to South Australia. She is tremendous in a crisis and has a sense of direction like a GPS navigator.

This was a lovely time in our lives, wherein we lived in what I suppose one might describe as a modern idyll. Patsy, who has a tremendous mind, gave herself over completely to being the perfect super-mother. I think she could be the perfect 'super-anything' actually. She made our children's clothes to a large extent, with her sewing machine and knitting machine, and they were turned out impeccably. She ran and managed our home to perfection and was the best wife I could ever have hoped for, in all respects. She faithfully brought up our children in the Catholic form of Christianity without compromise, and that in itself was a tremendous achievement. She created and still creates the 'hearth' and the heart of our home, like a sort of latter day Vesta except of course she is not a virgin. I will be chastised for using 'that' word. And she has recorded every jot and tittle of our family history with her incessant and thoroughly catalogued photography. I am so thankful to her for that, although there were many times she had to suffer torrents of silent abuse from all of us for having to stop to take photos.

When the children were young, up until the time David and Patricia became teenagers, I used to take them for family worship when I was home and we would read the Bible, sing hymns and pray. As they got older, it became impractical. Around this time also, I was and remained heavily involved in the church at Avon Street, in Hamilton, taking the Bible Study and studying for the Readership. This required a lot of reading and essay writing, the results of which were sent to a professor of Theology in Edinburgh, Dr. Ruth Page. She and I were not in the same camp theologically, she having what seemed to me, a strong leaning towards modern, liberal thinking which allowed one to drive a coach and horses through what I regarded as unshakable truths. I had read Calvin's Institutes of the Christian Faith by this time, and it established my thinking on a bed-rock of ideas which, although I have had to adapt and modify them over the years, nevertheless enabled me to build a structure of belief which I not only find to be in agreement with Scripture but which also accords with my observations of human kind and my own humanity, in relation to God. Particularly with regard to His sovereignty and the sinfulness of man. I still have these essays and I must look them out sometime.

I think the last essay I wrote for Dr. Page's scrutiny was on the Ontological Trinity; after she had scolded me for cavalierly discounting the work of two hundred years of Form Criticism and Hermeneutics, she was kind enough to say that my essay was beautifully written, 'of its type'; and that, having now seen five of my essays and sustained each one, she could see no reason why I should not be 'set apart' to become a Reader in the Presbytery of Hamilton. In fact I never did get 'set apart'; principally because I was too busy keeping all the plates of my life spinning at once. I recall having to sit before a board of ministers who were to judge whether I was fit for this office and one of them, who smoked a pipe incessantly during the interview, reckoned The Church of Scotland was 'not ready' for my strong evangelical approach to preaching. I thanked them for their time and privately thanked God that the Church was not ready for my preaching style and content. I sometimes wonder which Bible they were reading, if any! Anyway, over the years the Lord has used this preaching many times and my prayer is that I will die in the pulpit proclaiming Christ and Him crucified.

Part of the training for the Readership involved taking services all over Lanarkshire. This was arranged by Mr. Hugh McComisky who oversaw the deployment of Readers in Training. He was a kindly soul in late middle- or early old age, who had a bald head with a fringe of white hair, twinkling be-speckled eyes and a ruddy complexion. He looked 'benign'. This was great training, because one was left entirely to   oneself, to plan and organise the entire service, from start to finish. I found myself travelling to many churches, which lay within say thirty miles of Hamilton. I never felt that what I had to say was badly received, quite the contrary; it was humbling to be told that what I had said was 'Just what I needed to hear', or that 'It's a long time since we heard that kind of preaching'. It largely endorsed my view that people were, and are, weary of listening to 'nice wee stories to make you cheery' and would rather, in the main, hear the powerful, soul winning, life-changing, Word of God.

At one point during this period, I came upon a book which recorded the work of an evangelist who worked in the late 1800s preaching all over Lanarkshire, then up to the North East of Scotland and on to Orkney and Shetland. It was uncanny how I was to a large extent following in this man's footsteps, even preaching in the same hall at Ferniegair where he had preached one hundred years earlier. His name was James McKendrick. Of course I lent someone the book and never saw it again, but I have a new copy now. The other odd thing about this connection was that while I was preaching down in Greenock at the Mission Hall near the James Watt Dock, which I have done on quite a few occasions, I met a man with the same name (McKendrick) who referred to his 'Bible-thumping uncle'. I quizzed him as to whether his uncle had written a book and he quoted the name correctly. I found this quite uncanny, because not only had I already unknowingly followed this old preacher's path quite closely , but also in the coming years I would go on to preach in Orkney, Shetland, The Western Isles, the North East, and other places which I have forgotten, as the Lord gave me opportunity due to the deployment of my ships.

CHAPTER TWENTY-TWO
WESTRA (FIRST TRIP IN COMMAND)

In February 1981, the Marine Superintendent asked me how I felt about taking the *Westra* to sea in charge. This was brought about by a combination of circumstances wherein the regular Captain and the Senior First Officer would be off at the same time. He had actually asked me to take the research ship *Explorer* away a few months before this, but we were at a critical point in the building of an extension to our house and Patsy was expecting Rebecca. I had begged to call off. Thankfully another more senior First Officer was able to step in. But I was up for it this time and leapt at the opportunity, albeit with the sudden reality hitting home that this is what I had been preparing for the last fifteen years.

Like every other 'First', the first time one takes a ship to sea as Captain is indelibly etched on the memory banks of one's brain. Strangely, there is one thing I remember particularly; the men instantly took to calling me 'Captain' and it felt good. Maybe they were just 'Giving the kid a lift'.

It was blowing quite strongly from the west when we sailed from the Edinburgh Dock in Leith, comfortably negotiating the locks and docks which I knew well by this time. Then, when we arrived at the sea locks, the wind freshened some more and it was blowing quite hard. We landed on the eastern wall of the lock quite gently, gliding along the pontoons which kept us off the lock wall. Then came the time to break away when the lock had reached sea level and by this time the wind was holding the *Westra* alongside very tightly. I cannot remember if we had a bow thruster at this time but I realised I had to do something to get her off that quay wall, otherwise, when we let go, she would bump all the way seaward until she cleared the finger jetty which stuck out from the lock wall, and marked the eastern side of the fairway channel. Then it came to me; the Island Class, like tugboats, were built with a lot of 'cutaway' at the stern and if I got the after crew to heave hard on the breast line it would pull her stern in and her bow out. I could then give her plenty of power to get her going, then put helm onshore to lift her stern. That was the theory and that was exactly what happened. That was very satisfying because I had not seen it done before in the Fisheries ships although I had seen it in the tugs. The Mate came up to me after we were clear and said 'That was nicely done.' We had hardly cleared the Herwit Rock with the wreck of the *Switha* sitting on it when the wind backed southerly and blew a gale, so I decided to spend the night dodging in the Firth of Forth till morning to see how the forecast would develop. We got away in the morning and began one of the windiest trips I have ever experienced.

I was mentally quite unprepared for the degree of anxiety with which I was assailed in this new role as commander, albeit a very temporary one. It was not the running of the ship, or man-management, or the deployment of the vessel to maximise efficiency; it was the weather, which almost began to take on a life of its own as one day ran into another with no sign of respite. We were initially tasked to the Orkney area where pelagic vessels were allegedly fishing for herring, a species totally taboo at the time, there having been a moratorium on their catch, distribution and sale since the late seventies. We ended up dodging in the North Sound, at the north end of the Orkneys in ghastly southerly gales which had dogged us since we sailed. We would sally forth every now and then only to be turned back by the sheer absurdity of trying to patrol in these conditions. Even if we had seen anyone we could never have approached close enough to identify them because of these conditions. Anyway, we hung about there for a while and then, by degrees, utilising every short weather window which presented itself, we migrated to the Western Isles. For a few days we went around in the relatively sheltered waters of the Minches, boarding as many small vessels as we could until another very deep depression was predicted and I started to watch its progress on the weather fax machine as it lumbered malevolently across the North Atlantic, hourly gathering strength and deepening to a pressure I had not seen before.

Now, you should realise that I was not trying to bear this new type of pressure by myself. I had known pressure before in tankers but this was new because the buck definitely stopped with me, and I found myself often on my knees in the privacy of my cabin asking God for the strength and wisdom to deal with this challenge which was now accelerating towards us. I studied the situation intently and finally decided to anchor in Broad Bay in Lewis, not to one anchor but two. Now, this was not done very often in the Fisheries in the bigger ships like the *Westra* but I kept on being prompted to do just that. *Moor the Westra with two anchors.* So I took her to Broad Bay having been dodging off Loch Ewe where it so happened that the *Brenda*, with none other than the erstwhile Captain of the *Jura* aboard in command, was already at anchor and had been for some time. It blew hard across the North Minch with the wind offering to veer out of the south-east into the south. As we sped over the ever-growing seas, I continually went over in my mind if this was the best thing to do, when suddenly the VHF came to life and the unmistakable clipped tones of the Captain of the *Brenda* rang out. There was the usual exchange of identities. Then 'Oh hello, (no name) what are conditions like in the Minch'? I told him.'How do you think the *Brenda* would manage?' He was asking me! I told him I thought she would manage fine if he moved now but it was deteriorating rapidly. 'Good, we will go there as well; it's the only thing to do in weather like this.' I liked that because in a way it endorsed what I was doing, and he was much more experienced than me. So we made our way down to the root of the bay and anchored with one anchor, in the relatively calm water of Broad Bay. I listened intently to the next forecast and it sounded very grim:

HEBRIDES Southerly Violent storm 11 veering south-westerly and increasing to hurricane force 12 soon.

When you receive a forecast like that, there is a sense of foreboding which falls over the ship, particularly the Deck Staff. Even the Engineers will mention it at mealtimes, and the Steward will say as he delivers your tea, 'Bit of bad weather coming, Sir?' and you say 'Aye, a breeze right enough, Jim', or Hughie or whoever it is, and he goes down to see about the evening meal and you mull over all the 'What ifs' that keep assailing your peace of mind. And the sense of tension grows.

Sure enough it started to pipe shortly before tea time and I decided to cast another anchor, which is what I should have done on arrival. I made a mental note to listen to what God, working through my native wit, told me to do and not what folk usually did. Thankfully I had an excellent Bosun, who had been in the Fisheries since he left the fishing just after the War. As I outlined what I wanted to do, he was able to make suggestions and correct me on a couple of points and I thanked him, and thanked God for him.

We had been lying to six shackles in the water (a shackle is fifteen fathoms, or ninety feet). So we hove up to three shackles then I gave her a touch ahead to get her going, and I am now remembering we had a bow thruster which, combined with the engine, was able to allow me to reposition the ship for dropping the other anchor, with a good spread between the two. We then payed out to six shackles on each, screwed up the brakes, put the chain stoppers on, and that was that. During this evolution, the Mate up forward had needed to get down below the bulwark and roar through the VHF to pass information, so strong was the wind. In the meantime, the *Brenda* arrived and moored just like us, with both hooks down. Then we waited.

One of the longest nights I can remember ensued, with the wind howling and screaming like a demented creature. I could not rest or settle to anything and kept going up and down to the bridge until eventually I just stayed up there. We were anchored 1.2 miles off the point of Melbost pier; I know this because after that night I would return many, many times to the same spot to wait out other storms. Even at such a short distance from the land she was pitching and taking spray over the bow, and the anchor cables, each link made out of thirty six millimetre steel, were stretched like bow strings, disappearing into the spray and thick glaur. The wind blew so hard our anemometer could not record it, and for long periods it sat up at ninety knots. It could go no further. I had the engineers on standby with the engines warmed through, so that should the cables part we would be able to do something. So it carried on all night and it was not until dawn began to infuse a wan light into the anxious darkness that the wind began to ease to a less frightening sixty knots. That incidentally is still a force 10. I stood down the engineers, went down below and lay on my day bed with the words *'Thou shalt keep him in perfect peace whose mind is stayed on Thee, because he trusts in Thee'*, going round in my head, and fell into a dreamless sleep. I was wakened at eight in the morning by the Chief Steward, who hailed from Leith and had been to the whaling, with a cup of coffee and a cheery, 'Better day now, Cap'n!'

And he was right. The sun was shining, the sting had gone out of the wind and it was beginning to look like a good day. After exchanging pleasantries with the *Brenda* at the morning 'Chat Show', which is what we called the communication schedule during which all ships exchanged their positions and status, I decided to run down the Minch and poke the *Westra's* nose out into the Atlantic. I could hear the eyebrows being raised in the wheelhouse of the *Brenda* but I knew that it would take us all day and night to get down to Barra Head, by which time the weather would be more settled. So we weighed anchor that afternoon and trekked southwards in the North and South Minches and into the Sea of the Hebrides. By morning we had reached, Barra Head which we rounded at about four miles and stood westerly into the Atlantic.It is difficult to describe what it feels like to forge into a great ocean in a small ship in winter. Even though the conditions are currently benign, one knows that in February they will not stay that way for long and there exists in the mind a constant nagging sense of something akin to foreboding. It is like having to look over one's shoulder all the time to be aware of the unknown beast which lurks in the undergrowth. I have to say this feeling is particularly prevalent after a night like the one we had just experienced. It is as though we have glimpsed how vicious the weather can be and we are on guard, in case it tries to best us again. May be it is just me.

A big residual swell was loping in from the west which the *Westra* lifted her bow to as we crossed the White Strip Bank, the shallower water tending to shorten the period of the swell and make it uncomfortable for the ship and ourselves. But I was determined to get out at least as far as the Continental Shelf, some fifty miles west of Barra Head, where most of the fishing activity took place. The Continental Shelf, or as we referred to it 'The Hundred Fathom Line' is a phenomenon which occurs off every continent where the shallow water which surrounds the land mass suddenly falls away very markedly into the abyssal depths of the real ocean. All over the world this occurs at roughly the same depth; so much so that for hundreds of years mariners have used this rapid change in depth as a kind of position line, the point being that if one watches the depth decreasing to one hundred fathoms, or six hundred feet (it is now prosaically called the two hundred metre contour, which does not have the same ring somehow), one knows that one is on that line 'somewhere'. If that position line can be crossed with another from say a radio beacon then one has an idea of where the ship is. This of course was much more important in the days before GPS, radar and all the other modern paraphernalia. In addition to this, the Hundred Fathom Line is where the great plankton-laden currents sweep past, providing the nutrition for the food chain which climaxes in edible and marketable fish. So, for our patrols we knew that if we got out to the 'Line' and followed it northerly or southerly we would come on fishing vessels. But I had another reason wanting to head westerly. The *Westra* carried a 'Bond' which permitted the Master to purchase cigarettes, beer, spirits, wines and perfumes and sell them on the ship to the crew at bonded prices plus a small profit for the trouble of organising it. It was a nice perquisite in those days, which has now been removed. It was a fair bit of work for the Master to organise all this, but the whole arrangement was predicated on the vessel sailing either west of twelve degrees West or north of sixty one degrees North.

Now, it is much easier to reach sixty one degrees North, using the Orkneys and Shetlands as a means to shun adverse weather, than it is to forge westwards to the twelfth meridian of westerly longitude. For this reason, plus the fact that there was a general dread of going out that way in winter anyway, (and summer in some cases) few Commanding Officers would 'Clear the Bond' by running westwards. On this voyage however, it was looking most unlikely that we would be tasked to the Northern Isles so I began to form the idea that perhaps I could not only clear the bond but perhaps even get to Rockall, which was a kind of obsession with Headquarters because so few people were willing to tackle it. I began to study the weather charts, which in those days were not so accurate or helpful as they are now; neither did they give a prognosis much beyond seventy two hours. One had to be pretty sure there was a settled patch before travelling out there, because one had to get all the way back in. In winter time, conditions could develop and deteriorate very quickly. I had been out this way in January before with my Scottish Nationalist Captain, but that was an exceptional period of calm weather and I can remember we were all astonished at how long that particular spell lasted.

Of course, I brought my plan to God in my prayers, and in a way, similar to Gideon of old I put my ideas to God with conditionals that if so and so was the case I would carry on. You should not conclude from this that I was in any way behaving irrationally; as a man of faith, I was merely seeking the reassurance that my inexperience lacked. So we trundled on to the hundred fathom line then carried onwards with doubtless much comment from the whole crew, to the far west and Rockall. I began to become anxious when I considered how I was seeking to achieve something which very few would attempt in winter at that time, and made continual visits to the Book of Samuel and the Psalms to see how my namesake King David coped with the strain. The weather forecasts continued to predict reasonably fair weather, and I began to fix in my mind a 'cut off point' in terms of the weather forecast, which I would not exceed. It became my 'bale out' conditional. All went well until the evening was coming on, when the Shipping Forecast at ten minutes to six gave the wind increasing to force eight, which in itself was nothing to worry about, but which on top of a large(albeit decaying) swell could produce plenty to exercise the mind. I was distressed in my mind about turning back. Was I failing God? Was my faith not a match for these doubts?

I prayed about it for some time; then, reasoning that even if we got to Rockall we would not be able to do anything in terms of boarding any vessels (should there be any out there) I decided to put about, and stand east north easterly before the freshening wind, with the big swell now shooing her back towards the Hundred Fathom Line. I asked the Mate to fix her position by the Magnavox Satellite Navigator and on looking at the chart found we were in twelve degrees and one minute West! I had made us legal at least, although I continued to lambaste myself as a craven for some time afterwards. We continued to run easterly till morning and found poor weather as we rejoined the hundred fathom line west of Saint Kilda, so we had to content ourselves with interviewing every fishing vessel we passed, asking how long they had been fishing, how long they intended to continue and what their catches were. This was called a *FISHREP* and the information was routinely transmitted to Headquarters at least once a day. In those days there were many ships fishing, Frenchmen, Norwegians, Germans, Danes, Faroese, as well as British. Of course all of this was carried out at close quarters usually within a quarter of a mile, as most of the fishing numbers were illegible beyond that distance. Moreover at that time we did a lot of night work using the searchlight, but this practice became less and less frequent in recent years, due to the inherent danger of closing other ships at night to within two cables. That is two tenths of a mile.

Time had worn on by now and it was coming to the point in the trip when I had to arrange for the half-landing or stand-down. The obvious choice was to go into Stornoway since we were working the West Coast, so I made the usual overtures to Stornoway Harbour, via Headquarters on telex, and began to plan how I would do this. One of the big 'bogeymen' of Stornoway was a south southeast gale which assailed the harbour in ways that no other did. Stornoway is a wonderful harbour except for anything from the south east. I knew, having been alongside there previously on the *Westra*, we had thirteen parts of rope out aft to stop her carrying away and ending up in the Caledonian Hotel! In time to come, the *Vigilant* when she was quite new, under the command of my friend, spent a most objectionable night there on the East Side of Number One Pier, with all their moorings out, including the insurance wires, and with engines running. This did not prevent her sustaining damage that night, to her hull plating which went with her when she was sold, because it would have been too expensive to repair.

I decided that if I was to go on the east side of number one pier, I would turn her round on her port anchor and sit head to sea so I would lie better and get away easily if need be. I agonised over this for some time because no one had reported doing this before, but I reckoned it would be a good plan. As always, I considered it prayerfully and was mentally prepared for it as we approached Arnish Point, at the mouth of the harbour. I had just lined her up for the leads into Stornoway when we were called on VHF by Oban Radio, who had a coded message for us. I put her about and stood slowly back into Stornoway Bight. In those days, whenever HQ wanted to send us something sensitive we would receive a coded message, which of course had to be de-coded. This was achieved by use of the 'Red Book', which was a really versatile code book, adequate for most of our needs. Anyway, we were not to go into Stornoway but to return to the Orkneys at best speed to investigate the same alleged herring fishers who had featured in the early part of the trip. I arranged for two engines and set off at full speed for Cape Wrath.

The weather was not particularly favourable at this juncture but the *Westra* and the *Jura* really came into their own in these conditions and we tore up the miles at about sixteen knots, which is pretty fast in a small ship in poor weather. We did not find any herring boats in the Orkney area, or anywhere else for that matter, and I began to wonder if they were the figment of some crazy fool's imagination. After searching, we could hold off our stand-down no longer, so HQ allowed us to go into Kirkwall, in the Orkneys, which we did. I always remember the Mate getting very twitchy as we approached the pier, which was built of the slate-like sandstone formed on the sea-bed of the great shallow sea which once covered these islands, and which was quite uncompromising with the lightly built hulls of modern ships. He need not have worried, because I was beginning to 'wrap' her round me and could feel her like an extension of my own body. This is not fanciful; you do it with your own car on a smaller scale.

I think I went to St. Magnus Cathedral that night, and in that ancient quiet got down on my knees and allowed the weight of my care to seep out of me, to be taken up by my Saviour. *"Come unto me all ye that labour and are heavy laden and I will give you rest"*.

I do not remember much more about my first patrol in command except that we must have arrived safely into Leith without any mishaps. As I made my report to the Superintendent when he visited after we berthed, I said I had never encountered so much ferocious wind. He replied 'Don't you know it always blows harder when the Captain of the ship is on leave?' I do not know what that meant, whether he thought it was just in my head, but it never seemed to be so bad again. I have just written that, but it is not true; in fact it was often as bad and sometimes even worse, but I think if there was anything worthwhile to come out of this experience it was that I was better prepared for the times that would follow, and had gained the knowledge that God was not a hard task master.

Now I should have mentioned this before, but I had a colleague on the *Westra* during this time who was and is, my brother in the fullest sense of the word; and during this period we sailed together as opposite numbers, I on deck and he down below. He was the Second Engineer. Once we knew that we were both Christians we would have a time of prayer and reading the Scriptures in the evening after supper. These were good times, which helped us to develop our faith and prayer life. It taught us that prayer really makes a difference and changes things, and often we would be astonished at how apt our readings would be for the particular events that shaped our lives day by day. Let me give you an example. My friend and his wife had been trying to have a baby for quite a long time, and hope was turning to acceptance that it would never happen. On the other hand, we both believed that with God all things are possible and our reading of Abraham and Sarah was most encouraging. We believe that God does not change, and is all powerful, and so we prayerfully committed the situation to Him. I do not remember how long we went on in this way but I do know that they now have three children and are a happy, loving family.

I am not saying you always get what you want. I am saying prayer makes a difference.

One night, my friend and I were returning to the ship from the Thursday prayer meeting in St. Columba's Church in Stornoway. We had just passed the Evangelical Bookshop, and were discussing this and that when a man burst from the door of the fish and chip shop at the foot of that road and literally fell upon us. He was very drunk and blurted out 'Sorry boys, sorry. I'm in an awful state can you help me?' He was reeking of whisky and swaying like a reed in a breeze. He asked again 'Can you help me?' his eyes only intermittently focussing on either my friend or me. I have told you I am not good with drunks, but there was something in the plaintive and heartfelt way this man besought our help that I realised that this was different.

I said 'What's the problem? ignoring the obvious battle he was having with keeping an even keel.

'I'm in terrible trouble boys; my life is falling apart before my eyes.' This was all conveyed in the soft lilt of the Lewis man, and the complete sense of hopelessness was heart-rending.

'Well,' I said, realising that that this was clearly a challenge from God to put our notions of service to the test, 'You have come to the right men. We have the solution for you.'

'What do you mean?'

'We believe that the Lord Jesus Christ can and will save any man who will be saved, and He has the power to give you and yours new life'. These were maybe not the exact words but it was along these lines.

'Are you evangelists?' he says.

'Yes! 'Said I, and for the first time in my life realised that this was what I really wanted to do.

'How can you help me?'

I asked him for his address and said 'We will come to visit you tomorrow when you are sober and we can talk'.

So we did. After our day's work (in those days we had two nights alongside at the half-landing) we both set out and I think we walked to where he stayed. He and his wife had six or seven children, I forget exactly, and their home was pretty squalid. However, we told them about Christ and carefully explained the Gospel. It was clear, as we spoke to them, that there would be no miraculous transformation, no easy fix; say a few well chosen words and depart. And so began an association with that family lasting for many years, which both my friend and I were as faithful to as we were able. Even on different ships, for we would soon be split up, we would visit, to encourage and assist in practical ways, to help the family turn around its life and well-being. I cannot say how they are now but I know that several of the children went on to give their hearts to Jesus, one of them becoming a pastor in Paisley, and another who owns his own van selling fast food, with a Bible always lying on the counter! The family, who were originally travelling folk, are well known in Lewis, and it well known that God did a work amongst them.

CHAPTER TWENTY-THREE
SCOTIA (SECOND TIME)

I think I went back on the old *Scotia* for one trip just before she went in for refit. For some reason I always seemed to join her when the refit specification had to be made up and typed out. No computers in those days. Typewriters and carbon paper!

She was being commanded by a very experienced Officer in Charge, who was about to retire after this trip. He had been in command for years in the Far East, but the Department had never made him a substantive Commanding Officer. They used to try to assign command to chaps who were about to retire, to enhance their pensions a bit. He was a really nice fellow and in fact I still have his uniform which he bequeathed to me when he retired. It is up in the loft.

We were carrying out some kind of larval survey again, and had worked at stations all over the West Coast. We had only to do a few stations to the west of the Uists to complete the work for the trip, when we started receiving very disturbing weather forecasts. As I recall, an enormous area of polar air was hurtling down from the Arctic, borne on very strong northerlies. I made a point of thrusting these facsimile charts and forecasts in front of him at every opportunity but for some reason he was not joining up the dots as far as I could see. At that time we were working to the west of South Uist. I looked longingly at the relative shelter of the Sea of the Hebrides and mentally prepared for what was coming. My Captain was unshakable. To this day, I do not know why he kept us out, unless it was simply to experience one last time, the vicious, animal ferocity, of an Atlantic storm.

Well, it hit us in the late afternoon. I remember going round with the crew, lashing everything that could move and securing everything that could be secured. I think they liked the fact that the Mate was out on deck with them, because it did not happen that often on research ships. Maybe it was I who enjoyed it! As the afternoon wore on, the seas began to build; iron grey, with combers forming in slow- motion malevolence in the failing light, accompanied by a bone-chilling wind that cut through clothing effortlessly. The *Scotia* was a big stern trawler and well-built, but the seas which were growing as night progressed were stopping her in her tracks. The Captain had decided to try to make for the south side of St. Kilda to obtain a lee, but the size of the seas and strength of wind were slowing her right down to a crawling pace. I did not sleep; the continual, laboured climb to the crest of the next mighty sea, with protests from every particle of her structure, followed by the sickening headlong plummet into the next trough, terminating in a withering crash which made havoc of anything which was not secured, ensured sleep was impossible.

The Captain was on the bridge when I arrived there for the four to eight morning watch. It was still black dark and he had on a fleece. He had not slept either and had been up most of the night. His pale aquiline features lined with weariness and anxiety as he nursed his ship through the night. Little by little the dawn came on and huge masses of water began to become visible beyond the immediate loom of the ship's deck lights. At every plunge she shipped heavy water on the focsle and down her sides, and the spray and spume flew mast high, overall. One of the seas smashed the sampling platform into an unruly and chaotic tangle of metal, and here and there on deck could be seen bits of debris which the merciless wind and sea had discovered and tossed around like a spoiled child. Our anemometer had been ripped off its mountings at the top of the mast at some point during the night, for we noticed that the needle on the gauge in the wheelhouse had not flickered from ninety knots for several hours, and the noise of the wind-cups crashing to the deck had been lost in the general cacophony. But, in the main, the *Scotia* had come through the night unscathed.

Grey. So many shades of grey!

As we gazed out on the furious sea, we could at last see the outlines of some French trawlers, as big as us, making huge mantles of white water as they dived with us into the great troughs, on our way to the sheltering cliffs of the south coast of St. Kilda. During the night, there had been some excitement amongst the ships which had already made the lee of St. Kilda, and the crew of a German Fishery Protection vessel (whose name escapes me, it might have been the *Seefalke*) had put their boat away with a doctor on board to assist a Frenchman with broken ribs. Another Frenchman had died of a heart attack overnight, and there were several other injuries to seamen. Eventually after eighteen hours we covered the thirty two miles to St. Kilda and came under the lee of the grey black cliffs which glowered over us. We all breathed a sigh of relief and were just settling down when the German Fishery boat, maybe it was the *Fridtjof*, called us up to say that they thought they could see storm damage at our bow. The Captain and I immediately investigated but there was nothing. It was the shape of the *Scotia*'s focsle which had confused them, and I think they were a bit keyed up from their escapades overnight with the doctor.

I am fairly sure there were not many atheists on the Western Ocean that night!

ST KILDA RECOLLECTIONS

St. Kilda is an amazing place. The word 'amazing' has been badly devalued in recent times but in its purest sense it describes that combination of wonder, awe and excitement which assails the visitor on their first sight of this collection of islands and rocks rising unexpectedly and defiantly out of the waters of the Atlantic. On my first visit, I think it was on the *Westra*, we anchored in Village Bay and put the boat ashore. In those days the Army were a big presence there, guarding and operating the tracking radar for the missiles being tested from Benbecula , their buildings (still in use) strangely out of place and ill at ease; set as they are, amid the 19th century school, church and minister's manse, and the much older houses of the original inhabitants. On stepping ashore there are very few people, I think, who are not sensible to the aura of the place. It is like a deep melancholy, like a Gaelic lament which croons to you from the ancient stones and whispers tales of the old people who were spirited away, never to return.

The landscape is remorseless, and uncompromising, jagged and lunar and yet I have been there on days when the scents of the summer wild flowers are wafted across the hardy grasslands and heathers, when the skuas wheel belligerently overhead, and I am sure I have heard pewits and skylarks, although I am no expert.

This was not one of those days... It was cold and hard and terrifying and the last place you would want to be, and we were all glad when the wind finally took off the next day and we could run southerly, away from St Kilda in bright blue skies and a big following swell. We had survived without serious hurt, but I remembered that storm for the next twenty six years and made it my study to avoid putting a ship through that kind of weather if I could help it.

Before leaving St. Kilda for the time being, it has come into my memory just now that while I was on the *Westra* during this period, that is to say my first five years in the Fisheries, we were patrolling one day in late summer looking for Dutch herring super-trawlers. We had drawn a blank and decided to go down to St. Kilda to anchor because it was Sunday. We approached from the North West, and on rounding the point into Village Bay were assailed by the sight of thirteen massive Dutchmen lying at anchor. In those days the Dutch, like many of the Scots boats, tried never to work on the Sabbath. Anyway, it presented a first class opportunity for me to go round them all and inspect them at my ease as it were. I did this, and within a couple of hours I had done the lot and finished in time to catch the Sunday service on the Dutch Hospital Ship *De Hoop*. You see, in those days the Dutch were still taking their religion very seriously and I for one was glad. I did not understand a word of the sermon, nor could I sing the hymns, but it was good to share in worship in such an extraordinary place.

ENFORCEMENT IN 1983

You must be wondering why I have not mentioned capturing many offending fishing vessels up to now and I have to say the fact is that, at this time, we were not doing anything of the kind.

There would be the odd case of flagrant trawling within the Three Mile Limit but very few foreign vessels were apprehended. The big exception to this run of events was the case against the Scottish purse seine net vessel the *Chris Andra*, which was alleged to have tried to ram the old *Norna* while her officers were attempting to identify and board that vessel with a view to ascertaining how much fish they had on board. This was at the time of the great mackerel fishery which was pursued on the west and north coasts of Scotland. That fishery was a huge seasonal operation, and Annat Bay outside Loch Broom, where Ullapool is situated, was literally full of very large trawlers, generically known as 'Klondykers' from all over the world, who would buy the mackerel off the Scottish and English boats, since they were not allowed to fish for it themselves.

The Department arranged for a guardship to be in position at the entrance to Annat Bay to intercept each catcher as it arrived, to measure the catch by dipping the tanks. This of course was not physically possible if a lot of boats arrived at the same time, as they frequently did, or if the weather was unworkable. I think the guardship concept first appeared in 1980 and was an annual task for all fishery cruisers, as they took it in turn. The routine was to anchor at some strategic point in Annat Bay thus permitting the boarding boat to be rapidly deployed night or day, so although the guardship was at anchor, it was by no means a holiday and there were many times when the boarding boat had a hard time either chasing the new arrival or coming back.

The *Norna* incident with the *Chris Andra* did not take place in Annat Bay, but near the Pentland Firth. This case saw almost the whole of the Marine staff and many from Headquarters attend the High Court in Aberdeen. I myself had to give evidence to the effect that I had seen the *Chris Andra* on the North Coast off Loch Eriboll. It virtually brought the enforcement arm of the Department to a standstill for a few days and in the end did not result in a huge fine. Of course, the charge of 'attempted ramming' was always going to be difficult to prove.

The legislation was still in a settling-down phase following the introduction of the Common Fisheries Policy in 1983 and this is the period I am describing. My recollection is that nothing was organised, there were no protocols or procedures to meet the needs of the enforcers like us and we were largely writing the book as we went along. There was little or no structured training for new British Sea Fisheries Officers which dealt with 'managing' the legislation and 'implementing' it, and it would be another couple of years at least until we were able effectively to take offenders to book. That is as much as I can remember about this period, from 1978 to 1983, but something was about to happen which would completely refresh my sea-going career. The Department had decided to build two sixty five foot fast patrol boats.

CHAPTER TWENTY-FOUR
1983 - 1985
MORVEN

You may recall that I told you that my fellow Second Officer and I, who survived the moody Captain of the *Jura,* used to sit and dream about how we would run the enforcement at sea if we were given the opportunity. As I said, one of our ideas was to build two fast patrol boats based on an Aran lifeboat design to patrol and manage the inshore fisheries. In those days there were still numerous vessels around the fifty foot mark, many of them being demersal trawlers. Demersal means trawling a net on the sea bed as opposed to pelagic trawling, wherein the net is trawled in the mid-water. Demersal trawlers catch fish like haddock and whiting, whereas pelagic vessels catch shoaling fish like herring and mackerel. There were literally thousands of these smallish vessels engaged in demersal trawling which of course was banned inside the Three Mile Limit, so there was huge scope for breaking the law if the only deterrent was a big fishery cruiser which could be recognised eight to ten miles away. If, on the other hand, one had a low profile rapid patrol boat, the element of surprise could be maintained until the last moment, thereby preventing offending vessels getting their gear up on time. You will understand my excitement when the Marine Superintendent announced that the Department were going to build two such craft. I made it very clear to him that, without reservation, I was completely seized with the concept and did my best to show that I would be an ideal candidate for command of one of them. Gauge my joy then, when I was posted to join one in the building yard at Cheverton Boats, on the Hamble River, on the Isle of Wight.

Four of us were to command two boats so it would be a shared command, but this had the advantage that the patrols would be of two weeks' duration which on looking back was sound thinking. Two weeks is long enough on a small boat. The boats were beautifully built with a first class finish more like yachts than work boats. Their bulkheads and fittings were teak or iroko with subdued green upholstery, and Flotex carpeting throughout. The Officer in Charge (Skipper) and Second Officer (Mate) slept aft, with their own mess beside the Galley on the main deck level, while the Engineer, Bosun and Steward slept amidships around a cosy mess, down below. To me they were nearly perfect in concept, although I thought there were certain things that were too 'yacht-like', and these misgivings would prove well-founded in the months following their commissioning.

We were not given a long time to familiarise ourselves with the boats; in fact about half an hour manoeuvring off a buoy was all the handling practice we received, although we had time enough to become acquainted with the build of the boats and the management of them.

The boats never achieved their design speed even with almost no fuel or water on board, but to be frank that did not trouble me. By now I knew the waters round Scotland pretty well and the times when thirty knots can be sustained are few and far between. When they were new, I think they made twenty fours knots on trials which was enough for me. The preparations for sailing were very frustrating because I found myself having long discussions about the colour and quality of table place-mats, the type of cutlery, crockery and cushion covers, and the maxim 'never get four fairly intelligent men to make a decision about trivia' was proven to be true in all respects. If that is not a maxim it should be! In the end I let them get on with it and studied the weather charts for the journey north.

I, along with several others, was lodged in a beautiful guest house which was as clean as a whistle, for the time we were down there which I think was not more than a week. Looking back we should have been given longer; after all, the boats cost seven hundred and fifty thousand pounds each, but the Superintendent had decreed so that was that. But to get back to this house, it was just so well painted up and cared for, with oar blades and other memorabilia and photos on the walls, and discreet wallpaper, that it informed what I liked about houses and required from them ever after. Thankfully Patsy is of a similar mindset, for I could not live in a 'minimalist' house. The night before we were due to leave I went to the Anglican Church, there being no Non-Conformist churches open. It was a small congregation in one of the small halls or rooms of the church, made up of the usual disparate characters who are wont to gather for prayer and hearing the Word. The priest, as Anglican ministers call themselves, was a kind soul and I found the opportunity for open prayer unexpected and welcome. I had great liberty, because my mind was filled with anxious thoughts for the next day. We celebrated Communion after prayer and a short sermon, and it was the first and only time I have taken a wafer as opposed to bread in the Sacrament. I see no need for wafers myself. The wine was real wine though, which I was pleased about. There is a common practice in the Kirk now to use grape juice, but the scripture says bread and wine. That is good enough for me. I loath the tendency to 'sanitise' the sacrament. After the service, a woman came to me, with tears in her eyes, who said that my prayer had helped her profoundly. I felt good about that and went back to my lodgings to sleep soundly.

Next day was filled with final preparations and we were ready to get away in the early afternoon, I think. The other boat, the *Moidart*, was tied up outside the *Morven* and when the time came to leave she was able to simply go ahead and was instantly into the stream. When it came our turn to cast off, I had control of her and I noticed my partner skipper being called out to the deck by one of the Cheverton guys, when he came back into the wheelhouse he said 'The fellow ashore says there is plenty of water to starboard past the berth'. I took that on face value, because we had to do a sharp turn to port on leaving the berth and it would be good to have a bit of room to swing. She came away beautifully, then as we cleared the berth I let her come to starboard a little as advised, when suddenly she lifted her starboard quarter as she ran over an underwater obstruction which turned out to be a huge sewer outfall pipe. I heard the tell-tale 'THUMP THUMP THUMP' of the starboard propeller hitting the pipe then it stopped as we cleared. It was one of the most sickening moments of my career for I felt it was so unjust. I could handle this boat without thinking and I had been the one to suffer this ignominy. I felt angry and betrayed for if no one had said anything at all it would not have happened. I told my partner to go down below and check her bilges to make sure there was no water ingress, while the Engineer checked the stern seal. We were watertight, but I knew I was going to have to get her onto a hard somewhere to sight the bottom and ascertain the damage. I decided to press on to Newhaven where there was such a facility.

It is funny how suddenly, because I was in control when this happened, I felt my fellow skippers distancing themselves from me and yet at the same time I was definitely aware that in some perverse way I was the leader. I suppose they reckoned I had become one of the 'condemned', just like when I was taken to task for drawing naked ladies, and therefore separated from the 'group'. I could not have cared less what they thought; all I wanted to do was get this charge safely back to Scotland and report to the Superintendent. So we pressed on to Newhaven where we tied her over the hard and waited for Low Water. Sure enough, her starboard propeller was badly damaged. On a more positive note, her hull was undamaged so that was fine. I got on the phone to the Superintendent, and made my report. He could not have been more understanding, with words of wisdom and kindness which I had not expected. You never really get to know people until the cold winds of adversity blow.

Next day before some poor weather closed in, we made for Lowestoft, arriving there safely on the centre and port engines, which gave the boats about fifteen knots in those days. We were stuck in Lowestoft for a couple of days because of the weather, during which time the son of the old Superintendent who had hired me joined to be my Mate. I took the opportunity to go up to the Fisherman's Mission, where I met some dear people to whom I would write and exchange cards for many years. I felt a strong connection with the place since my forebears had fished down there for generations, and my grandmother had packed herring in the curing yards, now long derelict.

When we came to sail, the *Moidart*, which was lying outside us as she manoeuvred to turn in the river to head to sea, drifted down on us and damaged the apron on our bow. I was beginning to feel that I was being singled out for special treatment on this trip, and I must say with one thing and another I was being tested quite hard; however, at all times I felt not only 'protected' but 'at peace'.

For I, the Lord thy God, will hold thy right hand, saying unto thee, Fear not; I will help thee.

When we sailed from Lowestoft, the weather had improved somewhat with the wind settling down to a south-easterly force four to five. We made good speed up the coast with the wind more or less astern and I managed to turn in for a spell while the other two officers took her. By the time we reached the Farne Islands the wind had freshened a bit and she was becoming quite lively and taking spray on the deck. It was not bad enough to waken me because the first thing I knew was the Mate at my door telling me:

'We're taking water. [LONG PAUSE, with sufficient time lapse to allow appropriate exclamation]. 'But it's OK I've fixed it. [PAUSE, with anxious air of expectancy on part of the skipper, and full development of comic timing].

'With a carrot!'

I was never given to roaring at folk when I was called and I think I always responded with courtesy. So also tonight. My initially exclaimed 'What!!' was replaced by a more subdued 'OK, I'll be up directly'. I bobbed around in my new cabin, bumping off all the new protuberances, mentally noting that in future my clothes would always be left at the ready for just such an exigency. Sure enough, my new Mate had indeed cured the leak temporarily with a carrot, which served to prevent us sinking until a more permanent solution could be found. I was glad I had this fellow as my Mate, and I was glad to get her up to Granton where we berthed. Before long the Superintendent was down and we went through the incident with the propeller and the sewer pipe, and he arranged for us to go on the slip at Cockenzie, to effect repairs. This did not happen immediately and I am sure there was a spell where we continued our 'shakedown' cruise before we went on the slip. My Mate, who is now Marine Superintendent of Marine Scotland, reminded me the other day that it was several weeks before we were ready for the naming ceremony and I seem to remember this as being an extremely frustrating period. Several other things happened including the bunker tanks developing cracks and leaking gas-oil into the bilges. I resolved however, never to fall into the trap of despair, and I think in the main I was successful, for the last thing I wanted was for the boat to get a bad name.

We have photographs of the naming ceremony, which took place on a lovely sunny day in Leith with both boats immaculately turned out, lying astern of the *Sulisker*. The man who was my Bosun was from Carradale in Kintyre, one of the best men you could ever want on a ship. He would become a brother in Christ and works tirelessly for the Lord. He attributes his faith to me, but he is wrong. He got it from God; I just showed him the way. My Engineer was from Buckie, an excellent practical man who was not only a good engineer but the most knowledgeable man I ever met concerning the identities and particulars of Scottish fishing vessels. His great forte was collecting all forms of scrap 'Which might come in handy' Sometimes they did. And last but by no means least, a man from Findochty was the Cook/Steward, whose constant cups of coffee have probably contributed hugely to my high blood pressure today; but who never failed, whatever the weather, to produce a lovely meal.

We are all there on the fore deck of our little boat, looking quite the thing. Patsy and the five children we had at the time were there looking as smart as paint, and of course Patsy made sure that the event was well archived. Lady Mansfield (wife, predictably, of Lord Mansfield, the Minister for Agriculture and Fisheries) named the boats, very graciously, and a lovely spread was laid out on the *Sulisker*. All in all it was a nice day, but there would follow months of frustration as one thing after another had to be repaired and ironed out. From broken crank-shafts, caused by a bad batch of 'dampers', to problems with the 'Feathering gear' on the propellers, one thing after another cropped up to inhibit our efforts. Despite this we did our best to do a good job and prove the concept was sound and I actually looked forward to returning to my little boat, at the end of every leave. I had never felt like this before and I really cannot account for it except that the small crew size and the feeling of self-contained autonomy were a strong concoction for making me happy. You see, no one had done this before. The Department had run a couple of 'Fairmile B' launches after the war, but that was a world away and whatever they had learned had been forgotten. We were starting afresh and there was no one to say 'what doest thou?'. I thrived, on it and the thought of exploring the coast of Scotland in a millionaire's yacht with all expenses paid was exhilarating to say the least. I served on the *Morven* for two years and had some interesting experiences, but for the life of me I cannot set them in any kind of chronological order, so if you will bear with me, I will relate the events as they come to mind.

When the *Morven* and the *Moidart* entered the scene, they had a disturbing effect on fishermen who habitually poached on the wrong side of the line, and I can recall several skippers being very shaken having been caught 'bang to rights' because of the speed of the launches, combined with their low profile and the sudden appearance of the small Searider RIB working in tandem with the mother vessel. I know that our presence seriously unsettled would-be poachers, so much so that on one occasion when we had been working on the West Coast Lochs, which had several areas closed to demersal trawling, one skipper really lost control.

We were lying in Oban one evening, tied up to the pier, having our evening meal. It was peaceful and mellow after a day charging around in a small fast ship. Suddenly we became aware of a boat passing very close alongside, followed almost immediately by the wash of the boat which set the *Morven* rolling as if she was at sea. We leapt up to see what was happening, only to see the fishing boat make a hard turn to come round and do the same thing again. I was seething inside and demanded to know what the skipper thought he was playing at. To say his language was bad is to understate the case severely. I have seldom heard such a vile outburst of pent-up hateful invective, all of which terminated in his claim that we were taking the food from his children's mouths. So I began to understand the problem.

We had actually never seen this particular boat, nor the skipper, but so concerned was he with the presence of the launch that it completely disturbed whatever illegal fishing he had been engaged in not to mention the equilibrium of his mind. That was the value of the launches; once they were known to be in an area, fishermen felt inhibited and unable to carry on as they had in the past. I am not saying they did not find ways round this as time went on, but in the beginning they were seriously on edge. I was not about to let this go, and went to the police station to obtain the services of a policemen in the hope of defusing the situation, and for my own protection. A uniformed policeman accompanied me to the pier where the fishing boat was now tied up and the skipper who had done the roaring was washing some baskets of prawns. At this stage he was utterly unrepentant and indeed I am not sure the policeman did not incite him to even greater paroxysms of rage, which made me wonder if he was in full possession of his faculties.

I later found out that he had been charged at some time in the past for being in possession of a sawn-off shotgun. In the end even the most excitable will run out of steam so I just waited till the tempest in his mind had passed then said I was coming down. I think this surprised him and in a moment I was on the deck of his boat. The incident had gathered a little crowd of onlookers, some of whom were fishermen who were at pains to disassociate themselves from this man, whom they deemed to be a 'nutter'. I said to him that we seemed to be attracting some attention and invited him to lead me below to the cabin. In hindsight, knowing what I knew later, that was perhaps not such a good idea, but he acquiesced and it gave me the opportunity, once we were seated to ask him what his problem was. As I suspected, it was not anything the Department's vessels had actually done; he was simply afraid that his livelihood would be put at risk, particularly since the advent of the *Morven*. I spent some time listening to his woes and sympathising to some degree but in the end the enforcer has to enforce. He understood this, he said, and I said that he would need to take it up with his Member of Parliament. I also told him that he had made no friends tonight either with his fellow skippers or with the Department and that if he wanted to put his area in the spotlight for increased patrol activity he was going the right way about it. I sensed I had struck a chord with this last remark and left, at least having been able to come to some kind of personal satisfaction. I think the whole thing had taken about two hours. I thanked the policeman who had remained on the pier throughout. In my twenty nine years in fisheries he was by far the most unpleasant person I met, a man whose own sense of self interest went far beyond his real significance. I have apprehended men who were running multi-million pound ships but they were for the most part gentlemen, who accepted they had crossed the line and faced the consequences.

We would sometimes be tasked to salmon patrolling to deter illegal fishing for salmon at sea with mono-filament nets. These nets would be set either near to shore or allowed to drift in the tidal flow either anchored to the shore or free floating. For a while we worked out of Wick and I cannot tell you how much pleasure it gave me to take my little ship into ports like this. Why, in the first year, we went Montrose, Peterhead, Fraserburgh, Buckie, and Wick as we worked our way up the East Coast. We would usually be alongside at night unless we were required to do night work, and then we would rest accordingly during the day and slip away at night. I say slip away, but in fact that was impossible in the launches because of inadequate silencing systems. As soon as power was increased, the noise was similar to that of a Shackleton bomber, which I once heard.

Of course, it was also very pleasant to go to church to attend various prayer meetings on these overnight visits, and the Bosun would usually accompany me. We became quite well known up and down the coast.

One day, while alongside in Wick for something, we were getting on with this and that when we were hailed from the quay by a chap dressed in a comprehensive set of what I can only describe as 'country clothes'. He had the full regalia including a shooting stick seat. He asked if he could come aboard and I said it was all right. We got that a lot. Anyway, he came aboard and I gave him a brief tour, then for some reason I had to usher him off rather brusquely, because he was becoming objectionable. I showed him to the wheelhouse door and noticed the binoculars lying on the table and said, 'And take your binoculars with you!' He departed without more ado and never a backward glance, and we all got back to what we were doing. It was not till later in the day that I needed to use a pair of binoculars and realised that a pair was missing from its box. In one of those moments when you see and understand, with a degree of clarity which has hitherto eluded you, that the reason for the missing binoculars was your own crass stupidity. I had been utterly taken in by his country look which to my eyes would be incomplete without a set of binoculars, and so I forced the boat's pair on him before he departed! Naturally, I had to confess that I had given away a set of the Department's binoculars to an itinerant countryman, and have to suffer perennial reminders of the incident to this very day from my Mate, now the Marine Superintendent of Marine Scotland, who thought the incident quite hysterical.

On another occasion we were patrolling south of Wick with the Mate and Bosun away on the Searider looking for illegal salmon nets, when they came very close to actually apprehending a boat in the act of hauling the net; the poachers, however, managed to escape up steps cut into the rock face of the cliff. I do not remember the name of this tiny cove but it is very impressive. Actually, this entire coastline of Caithness is impressive, in a sombre and rugged way, the cliffs rising dark and sheer from the sea; and one can only appreciate the complexity and intricacy of the rock formations from very close quarters. On the *Morven*, meanwhile, we carried on searching and sure enough the new Engineer, from the Black Isle area, who was keeping lookout up in the pulpit at the bow, sang out that he could see a net. I manoeuvred *Morven* round to avoid getting the net in our propellers, and approached gingerly. The Engineer and the Cook got a grapnel on it and began to heave it in. In no time at all, salmon were coming up as nice as ninepence, and in fact there were nine salmon in the net. Six were dead and three alive. The fisherman in me (please bear in mind that on my mother's side, no one did anything but fish for at least ten generations, and I have not finished that search into my ancestry yet) was delighted with the catch. The British Sea Fishery Officer in me rather naively reported by telephone to the Marine Superintendent to that effect, later in the day. I received a welcome 'Well done' and then he stated that he assumed the live fish had been returned to the sea. Stunned silence from Beveridge for a moment then 'Two of them died of shock on hitting the deck, Sir, and the other of exhaustion despite our best efforts to revive it!' More stunned silence this time from the Superintendent, then gales of laughter from him and the Assistant

Marine Superintendent.

I enjoyed working out of Wick but it retains a sense of melancholy, as if the harbour was waiting for the return of the great herring fleets which massed there in the late 1800s. I do not know if it is the same today, but the Fishery Office there was like a time capsule from that period, with the only acknowledgement of this modern age being the bits and pieces of new stationery which inhabited the desk. The rest is unchanged from over a hundred years ago and provides a vital link with that period which is so much a part of my own background. On the tongue and groove, varnished, pitch pine-clad walls, hangs a map of what was intended and planned for Wick in its heyday. It is a large coloured chart, mounted on oilcloth, showing the drawings for the projected breakwaters which were started and never finished. Sadly, the herring fishing collapsed before it could be realised, and the breakwaters which would have provided a refuge similar to Peterhead, remained simply an aspiration. This is to be lamented, for in an easterly gale Wick is a poor place, where the scend from the swell in the bay causes much disturbance to vessels alongside, and I remember the old Superintendent who hired me telling me he was caught there once and his ship was 'bouncing' off the bottom because of the swell at low water.

We got to know the congregation of the church we visited quite well and kept in touch for many years afterwards. The Bosun was especially good at keeping in touch.

Eventually, as autumn drew closer the Superintendent very sensibly had the Operations Room arrange for us to work on the West Coast and so we began the migration westerly via the Pentland Firth and along the North Coast, visiting Loch Eriboll where the German U-boat fleet was moored after their surrender at the end of the Second World War. It is a doleful place in a southwesterly gale. I think we stopped at Scrabster for a night and then on to Kinlochbervie, which fishermen from the northeast call Clash. Clash in fact is a tiny pier in a little bay on the north side of the entrance to Kinlochbervie. Loch Bervie was where northeast fishermen left their boats at the weekend, for it is virtually landlocked and very safe from all winds. In time, the obvious attractiveness of the loch as a safe haven was appreciated and funding obtained to build it into a proper harbour with quay walls and a fish market. They had to blast the entrance channel which was too shallow for modern boats.

From Kinlochbervie we made our way to Ullapool, which at the time was still going like a fair with many klondykers lying at anchor to be supplied with fish caught mostly by Scottish boats.

BRIEF DIGRESSION TO *WESTRA*

As I write this I am remembering that, while there on guardship duty on the *Westra*, I was carrying out an inspection of a Russian factory ship which was loading herring. Having introduced myself to the Captain and Commissar, who always accompanied the Master in case he defected or said the wrong thing I suppose, I went below to inspect the hold. It was cavernous and poorly lit by unprotected bulbs. On surveying the scene from the top of the access stairway, I could not help drawing comparisons with a Dickensian workhouse. Men and women were toiling away to process a seemingly never-ending river of fish, which was shovelled into pre salted barrels then salted again on top. In another area workers were putting herring fillets into tins, combining the fish with a radioactive-looking tomato sauce. I was offered some but graciously declined. It was quite depressing.

On completing my inspection, I was conveyed back to the Captain's cabin and offered hospitality in some form which I cannot remember but almost certainly included Vodka, which I again declined. After a bit of chat, the way you might with your next door neighbour I said 'I have a gift for you.'

The Captain and Commissar looked quizzically at each other, and visibly brightened up. I took out a copy of the New Testament left on my ship by the Gideons. They left these on all our ships and I was delighted about that; the great thing about them was that in the first few pages the words of John Chapter Three and Verse Sixteen were written out in the script of several different languages, including Russian Cyrillic. *'For God so loved the world, that He gave His only begotten Son, that whosoever believeth in Him should not perish, but have everlasting life'.*

I gave it to the Commissar and said 'Read it please'. He read aloud, in Russian and then stopped in his tracks. He looked at me with a very startled expression, then realising he was being watched by the Captain, said 'No, no! Now, in Russia, no one believes this. Maybe only some old women in villages, in country.' This was delivered in a strong Russian accent, as you might expect.

I said 'Whether you believe this or not I have a duty to tell you, and you have a right to hear the Gospel. This book can change your lives for the better, forever! It is the greatest gift I can give you.' Whereupon I bade them farewell and departed.

Now I mention this because after this interlude, my friend the Christian Engineer and I got together and decided that we would arm ourselves with Russian Bibles, for which he knew a source, and whenever the opportunity presented itself we would be in a position to distribute them and expose those Russians to the Word of God.

BACK TO *MORVEN*

Eventually the Bibles were available. I arranged with my Engineering friend from the *Westra* for him to leave them on another Christian brother's fishing boat, the *Morning Star*, which was a purse net boat from Peterhead lying in Ullapool. I cannot remember how I met this man, who I think was part-owner of the boat, but he agreed to let us leave the Bibles on her when they went home for the weekend, when I could pick them up from an unmanned *Morning Star*. So I suppose I collected them on a Saturday in Ullapool. I hope that digression has not confused you. That Christian Brother incidentally eventually left the fishing to become a full-time preacher.

Now, the weather was not good and I had been obliged to remain in Ullapool longer than I wished, to collect the Bibles. Forecasts for cyclonic winds up to force ten were forecast all round us. 'Cyclonic' simply means the wind will not come from a settled direction, but will change direction very quickly. In any event we got away in the early afternoon and made rapid progress out of Loch Broom and Annat Bay, past the many large ships lying there, on round Greenstone Point and on to Rubha Reidh lighthouse, where the wind freshened markedly from the south south west. As we headed over to South Rona Light on our passage to the Sound of Raasay and on to Portree, the wind freshened progressively and before long she was ploughing into the short steep seas. She made remarkable progress and maintained a good speed, and not for the first time I thought our little ship was made of stern stuff. By the time we rounded South Rona Light and stood into the Sound of Raasay it was pitch black and really howling, and even in that inland sea the waves were impressive. The

Morven was not discomfited however, and before long began to feel the effects of the land, which produced smaller and smaller water. We entered Portree Harbour with a full gale blowing and made our way towards half a dozen fishing boats which were tied to the pier. The wind must have been very strong for it blew off the Breton cap I had purchased in the Crinan Canal, which I have yet to tell you about. You see, the chronology may not be correct but the events themselves are true.

Anyway, I put *Morven* about and the Bosun managed to recover the cap with a boat hook, and it is still doing sterling service to this day. Then we went alongside and made fast with our storm moorings. These moorings were a story in themselves for I had been very unhappy with the 'bits of string' they had provided when the boats were commissioned. So I mounted a raid on our Store, which at that time was in the Customs House in Leith, and obtained some excellent stuff which came off the old *Explorer*.

After making fast, the Bosun, who had gone ashore to take our moorings, said 'There is a man ashore who knows you and would like to speak with you'. I was intrigued and asked him to bring him aboard. He was a Welshman with a red beard and curly red hair and had been there for us when we came in to take our moorings. His name was Iollo as I recall and I said 'How do you know me?' 'I have heard about you from the Missionary to Fishermen and his wife in Stornoway, and I have come down here tonight to welcome you and put myself at your disposal for the weekend.' I thought this was extraordinary and inwardly thanked God for this good man, an inshore fisherman, who had such an awareness of God's ordering of our lives.

In addition to this, the Bosun's old minister from Carradale was now working in Portree and Kensaleyre in Skye and we would also try to meet with him.

On Sunday it blew very hard and we would not be going anywhere, so in the morning Iollo appeared in his old van and gave us a run to Mr.McGuinness' church in Portree, where we enjoyed his ministry at morning worship. After service we were invited, all three of us, to the minister's house for lunch then out in the evening to the Free Church, I think it was, where we sang Psalms unaccompanied by any organ. It was exhilarating and deeply moving. From there we drove out to Kensaleyre itself, in the darkest of night, and there in a tin shack full of people young and old, we praised God and felt the powerful presence of the Holy Spirit. At the end of the day, which was close to midnight, we bade farewell to Iollo with a shared prayer and I never saw or heard of him again. It had been a most extraordinary weekend from every point of view and one which I have treasured all my life, having felt the intimate care and love of God through the ministry of his people.

A BAD STORM AT LAMLASH ON ARRAN

Among many others, I have two letters of thanks referring to the particular night of 4 and 5 of September 1983. One is from the Marine Superintendent and the other from H.M.Coastguard and they thank the crew of the *Morven* for the service we rendered to three vessels on that night.

We had been patrolling the Clyde for some time, varying our patrol patterns between day and night patrols. Much of our attention was directed towards monitoring fishing for herring. The thing about herring is that they will often swim with sprats, from which they are virtually indistinguishable, except that sprats are smaller and have 'keel scales' on their underbellies. At this particular point in time it was permitted to fish for herring but the fishery ceased at the end of October. I wanted to keep the *Morven* in the heart of things, as it were, and so this night decided to moor to one of the large mooring buoys in Lamlash Harbour on the Isle of Arran. In those days the harbour, which is a huge lagoon with channels at the north and south ends, and is made up of the coast of Arran and the coast of the Holy Isle, had two trots of these huge buoys for mooring warships. All the buoys except one have gone now.

I knew that the weather was going to be bad and had watched this equinoctial storm brew out in the Atlantic for a couple of days, my own observations being borne out by the BBC forecasts. On the night of the fourth we moored with two of our heavy mooring ropes to the buoy nearest to the land in Lamlash Bay and settled down to ride out the weather. I suppose you could call it a premonition, although I would call it forewarning, but I began to believe that tonight was going to be a challenge, and I could not settle to anything. I listened to the forecasts and the expected wind speeds rose and rose, until they were forecasting winds in excess of eighty miles an hour on shore, with violent storms at sea. I went to my cabin and spent a good while on my knees asking for courage, strength and wisdom and calm. Sure enough, the wind freshened as the night wore on, until around eleven o'clock it was howling up to ninety miles an hour on our yachty anemometer. Even in the bay, the sea was building and the *Morven* was pitching to her two moorings and shipping water overall. I was unconcerned for them for they were far bigger than she needed, and we had set them up well.

Shortly before midnight the VHF radio burst into life with the words 'PAN PAN, PAN PAN, PAN PAN this is Clyde Coastguard, Clyde Coastguard, Clyde Coastguard. PAN PAN yacht *Alva, Alva,Alva* has broken adrift from her mooring at the south end of Lamlash Harbour and requires immediate assistance, Troon lifeboat launching.' I immediately called Clyde Coastguard to inform them we were in the harbour and advised them not to send Troon lifeboat to sea, for I knew what kind of a boat she was, and I also knew what kind of a sea would be running at the entrance to Troon Harbour. I gave them a report of our on-scene conditions then called the yacht. She came back immediately, the voice being a young man's, clearly shaken. For some reason a great calm came over me. I asked the young man if he had the engine going and he said he had. He told me he had a young woman on board with him who had no experience of seagoing.

The words came out of me '*Here is what you are going to do. I am going to give you courses to steer to bring you up to my vessel. You must not attempt to make fast to my vessel; I will be observing you all the time on radar and will tell you when you need to correct your course. When you come near me, I will give you further instructions*'. We watched him carefully as he began to make his way northwards in the inky black harbour, the surface of which was whipped to a frenzy of spray and spume and was peppered with big steel mooring buoys. Thankfully our radar was behaving and I could easily advise him on which course to steer, and continually encouraged him. That young man did well to do what he did and before long we picked him up in the searchlight. The yacht was a Fisher, which are very able little craft. As she came into our vicinity, I directed the young man to make for a large yacht called the *Tycoo* which was on her own mooring, close to the shore, off the village of Lamlash, having already arranged with the skipper of the big yacht to take him alongside. After a little while they moored up alongside the *Tycoo* and that was the end of that.

We had hardly had time to get a cup of tea when 'PAN PAN PAN'. This time it was the fishing vessel *Fair Morn* of Dunure in Ayrshire. She had just run aground on the north end of the Holy Isle. We had heard her and her partner vessel the *New Dawn* on VHF earlier, bemoaning the weather, the like of which they had never seen. Again I got on to the *Fair Morn* to find out their condition. The skipper came back that they were hard and fast on the shingle beach and the tide was ebbing quickly. In other words, their condition was not critical from the point of view of safety of life. I reported to the Coastguard accordingly. In the meantime, the *New Dawn* had crept into the harbour making for the small water near the head of the bay. Before you could say the words 'PAN PAN PAN. Fishing vessel *New Dawn* aground in Lamlash Harbour,' they had crept so far into the bay that they had run aground! At this, I decided to slip our mooring to see if we could get them off. It would be a one way passage, for we would not be able to re-secure to the buoy again that night. I reckoned it was worth a try so I told the skipper of the *New Dawn* to tie a big dahn buoy to a messenger (a light line used as a preliminary connection for passing a towing hawser), and let it carry downwind towards us. In the meantime, we got the port and starboard engines on and slipped from the mooring buoy. I cannot describe the strength of wind or the state of the sea as the wave tops were ripped off to be hurled against the *Morven*'s wheelhouse casing and windows. The wiper blades were no match for the solid water and we had to rely on the radar and echo sounder as we nudged closer to the orange dahn buoy. We could see it clearly now in the searchlight but we were rapidly running out of water ourselves. The Mate was monitoring the sounder and I was steering and controlling the engines. The Bosun and the Cook were ready to pick up the messenger and the Engineer was tending to his engines. I suppose we were about fifty yards from the buoy when the Mate shouted that we were out of water. I immediately put the engines full astern and *Morven* shot backwards away from the shallow water and the dahn buoy. When we settled down, I called the skipper and told him it was not possible as we had almost been aground ourselves. He replied that it was all right, because the tide which was ebbing fast due to the strength of wind would leave his boat high and dry very soon. So that was that. We spent the rest of the night dodging in Lamlash Harbour in hurricane force winds which only eased with the dawn. The *New Dawn* re-floated with the next tide and we spent the rest of the day trying to pull the *Fair Morn* off the shingle on the north end of the Holy Isle with the *New Dawn* and another Ayrshire boat. It was no good, and they had to wait until another couple of tides had come and gone before she

came off.
The letter of thanks we received from the Coastguard reads:

Marine incident - 5th September 1983– Lamlash Bay- Yacht ALVA

I would like to forward our appreciation for responding to the yacht ALVA Pan Pan on the night of the 5th September during such filthy weather conditions. We believe that without the cool assistance rendered by your Vessel, a much graver incident may have occurred. Very many thanks and good sailing.

The letter from the Superintendent said much the same, but also mentioned the *New Dawn* and the *Fair Morn*. The thing that struck me about this incident was the calmness which had come over me as events unfolded. I felt clear-headed and confident, although excited inside. During the morning, I overheard the skipper of the *Tycoo* talking to another yacht, and as he rehearsed the events of the night he said 'That skipper on the *Morven*, his voice just calmed everything down. That was something else'. Little did he know the skipper on the *Morven* was as excited as all the others, and that the voice was inspired by Someone else!

ILLEGAL HERRING BOATS

We continued to patrol the Clyde for the next few months, engaged in enforcing whatever was required including a total herring ban which came into force on 28 October 1983. I know this because I have in my possession the draft of a case we took against two Campbeltown fishing vessels, the *Acorn* and the *Erica*. The draft runs to ten pages and was submitted by the Sheriff of Rothesay, where the case was heard, to the High Court of Justiciary in Edinburgh for an opinion of his judgement on the case.

What happened was, we were patrolling the Clyde Estuary as usual and came on this pair team who were fishing for sprats. It was 10 November 1983. I laid the *Morven* alongside the *Acorn*, and the Mate and Bosun jumped on board, just off Garroch Head. They went through the usual procedure of sighting the vessel's paperwork then carried out an inspection of the catch and nets. In the course of that investigation they discovered thirty boxes of herring in three stacks of ten neatly stowed under ten boxes of sprats. It was clear that the herring had been caught as a by-catch, and the intention was to hide them from view and sell them secretly. The Mate cautioned the skipper at that point, and then left the Bosun on board to 'guard' the *Acorn* for the passage into Tarbert Loch Fyne. He jumped back aboard *Morven* and we set off at full speed to board the *Erica*, which he did off Inchmarnock. We then all went into Tarbert and concluded investigations. I also cautioned the skippers of both boats after we had assembled the evidence.

The case was not heard until 4 June 1984, when a plea of 'Not Guilty' was recorded. There followed a period of 'sundry continuations' until the case was concluded on 17 December 1984! We lost this case not because of anything we had done, or failed to do, but because the Procurator Fiscal, guided by the Department's legal staff, had charged the skippers with 'fishing for herring' as opposed to 'retaining' herring. The fact that the Sheriff sought confirmation of his judgement from Edinburgh indicates some doubt is his mind. It certainly annoyed us intensely because it was a good case, well presented; we just did not charge them with the right offence.

On a lighter note the Sheriff, who was of 'advancing years' (a bit like myself) on the day of the trial was clearly beginning to suffer from courtroom fatigue as the afternoon wore on. Hours of technical data will do that to you, and for light relief he must tell us a story about how, years ago, an old fisherman had wanted to be buried at sea in Rothsay Sound. This pre-dated the advent of bottom trawling, and I suppose no one could have foreseen that one day trawlers would be rumbling over the Sound. Of course the inevitable happened and the poor old fisherman was trawled up, coffin and all. Naturally, everyone was upset and arrangements were made to rebury him with dignity. Unfortunately, this began to happen more and more frequently as the popularity of bottom trawling increased and the good folk's patience with the continual necessity to respectfully commit the remains to the deep on a regular basis diminished. In the end I am not sure if they took him out to deeper water or interred him, in the kirk yard overlooking the Sound. Whatever they did must have worked for after a while the problem disappeared. And the mood of the courtroom lightened up markedly.

The *Morven* continued to patrol the Clyde estuary and neighbouring waters, including Luce Bay and the Solway Firth area. We would work out of

Tarbert in Loch Fyne, surely one of the best harbours anywhere for really bad weather, or Campeltown, or Troon .or Lamlash. This carried on throughout the winter until one day the Superintendent informed me that there was an urgent requirement to have a launch in the Loch Linnie area. I had been working away at him for quite some time to let us go through the Crinan Canal (because it was there) but he had resolutely refused, fearing damage to his launches. I had no such reservations because I knew our capabilities. Anyway he wanted us up in Loch Linnie and it was blowing a severe gale of south west wind. I said that in this weather there was no way we could get round the Mull of Kintyre for the next few days, so he reluctantly agreed to let us go through. I was overjoyed; not only because I relished the opportunity to do it, but also because I had a Bosun who, before he joined the Fisheries, had been at the fishing out of Carradale all his life. He had been through the Canal more times than he could remember and would be able to keep me straight.

So off we went to Ardrishaig which is the beginning of the canal at the east end. I thoroughly enjoyed this inland waterway sailing. No big billows or concerns about shifts of wind, and the wind could blow as hard as it liked. And it did. That ended up a very heavy gale , and the canal was so full of water that the stretch at Ballindalloch looked like a massive loch, the sides of the canal only being discernible due to the lines of trees down each side of the canal! There is a nice wee Strathspey incidentally, called *O'er the Bows to Ballindalloch* which is written for the pipes. I was very glad the Bosun and the Cook were there, for they knew the workings of the lock gates and all I had to think about was not damaging the propellers. We spent the night at Cairnbhan and I went ashore to have dinner with some friends at the head of Loch Sween. They were the Ivisons; Ann had been a chum of Patsy's from Kilmarnock. They were vegetarians and she produced a lovely meat loaf with no meat. Quite an achievement! In the morning we were off again, eventually coming to the narrowest part of the canal shortly before Crinan itself. Again I was glad the Bosun was there because he knew what was coming next as the steep rock walls closed in on both sides, so much so that it felt like a tunnel. Well, we got through without damage and started patrolling Loch Linnie and the Sound of Lorne. As I say, we must have been effective because I think it was on that patrol when we were set upon by the 'Nutter of Oban', previously described.

As time wore on, we must have been ordered to wend our way back towards the East Coast by way of the Minches, with the advent of spring, carrying out salmon patrols and regular inspections as we went. This was a wonderful way to see parts of Scotland very few ever see, as we visited all the nooks and crannies on that incredibly long coastline. We briefly worked on Lewis, as I recall with some success, lifting the odd salmon net. I am blithely referring to salmon by their name here, but on the boats we never called them that. They were always referred to as 'red fish', out of a feigned respect for the fishermen's superstition that saying the name on board brought bad luck. Whatever that is.

Skye was another area of activity for us, where we worked out of the pier at Dunvegan. Many years ago this had been a base for fishery cruisers and indeed the bitts on the pier were ships' bitts, on which the vestiges of Fisheries Grey could still be seen. The pier was now used by scallop boats that make poor companions for fibre glass patrol boats, since their hulls are sheathed with steel plates and fenders to cope with the tremendous wear and tear they get with the dredges. It was while working out of Dunvegan that I received news that Patsy was going to be taken into Bellshill Maternity to have Martin. I contacted the Superintendent immediately and was told to get home as quickly as possible and handed the *Morven* over to the Mate.

DOMESTIC ASIDE 2

The journey home, from Kyle then down the west coast line was magnificent for the mountains were plastered with snow even in April, and I arrived in time to be there for his birth and safe delivery. I say I was there for his birth, but what I mean is that I was in the hospital. The only baby I saw born was Rebecca, and quickly realised that the birthing room was no place for a man. Of course I was instantly transformed from fast patrol boat commander to child minder and housekeeper, which requires a degree of schizophrenia or bi-polarity (a feature of my entire married life). One minute you are a law enforcer, the next you are cooking dinners, vacuum cleaning and trying to survive. I do not know how Patsy coped. After I had done this for a couple of days, I got a migraine which had the effect of creating semi-permanent zigzag lines across my eyes, leaving them looking like the ground plan of old fortifications. I was trying to stay on top of everything, you see, and just did not possess the gifts. - thank goodness! Martin was born on 5 April 1984 and has been a wee pal ever since. When he was a wee boy, he had long ginger curls and his own NATO jumper with epaulettes which his mother made for him. He is a lawyer now with Dundas Wilson and they seem to think he is all right. He is our sixth surviving child.

In fact I am very good in and around the house and cannot suffer dirt, untidiness, carelessness or disorganisation. A lifetime at sea making sure everyone is doing the right thing and that everything is in order impresses these things upon you. Mind you, I was pretty good at coping when we went away camping. I would take the children away in different combinations of age so that they could get to know each other outside the context of family hierarchy. Over the years we traversed the length and breadth of Scotland like a band of gypsies, but always with a different combination of children. Apart from family holiday time when Patsy would come, I did this myself. Sometimes the children would bring friends and it would turn into a species of mini jamboree. Some of the expeditions were quite adventurous depending on the ages of the children, and we climbed many Munroes, including Ben Nevis. The best times were to be had round a camp-fire at night in the spring or autumn when the midges were not too bad and we would sing and talk. If you want to be friends with your children take them away and teach them to survive.

We had built a two-storey extension to our house in 1981 I think, because we were running out of cubic capacity. That in itself was an exercise in faith for money was tight and the interest rates at the time were astronomical. However I obtained quotes from several builders, having drawn up my own contract, which included a stipulation that there would be no work on Sundays, and in the end we chose a young fellow from Stornoway who was just getting started. He was not the cheapest and on the day he arrived to start Patsy and I looked at each other with trepidation, for all the tools were new and we thought 'What have we done?' We need not have worried, for not only did he and his colleagues work solidly and consistently on our project, but they enjoyed six weeks of days without rain. The extension is still standing after over thirty years so it must have been well put together. I mention the extension because the advent of Martin caused us to yet again re-evaluate the accommodation situation, and Patsy began looking for a new cave.

BACK TO *MORVEN*

After our experience with the disenchanted fisherman in Oban, I looked round for a suitable alternative berth for us to lie. I had never been happy with Oban for it was a ferry terminal, fishing port and badly exposed in certain winds. I found the perfect haven in Dunstaffnage. There is a marine laboratory there with its own pier for their research trawler *Calanus*. They were happy for us to lie alongside her, or on the pier if she was away, and I felt much happier. It was a lovely spot. One night, returning from patrolling the coast of Mull, we were running down the sound of the same name when we saw our opposite number, the *Moidart*, lying on Lochaline pier. The forecast was not particularly good and that berth is quite exposed. I hailed them on VHF and my old chum from the *Westra* days answered. I passed my compliments and suggested he might want to follow us to my recently discovered bolt hole. He was concerned about us being in the same place overnight, but I promised not to tell if he didn't! My chum was quite a nervous chap and would sometimes have three cigarettes going at once, but I liked him a lot. There were no GPS navigators or mobile phones in those days and it was easier to disappear. I am glad he took my advice, because it blew quite hard that night and they would possibly have had to get off the berth.

As it was, we hardly knew anything about the weather in Dunstaffnage. That was the secret of enjoying the launches. One had to think like a fisherman to survive comfortably. We could end up in the most extraordinary berths. On the same migration, we patrolled up the Sound of Sleat through Kyle Rhea to Kyle of Lochalsh, with a very bad forecast. In those days the ferries were still operating and the only berth we could obtain was alongside the standby ferry, on the west side of the railway pier. Well, it blew like nothing on earth all night although we were comfy enough, with our big ferry alongside sheltering us from the worst of the wind. The only thing was that the strength of wind blew the ferry so far off the berth that there was no way to get ashore during the height of the gale, and so we were marooned with nothing to do but watch the squalls of driving rain lash the Kyles in the yellow light of the pier lighting. Getting ashore was important because it enabled us to phone home, which is normally a great boost to morale.

You will notice there is not much structure to this voyage, because having been given a general remit, I was at liberty to deploy the boat accordingly. This suited my mentality to perfection, and as long as the boat ran well I was completely happy. I will not describe the times when we had to withdraw her from service, particularly in the first year, to effect machinery repairs; for they were times of great frustration which I have chosen to forget. Except for one instance, when we had been up on the slip at McGruer's Yard at Roseneath for some reason; I think it was the deep sea seals which stop water coming into a boat via the propeller shafts. They lowered us down the slip, allegedly fit for sea, and almost immediately water started leaking in round the seals. Unfortunately the *Moidart* was to be put up on the slip as we came off and this could not be delayed. So rapid was the ingress of water that I worked out with the Mate a strategy for how we would beach her if it came to that. McGruer's sent us to a mooring buoy up Loch Long to spend the night. Technically we were sinking but we had two bilge pumps and our Engineer kept the bilges down overnight so that we did not sink at the buoy. I think we got up the slip again shortly after that.

In time, we got back onto the East Coast and I will relate one more recollection before leaving the *Morven*. In fact I can do no better than give you an actual transcript of a combined helicopter patrol off Cairnbulg, which took place on 29 July 1984, and shows what our officers sometimes had to put up with. It was sent to the Superintendent.

At 1830hrs, on Sunday 29 July 1984, I took Morven to a position some 7 miles to the north of Kinnairds Head Light as pre- arranged, to await the arrival of a Department helicopter between 1830hrs. and 1900hrs. Snatches of radio conversation were heard on Departmental private frequency at 1843hrs. And it was deduced that this was the helicopter speaking to someone in the Findochty area, therefore at 1853hrs Morven was put on 3 engine status and searider launched, by which time she was about 6 miles north of Fraserbugh Bay. The helicopter was sighted at about 1900hrs. And at 1907hrs, the helicopter gave the report that a small craft, a speedboat, with an orange hull and cream upperworks, had been sighted in the vicinity of St.Combs, hauling a net. Morven and searider immediately set off at full speed for the indicated position which was being marked by helicopter. Between 1910hrs, and 1915hrs, various reports were received from the helicopter to the effect that the net had been retrieved and the boat making for Cairnbulg and then, that the boat had stopped to work hand lines. At 1920hrs, Morven's speed was reduced to permit the searider to make an undetected approach, and during this time, the helicopter advised that the boat was making for Cairnbulg, having first feinted towards Fraserburgh.

At 1927hrs, having been advised by the helicopter that the observer, the Fishery Officer of Buckie had landed at Cairnbulg, Morven proceeded towards Fraserburgh to head off the speedboat should this be required. In the event the boat went to Cairnbulg to be met on arrival by the F.O. [Fishery Officer], who was joined by the Mate from Morven's searider at 1933hrs. Shortly after this reports from the shore party were received to the effect that the occupants of the speedboat would not be interviewed, and had left in a blue hatchback car, registration number etc., and that a mob had gathered on shore and was attempting to remove the boat. At 1945hrs, the Mate reported that the net had been removed to a blue Transit van, registration number etc. This van was kept under surveillance by the helicopter. In the meantime I took Morven to Fraserburgh to call the police as the situation was becoming ugly at Cairnbulg, and having berthed at 1947hrs, contacted the police at 1948hrs. [No mobile phones in those days].At 1950hrs. the Mate reported that the engine of the speedboat (a Johnson type) was being removed to a blue Cortina, car registration number etc. I then kept Morven alongside at Fraserburgh to monitor radio conversation and provide a land link for all parties, during which time the following exchanges took place.

At 1953hrs, the helicopter reported that the Transit van had returned to Cairnbulg, having done a short tour of the surrounding countryside, and shortly after this the Mate was able to pass a description of the speedboat as a CRESCENT 425, GRP moulded, about 16 feet long, orange hull, cream upperworks and two hatches with orange lids. At 2005hrs, at the request of the helicopter, I called the police a second time to advise them that the blue hatchback car had stopped at a house (the first on the left entering Cairnbulg). Between 2010hrs and 2015hrs, there being no advantage in remaining at Fraserburgh, I took Morven back to Fraserburgh Bay, to await the return of the searider, and during this time overheard the helicopter direct the police car, with the Buckie F.O. inside, to the location of the blue hatch-back. This concludes Morven's involvement in the salmon patrol, because at 2023hrs. Morven responded to a distress call in the Kinnairds Head area.

Throughout the above operation, my men and the Buckie F.O. were continuously verbally abused, jostled, stoned and threatened. Despite my orders to withdraw if they feared for their safety they stuck it out, and as a result of their tenacity, in the fullness of time these people were taken to court.

Their boat was confiscated, and they were fined £2000, which was significant at the time.

I was conscious around this time that I was becoming better at recognising how to detect and anticipate the situations in which fishermen would be likely to bend the law and ignore the regulations. I had been in the Fisheries for six years but it took me that long to see how to apply the regulations which were coming from Brussels on a frequent basis. I could see that the secret was to study to gain a working knowledge of the law as it pertained to fishing, understanding the principles in play, then apply the specifics as they changed from time to time. European law was good at conveying the spirit of the intention of the law whilst United Kingdom law hardened the intention into detailed requirements. This approach, combined with a developing understanding of human nature and the frailty of man, enabled me to achieve some success in my fisheries work

I have already mentioned that the first year on the launch was very frustrating at times due to the problems we encountered with machinery and equipment issues. These problems would bring us back to McGruer's yard at Rosneath on the Gareloch from time to time, and in a way I quite enjoyed it because we would stay in the Kilcreggan Hotel which had originally been built for the owner of the Donaldson Line. I suppose he, or they, for the company was owned by brothers, would be able to observe the passage of their ships as they sailed from and arrived at the Clyde on their voyages to Canada and South America. Oddly enough my Uncle Vincent sailed in that company as a refrigeration engineer for a while, tending to the machinery which kept the carcasses of beef frozen from South America. But I digress. The point was that the Kilcreggan Hotel was a delightful old Victorian manor and I for one thoroughly enjoyed the ambience. It allowed one to pretend to dwell in a time now long gone, to co-exist with the feelings of a bygone age, to mingle as it were with borrowed experiences out of time. I realise this sounds fanciful but that is how it felt for me. It was also a wonderful place to study at night when work was done at the boatyard, my particular study at the time being 17th century Calvinistic theology. It was in this frame of mind that I covenanted with the Lord, Whose presence I was now acutely aware of, seeing as I did His hand in the ordering of every department of my daily life. I have pondered whether or not to record this covenant for you and since this is a record for you, my family, I will.

Oh Lord God Almighty, Who by Your powerful hand and for Your mercy's sake alone, have taken me from the miry pit and from sin and bondage to sin which is death, and have set my feet upon a Rock, Who is no less than your Dear Son Jesus, and Who I believe has died in my stead and taken all my sin upon His Blessed Shoulders, and fully paid the price of sin and purchased for me a plenteous redemption, full and free, and nothing lacking, so that believing this, I am able to come near to Your Presence not as a rebel but as an Adopted son, whereby I am able to call You Father; my Father, I this day hereby covenant to, by Your Strength, to look always to Your Son Jesus My Saviour for salvation and so far as I am enabled by Your Strength, to keep Your Commandments and so live a life, godly and pleasing to You, and I further covenant, that if it please you I will declare each and every message of Gospel news which You entrust to me. To this end Oh Lord, I beseech You that You grant me such Wisdom, Courage, Strength, Power and above all Love, that I may fulfil this Covenant in every aspect so far as I am enabled by You. And I further beseech You, Lord that You grant me such opportunities as it please You, to declare your Gospel to Your people wherever they may be. For my part I pray, Lord, that if this covenant please You, that I may lay hold of, and take as my own, all the promises You have made to Your people as written down in Your Holy Book called the Bible. Lord, help me in this covenant, for I have no strength of my own. Keep me humble and keep Satan far from me. Forgive my unbelief.

Done this thirteenth day of December nineteen hundred and eighty four.

David Littlejohn Beveridge.

I remember writing the covenant in the back of my Bible on my knees at my bed in the Kilcreggan Hotel, and it remains in my Bible to this day. The words poured out and I have recorded them as they appear in the Bible. I realise that I was heavily influenced by my reading at the time but the fact that I have never felt any need or desire to change a word of it shows me that I meant, and mean, every word. I have renewed the covenant several times, the last time when I retired from the sea.

In the Spring of 1985 my two years on the *Morven* were up and although I wanted to stay on her, the Superintendent had other ideas and wanted me to join my old favourite the *Jura* as Junior First Officer. So I handed my lovely little *Morven* over to my replacement in Troon harbour one afternoon after putting her through her paces and showing him what she could do, and never took her to sea again. It had been the happiest time of my sea-going life and had occurred at a pivotal moment in my development. Running the little ship had taught me so much about independent command, teamwork, trust, and weather awareness; it was and is, in my opinion, the best training ground one could ask for.

Before we leave the *Morven*, I should tell about Bill Knox. You may not be acquainted with the name but Bill has written several books about the Scottish Fisheries. They are good yarns and many people have read them. One day he came down to the *Morven* in Leith, having obtained permission from the Superintendent. We made him very welcome and laid on tea and tabnabs (which is sailor speak for fancy cakes), sitting round the table talking about the *Morven* and what it was like to operate her, and our feelings and how we went about the job. He took copious notes, thanked us for the hospitality and left. Maybe a year later the Bosun appeared with a copy of a book Knox had written, which I think he called 'Box Tango'. I read it and one of the first things which struck me was the hero had brown eyes and did not suffer fools gladly. Very seldom do heroes have brown eyes but I do, and I certainly do not suffer fools gladly. So there you are.

On 9 May 1985 our lovely baby Hannah was born. Her name means GRACE and she is well named for she has brought grace to our family. From the very beginning of her life she was different and put a different skew on things, refusing to fit into any familial mould. Everyone loves her because she is so different. As I write this she is about to embark on a holiday (expedition) to Nepal to walk part of the Annapurna Trail. I have simply committed her into God's loving care.

Her arrival also ensured that we would have to obtain a bigger house, for we had now outgrown Five Pine Park in Hamilton by some long way. Patsy seriously set about discovering a place for us to live, and after a great deal of research on her part and prayer by both of us we bought the big house in Cambuslang, where we now live. It is referred to as the 'White House' by the children for some reason.

CHAPTER TWENTY-FIVE
1985 - 1987
JURA (THIRD TIME)

When I rejoined the *Jura* it was like stepping aboard a battleship. She felt huge! She was now commanded by a chap who had been Senior First Officer on her in 1979 with me, and her Senior First Officer was an old acquaintance from the same period. I do not know why, but between the two of them they seemed to think that I would join the ship with some kind of personal agenda, having been in charge of my own boat. Nothing could have been further from the truth; for I was actually quite happy to let someone else do the worrying for a while. The Captain was a good ship-master in that he had great pride in his ship and the Senior First Officer was a good efficient Mate. I was happy to try to slot into the team they had forged together and the *Jura* looked as well as I had ever seen her. On one occasion we were patrolling to the north-west of Lewis and the Captain made a big production out of the fact that we were not quite in the exact spot he had marked on the chart to be at a certain time. Now this was absolutely normal in cruisers because after all we were at sea to look at fishing boats and had to divert to do so. We were not a ferry running to a schedule. Anyway, he wanted to be told in future of any and all targets which appeared on my watch. No problem with me. I called him every time I saw a boat and within a short while he got fed up.

For my part I wanted to make her legal and fisheries paperwork as good as I could make it. That was in my job description. The Captain and I did not always see eye to eye on this subject, and on one occasion, having given me a job to do, I forged on doing what I thought I was supposed to be doing when he came up to the wheelhouse and started ranting on about 'Change,Change, Change, it's always change with you!' This was delivered with some vehemence, which in itself did not trouble me; what bothered me was that this was imparted in front of the rating on watch. I regret that the haze which, so many years before, old Duncan had warned me about in Calcutta, swam over my eyes.

I said 'You listen to me; you do not talk to me like that under any circumstances. I do not know who you think you are but you do not impress me. You gave me a job to do which I have done in good faith. You did not leave specific instructions about how you wanted it done; had you done so I would have followed them. Since my work is not satisfactory I suggest you do it yourself.' With that he left the bridge and I later saw him thick in conversation with the Mate, but I could not have cared less. It was becoming clear that my face did not fit in their regime and I was not in a position, nor did I feel inclined, to do anything about it. So I just got on with what I had to do, but it was an uncomfortable time and completely unnecessary. For some reason they both seemed to feel threatened.

Now, the *Jura* had not detected any illegal activity for a long time, the Captain was on leave and the First Officer was Officer in Charge, so I was Mate. On 6 July 1985, I was on watch in the early hours of the morning cruising off St. Kilda, when I noticed a radar target inside the twelve mile limit of St. Kilda. I stood the *Jura* over towards her and after a while saw it was a Danish industrial trawler, the *Bodil Gjedsig*. I called the Officer in Charge and we checked the fishing vessel's position and sighted him hauling the net over the starboard side. I repaired on board to find that not only was he unaware that he was not allowed within twelve miles of St. Kilda, but also that his by-catch of what we called ANNEX V species (stuff like haddock, whiting, cod etc.) was very high. Norway Pout, which is what he was targeting, was an industrial species; the only problem was that immature, good quality fish would sometimes swim with them. Hence the need for vigilance. Even without sampling I could tell he was way over the permitted percentage, and recommended that a proper sample be taken. So the OIC concurred and we started out for Village Bay in St. Kilda as the weather was deteriorating.

En route, we were instructed by HQ to proceed directly to Stornoway which was good news, for the facilities were better there and there was space to work. In the meantime I enjoyed my breakfast on the Danish ship, which was very kindly supplied by the skipper. It was delicious! They do not eat breakfast like us. They have cold smoked meat, pickled fish, hard boiled eggs and good coffee, and when you have been up since quarter to four in the morning it is just what you need. We got him to Stornoway that evening and I detained the vessel with a Notice of Detention. Then we drew samples which showed he was well over the limit. Next day we went to court and he was fined a total of £5000, which although not a big fine was enough to have made it worth our while. The Officer in Charge said to me afterwards, 'If it had not been you doing the boarding, I would not have taken it'. I do not know what that meant.

In those days, as in all ships, there was a culture of drinking which was seldom abused at sea but which could be in port. At that time we were still going in for two nights so there was plenty of opportunity to drink. I had stopped taking drink when our David was born and that may well have been another reason I was not 'one of the boys'. That, plus my overt Christianity, more or less guaranteed I would be unacceptable in some circles. One of the bad things about drink of course is that men will start to fight over stupid things. I cannot tell you how many times I have been called in the middle of the night, to settle punch ups in the lower deck. For this reason I did not enjoy being alongside although it gave me an opportunity to go church from time to time. All in all, I did not enjoy this period on the *Jura* and was glad when I received orders from the Superintendent to join the *Vigilant* around the end of 1985 as Senior First Officer. This was a promotion for me because it meant that four times a year I would be taking her to sea as Office in Charge and that was just what I wanted. In addition to that my old friend and mentor was the Captain, and that was just fine by me.

At this time she was the flagship; the newest in the fleet, captained by the Senior Commander, so I felt honoured to be sent there. I resolved to excel. By now, after three years of the Common Fisheries Policy, I was beginning to see where detections were likely to made and I was being placed in situations where I could hone these skills. This Captain was an excellent fishery man and knew his job well. He taught me a lot about the whole range of fishery skills and I am indebted to him. He had gone for the job of Assistant Marine Superintendent in competition with another Captain you have met before, who favoured a separate Scotland, but he did not get the job. He was hurt about that because he was the better practical man but I believe the other man was more polished and could talk the talk of the politicians. Even if most of was of dubious merit. I am not saying the new Assistant Marine Superintendent spoke rubbish but he knew how to deal with it. My friend was more direct and plain spoken, and everything was delivered with the Campbeltown accent which I have mentioned before.

VIGILANT (THE FOURTH OF THAT NAME)

I have only a few memories of this time on the *Vigilant*. I know I enjoyed the posting and was on her for about a year. Soon after I joined we were sent out to a position about seventy miles north of Cape Wrath to investigate some Irish pair-trawlers which were fishing for mackerel. These were large trawlers which towed a huge net between them. It was 13 December 1985. At that time they had no licence to fish there, and our orders were quite clear; to order them to cease fishing and escort them to port. Sure enough we found them, and they were fishing so we had to bring them in. The Captain was always very apologetic to the Irish because they were really nice blokes and we regarded them as just like ourselves. Anyway they came like gentlemen and we took them to court the next day. The boats were the *Sheanne* and the *Paula* and they were fined £10,000 and £15,000 respectively. This experience did not put them off their stride, because the names *Sheanne* and *Paula* went through several manifestations, each time the boats getting bigger and bigger. They were good fishermen.

My Commanding Officer, although a good teacher, was never keen on letting his First Officer handle the ship in port. He was quite content to allow the officers to anchor her but not take her in and out of port, so it was with some reluctance that he allowed me to take her away from the berth at Stornoway. I knew that next patrol he would be on leave and I would have to do all the manoeuvring as Officer in Charge. Of course, this was a big thought because she was the newest in the fleet. But that chance to take her away was all I needed to get the feel of her and although sometimes challenged by conditions, with twin screws and a bow thruster she was a much handier ship than the *Jura* and the *Westra*.

I have nothing much to report about the times I took the *Vigilant* away as Officer in Charge, until 9 April 1986; patrolling about forty five miles to the north west of St. Kilda, we were identifying and ascertaining the catches of the big Norwegian pelagic trawlers fishing for Blue Whiting. This is a fishery which still takes place every year and is prosecuted mostly (but not exclusively) by Norwegian vessels. They are huge efficient ships, towing enormous nets and very long warps (wires which attach the net to the ship).There are usually dozens of these vessels trawling up and down the hundred fathom line, which I have already told you about, and one has to concentrate to pass through them safely and obtain the information required. They are all moving about 3.8 to 4.0 knots and you will be passing through at about eleven knots. Here is a report I had to make to the Superintendent:

I write to inform you of an incident which took place at about 1400hrs. On the 9th of April 1986 while the Vigilant was engaged in interrogating vessels fishing for Blue Whiting in the area 061282 about 45 miles NW of St. Kilda.

I was on the bridge supervising the manoeuvring and interrogation and, having seen that the Vigilant was set on a course to pass about 3 cables [3 tenths of a mile] astern of the next target vessel, had gone to the chart table to check a licence list, leaving the Officer of the Watch to keep lookout. As I returned from the chart table a call was heard on VHF in which the word 'net' was discernible. The OOW and I immediately looked for a net and simultaneously saw a cod end which had broken the surface about 200 to 300 yards on the starboard bow. The OOW immediately began to alter course to starboard, but as I could see there would be insufficient room for this I instantly stopped and de-clutched both engines. The Vigilant carried her way harmlessly over the back-straps of the net, turning slowly to starboard as she drew clear. As this was happening I called up the Norwegian whose name was Vestraal M.9.VN, and told him my engines were de-clutched. He replied that he thought the Vigilant was clear. This was confirmed on board as the cod end had not altered position throughout and was therefore not being dragged. As soon as the Vigilant carried well clear I engaged the port engine and very slowly built up revs and pitch, until when about a mile clear of the cod end I engaged the starboard engine. Both engines and stabilising fins worked perfectly, as did all bridge equipment. I then had the Officer of the Watch contact Vestraal to carry out routine fishrep (fisheries report) during which the Norwegian indicated that he thought all was well. The Vigilant remained in the area for some time and there was no more from the Norwegian.

In commenting on this incident, I am bound to say that I am certain that both the OOW and the lookout were keeping a sharp lookout and were alert to the situation. Moreover, in my judgement the Vestraal's net surfaced at an exceptionally large distance from the stern of the vessel and appeared suddenly. In addition to this its presence was not easily discernible due to the fact that the cod end did not appear to contain much fish and that there was a rough sea generated by Northeasterly wind force 6.

Yours etc.

If we had caught that trawler's net, the damage could have been catastrophic. Net destroyed, wires tangled in propellers, propeller blades mangled, engines damaged by an enforced stop, probably a tow required for the *Vigilant* and I would probably never be trusted with command again. That was a moment of truly ardent prayer, and I was not afraid to voice that prayer on the bridge.

I was happy on the *Vigilant*. My Captain, as I said, was very knowledgeable, professional and competent and an excellent man to learn from. I studied the way he did his job and took on board many of his ways. His great secret was being interested in the fishing boats. It sounds simple, but in fact without that interest the job could be crushingly boring. This was the case with quite a few individuals and they must have had a hard time of it, not possessing this abiding interest which made every appearance of a mast over the horizon a reason for anticipation and guesswork until the vessel was identified. It was like a game, based on our experience and ability to remember the design and build of the ships we saw. The more we got to know the vessels and their owners and skippers, the more complex the 'game' became; so that in time we would remember a host of facts about different vessels. Bear in mind, most of the time the weather is very poor in the North Atlantic and our job was to cover our area, patrolling and investigating at a moderate speed. Without this approach to the job it would have been very grim, for the days were more often than not, a thousand shades of grey, accompanied by the interminable restlessness of the great ocean.

As we approached each fishing vessel our next question was 'Can we get on board?' For this reason, we were always studying the condition of the sea and the movement of the weather systems. Of course, there could be long periods when the weather made boarding out of the question, but each encounter was evaluated with a view to inspecting the boat, bearing in mind not only the condition of the sea and swell and the motion of our own ship, but also the conditions alongside the fishing boat for the boarding party. Each boarding was a risk assessment in itself, and we did it all the time without having recourse to bits of paper to guide us how to think. I think the paperwork nowadays associated with doing potentially hazardous work like boarding ships at sea is laughable. If you cannot make these decisions you should not be doing the job. Take up market gardening or something!

I see from my collection of reports submitted to the Procurator Fiscal that on 12 September 1986 we were patrolling about forty miles south west of Barra Head when we came upon two Danish Industrial trawlers fishing for

Norway Pout. I have already mentioned this species which is fished mostly by the Danes in our waters. They are members of the gadoid family like cod; the Danes catch them with very fine meshed nets, and of course anything which is also swimming in the shoal will be caught, including marketable fish like juvenile cod and haddock, and herring. Norway Pout is very oily and it is processed into feed for pigs in Denmark. That is why you sometimes get a faint taste of fish from Danish bacon. It is an advantage for the processor to have an amount of herring in the catch as this increases the oil yield. Norway Pout occurs quite low down in the food chain and I was never very keen on it being caught industrially. I always reckoned if one hit the food chain at that level then it would have a knock on effect much further up, but I am not a scientist. The other thing about Pout is that it stinks.

So I and the Second Officer, who was new to the Service at the time, repaired on board the Danish trawler *Morthorst* at quarter past eight in the morning. We went through the usual paperwork then inspected the catch. It did not take long to realise that we would have to sample the catch, and sure enough he had a very large percentage of herring on board. He was allowed five percent but he had something like twenty five percent, not to mention the good stuff like cod and haddock, which he had separated into a freezer! So I left the Second Officer to stand guard on him then, having picked up the Senior Second Officer who was also quite new to the Service, and boarded the *Sonja Gronberg* at half past eleven. His catch was not quite so bad, but still bad enough to be reported. It took us till about two o'clock in the afternoon to finish our investigations, on conclusion of which we left a seaman on board as guard and all three ships set off for Stornoway, where we arrived at five in the morning. When we got there I detained both vessels, re-sampled the catches and cautioned the skippers, in the afternoon of 13 September 1986. We had been at it all that time, escorting our captures, standing watches, writing statements, checking the law, preparing paperwork and so on. We grabbed sleep when and if we could, and I loved it. We had made another 'double' capture and were beginning to make a name for ourselves. I see from my signature at the bottom of my statements that I was feeling both confident and competent.

On 11 November 1986 Esther Anne was born. To say she was not planned is an understatement, and I well remember the sense of shock when Patsy told me she was expecting another baby. However let me say it took precisely ten seconds for us to recover and prepare mentally for this new wee one, and as I write this I realise with a new intensity what it meant for Patsy. Esther brought with her a huge capacity for love, not only for us her family, but also for all creatures, and this manifests itself now in her ability understand and heal animals. In fact I sometimes think she likes animals more than humans.

Now we come to a juncture in my life where I felt a strong compulsion to give my life more completely to the service of God. I felt He had given me great gifts including an ability to talk about my faith, to study and understand it, and a voice to declare that belief. And yet at the same time I was married to woman whom I loved with my whole heart and with whom we had brought eight surviving children into the world, with all the attendant responsibilities which went with that status. To be frank, at this time my mind was in turmoil. This compulsion to go into the ministry full-time was very strong, and I was constantly asking God what I should do.

There came a day when I was coming home from Leith. *The Vigilant* may have been in dry-dock, for we were not normally on that side of the country. As I approached the concourse at Waverley station I suddenly became very aware of the immanent power of God focussing on me like an enveloping beam of His attention. I was saying to Him 'What does this mean Lord? What am I to do?' It was simultaneously distressing and exciting. I became aware that I had a choice of two trains to take me home to Hamilton and I prayed 'Which one? I know You are going to show me something, so which train?' In the end I chose the slower train. I climbed aboard and sat down. As I looked down the packed train I silently asked 'What now?', and there at the end of a packed carriage saw a face I had not seen since I left secondary school. It was my old Religious Education teacher, Harry Melrose. I was astonished and exhilarated. That God should arrange such a coincidence as this was extraordinary.

I debated with God: 'I realise that this is an important moment, and that I am to speak to Mr. Melrose, but I cannot speak to him in a train carriage packed with people. If I am to speak with him, Lord, I will know that I am doing the right thing if the carriage empties.' Before we had gone three stops, only Mr. Melrose and I remained in the carriage! I made my way forward and stood over him. 'Good afternoon, am I right in thinking it is Mr. Melrose?' He looked up slightly bemused and said that he was. I said 'You won't remember me, sir, but you taught me in Hyndland Secondary back in the Sixties'. He said he did not but then he guessed I did not have a beard then. We laughed. I said 'You once had occasion to clip me round the ear because you thought I was asleep [his brow furrowed], but that is not why I want to speak with you. Far from it.'

Actually what had happened all those years ago was that Mr. Melrose was teaching us comparative theology, comparing Judaism, Islam and Christianity, and I was very interested. I had put my head on my desk just enjoying the thoughts which his talk inspired and the next thing I knew... THWACK! Across the head, and 'Don't fall asleep in my class!' delivered with huge indignation, I may say. I was up on my feet like a shot and the old haze came over me. Old Duncan had been right enough, I suppose. I looked down on Mr. Melrose for I was a bit taller and said 'Don't you dare hit me. I am the only one listening to your talk!' I remember looking round the class through a red mist and thinking 'I wonder what the girls think of this?' He dissembled a bit and left me with 'Sit up straight in future' in a more measured tone.

Anyway I said 'This is going to sound a bit strange but I believe God intends to speak through you to me, for my mind is most disturbed and I need a solution.'

I know this sounds nuts, he probably thought so, but he asked me to describe what had been my experience thus far and I related it to him. He did not give me an opinion there and then on the train but invited me to his office in Hamilton College where he was advisor for religious studies.

I attended at the due time and date and basically he said, and I took this as advice from God, that if I was to make anything out of a ministry I would have to have the full backing of my wife. I see now that these were wise words, and at the time it was comforting after a fashion but I would need further proof whether or not God wanted me to embark on a new career. I said as much to the Lord. 'If You want me to stay at sea, Lord, I am happy to do so, as long as I know that is Your will. I need a sign so that I can be sure.'

CHAPTER TWENTY-SIX
I BECOME A SEA CAPTAIN

It so happened, that very soon after this one of the senior Captains retired and a post became vacant. I was one of about six Senior First Officers who were invited to the promotion board. I think they were all senior to me and I thought I was invited as window dressing. When I sat before the board I felt inspired and ideas flooded into my head. I had clear views about everything they asked me and felt that I had a real contribution to make as a Commander. That is what we were called in the Service officially: Commander, Marine. I went home thinking 'That was that' and related the interview to Patsy. We were reconciled to not hearing any more about it, when either that same night, or the next morning, the Marine Superintendent phoned me and greeted me as Captain Beveridge! I was thunderstruck, overjoyed and utterly thankful. I thanked the Superintendent who said *'remember to keep plenty of water under the keel'* and, in a state of blissful shock, I told Patsy.

I then thanked Almighty God from the depths of my heart not only for this promotion but more importantly for this sign that I was living in His will.

In fact the large rise in salary did not come a moment too soon for things were very tight at that time, the interest rate on the mortgage being very high at around thirteen and a half percent.

So I was now a Sea Captain. I was thirty eight years of age, I had a wife whom I loved deeply, eight wonderful surviving children. We had a large house which was expensive in every department and needed a lot of work to be done to it but it was ours and we were a family. We had health and strength and faith in Almighty God. Psalm 127 has always been a favourite of mine; here are some extracts:

Except the Lord build the house they labour in vain that build it.

Lo, children are an heritage of the LORD: and the fruit of the womb is his reward.

As arrows are in the hand of a mighty man; so are children of the youth.

Happy is the man that hath his quiver full of them: they shall not be ashamed, but they shall speak with the enemies in the gate.

That is how I felt and feel about my relationship to God. He has been in all respects faithful to His covenant with a poor sinful man like me; I cannot say I have always been faithful to my dear heavenly Father. I must have grieved Him many, many times.

It was February 1987. I was now to join the old *Norna* built in 1959 and launched by William Denny and Brothers Limited of Dumbarton, the same stable as the *Cutty Sark*. She was one hundred and ninety five feet long, twenty eight feet in the beam, and nine feet moulded depth. In other words, she long and thin with very little draught. This made her a poor sea boat for the deep water but she was fine for coastal work, which is what she was used for. She was beautifully appointed in her accommodation, with bird's eye maple wood panelling, lovely old moquette-covered Westminster chairs in the lounge and all the original fittings appropriate to the time of her build, for she had been lovingly maintained. She also doubled as a Ministerial Yacht for the Minister of Agriculture and Fisheries to go on tours of the Hebrides whenever he deemed it appropriate. She was like a time capsule. I liked her very much of course, because she was my first command, but I never felt possessive about her, I think because she had had so many masters over the years. A bit like claiming ownership of a mountain, or a bit of the sea. As I started writing this part, I thought there was little to tell about the old *Norna* but as always the memories and feelings come flooding back.

I remember taking her away from Edinburgh Dock in Leith for the first time. She had twin screws but only one rudder, and her propellers were quite close together, so much of the advantage of being able to work the screws independently was lost. Also, her rudder was too small for such a long vessel, so she was unwilling to turn in a restricted space. Moreover her 'DEAD SLOW' was a misnomer. When that movement was rung on the telegraph she set off like a greyhound so one had to be ready immediately to ring 'STOP'. One great advantage of such a long narrow boat, however, was that once she was set going in a straight line she was virtually unaffected by leeway and stuck to her course like glue. All of these things I learned on taking her away from the quayside. She had a very heavy rubbing belt along her sides at the water line, made of American Rock Elm. It was amazing stuff, better than steel or iron, and it protected her riveted hull, which had very thick plating, wonderfully.

So my first weeks in command were spent getting to know the ship and finding my feet as a Captain. I had to experiment with her to find out what she could do and this included launching the boarding boat at sea. The arrangements were primitive but I had a good Bosun from Lewis, who had been on her a long time, and under his direction the men were able to cope fine. Our job initially was to patrol the East Coast from Marshall Meadows on the border with England to the Pentland Firth, so we had plenty of scope, and it was an excellent way to cut my Master's teeth. I always remember my old mentor saying to me that the Superintendent was breaking me in easily. Which I suppose he was.

The *Norna* had a great feature, which was exclusive to the Captain and Chief Engineer. She had a bath! Now, except in big ships, I had never sailed on a ship with bath, which was for the use of patients in the Hospital. This was something else. I can remember my first experience of this at anchor one night in Musselburgh Roads outside Leith. The *Norna* was rolling gently to the swell which was managing to creep up the Forth; otherwise it was calm and a dense fog hung over the ship. We had been groping about all day in this fog and I was weary so I decided to put the hook down, and hope for a better day on the morrow. I can still remember sinking into that deep, warm water and feeling the tension of the day soak out of me. What I was unprepared for was the effect the roll of the ship would have on the bath. The *Norna* went one way and the bath water went the other! I was soon caught in a bewildering mini maelstrom of cross swells which took some time to cope with, and indeed it was only when I let some water out and settled my backside on the bottom of the bath like a grounded iceberg that I was able to regain some sense of tranquillity and poise, not that anyone other than I was aware of it.

We did not have many incidents on the old *Norna* but I notice that in late August we were sent round to the West Coast to deal with a situation of conflict existing between trawler-men and static gear fishermen in the Gairloch Area. Going round to the West Coast was always interesting, particularly in my own command, and this time I had the added interest of having my eldest son David on board. I remember he was bemused and delighted when he received his ration of crisps, three two litre bottles of lemonade and a dozen Granny Smith apples from the Chief Steward.They were intended to last the entire patrol but despite my warnings to be controlled in their consumption, our Davy got stuck in. Unfortunately for him we were soon up at the Pentland Firth where the tides are colossal and no matter how calm the weather one always meets swell at some point or another. Of course by the time we reached the Cape the apples, crisps and lemonade refused to remain where he had stowed them and were in due course delivered up as an offering to Neptune, which I do not suppose the Greek deity would have relished, had he existed.

The conflict between mobile and static gear is a perennial problem, not only around the coast but also in the ocean. It always takes the same form and it will remain a source of trouble until either everyone uses the same type of equipment to catch fish or they cease to fish. On this patrol we went round to Gairloch to investigate and I have my report in front of me which I think is the first I sent in as a fully-fledged Commander. It is well enough written, if I say so myself, and exists as a flimsy carbon copy written on a typewriter, containing recommendations which were eventually put in train. However, men being what they are, I do not expect that gear problems will cease any time soon, and they are probably still threatening to knock lumps out of each other. My own belief is that the Minches should have been closed to all forms of mobile gear without exception, so that an inland sea, bounded by a line from Cape Wrath to the Butt of Lewis and from Barra Head to Skerryvore and Dubh Artach, could be created which would allow a fishery for small vessels to re-generate, thereby encouraging the capture of high quality fish for the markets in Europe. I know for a fact that at one time large fish of every species could be caught on baited lines in the waters I have described, because I was privileged to talk to old line fishermen who had fished at the turn of the century. The idea was floated in the thirties by the 'Sea League', of which Compton MacKenzie was a member, but it was politically impossible to enact. Perhaps now that there are almost no fish in the Minch they will manage to do something about it.

That is the only report remaining from my time on the old *Norna* and for the remainder of the patrol I tried to get to as many places as I could, for David's sake. So we went to Ullapool, Loch Eriboll, Scrabster, Kirkwall, Stromness, and eventually ended up putting him ashore at his grandparents' in Gardenstown, or Gamrie as we call it. I think he enjoyed it and regaled his friends with his salty tales for some years to come.

Hygiene is very important on a ship, for living in close proximity requires that all hands endeavour to be acceptably odour free as much as possible. One day I received a deputation from some of the crew that one of the motormen had failed miserably in this department and something had to be done. I had the offender up to my cabin and I can tell you that the men's complaint was well founded. Words desert me as I recall this interview for I have never come across such a foul smelling individual before or since. He was putrid and whilst not wishing to hurt the man I was duty bound to order him to have a shower and clean his clothes. I am surprised the men put up with it for so long. Apparently he had been a tail gunner in a bomber during the war and it had tipped his brain into eccentricity. I think his name was Magni, which inevitably on a Scots ship became Manky.

This was not the first time I had come across exotic tail gunners. We had one on the *Port Victor*, whom we dubbed 'The Bird-man' because he refused to sit on a seat unless he was in his cups. He 'perched' everywhere as if constantly in a state of preparedness to make a quick exit. I suppose sitting in the tail gun of a bomber will encourage that sort of behaviour. His name was Keith.

In the end his remedial measures were deemed inadequate and the men took him to the shower and arranged the necessary ablutions. I think he left the service shortly after that to find employment more suited to his personal habits.

Only one other incident comes to mind from my six months on the *Norna*, and that was in September 1987. The weather was very poor with a strong northwesterly gale blowing. We were anchored in Largo Bay I think, when the VHF burst into life with a MAYDAY call from Forth Coastguard regarding a Russian vessel which had dragged anchor in St. Andrew's Bay and gone aground on the south shore. Of course, I offered our services immediately although I was not sure what we could achieve for the *Norna* had very few of the pieces of equipment required for rescue or towage. However, they asked us to go round and stand by, which is what we did. It was a poor night and very uncomfortable, and I remember sleeping in the chartroom for a couple of hours while the Mate kept watch. In the morning the wind eased and they were able to get her off and that was that, but we were mentioned in the coastguard magazine for that quarter.

I had the privilege of being the last commander of the *Norna* before she was sold by the Department to Norwegian interests who would run bird-watching trips to Spitzbergen. A big welcoming party was arranged for her when she arrived in Leith and lots of people came down from the office. Previous incumbents had always made a big thing about how difficult the *Norna* was to turn, and she was, but I reckoned I had mastered her. So when she poked her head into the Edinburgh Dock I set about turning her in front of this big crowd and backing her down the dock. A ship should always be ready to sail. The manoeuvre went well and I was pleased with myself. I always hated 'taboos'. It is just the way I am built. The Superintendent asked though, 'Why did you turn her?' and all I could say was 'I felt like it'. I do not know if he was very happy about it; maybe he had something else in his mind.

That night we had a fabulous party organised by The Mate's wife, the Second Engineer's wife and the Third Engineer's wife, and if I have forgotten anyone I am sorry. It was really most enjoyable and the ladies did us proud. The entire crew was there and some previous skippers. I think the ladies baked a cake which looked like the *Norna* and we have photographs of it. We all look so young and some are no longer with us. That night as we were leaving I asked the Superintendent about the ship's barograph and he told me to put it in the back of my car as keepsake. I still have it and look after it with loving care. I also have one of her telescopes, which is also carefully protected. I have it in my mind to set up a museum of Fisheries someday, but not yet.

The next time I saw the *Norna* she was called *Eisprinzessin* and painted white overall, as I proceeded to join my new ship the *Jura*.

CHAPTER TWENTY-SEVEN
JURA (FOURTH TIME)
1987 – 1988

In a way my posting to the *Jura*, in early September 1987, saw the completing of a circle which began years before with a picture in a union newspaper. She had always been my favourite and now I would be her Captain. It had been a remarkable period in my life covering more than ten years and I was very aware that I owed everything to God. I have to give Him the glory.

My Senior First Officer (the Long John Baldry look alike) was an old friend with whom I had had many a laugh. My Junior First Officer and my Second Officer were both sound fellows and together were a good team, and all individually, had strengths which I was happy to draw on.

On Saturday 10 October 1987 during the Mate's watch, we came upon a Faroese coaster called the *Atlantic Cloud*, lying four miles west of Dubh Sgeir near Loch Bracadale in Skye. She was as quiet as the grave with no sign of life, lying, rolling easily in the low swell which was running up the Sea of the Hebrides. We hailed the vessel for quite some time and were becoming concerned when a voice replied and explained they had suffered a minor engine failure, but thought they could repair it. I said that was fine and was considering leaving him to his lawful occasions when he came on again and asked for assistance. The Mate and I looked at each other with pound note signs beginning to swim unbidden before our eyes. I asked our Chief Engineer to have a look and he went over with the Third Engineer. The Chief reported back that the main engine water cooling pump had broken and they had no spares but that he would try to fix it. In the meantime I told the Mate to start getting ready for a tow just in case, for there was a south-easterly gale forecast which could have driven the coaster onto the coast of Skye. I always assumed the worst with incidents like this and reckoned delay in remedying a situation was a recipe for disaster. This he did with a will, for I had shown him the towing arrangements which the Navy had made up when they 'borrowed' our ship back in the Seventies, and he was like a dog with two tails. He was a man after my own heart, as far as salvage was concerned, and it said a lot for him to be so supportive of me for he had been one of the men I had jumped over. If he held any resentment he never showed it. By eight o'clock in the evening The Mate was all ready for towing when the Chief appeared like McPhail in Para Handy clutching something wrapped up in an oily rag. Away he went again in the searider. I suppose it must have been twenty minutes later that a puff of smoke appeared at the funnel of the *Atlantic Cloud* and our dreams of salvage money evaporated with the smoke. The Chief had been able to fabricate a part and the skipper of the coaster, when he came on VHF to thank us, said that the pump had never run so well. That's what happens when you have talented engineers. We escorted them till they got through the Sound of Shiant at one in the morning, then resumed our normal patrol.

Five days later the Chief was in action again when we were asked to give assistance to the Scottish seine netter *Courageous INS.146*. I do not have any more details for the report is long gone and only the letter of thanks from the Superintendent remains.

It was December 1987 and I remember saying to Patsy as I was preparing to leave again 'We'll probably get blown inside out again', and she replied. 'No, you'll probably have glassy calms'. I do not know how she knew, but she was right. I do not remember another December like it, and I was so relaxed that I even did a couple of small watercolours, one of which I still have. As I look at it, it exactly coveys the late afternoon anticyclonic light off the coast of Lewis. The second of December saw us thirty miles southwest of Skerryvore alongside the Lowestoft registered fishing vessel the *Pescafish 1* which was as British as a plate of paella. The Mate discovered they had a British skipper on board but no British Engineers. They had also caught and retained 27 boxes of plaice, which at that time was not to be retained by UK vessels; in addition to this they had falsified the EEC logbook. All in all it was a good case. In later years we would have taken him straight to Stornoway but at this time he was treated as a *bona fide* British vessel. Of course he was a Flag of Convenience Spaniard but we had not yet realised the difficulty of bringing these so-called Anglo-Spaniards to court once they disappeared over the horizon. I think he was fined in the end but it took a long time.

The next day saw us out on the Rockall Bank boarding the Anglo-Spaniard *Juan Mari*, registered in Milford Haven. Again his engineers did not possess British Certificates of Competency and so we reported him to HQ for forwarding to the Procurator Fiscal. I do not know if that case came to court but that was normal at that time for we seldom heard if a case was successful if it was heard in an English court. I recall the eyebrows being raised on other ships because the *Jura* was out on the Rockall Bank in December but I knew what I was doing and years of poring over weather faxes was definitely paying off, for without relying too heavily on the charts, I found it quite easy to identify the trends in the weather.

I regret that I was not to enjoy the *Jura* for long because early in1988 it was decided, under a rationalisation plan instigated by the Thatcher government, that the Department come under scrutiny with a view to the privatisation of the entire Fishery Protection fleet. It was a very unsettling time, and they sent up a young financial genius (who must remain nameless) whose job was to make recommendations about whether or not we should be allowed to continue. In the end, after a great deal of questioning and delving into statistics and so on, and visiting our ships in port, he came out with three possible 'scenarios'. He made an analysis of each possibility then came down in favour of a plan which involved selling the *Jura* as part of his cost-cutting exercise. We Commanders were all invited to respond to this proposal and I for one gave a clause by clause analysis of the flaws in his thinking. I have the paper to this day and I am glad I wrote it. I was right and he was wrong. In this cost-cutting exercise, the *Jura* was expected to raise one million pounds. In the end she was bought by Marr Trawlers for about three hundred thousand.

At the beginning of 1988 I was ordered to take her to Edinburgh Dock where she was to be laid up. In the end only the Chief Engineer, a Steward and I remained on board until she was sold. I had the job of handing her over to a skipper from Marr Trawlers, who oddly enough had been in Cunard. He did not have long to become acquainted with her because they sailed next day, on 8 April 1988. I took her out to the locks for him and the *Jura* did not behave well. I do not think she wanted to leave and I certainly did not want her to go. She was eventually re-named the *Crisilla* then the *N'madi*, while she worked out of some port in West Africa. She was broken up in Portugal in 2001, as fine and brave a little ship as ever sailed. She was the first of the Island Class followed by the *Westra*, which is still doing sterling service in the Southern Ocean as the *Steve Irwin*. The Navy went on to build seven Island Class Patrol Vessels after they borrowed her so she certainly proved herself. And I was getting a name as the guy who got rid of ships.

For the next few months I had a roving commission, going from one ship to another in temporary command. This has much to commend it because one cannot become involved in the domestic problems of the ship. I sailed on the *Sulisker* (30/04/1988 to 12/05/1988), the *Scotia* (7/06/1988 to 28/06/1988), the *Norna* (new ship) 12/07/1988 to 27/07/1988) and the *Vigilant* (31/08/1988 to 21/09/1988).All were enjoyable in their own way but they were not 'my ship'. I can remember only two things from this period. Firstly that I had the pleasure of making the new *Norna*'s first foreign detection down in the Irish Grey Zone; as I recall it was a Danish industrial trawler, which was very fortuitous for I had failed to recognise a potential case with a Spanish trawler only hours before. By the time we returned to apprehend the Spaniard he had fled across the boundary.

Secondly I designed the davit, which I believe, would eventually become known as the Caley davit. This davit was created in my mind after being so frustrated with the new *Norna*'s boarding arrangements. It required three seamen to safely launch the boarding boat, which was an Arctic RIB like an inshore lifeboat. It was a big boat and in a swell it could be dangerous swinging at the end of the HIAB crane's wire. (The HIAB is a hydraulically powered crane with articulated arms) I experimented with the design of a davit in a 'C' form controlled by a massive hydraulic piston or ram-jack, which was retracted when in the stowed position. I cut out cardboard experimental forms and finally hit on a shape which would fit the bill. I then worked out the loadings and moments of the set up and gave them to my brother in law William Lawson who at the time worked for Anderson Strathclyde Engineering, builders of ram- jacks amongst other things. I asked him to have their engineers check out my maths and virtually forgot about it. I remember showing my designs to the Superintendent and the regular master of the *Norna* who started shaking their heads before I had finished my presentation to them. They did not have counter arguments; it was simply resistance to change. I just folded up my plans and calculations and told them that they had no right to discard my idea without even having the grace to hear about it fully.

Shortly after this the old Superintendent retired and I have yet to tell you about that.

Sometime went by and Patsy reminded me about my drawings in Willy's firm. In the meantime a merger would take place between Willy's firm and a firm owned by a certain Bob MacCallum. That consortium would become

Caley Anderson, with a play of words on the CAL of Bob's name. After the old Super retired, my old nationalistic Captain became Marine Superintendent and I remember the day he proudly displayed to me the notional drawings, which he had been shown by this firm Caley Anderson, for a davit for deploying RIB boats at sea. What he failed to mention was that I had been waxing lyrical about this idea for a very long time before Caley Anderson came out with a market tester for the idea. On the front cover of the handout, was an artist's impression of what I can only describe as my davit! Nothing was more certain to me, for the drawing showed the winch which would heave up the wire, lifting the boat on and off the ship in the position I had placed it. (This would later prove impractical and it would not reside there, but no one knew that yet because the davit had not been built). The basic geometry was all the same although there was an imaginary docking head at the top of the davit which was not part of my design. I asked Willy to get my plans back, and described the notional plans which Caley Anderson had come up with. I could see the penny drop as Willy, postulating that was why my plans had disappeared for so long, went on to explain the comings and goings of the merger. In fact I did not and do not feel bitter about this use of my idea, if that is what happened

I did not and do not possess the business acumen to develop a project like this and I think the idea gave Caley Anderson a lead in the market. I was just glad that the amazing Providence of God had given me an idea which better engineers than I could exploit, and actually bring into reality. I was invited to be present at the testing of the first ever Caley davit, which was later installed on my ship the *Vigilant,* and I can tell you there was a lump in my throat when I saw it put through its paces. They had built a mock-up of a ship's deck in an old engineering shed down on Clydeside, I forget where. It was very ingenious because they could alter the angle of the deck and do drop tests with the davit in different attitudes. It was so typically British. A brilliant idea in a dirty old shed on the banks of the Clyde.

That davit, or rather its offspring is now a standard fit all over the world in many different navies and organisations, but it is my firm belief that it started on a piece of chart paper, which resides to this day in my loft, on the *Norna.*

I would later show many people the Caley Davit installed on the *Vigilant,* from the Indian Navy to the German Sea Fisheries Laboratory, and in the fullness of time Caley gave me a plaque for *'help and good guidance with 'World's first Caley Davit'*. The plaque is there to this day along with photographs of some of the folk I demonstrated it to. It took a good while and quite a few frights to perfect it, but we did and I was able to deploy my boat with infinitely greater safety and that was all I wanted.

Poor Bob MacCallum did not live long after that, I'm sorry to say, for he was a really nice chap.

It was not until 28 November 1988 that I was sent to take over the *Westra*. As I recall, this was because there was a general re-shuffle of personnel following promotions. Maybe I am not getting that quite correct. I cannot remember.

I remember, sometime after taking command of the *Westra*, I had a terrific falling out with the old Superintendent because I brought the *Westra* in early. I had phoned him up when I saw a storm coming and asked to come in the night before we were due. Of course the BBC weather man was still maintaining that it would just be a regular gale, and the Super said 'I do not want that ship alongside early!' I knew he was making a point because some of the skippers had been making a habit of coming in early for convenience. In fact coming in early actually made sense, but of course the number crunchers picked up on it and started whining. Oh how I wished I could get some of these guys out into a gale for a few days. Anyway I had my orders and actually looked for an anchorage to weather this lot when it came.

But as I watched it develop I knew the right thing to do was get alongside. So that is what I did. That night it was blowing fifty knots westerly at the locks and she was awkward to handle, but manageable. When we got into the Edinburgh Dock I decided to turn her for I knew she would be easier to control. I remember the First Officer thinking I had gone crazy but I knew what I was doing. And so we came alongside ready to go into dry-dock the next day on schedule. In fact we could not do so because of the strength of the wind which had closed the port. I can still see the waves lashing the lock breakwater at the Western Harbour. The old Superintendent came down for his regular visit in the morning and when I told him I had come in the night before he erupted.' I ordered you to stay out and you disobeyed me!' He was raging. I replied as quietly as I could after he had vented his anger and said 'When you promoted me to Master you gave me a command to do everything in my power to preserve this ship and her crew. I believe I have and am discharging that duty. You cannot run a ship from a desk. This ship was programmed to go into dock today. If she had not been here we would have been liable for dry-dock costs. As it is, the Dry Dock Company must accept the cost of any delay. You only have to look at the Western Harbour to see we are experiencing hurricane force winds;

in these circumstances I believe my actions were reasonable and given the same circumstances I would make the same decision. If I have offended you and caused you distress I am profoundly sorry; it was not my intention nor do I take your orders lightly.' With that the incident was over as far as I was concerned although he did say quietly, later, that that was as close as I would ever get to being sacked. I still say I was right.

THE OLD SUPERINTENDENT RETIRES

I had been doing a large painting around this time of the *Westra* out on the Rockall Bank in poor weather, approaching a couple of Spanish trawlers. It turned out very well and my friend Rob Anderson, a fine artist himself, gave it the stamp of approval and said 'It's the sort of thing you would give someone on their retirement'. I pondered this for a while, then, because the words kept going round in my head, decided to present it to the Superintendent when he retired. He was not a man to make many friends with his subordinates; he could be very hard and stubborn, but I reckoned I owed him a lot. So on the day of his retirement celebration I took my painting over to Edinburgh and set it up in the room arranged for the soirée. It was a big painting with a beautiful swept guilt frame. Thanks to Patsy I have a photograph of it. I covered it with a cloth and waited for the arrival of his guests. The entire office staff turned out to see him off but only I and one other were there from the fleet. I was very disappointed in my colleagues. When I revealed the painting I could see he was delighted, as was his wife, and he later wrote to me thanking me and informing me it was hung somewhere in his home. The poor man died not long after his retirement and I seem to remember he had a better turn out for his funeral. The painting is probably in a skip now somewhere.

EEC INSPECTORS

We did not catch many offenders on the *Westra* for quite some time, with the exception of the detection of a big Hull trawler the *Kirkella* which was reported for a manning contravention, on the first voyage I took her as Master. That detection was Saturday 22 October 1988. We had sailed from Leith on 19 October with two EEC inspectors on board, who were to observe how we did the job. The Department was being criticised at the time for failing to pursue the illegal catching of mackerel rigorously enough, and the EEC wanted to see for itself. We sailed in a gale of South-east wind and wallowed our way to the Shetlands to try to pick up the trail of the big pelagic trawlers. We found them but the weather was boisterous and precluded launching the boat although on 21 and 22 October, we did manage to get on board a few vessels in the lee of the land. The fleet was a mixture of nationalities, including the Dutch. I employed every trick in the book to try to get close to these vessels, including running with trawling lights up, and blacking out the ship. I was quite successful sometimes, and on a couple of occasions had a big trawler fall in astern of the *Westra* at night to see if they could share in what she was catching! You only get away with that once or twice. I even had my officers away at ten o'clock at night to board our old sparring partners the *Taits*, sister ship to the *Chris Andra* which I told you about before. My officers and the inspectors could not find anything to report. All this clandestine activity and night work was out of the ordinary but we had to show that we were being energetic over the issue of the misdeclaring of species and amounts caught.

The Department was very concerned about the bad impression the EEC were forming about us, and wanted to see all the Commanders who were at sea so I arranged to rendezvous with the C.O. of the new *Norna* off Brough Head on the west side of the Orkneys, took him on board, and went down through the Westray Firth to go alongside at Kirkwall. Our two inspectors transferred to the *Norna*, with whose Captain I flew down to Edinburgh next day for a meeting with our bosses about the whole question of policing this fishery. I left my First Officer in charge with instructions to get off the berth if the wind came away from the north, which I knew it would. We flew down on the Titan twin engined spotter plan we operated. Our bosses were at pains to tell us how important it was to fend off criticism and then said that we were doing a fine job. So I went home for the night and caught the Titan next day at Edinburgh airport, to return to the *Westra*.

EMERGENCY LANDING

In a small aircraft like the Titan, one is very close to the nerve centre of things, being seated immediately behind the pilots. I could not help noticing the co-pilot frequently tapping the oil pressure gauge for the port engine and drawing the pilot's attention to it. Much can be conveyed in a look and it did not take an expert in body language to realise that they were concerned about it. We had just crossed the south shore of the Moray Firth with a very strong northerly wind blowing, when the pilot announced we would have to make an emergency landing at RAF Lossiemouth. I do not remember being all that concerned about it, though I must have been because I knew that Titans could not run indefinitely on one engine. Anyway, we landed safely with the foam truck running alongside us as we touched down. We were eventually picked up by our Fokker F27 around two in the afternoon and taken to Kirkwall. When I got down to the pier, the wind was howling from the north north west and the *Westra* was banging the quay heavily at times, and had already bent a couple of plates on her starboard quarter. I was very angry with the Mate but refrained from making a scene. I got her off the berth as soon as I could and went to anchor in the lee of Shapinsay. I was disappointed that my instructions had not been followed but I suppose I had to learn about how to deal with that as well. Funnily enough when the C.O. of the *Norna* had transferred to the *Westra* on our way to Edinburgh, he had said to me 'You have a right bunch of Jobs Comforters here'. I was not sure what he meant but I was beginning to catch his drift. As the months went on I would understand more and more. The *Westra* patrolled mostly on the East Coast to the Orkneys and Shetlands, and when I took her over we were seldom allowed to go beyond the twelve mile limit. The reason for this was that the Royal Navy were hired by our Department to patrol the North Sea for Fisheries, a task which could be done in tandem with their commitment to protect the oil interests. As time went on, the cost of this arrangement became prohibitive and our Department did not renew the contract. This left an opportunity for our East Coast vessels, and I was happy to exploit the new areas which became available to us. The problem was that opportunities for detection and capture were far fewer on the East Coast and North Sea generally, and I found this very frustrating. In addition to this the low level of keenness, which the Captain of the *Norna* had so quickly identified pervading my deck officers when he came aboard for only a few hours, became more obvious as time went on. Lack of commitment to the task is something which good leadership ought to be able to address but there is only so much one can achieve and I had the feeling that there were always forces 'putting the brakes' on any outbreak of enthusiasm I might be able to generate. This phenomenon showed me that you are only as good as the men and women who support you. You rely on every member of your team and if the hunter instinct is not there in the task of law enforcement, one cannot impart it or force it. I know that this was the case, because when my old Christian friend joined us on the *Westra* he would sometimes pass on what was being said behind my back. I am sure he did not tell me everything. When I eventually had officers who possessed a similar commitment to the task as me, posted to my ship, the change was instant, radical and most enjoyable.

My recollection is that the end of the Eighties was a particularly windy period with incessant gales from all directions, and periods of calm were few and far between. The weather probably improved in summer, but it did not feel like that. Here is an extract from my diary from the 13 November 1988 to the end of the year:

Wednesday 30th November
Sailed Leith

Thursday 1st December
Continued northwards towards Fair Isle in very heavy easterly swell. 1822hrs, west of Foula – continued north. Exchanged information with VIGILANT. 2300Hrs reached 61 degrees North.
Wind SSE 7/8

Friday 2nd December
In vicinity of pelagic fleet. Various boardings in lee of Yell Sound. Entered Whale Firth. (To check vessels anchored there)
Wind SSE 7/8

Saturday 3rd December
In vicinity of pelagic fleet. Various boardings in the lee. Instructed GENESIS N 338 to proceed to Ronas Voe.[This would have been for further investigation].
Wind SE 9

Sunday 4th December

Wind E by S 9/10 dodging with VIGILANT off Blue Mull Sound. Stood through Blue Mull Sound to anchor in Basta Voe at 1430hrs.
Wind E by N 5. [The wind had fallen lighter as it backed northerly].

Monday 5th December
Hove up at 0800hrs and investigated Balta Sound then patrolled north and east of Muckle Flugga. Returned at night to dodge south of Fetlar.
Wind NW 8

Tuesday 6th December
Wind N by W 8/9. Various inspections in the lee then out with the fleet. Remained with the pelagic fleet.
Wind SW 5/6

Wednesday 7th December
Stayed variously with fleet. Fleet ran for shelter at 2000hrs.
Wind SW 8

Thursday 8th December
Dodged north of Out Skerries till daylight, then did some boardings alongside at Balta Sound. Ran down the coast to dodge south of Bressay.
Wind WSW 8/9 veering WNW 9.

Friday 9th December
Berthed in Lerwick in light westerly airs at 10000hrs. Chief Engineer discharged, Replacement Chief joins.

Saturday 10th December
Alongside in Lerwick

Sunday 11th December
Stormbound at Lerwick.
Wind NW 10. [The pelagic fleet remained tied up. I went to church with James West and his son. They owned the Crystal Sea].

<u>Monday 12th December</u>
Sailed at 0630hrs and followed fleet to grounds about 60 miles west of Shetland. Very heavy swell wind NW 6/7.Unable to close vessels due weather.
Weather deteriorating.

<u>Tuesday13th December</u>
0130hrs Wind westerly 9 gusting 10 – fleet disperses – run for Orkneys.
Mail pick-up at Kirkwall 0930hrs – 10 30hrs.Dodged in lee of Orkneys. Patrolled slowly south to Clythe Ness.

<u>Wednesday 14th December</u>
2 boardings off Clythe Ness – Caithness.
2 boardings off Buckie (I infringement – LUNARIA BCK65)
The only day without a gale at sea this trip.

<u>Thursday15th December</u>
Continued southwards and came to Leith in light south-westerly winds.

The Westra remained in Leith for normal turnaround finally sailing on Friday 23rd December, her sailing delayed due to manning shortage. I remember feeling under a strong compulsion to clear the bond before Christmas and so my diary reads:

<u>Friday23rd December</u>
Stood up coast wind freshening from SW.
1943hrs Fair Isle. 2200Hrs Bard abeam stood for Muckle Flugga.
Wind fell light in lee then freshened northwesterly to north of Fetlar.
Wind NW 9

<u>Saturday24thDecember</u>
0326hrs reached 61 degrees North.
Wind north westerly violent storm – stood for lee of Shetlands and continued southwards to Orkneys- coming to anchor in Inganess Bay at 2200hrs.
Wind NW 10/11 (over 80 knots).

<u>*Sunday 25th December Christmas Day 1988*</u>
0730hrs Hove up and stood through the String to Kirkwall – 0930hrs all secure.
A very fine and civilised meal was had by all, the Stewards excelling themselves.[I still have the actual menu for this meal prepared by the First Officer on his Sinclair ZX computer!]

I remember this was the occasion I discovered that the *Westra* was much easier to back onto a berth in a very strong offshore wind, and I put that fact in my pocket and used it many times in the years to come.

<u>*Monday 26th December*</u>
A very pleasant quiet day. Walked to disused airfield with the Chief Engineer.

<u>*Tuesday 27th December*</u>
Sailing delayed due 50 knot winds. Came north to dodge in North Sound.
Wind SW 9

<u>*Wednesday 28th December*</u>
0400hrs stood north by west towards Hundred Fathom Line.
0930hrs stood north eastwards on Line - nothing seen.
1510hrs reached 61 degrees North and came down east side of Shetland. Wind had backed a couple of points round the land. Not much lee. Stood south, well to leeward of Shetland and Orkneys.
Wind SSW 8/9

I well remember that night as boisterous and uncomfortable as the *Westra* punched the gale.

<u>*Thursday 29th December*</u>
0600hrs Stood south-westwards for Moray Firth – wind and swell fell away to calms and light airs.
1335hrs – 1545hrs boarded CELTIC PRIDE CO.365 and BUDDING ROSE BF.156, then stood round Kinnairds Head for home. Wind freshened to Southerly 8.

<u>*Friday 30th December*</u>

Entered Leith at the top of the water with strong southwesterly wind.

The above is an extract from my personal diary which I happened to keep over this period. I was never a faithful diarist or journal keeper, but I do have a collection of some partially completed diaries to enable me to join up the pieces of this story.

RESCUE OF *PROTECT ME*

As we near the end of my recollections of the *Westra* I must relate one stormy night when we lay at anchor avoiding the worst of a southeast gale in the Deer Sound in Orkney. We had not long been anchored, after a typically arduous patrol in winter, when the voice of the operator at Wick Coastguard broke through the drone of the wind on the handrails round the wheelhouse top. (Handrails will drone at around thirty knots) 'MAYDAY MAYDAY - Fishing vessel *Protect Me* sinking in position eight miles southeast of Copinsay Light house, requires immediate assistance. Kirkwall lifeboat launching.'

Well, Copinsay is not far from the Deer Sound, so I reckoned this one had our name on it so I immediately responded that we were getting underway and proceeding at best speed. In no time the duty engineer had the engines on and the crew were turned to for anchor stations, and I think we cleared away from the anchorage in not much more than ten minutes, which is very fast even for a small ship. With the navigation lights on and the diesels throbbing out their tireless beat, the *Westra* sped through the inky darkness of the gale towards the stricken fishing boat. Eight miles is not far at sea so we were on scene in a little over half an hour. I spoke to the skipper and he told me he had severe flooding in the fish hold but had managed to get his engine going. If the *Westra* stood by he might be able to make his way into the lee. I was very pleased about this piece of news for it would have been very awkward to connect a tow in the prevailing conditions; we took up station close by him and wallowed our way towards the lee of Orkney. The Kirkwall lifeboat had come on the scene by this time and was offering the use of his portable pump, and I think I recall it being passed over to the fishing boat. Anyway, by this time I had come up with a plan; assuming the fishing boat could make it to Deer Sound, I would anchor the *Westra* in the usual anchorage and the *Protect Me* would lash up alongside. The lifeboat would also tie up to the *Protect Me* on the other side. That way, she could be supported by the buoyancy of both vessels if need be. We would then rig our high volume salvage pump and attempt to pump her out.

This is what we did, and my Christian friend the Second Engineer had the suction of the pump over the side as soon as the fishing boat tied up. Our pump was exactly what was needed and he kept it going at a great rate. One of the problems was that the suction end kept clogging with fish and debris, but eventually some bright spark came up with the idea of using an empty fish basket to keep the suction clear, and with that we were able to bring the level in the hold down to virtually empty, which revealed that a plate had fractured along a butt weld and was allowing the North Sea to pour in. During all this, I was on and off the *Protect Me* to talk to the skipper and give him the rest of my plan face to face. What I explained was that we would heave up in time to allow us to reach the String, which is the eastern entrance to Kirkwall Bay, just as the tide started to run westerly. The *Protect Me* would remain lashed alongside the *Westra* and this would allow us to keep pumping, permitting the *Westra* to provide the power and steering to negotiate the relatively narrow channel. The *Protect Me* would have her engines running, so that as we approached the berth at Kirkwall she would be let go and make her way, accompanied by the lifeboat, to the berth where she would be met by the Fire Brigade.

I think it was about four in the morning when we passed through the String, just as the tide turned westerly. The plan worked perfectly and I was very thankful to the Lord. Again, He had answered my prayers for strength and calm and ability and my friend told me later that the skipper was impressed by the air of calm I brought, for he had been very anxious. I wrote a report, which is long gone, about this rescue and managed to say nice things about everyone, although my 'Job's Comforters' did not make a big contribution, for they were not much use to me. I do not think it was their fault really, they just did not want their routines and peace disturbed. *Quieta non movere.* They would have been happier on a cargo liner. They were polar opposites to me but as I said, in the fullness of time the staff changed and my sense of bearing the load alone diminished. Eventually my quiet and stolid and reliable and very capable new Senior First Officer, arrived. My new Junior First Officer was smart, energetic, ambitious and great fun; and my Second Officer had driven a rescue boat during the Piper Alpha disaster. He was brave, keen, able, and fit for anything. My relief Second Officer was suave, dapper, hard-working and willing. Men like that made my task much more enjoyable, and three of them went on to serve as Commanders in their own right. They all served as my First Officers at one time or another and I had the great pleasure of recommending each of them for command. One of them left the Service and, last I heard, he was a crew member of the Broughty Ferry Lifeboat. Mind you, two of my 'Job's Comforters' went on to command their own ships and one became a very efficient Marine Superintendent in the fullness of time, so it just goes to show...something!

FOGBOUND!

I served on the *Westra* for about three years which I enjoyed very much and one never knew when a new adventure was round the corner. Simple things like being fog-bound in Leith could sometimes be a cause for increasing the adrenalin levels.

On one occasion the port was closed due to a fog which was as thick as I had seen since the great fog of 1953 which I told you about. All day nothing was moving and we had been due to sail around mid-day. As the day wore on I began to think about cancelling the sailing when just after tea time the control tower on the locks called to say the fog was thinning. I decided to have an attempt at sailing for it had also thinned a bit in the Edinburgh Dock where we were tied up. By now it was pitch dark. Within a short time our engines were running and the crew assembled at stations. All round the old dock and warehouses the fog swirled and flowed in amorphous banks, playing with the reality of substance and alternately dimming and intensifying the yellow light of the dock-side lamps. The boatmen duly arrived and slipped our moorings on my command. We lay on the cross berth at right angles to the narrow exit from the dock. I could just see the other side of the dock as I worked the *Westra* off the berth to turn her through ninety degrees and point her bow out of the cutting, leading to the Albert Dock. We had just entered the narrow cutting in the middle of the channel when the dense, enveloping miasma returned. We could hardly see the sides of the narrow cutting as we glided through, when I realised that we would have to negotiate a similar gateway to exit the dock! I called to the Mate to give me a course to steer from one cutting to the next and that is what we steered through that thick, blind blanket. Of course we had radar but the cuts were so narrow that they hardly showed on the screen and so the course was essential. As we transited the Albert Dock the distance to the cutting reduced and reduced; the quay wall coming closer and closer with no sign of the cutting until, barley yards from it and crawling at a snail's pace, we glimpsed the lights. I corrected our course with the bow thruster and engine and we slipped into the next cut. Thankfully, as we cleared the cut the fog lifted slightly again and we were able to grope our way to the locks. I was glad to get to sea that night and I cannot remember whether I took her to an anchor or not, but that was the first and last time I ever had to steer a course across a dock!

My Christian friend eventually took over as Chief Engineer, which pleased me immensely; not so much because we could resume prayer and Bible reading together (which we did from time to time, although less frequently than in the past) but just to know that there was a brother aboard who one knew would be praying for strength and wisdom to inform one's decisions and actions.

We did not often manage round to the West Coast on the *Westra* but when we did it was a cause for great rejoicing on my part, just to see that beautiful coast again and relish the never-ending change of scene as we made our way to the grounds west of the Hebrides. It was priceless.

SUNDAY OFF IN ST KILDA

I recall one day after we had been working to the west of St. Kilda, I decided to have a Sunday off and anchored in Village Bay. I remember I sent most of the men ashore to see the place, which many of them, having been stuck on the East Coast for so long, had never done. The Chief Engineer and I and one or two others kept ship. They loved it and it was most appreciated. Years afterwards when I was in command of the new *Jura*, the Chief Steward on the *Westra* at that time came to visit me and brought down a DVD of which he said mysteriously' I think you might enjoy this, Cap'n.' I played it, and there from around 1990 was me navigating the *Westra* through the Stacks at St. Kilda and again taking her away from Lerwick. It was a very kind thing to do and reminded me that I had been very happy there before I left her. I look very young.

My time was up on the *Westra* and I was now being sent to command the *Vigilant*. It was 1991, and she would be my ship for the next eight years and four months.

Before we go to the *Vigilant*, I see I was moved to put some thoughts down in poetic form on 13 August 1991. I think I was experiencing an arid patch in my religious life at the time, and the words were a response to that. I was also thinking about the forbearance of God and the humanity of the divine Christ.

POTTER
It's all inside,
It's there.
You put it there
Now it's coming to life.
You thought it,
You made it,
Now it's coming to life.
Why does it take so long?
It's Yours for the asking
Yet the mystery is You wait.
Wait for the clay to harden,
Wait for the glaze.
Wait for the furnace
Wait for the incandescent heat
Wait till the hardness comes
and the colours are fixed.
Till the bright colours sparkle
and sunshine - Your sunshine
Shines off me and spreads all around.

BOXES
I guess I never opened the parcels before,
And it came as quite a surprise
To find these boxes where light had not shone,
And what was mine to have, had lain unexplored

But I'm beginning to see that there's more to these than meets the eyes,

These parcels are gifts and they're my own.
You gave them to me and I should open them,
And I will -but I'm scared.

Scared to find the gift is loaded,
Loaded with some kind of pain,
I wish I could trust the instructions,
I wish I had the guts to believe You

Did you feel like that when You opened the box?
When You said 'Yes' to the awesome proposal,
Did You see the implications?
Did you study the form?
Did You ever doubt just a little?
When You cried out 'Why? 'I guess You really meant it.
I'm glad You had the guts to get involved.

DRY TIMES
In dry days when there is no life in me
When my soul is panting like a dog in summer sun
When lethargy clings to my heart like lichen
In the dry days the yearning is strong

In these days I know the problems, deep in deep places
I can see what's wrong in the half light,
I know all the answers — haven't I read them?
But the answers I'm beginning to forget,
And the dry days drag on and on.

I remember the sunshine times,
When the days were as full as ripe plums,
And juice of joy flowed freely
And my soul was up, always up
High and lifted. High soaring soul
Free as a bird. Skylark soul,

Reaching for my Lord. Singing with my all,
Winging soul, glinting in the beams of my Master's smile.
Where are the blue skies now?
This is a dry place. A place for old bones,
It needs wind and rain. It needs Spirit wind and Spirit rain.
It needs dew. It needs You.

In April 1991 the Department of Agriculture and Fisheries for Scotland became the Scottish Fishery Protection Agency.

CHAPTER TWENTY-NINE
VIGILANT
1991 TO 2000

PORT KING LO.75

In some ways my command experience up to now had been a preparation for being given command of the *Vigilant*. The barren years of patrolling the East Coast were about to fall away and I would be given the opportunity use the expertise I had gained through my experiences thus far. I now had a good grasp of the law and understood, at least in part, something of the business of being a ship-master. The *Vigilant* was a splendid ship, quite warlike in aspect, with dimensions not dissimilar to a large wartime corvette; for me the only detraction from a very satisfying look were her twin funnels which some wit referred to as 'biscuit tins'. I think it might have been the new Superintendent, who could turn a phrase with the best of them. They did look a bit like biscuit tins.

I joined her in Stornoway at the beginning of September 1991 and was immediately impressed with the officers I inherited from my old Campbeltown mentor, who was transferring to the new *Norna* on the retirement of the present incumbent. On this first patrol, my Senior First Officer was a man who hailed from the Wirral, an old shipmate and good, efficient officer. My Junior First Officer came from Stornoway, unknown to me but impressive in his keenness and knowledge of computers, and the Second Officer was a quiet older man to whom I instantly took a liking. Our orders on sailing were to proceed to the George Bligh Bank and patrol the area. I think we were sent out on a whim of the Operations Room Controller, because no one had been there for some time. I liked him, a fellow Christian and decent man.

I cannot remember if we sailed immediately or next morning, but by the morning of 5 September we were on the George Bligh and closing on a couple of targets. They turned out to be Anglo-Spaniards. I sent the Mate and Second Mate away in the boat and on the first vessel the *Robrisa FH.566*, they found everything in order. On the next, however, the *Port King LO.75*, things were not good. In the first place the Mate reported that she had no British certificates of competency on board and no fishing licence to fish at all! The entire crew were Spanish, and after some time we were informed that she had been arrested in Faroese waters the previous month. In addition, she was recording her catch wrongly and there were pages missing in the logbook. All in all it was a mess. There was considerable delay and prevarication on the part of HQ over this, and it was the Mate (who had his claws into this boat) who kept up the pressure to bring him in. I agreed with this entirely and was very comfortable with the situation for I trusted my First Officer, and I threw my weight behind arresting the vessel. At three o'clock in the afternoon we were instructed to bring him in. I was delighted that we were into some action so quickly. It took over twenty four hours to reach Stornoway, during which time we prepared our case documentation, writing statements and so on. At all times I had two men on the *Port King*.

We went to court soon after arrival and the Procurator presented our case. The result was that the owners of the *Port King* were fined seventy thousand pounds in total, and the boat detained until payment was made. She remained tied to the quay at Stornoway for quite a long time, but in the end the fine was paid. We heard shortly after she sailed that she had foundered approaching harbour in Spain and I think one can deduce that she was scuttled for the insurance. Maybe I am just being cynical. I was delighted with the result (as were the whole crew) and I think we all felt exhilarated, especially the deck officers, although everyone shares in the good feeling a capture gives. It was the biggest fine anyone had seen in a long time and the Operations Room Controller was the first to congratulate us. It was the best start I could have hoped for in my new command. What made it even better was that Operations Room had been requesting the presence of a ship out there for some time.

On the next two patrols we made two further detections of Scottish vessels, one on each patrol, and whilst providing grist for the mill they were much less satisfying than a foreign capture. This was partially because they were not taken straight to court, but also because they were our own people and most of their misdemeanours were of a less high profile nature. However, there were times when people could behave in unaccountable ways which can only be explained by the pressures created by anomalous regulations.

There is a fishing family called the Buchans who come from Peterhead. They are actually related to the family which owned the *Chris Andra*, of which you have heard. They are an extremely successful family and in so far as a family can be generalised, a very good living family. They were not given to piratical behaviour and indeed from what I know of them they led model lives, and yet I note in my records that when their vessels the *Ocean Way PD.465* and the *Vigilant PD.365* were boarded by two of my officers on 6 January 1992, some twenty one miles west north west of Esha Ness on the west coast of Shetland, they were far from cooperative, bordering on obstructive. Now, this was not normal for this family, who had hitherto steered a more or less exemplary course as far as relations with the authorities were concerned, and yet as I recall the case I realise that their behaviour was easily explained by the fact that they were being prevented from fishing their own grounds because of lack of quota, as some bureaucrat had failed to negotiate a decent deal for them. On this occasion we were in amongst a large fleet of several nationalities who were fishing legally, twenty one miles off our coast! Small wonder they were uncooperative. Nevertheless we reported them but I think it came to nothing. I hated situations like that.

THE CALEY DAVIT

Now, there is something I have omitted to mention in the midst of all this fishery activity; that on a dark night at the end of 1991, Garvel Dry Dock Co. Ltd. in Greenock began installing the world's first Caley Davit on my ship the FPV *Vigilant*. That was a great moment for me, not simply because I had thought of it first (which no one in the universe acknowledges but me) but because it had become a reality, and would allow me to launch little boats more safely from a small ship in a big ocean. Installation and commissioning did not proceed without a hitch; much fine tuning, experimentation and adjustment had to be carried out, but in the end we had a system second to none. I used that davit with complete confidence in some difficult conditions which we would not have contemplated with a HIAB crane. I have my plaque to note the help I gave, not just at the beginning, but for years to come, writing a paper for the Canadian Coastguard on how to get the best out of it, demonstrating it to many different concerns and finally before I retired, showing BAE Systems people how to use it on the frigates they built for Brunei. I was paid for that, but the tax man took a third of it. However, I am running ahead again.

CHAPTER THIRTY
DOMESTIC ASIDE THREE

I have not mentioned my family for some time, but I can assure you that the huge activity which that generated was unimaginable. I have just been scanning through the acres of shelves of neatly documented and catalogued photographs to try to convey some idea of life at home; I have come to the conclusion that if you want to find out what our lives were like at home, you must enter Patsy's, Alexandrian-type library, select a year and indulge yourself. There, you will find every twist and turn, cut and thrust of our family's life, recording births, christenings, deaths, holidays, Christmases, Easters, First Communions, projects (oh the projects!), arrivals, departures , graduations, promotions, new jobs, new homes, new everything. On balance there is very little sadness, for which I thank Almighty God.

The lines are fallen unto me in pleasant places; yea I have a goodly heritage. Psalm 16.6

What I can tell you is that I was there for almost all of it. When I came home I gave myself to the family with a whole heart and held back nothing. Neither Patsy nor I ever felt the need to escape or get away from our children, nor did we seek to serve our own desires. I have found this way of life both effective and satisfying, and will continue in the same way. To be sure, there is more time now for solitary pastimes, but that is what one would expect.

MY FATHER'S PATROL

In the summer of 1992 my father was dropping heavy hints that he would like to come away on patrol with me, just to feel the life of a ship and the sea again, so I spoke to the new Superintendent about it. By this time my father was seventy two years of age and so the Superintendent had to think about it carefully, bearing in mind the liability the Agency might bear in the event of a disaster. On the other hand my father had been at sea the greater part of his life and was still fairly fit, and in any case we would have to sign a waiver to indemnify the Agency in the event of problems. This was done, and around 13 June we sailed from Greenock with a view to going out to the Empress of

Britain Bank. I had been thinking about it for a long time after the *Port King* and I reckoned there might be some incursions into our limit generated by the two hundred mile limit from Rockall. I knew the weather was going to be boisterous on the way but I could see that it would fair away once we arrived, so it was worth punching all the way there.

My father was like a dog with two tails and quickly engaged with everyone on board, making friends very easily as he always did. Of course, he went down the Engineroom and had a tour with the Chief, but I think he was content just to relax and be at sea with nothing to do but read books, watch videos and enjoy the food. He missed not one meal and the breakfasts he consumed were epic. For his cruise I had bought him a bottle of brandy, which he loved, and at night in the wee small hours he could be found in the Officers' lounge in front of the television watching horror movies, which he also revelled in. With a glass of beer and a brandy he wanted for nothing.

Sure enough, on the morning of 15 June, the Junior First Officer, keeping the twelve to four watch, phoned down at three in the morning to tell me he had passed some dhan buoys further to the north and now had a target on radar, on the Empress of Britain Bank. I told him to stand further south and arrange to return to the vessel when daylight came on. At that time it was blowing a westerly near gale although the swell was not heavy. The Senior First Officer called me at five o'clock to say we were getting close, so I rose and we both identified a Belize-registered vessel called the *Swan*. She had no fishing number and had no business being there. I spoke with the skipper and ascertained that he came from Belize, had no fishing number and had allegedly run easterly before the weather. We waited for the weather to improve, and sure enough by ten past six we were able to launch the boat with the new Caley Davit. The Mate and the Second Officer scrambled aboard, in a position one hundred and forty six miles south west by south of Rockall.

I should say something about Rockall. It rises out of the Rockall Bank to tower about seventy feet above the sea. It is the core of an old volcano or volcanic plug. The Rockall Bank itself, rising from the abyssal plain, is a huge area of relatively shallow water, which is seasonally very abundant in marketable fish types. Britain, or should I say Perfidious Albion, has claimed it for a long time and so has Ireland but I think the British claim is better and older, although perhaps St. Brendan managed to claim it during his voyage.

Between Britain and Ireland there exists a 'Grey Zone' within which we have a gentleman's agreement not to bother their vessels and they do not bother ours. At this time we were policing and enforcing what were called the 'Rockall Generated Limits' (that means two hundred miles from Rockall) and would prosecute any nationality found breaking the rules within that area. Of course, if Britain's claim were ever internationally recognised then it would mean that we could legally claim a large chunk of the North Atlantic half way to Canada! (I exaggerate). At that time that is precisely what we were claiming.

To return to the *Swan*, the officers got on with their inspection, revealing that there were about three point seven tonnes of crab and eighty kilos of monk (anglerfish) on board. In the meantime I had asked the Mate to get him to steam back to the position where he had been seen at two in the morning while I carried out a box search of the area to locate the gear, so we could compare the gear set in the water with the gear on the *Swan*. By late morning we found the dhan buoys which were unmarked, but the skipper was wise enough not to claim them. So we hove the gear to get a sample of it, and this is where my father came into his own. My men were not used to fishing gear and were toiling to control the multi-filament netting, but my father had spent a great deal of his life handling gear and had them organised in no time. I was glad, for he was obviously enjoying himself and felt like one of the boys.

As we were hauling this netting, the Agency's aeroplane over-flew us and reported that there were no other vessels within a thirty mile radius. By four in the afternoon we had recovered eight panels of nets and about a box of crabs. We took this netting as a sample and reset the nets. The skipper asked to come over to see me to explain the differences between his gear on the fishing boat and the gear we had recovered, but they were minimal and more alike than unlike. I was satisfied that all the nets set in the area were his and this proved to be the case when the Junior First Officer heard him passing positions corresponding to the ones we had sighted to another vessel. We got permission from Operations Room Director to take him in at ten to seven in the evening on 15 June and arrived in Stornoway in the late afternoon of Wednesday 17 June.

It is a long way from Empress of Britain Bank to Stornoway. He was fined £5000 by the Sheriff next day and we had a night in. My father was delighted to have witnessed and been involved in this capture and had never appreciated how much effort it took to bring a case to a successful conclusion. I did not discover how impressed he was until I was tidying up his things after my mother died and found his own account of the arrest, written 'just for fun' on his old typewriter, which I had given him. He had a great writing style and told a story beautifully. That account is very precious to me.

After the court case, having left Stornoway, my father stayed with us for a while longer and I took him out to St. Kilda where we landed together and roamed around. It was pleasant just wandering through the old village, in which the houses of the 18th and 19th centuries are interspersed by the much older 'black houses', retained as stores. Time always seems to slacken its hold on the present reality as one walks the long street of the village. It is as though the old people had slipped out of sight for a moment, but not permanently. They won their right to exist there by sheer tenacity and courage over millennia, and it was only the rude and thoughtless invasion by the modern world which destroyed the integrity and resilience of their community. My father felt that same sense of parallel existence with the old people. Maybe it is just old buildings which create this feeling; I felt it in Fort Jesus in Lourenço Marques, Mozambique, and one or two other places, but nowhere is that deep sense of melancholy as strong as St. Kilda. One very interesting feature of the Island of Hirta is the proliferation of bee hive shaped 'cleits' or stores which have been constructed all round and up the hillside surrounding the village. Built out of large, naturally occurring stones they provide excellent drying and storage huts which must have taken enormous effort to construct. I have a theory that the moving around of large boulders provided much needed entertainment and purpose for the men, during the long periods in between fishing trips and bird collecting. Neolithic therapy, if you will.

I now treasure that time I had with my father, and am so thankful that I had the good sense to organise that trip. We had never before been so close, for so long. Both being at sea in one form or another, most of our lives, ensured that close contact was impossible. This time was priceless, I see now, for in another couple of years he would be gone

From this point forward we entered the busiest and most productive time for detections of my entire career. From 1991 to the turn of the century we seemed to turn up infringements with great regularity. A combination of opportunity and a growing expertise amongst our officers accounted for this.

I was invited by the de-facto managing director of the Agency to write to him with my suggestions for making the Agency Marine Side more commercial in operation. Many of my suggestions would become integral parts of our organisation as time went on, and as I re-read it the other day I realise that it formed a partial blueprint for development. Not the least of these suggestions was a far greater emphasis on training our sea-going staff, and I must say that the administrators are to be commended for the resources they put into this. There can be little doubt that this emphasis on training paid off in greater competency and effectiveness as time went on, so much so that into the new millennium we became victims of our own success, and this coupled with new regulations produced a significant reduction in the number of vessels being prosecuted.

CHAPTER THIRTY-ONE
LESIVY AND SWIFT

I do not intend to bore you with one fisheries case after another, although one or two are perhaps worth recalling. Suffice it to say, my great pleasure was to patrol the limits of our jurisdiction searching for interlopers and fishermen seeking to bend and break the law. The frontier is always the place where offenders feel safest and that is where I was happiest to hunt. I cannot describe how much pleasure and satisfaction it gave me to apprehend foreign vessels and bring them successfully to book.

From 1991 to 1999, we on *the Vigilant* submitted about thirty cases which I can find statements for, to the Procurator Fiscal Service. The majority of them were foreign vessels or flag of convenience vessels, but there were a significant number of British boats, mostly Scots.

LESIVY – NEW YEAR IN LERWICK

The Department, or Agency as it became in 1991, always ensured that there was a ship on station somewhere in our little empire, should a vessel be required over the festive season. In 1992 it was the turn of the *Vigilant*. After Christmas we were patrolling quite far to the northwest of Shetland in an area called the North of Scotland Box. This was an area in which the number of foreign and UK vessels allowed access was strictly controlled by licence list. The purpose was to ensure it was not over fished, to the detriment of communities like Orkney, Shetland and the North Coast which relied heavily on fishing, with few other resources. So vessels over a certain size, fishing in the North of Scotland Box had to be on the list. On 28 December we came on the French trawler *Lesivy*, which was not on our list. Naturally the French skipper swore that he was on the list and I reported this fact to Operations Room and continued to patrol the area. It was not until mid-day the next day they came back to me to tell me the French authorities had confirmed he was not on the list, nor had he been for over a year! I should wait for further confirmation which came in the late afternoon. The *Lesivy* was to be arrested and escorted to Lerwick.

Now that sounds pretty straightforward, except that by now we had come some one hundred and thirty eight miles from the original point of contact, and the North Atlantic is a big place. However in circumstances like that, one always returns to the last sighting unless there is intelligence to the contrary. Sure enough, after a brief search on the morning of the thirtieth, the Mate and I sighted him a bit south west of where we had last seen him. I spoke to him again, and he held to his original story. I ordered him to heave his gear and we set off for St.Magnus Bay as the weather was too boisterous to board him out on the Hundred Fathom Line. By half past one in the afternoon we had boarded him and he could not produce any licence of any kind so I ordered him to Lerwick. We arrived there later that day and just managed to convene a court before the New Year. The sheriff took fishing in 'their' waters very seriously and fined him £4000.

Now the reason I told you about this was that firstly it was a wonderful way to end a year, and secondly it was the last time I ever played football. As it happened *HMS Shetland* (an Island class patrol boat like the *Jura*), was in and I think they were quite impressed that we had arrived with a capture at the tail end of the year. We mingled amicably with the Navy lads and we organised a football match for New Year's Day between the ships. A considerable amount of ship visiting took place between the two crews and I always remember how impressed the Naval Officers were with the quality of our accommodation. I unashamedly tried to recruit some of the bright young men, for I liked their keenness and commitment. The football match was inevitably won by the Navy for they had youth on their side and a far bigger crew to choose from but I think we gave as good as we got. I was yellow carded several times for behaviour unbecoming a gentleman, and only remained on the park because I was the Commander of the *Vigilant*. It was great fun and a healthy way to spend New Year.

During 1993, we came across several Anglo-Spanish vessels whose officers and engineers did not possess qualifications appropriate for British fishing vessels of their size. Now this was an important issue because these vessels were being treated as *bona fide* UK boats, possessing licences to fish, albeit sometimes for what we would think of as less marketable species, although they were to all intents and purposes Spanish vessels. They were flag of convenience vessels which were often being run by companies which were simply a name plate on a portacabin. It was annoying that these companies did not take the trouble to man their boats with properly qualified men. These were the days before 'equivalency', when there would be a table of certification showing which foreign certificates were equivalent to UK tickets.

So every time we came on these boats I was happy to bring them in until eventually the situation was rectified. The period is a sad one in some ways, for I had a young officer on my team who was involved in several of these detections. He was a fine sturdy red-headed swain who fitted in very well and did a good job. He was shifted to another ship after this period and I was saddened to hear that he had fallen ill and died a very short time later. I think it was leukaemia. I attended his funeral, which was heart rending.

The fines for these offences were not large, usually around two or three thousand pounds, but the work was more or less the same as for a big case of say illegal fishing or fishing without the authority of a licence.

For instance, I think I mentioned the area called the Irish Grey Zone. This, as I said before, is an area of disputed water between UK-claimed limits and Irish-claimed limits. It was a good place to search for poachers of all types and nationalities, again because it was close to boundaries.

SWIFT

One day in May 1993 we came on an Anglo Spanish vessel called the *Swift* working in the Grey Zone. My First Officer jumped on board at quarter past seven in the morning. He discovered the nets the vessel was deploying were illegal and spent the whole day measuring his nets and checking the catch, returning to the *Vigilant* at two o'clock in the afternoon. Course had already been set for Campbeltown to take the offender to court. In such circumstances we would send over coffee and sandwiches to keep the boarding party going. I always remained on the bridge when we were involved in a capture and ate there. When the boarding party returned we had to prepare statements and navigate to the port of arrest, so I would sometimes be on the bridge for many hours, occasionally grabbing a nap on the passage in, when I could be relieved by one of my Officers. I loved it and was always thankful for my time in tankers, when my stamina for long hours of hard work was developed. Anyway we took *Swift* to Campbeltown the next day and convened a court for the following day. Because he had caught all his fish with an illegal net in UK waters, it was all confiscated as was his gear. He was permitted to buy it all back plus the fine levied for the offence. It came to £24,500! Good results like this helped morale and none of the crew complained about being alongside for a couple of nights.

In 1994 my father was diagnosed with cancer. This was desperate news, and put a huge burden on my mother and my sister who nursed him through it. I was hosting a meeting on the *Vigilant*, attended by a Minister of State Sir Hector Munro, who at that time had a portfolio for just about everything in the universe,(the Tories had no one else to put into position, having lost all credibility in Scotland) when I received word that I should come home to Gardenstown. My Chief Engineer immediately offered to run me up there and I will never forget that act of kindness. I forget who my First Officer was at the time, but I think it was the son of the man who gave me a start in Fisheries. I had no qualms about leaving the *Vigilant* with him, for we went back a long way, to the *Morven*, and trusted him completely.

CHAPTER THIRTY-TWO
THE GIRL MAUREEN

So the nineties continued, very busy and very successful for the *Vigilant*. I found that I was being increasingly asked my opinion by the Management Team, on a whole range of topics from enforcement to building new ships. This was partially because I tended to be outspoken at Commanding Officers' Conferences and usually had a point of view on just about everything to do with fisheries and ships. I could also make the assembly laugh, which is so important when grown men are impressed with their own self-importance. I loved the COs' annual conference, as it was called; later on, after the millennium, I successfully canvassed for its extension to two days, not just because there was a lot to discuss, but also because it allowed Commanders to talk to each other on the night between the two days. These were great opportunities for camaraderie, which one could not enjoy in the same way with one's crew. We could share concerns and points of view and generally 'chew the fat'. It was profoundly therapeutic, for me.

Scottish Fishery Protection Vessels seldom went abroad. Very occasionally a trip would be made to Norway or the Faroes, and on one very special occasion my old mentor took the *Vigilant* to Canada before I took command of her. She was out there for about six weeks and as far as know did sterling service, even coming into close quarters with an iceberg! But these trips were truly exceptional and usually planned with some care. In the summer of 1995 the *Vigilant* was obliged to visit not a foreign port, but an unlikely port for sure.

We had been patrolling one of my favourite hunting grounds southwest of Barra Head when we came on an ex-Scottish vessel called the *Girl Maureen K.100*. The vessel had been bought over by a family from Eire and was carrying on more or less as she had done under UK ownership, despite the fact that the owners did not possess a licence to fish for certain species. I duly sent my Junior First Officer (by this time we were calling them First Officer Safety) to carry out a routine inspection, and it did not take very long before he was reporting that the vessel was catching and retaining amounts of haddock in excess of the monthly quota.

This chap was an excellent catcher of poachers. He took the time to learn the law and possessed an excellent brain. This, combined with a large (if corpulent) physique and 'presence' made him a formidable law enforcement officer. His biggest failing was his lack of tact, which he conveyed in a not too cultured Glaswegian accent. He was an excellent officer, however, and never had any trouble with the crew, who responded well to his robust ways when he served as Senior Mate (or First Officer Executive in modern parlance). He eventually became an assistant harbour-master in Aberdeen and arranged to give me a nice berth a couple of times. He came round to visit me and I was glad he was getting on so well in his new career.

Anyway, he made this report and because the vessel was now 'foreign' I had to order the skipper to accompany the *Vigilant* to Campbeltown. That was where there was a divergence of opinion, for the skipper utterly refused to take his vessel to a Scottish port, fearing that it might be seized and confiscated; nothing I or my ambassador could say would persuade him otherwise. (I am not sure that my Junior First Officer was the best man for this job given his predilection for supporting the Rangers football club and the fact that these men came from the Republic of Ireland.). Finally, in the late afternoon, the skipper agreed to proceed in a generally south-easterly direction, with the J/1/O and his assistant on board. I began to wonder who was arresting whom. In the meantime, our Headquarters had come to a grumbling acceptance of the situation and arranged for the Department of Fisheries for Northern Ireland to meet the vessel in Derry, which was as close to Scotland as the skipper was prepared to go with his boat! I do not know what he thought we were going to do him, for his misdemeanour did not rank highly in the great scheme of things.

Around teatime I arranged to relieve the boarding party as we continued towards the Foyle, so the J/1/O and his seaman could rest until he returned to the *Girl Maureen* around quarter past three in the morning. The *Girl Maureen* arrived alongside in Derry about half past six in the morning, and the *Vigilant* cruised off the mouth of the Foyle. Once alongside, my Junior First Officer and the officials from The Department of Agriculture for Northern Ireland (DANI) weighed and counted the offending fish and after sometime it was agreed that the *Vigilant* should also proceed to Derry to take the illegal fish on board. I was very pleased about this for I had never been up the Foyle, and in fact I think I am correct in saying that no Scottish Fishery Cruiser had ever been up there. It is a river which changes its course over time and is subject to silting, so a pilot is essential. Not only that, but at that time there was a licensing arrangement, applying to the nations on both sides of the Foyle, which permitted monofilament gill nets to be deployed by small skiffs for certain states of the tide. At those times, the Foyle was covered by these little craft all shooting and hauling nets which on our side of the border would have been completely illegal!

I sagely arranged for a pilot to take us up the river, not only for the navigation but also for his communication skills in finding a way through this huge flotilla of tiny fishing boats. Passage up the Foyle was like a tour in a foreign land for it is a wide and mighty river, and the houses on the Inishowen Peninsula are generally painted in gaudy bright colours which lend a carnival atmosphere to the area. I mused over how many thousands of Irish men and women had been forced to leave their homes by this same river in years gone by, to be scattered to every corner of the world. Arriving at Derry at two o'clock in the afternoon, we duly embarked the illegal fish and arranged to pick up the skipper and his brother the next morning, on our way back downstream, at Greencastle in the Republic, where they lived. I could not let any of my men off the ship that night, for there was a lot of trouble in Derry at the time and I feared they might get caught up in it. I had visions of them telling some ardent Republican that there was a grey ship alongside in Derry and a squad of IRA men wanting to make a name for themselves by damaging the ship. The next day we picked up the skipper and his brother at Greencastle, and took them to Campbeltown, where the court had been arranged. The skipper was fined a couple of thousand pounds and there was never any question of taking his boat off him. There is a sad wee postscript to the story, for I heard from another Irish boat years later, that one of the brothers developed Crohn's disease and was very ill. All Irish stories seem to have sad endings.

CHAPTER THIRTY-THREE
THE ST CAROLUS

Towards the end of a patrol, the ship would start to get into the mind-set of going home, and all hands would suffer in varying degrees from the 'Channels'. This is a disease which has assailed seamen from the time Noah let the dove go. There is a kind of subdued jolly atmosphere which spontaneously generates then manifests itself in curious unguarded smiles creeping across the face of the lookout as he gazes unseeingly through the bridge window, his mind far away in Greenock or Livingston or anywhere but on the ship.

Men of all ranks start to run around with bundles of dirty laundry and officers can be found beavering away on end of voyage reports of all kinds. In such an atmosphere of incipient excitement, there is a strong temptation to 'put the blinkers on' and make for the Clyde, or the Forth, as appropriate; so it was with some dismay that on the lovely evening of 19 May 1997, just after dinner, we came on a Belgian beam trawler working west of Islay. Now I had never seen a Belgian vessel working on the West Coast before, and I was not only intrigued but highly suspicious that he would be breaking some rule or other. So, ignoring the glum faces which were slowly popping up here and there amongst my men like daisies in spring, I arranged for my First Officer to carry out an inspection.

Sure enough, before long he was on the radio informing me that the skipper was retaining several species for which he had no quota in our waters. I could not believe it! This was to be this officer's last trip with us; he had secured a place as a trainee pilot on the Clyde, so he had obviously decided to go out in a blaze of glory, as it were. We duly arrested the Belgian boat called the *St. Carolus O.231* and took him to the court in Campbeltown.

As I recall, there was no court available that day so I had to arrange for one of the launches to sit guard on him while I took the *Vigilant* up to Greenock so that the arrival time could be met, then returning to Campbeltown by some means with the officers involved in the capture. I mention this case because it shows that we worked from the moment we sailed until we came home. That happened a few times over the years and was guaranteed not to increase one's popularity with the crew, but it was just one of those things that went with the job.

My First Officer eventually went on to become a senior pilot on the Clyde and I had the pleasure of having him pilot me away from Ferguson's yard in Port Glasgow when I took the new *Jura* to sea in 2005.

MOTHER AND DAUGHTER – *SKUA*

Sometime in the summer of 1996, the *Vigilant* was selected to carry out a joint operation, acting as mother vessel while our large rigid inflatable boat called the *Skua* played the role of daughter, in order to provide an element of surprise when trying to catch illegal salmon poachers in the act. The *Skua* was a superb rigid inflatable of the Pacific 36 type, which were of course 36 feet long, with all the navigational gear and creature comforts to enable her crew to carry out prolonged independent patrols. With twin Sabre engines and watertight wheelhouses, they formed a formidable asset in the Agency's task of inshore water patrolling. At one time we had two of these vessels, the other being called the *Osprey*. I was never able to fathom why we got rid of them, but we did. The problem with them was they had to tie up alongside at night so the poaching community knew exactly when they left port in the morning.

The idea was that the *Vigilant* would provide a mobile base, affording not only accommodation and victuals for the crew but also replenishment and repairs for the boat. Over the course of one patrol we worked together with the *Skua*, which was commanded by my First Officer Executive assisted by another two chaps, one to look after the engines and one to look after the deck. These two boats were like mini launches. The Chief Engineer and Second on the *Vigilant* rigged up a pumping arrangement tailored to the size of the fittings on the *Skua* so that we could refuel her at the end of a patrol. Working this way, we could anchor the *Vigilant* in discreet anchorages then send the *Skua* away on patrol with no one being any the wiser. It was a tremendous idea and I wrote a glowing report about it on completion of that patrol, indicating the effectiveness of the set-up in allowing us to maximise the element of surprise. My 1/O/E had several successes even on that short trial, and I made the point that I would have preferred to be able to lift the *Skua* on board the *Vigilant* at night so that we could redeploy overnight in a completely different area. During that patrol we covered the whole of the west coast north of the Clyde learning how best to use the assets, but in the end the concept was never developed to its fullest potential. The 'mother and daughter' principle, however, is an excellent one, as we had already proved back on the *Morven*.

CHAPTER THIRTY-FOUR
CUSTOMS OPERATION *MUCKLE FLUGGA*

In September 1997 I received a signal from Her Majesty's Customs and Excise via our Operations Room. The signal had been generated by the commander of one of their small cutters to the effect that a certain yacht (actually a white hulled ketch) was suspected of carrying drugs and was possibly going to transit our area. So often intelligence of this nature comes to nothing; nevertheless it was placed on our 'Customs' bulldog clip and filed in that part of the mind where important information resides awaiting an appropriate prompt in the future. This is an important part of all police-type work. One carries around in the head a huge amount of information which simply needs a stimulus to be brought into play. On this occasion, the stimulus was provided on the morning of 19 September when we actually came upon the yacht in question!

I circled the yacht and exchanged waves then shared a good-willed conversation with the skipper, asking him where he was bound and where he had come from, then wished them bon voyage and stood the *Vigilant* southerly towards the Butt of Lewis. After about half an hour I pretended to call up a fishing boat and transmitted a one-sided conversation with this imaginary vessel. I knew the yacht would be listening and wanted them to believe we were carrying on as normal. As the masthead of the yacht began to dip under the horizon, I put the *Vigilant* about and took up station about nine and a half miles astern of her, matching her speed and course. At this range we still had the yacht on radar but he would be ignorant of our presence having a much lower height of eye. Even with his radar running he would not see us for we were firmly in his blind sector. In the meantime I contacted the Commander of the cutter who had generated the signal, and told him we were tailing his suspect. Customs immediately dispatched not only his cutter, based in Greenock, but also another from the Mersey.

For the next twenty four hours we shadowed the yacht, during which time the cutter which came up from England had broken down in Stornoway. I suggested we fly the officers off that vessel by rescue helicopter from Stornoway to Sumburgh in Shetland, from where they could be airlifted onto the *Vigilant* by the Shetland rescue helicopter. This plan was agreed to and put in train by the Customs Operations and our Operations Room, with the agreement and cooperation of HM Coastguard. The other logistical problem which presented itself was the fact that the cutter from the Clyde was now running short of fuel and would need to replenish her tanks before going into action. This would have meant a lengthy deviation to Scalloway in Shetland. I was able to offer them replenishment at sea because our engineers had already rigged up a fuelling arrangement for the *Skua*, as described previously. This was agreed to and we arranged a rendezvous north west of the Shetlands, a long way out at sea for a little craft like a cutter, but the weather was fairly good and I knew we could manage it. Accordingly, shortly before midday on 20 September, the cutter hove into sight and in no time at all we had her alongside and had begun re-fuelling. Well before one o'clock, her tanks were full and she was ready to complete her mission. Around half past four in the afternoon, the helicopter from Sumburgh arrived and within twenty minutes had deposited five men from the broken-down cutter plus all their equipment.

We now had everything in place for the operation and discussed the fine detail, including our communication arrangements and back-up for same. Communications are paramount in any operation of this type and I wanted to be sure that there would be no snags. By seven thirty, as the gloaming was coming on, I launched our sea-boat then embarked the Customs men we had taken on from the helicopter. The sea-boat set off to catch up with the Customs cutter which was now closing in on the yacht. We could see the capture develop on radar, which also showed that there was a fishing vessel between us, who were now steaming at full speed to catch up with the cutter, our boat and the yacht. I briefly mused that the yacht might have arranged to drop drugs off to the fishing boat so I stood in to identify it just in case. The fishing boat must have been a little surprised when I switched on our navigation lights, for we had been running blacked out. We identified him and pressed on. Around twenty past eight the Customs officers boarded the yacht from our sea-boat and after a search reported that they had found about three tons of illegal drugs aboard!

They reckoned it might have a street value of eight and a half million pounds. By ten o'clock our boat had completed all the ferrying of equipment that was required and I brought them safely back on board. By this time the wind was freshening and had increased to force six, gusting to seven. This was an outstanding result, demonstrating how well the different services could work together, and I was invited down to London to share in a dinner at Customs Headquarters for people who had assisted Customs during the year, and received a nice memento of a print of one of their old cutters called the *Vigilant*.

This was an extraordinary involvement by a fishery protection vessel, but I was certain that we could build on this experience and make a contribution to the fight against drugs. One of the elements which contributed to the success of this operation was the lack of involvement by the higher echelons of all administrations, other than their sanctioning it. The detail and execution were worked out on the ground, as it were. I arranged for the operation to be filmed from start to finish and sent copies to both HM Customs and our own headquarters.

Throughout this entire operation I was constantly aware of the promptings and guidance of the Lord, and I realised that I had an ability to organise and execute complex logistical issues.

Although the LORD *gives you the bread of adversity and the water of affliction, your teachers will be hidden no more; with your own eyes you will see them. Whether you turn to the right or to the left, your ears will hear a voice behind you, saying, 'This is the way; walk in it.'* Isaiah 30:20

I have always loved that quotation from Isaiah Chapter 30. It speaks to the experience of believers who are able even in difficulties to discern the guidance of the LORD.

CHAPTER THIRTY-FIVE
H M CUSTOMS APPRAISAL PATROL

Following on this success, H.M.Customs were keen to explore the potential of ships similar to Fishery Protection vessels for their own work and wanted a first-hand report by their own people, to get a feel for larger vessels. Accordingly in the late autumn 1997 a Commander Marine and Commander Engineering joined us for the first half of a normal patrol. We gave them access to every square inch of the vessel and all hands were keen to show off their ship and her strengths. I made a video of the ship for their superiors to let them gain a better appreciation of the reports which would doubtless follow and it was very pleasant to analyse all the scenarios in which vessels of the design and size of the *Vigilant* could be used. I do not think any of our crew was disenchanted by the possibility of coming up against dangerous criminals and in fact I think some of them relished the idea.

On the morning of 29 November 1997 we had been requested by the Coastguard to attend a distress situation then shortly after were released from this task as the situation had resolved itself. I cannot remember what the distress was. We were patrolling the Stanton Banks area which is south of Barra Head. It was good for the Customs men to see how diverse our services were and how we were more than ready to meet any exigency. This all took place before breakfast. When I returned to the bridge after breakfast, my new Second Officer, who would turn out to be a first rate fellow, was heading towards an old fashioned trawler which had all the hallmarks of an Anglo-Spanish vessel. I was immediately interested and arranged for the 1/O/E and 2/O to board her and find out what was happening. I was secretly hoping they would turn up something special by way of misdemeanours so that the Customs chaps could see how it was done. I offered them a chance to go with my officers and they accepted. Sure enough, it was not long before the 1/O/E was on the radio reporting that not only were the nets illegal, but the catch was misrecorded and she was carrying quantities of fish in excess of her monthly quota. The name of the vessel was the *Pembroke FH.635*.

We arrested her and made for Stornoway where we arrived just after midnight. Following the court case the skipper was bailed for £80,000 and I think the Customs men were duly impressed. I think we remained alongside to take the half-landing and our guests from Customs left with armfuls of photocopies of every aspect of the *Vigilant* and her work. As they were leaving I jokingly said, 'If you leave we will catch another poacher but if you stay we won't'. They just laughed, but on the tenth of December we caught the Spanish line fishing vessel the *Pilar Roca FE.2.2828* for retaining saithe for which he had no quota. He was fined £11,305. That was a good patrol.

CHAPTER THIRTY-SIX
1998 – 2000
VARIOUS ADVENTURES

THE *ECLIPSE* AND THE *NAVIGANTE MAGELLENES*

Over the next year, 1998, we made several other captures, including two Anglo-Spaniards the *Eclipse XI LO.532*on 2 July 1998, for fishing without licence in the North Of Scotland Box (NOSB), and the *Navigante Magellenes FH.548* on 4 October 1998, for fishing with a net of the wrong size north of 56 degrees North. They were fined £5000 and £6000 respectively.

THE IROISE

1999 proved to be another good year for capturing offenders, with three excellent results. The first, the French vessel *Iroise DZ.639931*, was arrested for misrecording quota species in an EU logbook on 10 March, southwest of St. Kilda. My new First Officer Executive, accompanied by the Second Officer who I told you died so tragically, detected the offence and my new Second Officer (temporarily serving in the superior rank) acted as guard on the way to Stornoway. As we made our way up to the Butt of Lewis the wind freshened markedly, and by the time we rounded the Butt and were heading southerly round Tiumpan Head it was blowing a full southerly gale. The officer on guard on the captured vessel remarked that the passage in the small Frenchman had been pretty gruesome. When we entered the harbour it really began to howl and for the first time I was really concerned about berthing the *Vigilant*.
My plan had been simply to go bow in to the west side of Number 1 Pier without trying to turn her, but as soon as I took the way off her she rapidly payed off to starboard and started to set down on the end of the pier. I put the bow thrust to maximum starboard thrust to keep her off, and tried to skew her stern with the engines, but there was just too much wind and she would not come up into the wind. So the best I could do was to listen to the 1/O/E singing out 'Ten feet, eight feet, six feet, four feet, two feet, landing now!' CRUMP! She shook all over. Well, we had arrived and now all we had to do was knuckle her round the pier end and we were alongside. As soon as we were all fast, I told

the Mate how useful and reassuring his intoning of the rapidly diminishing distance to the pier had been and we both had a good laugh. More soberly he said 'I'm glad it wasn't me handling her tonight'. As soon as we got a chance we checked her out and sure enough I had set in a couple of frames and bent some plating, but that's what can happen when you handle ships in gales. The court case was a success for the French boat received a fine of just over £7,000, but better still we received nice congratulations from none other than the Fisheries Minister.

The Minister had been our guest earlier, when I had picked him and his aide up from Wick, for a trip to Orkney. Our Chief Executive, who was really good at PR, had arranged it to let the Minister see what fishery protection was all about. He originally wanted the Minister picked up in Scrabster, but three days before the time I told him it would not be possible, because I saw a nasty set of northwesterlies coming in. So it was changed to Wick, and just as well. It blew hard. The Chief Executive was quite impressed by that, I recall. Anyway the Minister was supposed to get off in Kirkwall after having had dinner with us on the way north from Wick. We provided a lovely meal as always, and I suggested that instead of going ashore in the dead of night I could anchor in Inganess Bay and he could stay with us. The man was tired, anyone could see that, and he jumped at the chance. It was a lovely night and as we sat chatting about fisheries he asked me what I thought we should do to solve the problems of the fisheries world. So I gave him all my ideas and he sipped a nice whiskey and soaked them all up. Many of these ideas have come to fruition since then; I am not saying this is because of me necessarily, but I fear some may be a little too late.

BOSTON ARGOSY

Our next case was the *Boston Argosy LT.364*, whom we caught in the Irish Grey Zone for misrecording quota species in an EU logbook, on the second of June. We took him to Oban and I cannot remember the fine, but it was worthwhile.

DU COUEDIC

My last case on the *Vigilant* was another Frenchman called the *Du Couedic LO.288541*. It was evening time, after tea, and we were having a look at the

Anton Dohrn Seamount, which lies about eleven degrees west longitude, to the west of St. Kilda. The First Mate and I were having a yarn about this and that, and sure enough we saw the unmistakable profile of a big French stern trawler. It was Sunday 25 July and we would still have many hours of daylight. The two officers went on board and by nine o'clock had discovered he had failed to declare a load of Anglerfish.

We took him to Stornoway and he received a small fine of £1500. The skipper said 'C'est une erreur'. One could not disagree.

THREE MEN IN A BOAT

I cannot remember when it was exactly, but one night around this time, it must have been coming into winter, when we were creeping down the Sea of the Hebrides, trying to keep out of a north-westerly gale, we intercepted a Mayday from the Coastguard to the effect that a 'lugger' was overdue on a voyage from Coll to Tiree. There were three members of the same family (father, son and one other) on board and they were well overdue. Lifeboats were scrambled from Islay, Oban and Barra and about five fishing vessels responded to the call and were beginning a big sweep from the Treshnish Islands towards Coll and Tiree under the direction of the Coastguard. I put on both engines and made best speed to the Treshnish. For several hours the flotilla searched every bay and nook and cranny in the black dark without success, all the time working generally westerly towards Coll and Tiree. As dawn came on we were about six or seven miles from the coast of these islands when the Coastguard called to say they thought we might be looking for bodies now. That was a pretty solemn thing to hear, but I felt this job had our name on it and asked them to run their computer programme which, given all the information they had, would come up with a 'most likely' area of search. They ran the figures and gave us the position which was more or less on our course line.

By now the wind had decreased and as we approached the lee of the islands the sea decayed as well. I studied the radar screen and silently prayed that we might find and help these men. As I gazed at the screen I suddenly saw a tiny weak target about ten degrees to port of our heading marker. At the next sweep – nothing. And again – nothing. I began to think I was deceived when suddenly there it was again! I altered course to put it directly ahead and told everyone to direct their attention to that area. They saw nothing, but the target was now painting on every sweep, and I knew it was there. I took my binoculars up and tried to visualise what the boat would look like and there, right ahead, was a tiny black speck showing through the murky dawn light. One by one the entire bridge team reported that they also could now see the boat, and I passed a message to the Coastguard to that effect. Before long we were up on the 'lugger' and its crew of three and I sent the sea-boat away to check the condition of the men in the boat. They were cold and hungry but still very much alive. Shortly after we reached the lugger, one of the lifeboats arrived and took the three distressed mariners   on board, and another lifeboat towed the lugger to Arnigour. They had lost their rudder, and were unable to steer, so it was just as well we kept looking. That was the great advantage we had in search situations, our height gave us the ability to see much farther than lifeboats and fishing vessels, and our larger crew meant we could sustain higher levels of concentration. I was delighted with this rescue and once again felt the impress, guidance and encouragement of the Spirit of God.

Trust in the LORD with all your heart and lean not on your own understanding, in all your ways acknowledge Him, and He will make your paths straight. Proverbs 3 :5&6

ASSISTANCE RENDERED TO FISHING VESSEL *TENACIOUS BCK.219*

On 17 November 1999 we were in action again. During westerly gales I would often retreat behind the mighty bastion of the Western Isles to avoid the worst of the weather and try to get some inshore work done. It was a more efficient use of the ship than heaving to in a gale in the Atlantic, for these gales could persist for days and sometimes weeks. In these conditions it was difficult to sleep, men became exhausted and the ship could sustain storm damage. Apart from all that, it was downright dangerous to approach other vessels closely in bad weather. During one of the north westerly gales, we were ambling down the Sea of the Hebrides waiting for the weather to take off and allow us to patrol west of Barra Head. Here is a report which I submitted following assistance rendered to a fishing vessel called the *Tenacious BCK.219*. As I recall, she had been built in Sweden in the eighties and was now owned in Buckie.

TOWAGE OF FISHING VESSEL *TENACIOUS BCK-219*

At about 1030utc on Wednesday 17th November 1999 the Vigilant overheard the fishing vessel Tenacious talking to Clyde Coastguard, advising the Coastguard that the fishing vessel had lost all mechanical and electrical power on the night of the 16th and had lain for the last twelve hours dead ship. The Tenacious was some 20 miles southwest of St. Kilda with 4 persons on board. There were no other vessels of any kind in the area to render assistance. The Vigilant therefore offered to proceed and this was immediately accepted. ETA on scene was calculated to be 1730utc on the 17th. Preparations were put in hand to rig for tow and hourly position and weather reports sent to Clyde Coastguard.

The Vigilant arrived at the casualty at 1730utc on the 17th and having provided victuals and sustenance for the crew, who were cold and hungry, took the Tenacious under tow at 1845utc. Conditions for towing were good, there being very little wind and a moderate to heavy north-westerly swell.

Passage to Mallaig was uneventful, and opportunity was taken to pass hot food and drink to the crew whilst in the sea of the Hebrides. By this time the wind had freshened to northerly force 6-7 and whilst this transfer was being effected the sea-boat sustained damage to one engine when it connected with the Tenacious.

At 1226utc we arrived off Mallaig and towing arrangements were passed over to the Mallaig life-boat, which with the assistance of the local fishing vessel 'Sirach' managed to put the Tenacious alongside at 1400utc. The Vigilant then resumed patrol.

The Vigilant received written thanks for this assistance.

Losses:
1 Navico hand- held radio lost overside during tow connection
1 vacuum flask broken
Damage to port engine of the Arctic seaboat – outer casing smashed – arrangement in hand for repair. In the meantime the engine of the Searider is being transferred to the Arctic to allow operation.

Captain D. L Beveridge

One or two notes are required here for the layman. We were able to launch the Arctic seaboat when we arrived on scene for the wind had fallen light in a transient ridge of high pressure. The victuals consisting of soup and some hot food were most welcome to the crew, who were starting to get very cold. Steel ships cool down very quickly and it was the middle of November. The Arctic seaboat is a twenty one foot rigid inflatable, almost identical to an Atlantic inshore lifeboat; they can handle very difficult conditions. I used the seaboat to pass the tow line then recovered the boat. The lull in the weather did not last long and the wind came up again with morning from the Norrard, but by this time we were round Barra Head. A Navico radio cost about £300 at the time, and the smashed engine casing was pretty expensive. As we approached Mallaig I heard the dulcet tones of our Chief Executive calling me from the Fishery Office. He must have been up visiting and I think he was pleased to see his ship performing a service. The little fishing boat *Sirach* will appear again before this saga is finished. The thanks we received from Clyde Coastguard said:

Your assistance and professionalism in the TENACIOUS incident was greatly appreciated, many thanks.

We did not carry out these services to obtain thanks or praise but out of a simple desire to help people, so it was always appreciated when we received thanks and it gave us all a good feeling on board. It is surprising how often people, particularly fishermen, failed in that simple act of gratitude.

CHAPTER THIRTY-SEVEN
CUSTOMS OPERATION *YULETIDE*

Here is the narrative I sent in regarding the above operation. It is written verbatim with the identities of the Customs Cutters and personnel withheld.

At about 1230hrs, on 18ᵗʰ December 1998, whilst the Vigilant was alongside in Stornoway for half-landing, I received a call from Operations Room Controller, who informed me that the Vigilant was required to take part in a Customs operation in the Shetland area. To this end I was to proceed to Lerwick to make an arrival for 1200hrs, on Saturday 19ᵗʰ December. Foreseeing the need for extra LSA [Life Saving Appliance] equipment I left the extra Motorman at his home in Stornoway. On completion of storing and replenishment the Vigilant departed Stornoway at 1700hrs, and arrived at Lerwick at 1030hrs, on Saturday 19ᵗʰ. At this time HMCC [Her Majesty's Customs Cutter] X was already alongside and HMCC Y was expected at 1400 hrs. In the event Y arrived at 1420hrs, after a gruelling passage into a strong Northerly breeze. I then arranged for a conference on board the Vigilant which was attended by the commanders of the cutters named. The meeting was jointly led by two senior Customs Officers. The boarding officers of both vessels numbering about 12 men were also present along with our First Officer Executive and Chief Engineer.

During the meeting it was revealed that the target vessel was an old ex-German tug, registered in Belize. It was known to be transiting outside the Continental Shelf to the west of Shetland and was being monitored by an aircraft fitted with surveillance equipment.

The plan which was evolved at this meeting required the early deployment of cutter X at 2400hrs to Balta Sound, and the departure of cutter Y and the Vigilant at 0600hrs on Sunday morning. This staggered timing was due to the exhausted state of cutter Y on arrival at Lerwick. The idea was that the Vigilant would then provide her boat and crew and convey Customs Officers in two waves to the target vessel at a location about 25 miles north of Muckle Flugga. The Vigilant would be carrying 3 officers from cutter Y and 2 from cutter X on departure, and they spent Sunday night on the Vigilant. At about 0530hrs on Sunday morning I was informed that the spotter plane had lost contact with the target due to freezing of the surveillance equipment in the extremely cold conditions, but that the target had been overheard talking to a cable guard ship at 2330hrs on Saturday and that position indicated that she was still heading as expected. All future deployments were made on that assumption.

Weather conditions on Sunday morning were not good, with the wind blowing 25 knots inside the harbour. At a conference on board cutter Y at 0600hrs, it was realised that the cutters would not be able to perform at all and the operation went into temporary stasis, awaiting an improvement in the weather. As I made my way back to the Vigilant I suddenly realised that I was looking at a first rate ocean going patrol vessel in the shape of our own Westra which had remained alongside at Lerwick due to weather and so far had not entered the picture. Clearly, if we could arrange to cover these requirements then we would be able to carry all the officers required between the Vigilant and Westra up to the life-raft capacity on each side of our vessels. I then rapidly returned to cutter Y with this idea, which was warmly received, and immediately put in hand arrangements to obtain permission from the Duty Officer and Marine Superintendent. I regret this permission had to be obtained at 0630hrs on Sunday morning; LSA requirements were easily met by simply having each Customs Officer repair on board his temporary vessel with his own life-jacket and survival suit from his own ship. I then hurried to Westra to acquaint the Captain of Westra with my proposals, and he, being enthusiastic from the moment his bare feet landed on the deck following my rude awakening, is to be commended for having his ship ready for sea in time to leave with the Vigilant at 0730hrs, with 7 Customs Officers from cutter X. The Vigilant took 9 Customs Officers from cutter Y.

The passage to the north towards Muckle Flugga was rather unpleasant but uneventful in a Northerly near gale, and the deployment and tactics were left to the senior Customs Officer who had come aboard the Vigilant and who was continually liaising with the Senior Customs Officer who had remained ashore to control the aircraft. At 1000hrs, the aircraft was able to take off from Sumburgh having been grounded due to snow on the runway, and I later found out that it carried out extensive patrols to the west and north of the Shetlands following the projected track of the target, searching meticulously in all areas where the target was deemed likely to be, based on the original assumption. By lunchtime it began to become apparent that the target was not where expected and the Westra was requested to detach and patrol eastwards from the Balta Sound area towards the oil rigs.

The Vigilant, meanwhile, continued northwards until reaching 61 degrees 25 minutes North in a Northerly force 9 when course was altered to the westsouthwest to run down the original projected track. The Westra continued easterly until she came to the rigs then returned westwards.

As the afternoon and evening progressed, the Senior customs Officer on the Vigilant began to receive information from his opposite number in Lerwick, which was persuading them that the target had diverted to the Fair Isle Channel and consequently at 1954 hrs. the mission was stood down. The Vigilant then proceeded down the west side of the Shetlands and met up with the Westra off Lerwick approaches at about 0230hrs, where we spent the rest of the night in relative comfort. At 0730hrs on the morning of the 20th December both SFPA ships disembarked their respective Customs personnel with exchanges of genuine goodwill and mutual respect and resumed patrol directly.

The tug was apprehended as she approached the Dutch coast by Dutch Customs Officers and was arrested along with a fishing vessel into which the crew of the tug was transferring the cargo. She was carrying millions of pounds worth of illegal drugs and there were several arrests.

This concluded my time on the *Vigilant* for when I arrived into Greenock I received instructions to leave the *Vigilant* on 13 January 2000 after having taken her to refit, and join the *Norna* on 9 February. I would be taking over from my old mentor and found myself the senior master in the fleet. (Not the oldest, but the one with the longest command time). I had been in command for thirteen years.

PROMOTION BOARDS

Between my *Vigilant* years and the *Norna*, I was invited to two promotion boards, the first for Director of Operations who would be part of the Senior Management Team, and the other for Marine Superintendent, also part of the Senior Management Team. I came runner up to a 'proper' Civil Servant, a real amiable and very knowledgeable man who had all the gifts I did not possess to 'shmooze' his way about the portals of power. I remember during that board being asked by the author of the 'Quota Management Arrangements' what I thought of quotas, and I had to admit that I thought they were a bad idea. That did not go down well, but nothing has happened to cause me to alter my view. The first Chief Executive of the new Fisheries Protection Agency phoned me up next day to tell me I had been a close second place, and I silently thanked God, for I had no real desire to go ashore. The same thing happened with the Superintendent's job.

At these promotion boards there are normally three board members whose job is to ask questions and evaluate each candidate. A 'proper civil servant' is usually co-opted to provide a balanced view. I recall one lady whose specialisation was finance asking me how I would deal with several hypothetical scenarios predicated on the idea of shrinking budgets. I gave my ideas which ended up in a fleet of three ships (two big ones and a small one) and an aircraft. I am sad to say that I must have had my prophet's hat on that day, for that is exactly what we have ended up with. I went out of my way at that board to emphasise how much I enjoyed patrolling the frontier and pulling in poachers, and realised as I spoke that the office was no place for me. When I came home that night I said to Patsy that I really did not want to leave the sea. The next day the new Chief Executive called to say that another Captain had been successful and again I thanked God. He, that is the other fellow, was much better equipped for the task than me, although I am glad to say that he had the good sense to listen when I made good suggestions as the years went on. He ended up doing a good job in my opinion.

CHAPTER THIRTY-EIGHT
NORNA
2000-2005

No matter how long you have been in command, somehow a new ship requires you 'prove' yourself all over again. You are only as good as your last success. That is certainly the way I always felt when taking over a new ship. Of course your reputation went before you to some extent and there were always 'weel kent' faces amongst the crew in a small concern with only a few ships; but strangely, the bringing together of a new set of human beings so completely altered the dynamic of the crew that a new entity was brought about and had to be once again moulded into a ship's company. We never had a term 'Commodore' in the Fisheries but in fact that it what you were as the Senior Commander. I know I felt an obligation to show leadership to the other Captains simply by the way I went about the job, and I must have had some success in this aspiration judging by what people wrote about and said to me when I retired. I regarded this unofficial post as a privilege and responsibility.

I did not start particularly well. By this time I had earned a reputation as a pretty good ship handler and I well remember the first day I took the *Norna* away as her new Captain. Bear in mind that although I had taken her to sea some years before, I had been running the *Vigilant* for the last eight years and more. I had forgotten how effective the Becker rudders were and, having ordered the helmsman to put the wheel hard over to starboard, was totally unprepared for the rapid response of the *Norna's* stern as it flew towards the dock wall. Thump! The First Mate, whom I had known for many years, was completely taken aback, and I said to him 'There you are, that's to make me humble and remind me not to get too big for my boots'. That was the first and last time I bumped the *Norna*. She was a wonderful ship to handle and one could do just about anything with her. She had twin Becker rudders on twin screws and a powerful Brunvoll electric thruster.

This First Officer Executive was with me for about a year on the *Norna* and was a really kind hearted fellow. He had been with me the first time I took the *Vigilant* away as Officer in Charge and we ran over the Blue Whiting net. He did not possess the hunter instinct nor was he much of an individualist, preferring to 'go with the flow', but he had a kindly way about him and I think the men liked him, as an approachable and decent man. His biggest flaw, as far as I was concerned, was his garrulous tongue which nattered on incessantly until one was obliged to suggest he might wear himself out. On the other hand there were seldom awkward silences when he was around.

I liked him fine.

One of the first things I had to change on the *Norna* was the way they had rigged the painter for the sea-boat. (The painter is the rope which connects the sea-boat to the ship when launching and recovering). They had it rigged from a short boom about forty feet forward of the Caley Davit which meant that, because of the acute angle the rope made with the boat in the water, every time the boat pitched it put tremendous loading on the painter and all securing points. It also made the operation a two man affair. This incensed me for I had designed it to be a one man operation. I immediately approached the Chief Engineer, whom I had known for over twenty years, and asked him to rig up a temporary, longer boom further forward, to allow us to experiment with the rig. This had the effect of reducing the shock load on the painter and fittings, and after a bit of retraining made the operation a one man job. When we arrived home from the first patrol I requested the Superintendent to sanction the installation of a new boom in the correct position, to my own design, and he agreed. Not only that, I arranged for a set of bitts to be fabricated on chequer plate aluminium mounting to be installed in the bow of the boat, and this greatly improved the men's control in adjusting the tension on the painter. By the time the modifications were complete I was very satisfied with the arrangements.

I realise now that I have always made alterations, which I reckoned were improvements, to every ship I went on. I simply cannot help it and I am glad to say that one often finds kindred spirits amongst mariners. This Chief Engineer was an outstanding example of this and I never saw that man without some improving project or another to hand. It was great having him as Chief for not only did we get on pretty well, he was a good piper, and I wanted to learn to play the bagpipes. In two thousand and one I began my studies and it is entirely due to his patient teaching and merciless correcting of my appalling finger work that I can crank out an acceptable tune today.

I really took to the *Norna*. In many respects she was the perfect fishery cruiser. I have already mentioned her manoeuvring capabilities but I should also say she was a splendid sea-boat and, with her stability tanks and stabilising fins, as comfortable as a small ship could be in a big ocean. Over the course of time I would request and be granted several enhancements to her accommodation, which I think made her even better but opinion is probably divided on that, as would be amusingly revealed in years to come.

In my mind and personality I was experiencing a state of maturity which allowed me to enjoy life more, and I felt competent and equipped to deal with just about anything. It is a pleasant state of mind to occupy, for of all my commands the *Norna* would be the one which produced the greatest number of rescues and assistances to other vessels. There is a modern phrase which talks about being 'comfortable in one's skin' and that sums the feeling up quite well.

EFFICIENCY GAINS AND COST CUTTING EXERCISES

The desire of the Senior Management Team to save money on running costs was always present and we at sea were hard put to identify areas where we could cut down any more than we had. Our crews were as small as they could be and still do the job we were hired to do and we were very efficient and parsimonious in the consumption of consumables. Our victualing costs were not great and in any case I for one had no desire to compromise in this area, since it was one of the few creature comforts remaining to the mariner.

It was with some excitement therefore, when loitering off a fishing boat we were inspecting one day, that I happened on a phenomenon which I could see yielding potentially huge economies, if it turned out to be practical and feasible. You see, the *Norna* had two engines and two propellers and our practice was to run on two engines during the working day from about seven in the morning till seven at night. During the dark hours, we would come down to one engine and put the brake on the shaft of the other propeller. Much of our time during the day might be spent loitering around a fleet of boats; on the other hand we might have to cover considerable distances shifting from one target vessel to another, so it was reckoned to be more convenient to keep two engines running. On this particular day I needed to move the ship for some reason and, instead of clutching in both engines, clutched in only one but put the pitch control to full ahead on the de-clutched engine. That means the propeller on the engine which was not being used to move the ship was rotating just like a windmill in the water. The net result of this was that, for relatively little power being exerted by the engine which was driving the ship, a very noticeable and measurable increase in speed could be gained. The implications of this were great for it meant that we might be able to run on one engine almost all the time and save large amounts of fuel, which was one of our greatest expenses. I immediately shared this finding with the Chief Engineer, and he said that a predecessor, who had sailed on the *Norna* for a while, had reported the same thing, but no one had taken it up. We were now living in far more fiscally challenging times and I thought it was worth pursuing. I wrote to the Superintendent early in April 2000 and after he and the Engineering Superintendent had mulled it over we were given permission to experiment. That was all the Chief and I needed and by the end of May we submitted a joint report to which the Chief contributed by far the greatest part, with tables of technical details and comparators between different periods of running time and so on. Briefly, we reckoned the savings would be of the order of £50,000 per year for the *Norna*, and a similar amount for the *Sulisker* and the *Vigilant*. Following this, we were given permission to run in this mode from that time onwards, and the savings we predicted were at least matched in reality.

I am sorry to say we never even received an acknowledgement, either written or verbal, of our work and that left both the Chief and me somewhat disenchanted. I actually mentioned it to the Chief Executive during my Annual Performance Review, in the hope that some acknowledgement might be forthcoming, but the silence from HQ on the subject was absolute, and in my view it was an opportunity missed on the part of Senior Management.

TAHUME FH.666

On 16 September 2000, we made our first capture on the *Norna* under my command. We were operating to the northwest of Shetland when we boarded the UK gill-netter *Tahume*, for the second time in two days. The first time we boarded her, the First Officer (Safety) (Junior First Officer), had been unable to find anything wrong. In the meantime we had received a tip off from the Captain of the *Sulisker* that his officers had discovered that, on a gill-netter they had boarded and were now escorting to court, there was a practice of breaking off the claws of the crabs, retaining them and throwing the carapace over the side. This was illegal, not to say wasteful, for the crabs could not be checked for size. So my 1/O/S re-boarded the *Tahume* and sure enough they were doing the same thing. We escorted them into Lerwick and the skipper was fined appropriately. Funnily enough I did not realise it at the time, but this was third time I had taken this boat to court for she was none other than the *Boston Argosy* and the *Swan*! Her multiple identities demonstrate the rich and colourful imagination of the Anglo-Spanish owners.

THE ASSISTANCE TO *HARVEST REAPER* PD.142

About a year after joining the *Norna* we had our first major incident with a fishing vessel getting into difficulties. It was 24 January 2001, and we were just looking forward to going alongside in Stornoway for stand-down after completing a night patrol of the closed areas in the South Minch. These areas were closed to scallop dredgers due to the existence of an organism in the water which could cause paralysis if ingested by humans. This type of closure happens quite frequently and is closely monitored by government scientists. The report I wrote went like this:

At about 0930 the words 'MAYDAY' were heard on VHF followed by an immediate response from Stornoway Coastguard ascertaining that the vessel requiring urgent assistance was the Scottish trawler Harvest Reaper PD.142, aground at the north end of Loch Roag. On hearing this I promptly contacted Stornoway Coastguard on cellular phone and offered our services and was requested to proceed to the casualty. Stornoway lifeboat was launched and the rescue helicopter Mike Uniform scrambled. The fishing vessel Harvest Moon, a similar vessel to the Harvest Reaper (there may be a close association) sailed from Stornoway to render assistance.

Estimated Times of Arrival at the scene were 0945 for the helicopter, about 1230 for the lifeboat, and 1400 for the Norna at best possible speed, with the Harvest Moon around 1500. The helicopter arrived as planned and by 1000 had removed 4 men from the crew of 6 and taken them to Stornoway. The skipper and the Chief Engineer remained on board. In the meantime the work-boat Sirach [remember her?], which was local to Bernera was heard to offer assistance and managed, with commendable determination, to get a line onto the Harvest Reaper and pulled the fishing vessel off the cliff-bound shore. The Sirach then held the casualty in the loch awaiting the arrival of the life-boat, the Norna and the Harvest Moon. When the life-boat arrived she took over holding the casualty and intended towing the vessel towards the Butt of Lewis, but I intervened at this point advising against that course of action for two reasons:

1. *The wind had freshened to South-westerly 8 and the lifeboat would have difficulty making any way with a vessel the size of the Harvest Reaper.*

2. *There had been no survey done on the bottom of the casualty, and she could easily develop catastrophic flooding in a seaway.*

My advice was heeded thankfully, and the lifeboat attempted to re-enter Loch Roag with considerable difficulty.

    At about 1300 the Harvest Reaper reported that she was taking water and required a pump immediately. The lifeboat did not possess one. The helicopter, which had been stood down was scrambled again with two pumps which she deposited, along with a winch man, on board around 1330. By this time the Norna had arrived on the scene at the mouth of Loch Roag, and could see the helicopter, hovering over the casualty, landing the pumps. Contact was made with the skipper of the Harvest Reaper and I offered to take over the tow as the lifeboat was making nothing of it due to the weight of wind and the size of vessel. At this point the lifeboat and the Harvest Reaper were in the centre of the mouth of the loch. The skipper accepted my offer and asked if he could rig the pumps first as the water was now up to the plates in the engine-room. I agreed but reminded him he did not have much time as the Harvest Reaper and lifeboat were being driven slowly onto the lee shore of Aird Lamishader [there is a lighthouse above this point], being about 5.5 cables off the rocks at that time. [Just over half a mile – there are 10 cables to the mile.]Shortly after this the tow rope of the lifeboat parted and some minutes were lost trying to contact the Skipper and Chief Engineer of the Harvest Reaper who were below with the winch-man and unaware that the tow had parted. After some blowing of the Norna's horn they reappeared and realised the situation immediately. I told the Skipper that I would make one pass only then they would have to come off. In fact the helicopter wanted to take them off at that point, but I reckoned we could do it with a margin of safety.

    The Norna then approached and, the tow having been prepared well in advance, made connection in a handsome fashion and was able to begin clawing off the coast, being at that point still 3.5 cables off and in soundings of over 10 fathoms. Speed was kept to less than two knots lest the tow part, as the Harvest Reaper was quite lively in the strong breeze. Steady progress was then made to the shelter of the loch, where the towing hawser was taken in and the Harvest Reaper lashed alongside the Norna. The Norna anchored in the usual anchorage off Loch Risay at 1530 to await the arrival of the Harvest Moon. Hot victuals were passed to the Skipper and Chief Engineer, who had not yet broken their fast from the night before.

I boarded the Harvest Reaper to discuss a course of action with the Skipper and encouraged him to go to Breasclete to have the Harvest Reaper surveyed before contemplating the towage to Stornoway. He agreed with my observations and advice and at 1630 the Harvest Moon came alongside the Harvest Reaper to take her to Breasclete. At 1700 the Norna weighed anchor and proceeded to Stornoway for a belated half-landing, arriving there at 2200 with a Southerly gale forecast for the morning.

Our Chief Executive, who had been in the Royal Navy and commanded ships wrote to me:

'I have just read your fulsome report on the Harvest Reaper incident. The Norna's response was in the best tradition of mariners and much appreciated by the fishermen involved I'm sure. Well done to all concerned. May the stormy southerlies abate and the sun shine on the righteous.'

You see, he understood what was involved in carrying out such an operation successfully.

While the *Harvest Reaper* was lying lashed alongside us, I sent one of the sailors down onto her focsle to collect some pieces of rock which had fallen from the cliff when she drove against the rocks. I still have those rocks to remind me of the day. I also have lots of digital photos which I obtained from the helicopter crew. An article appeared in the Stornoway Gazette about this incident and thanks to one of my seamen who had met a reporter from the Gazette in a pub it was reported quite accurately, which made a change.

NORNA NEWS

During my entire tenure of the *Norna* I produced, every few days, a newsletter predictably entitled '*Norna* NEWS'. The idea of having such a newsletter was by no means novel and I think I mentioned that several officers had done this very effectively before. I felt it was a fairly good way of keeping everyone informed. As it happens I have retained most of the ones I wrote on the *Norna* and I suppose it did have the desired effect. I also have some of the early editions produced by several officers. As I read over the old copies, the minutiae of our lives in the Fisheries are easily recalled. In the main it makes really boring reading: Fleet Movements, Weather Forecast, Forthcoming Events, all the different initiatives which came out of HQ are all recorded. I am glad to say that the Chief Steward, on the *Norna*, a truly gifted raconteur, brought out an alternative production called 'NOT THE *Norna* NEWS' which was infinitely more amusing and often downright hilarious. He mercilessly poked fun in all directions including mine and I am profoundly thankful to him for his irreverent slant on life. He was also a good Chief Steward, and we served together throughout large chunks of our careers. As a final post script to the above incident I wrote in the *Norna* NEWS in 'Thought for the Day'

It is better to deserve honours and not have them than to have them and not deserve them.

I am not sure what brought that on but it may have been when the footballer Barry Ferguson received an MBE for – playing football!

It will be very obvious that I was extremely proud of every ship I sailed on, especially when I was in command. In the middle of the nineties we had begun to have shared commands whereby two masters were allocated to each ship and whilst this made for a 'trip on trip off' leave schedule, I always resented sharing my ship with anyone, even if I liked them. Of course, one had to give the other chap his place and consult on just about everything and I found it annoying and frustrating. Thankfully, most of the fellow commanders I sailed opposite were reasonable people and they were all junior to me, but it always irked me nevertheless and I was much happier when the ship was mine exclusively. Of course, I enjoyed the extra time at home and it made for a predictable and settled life, if you like that sort of thing.

In 2001 the 'Flagship', as the Chief Executive referred to the *Norna*, was earmarked for a visit to the International Festival of the Sea in Portsmouth, and this was exciting from several points of view. It would be an excellent opportunity for the world to see a Scottish Fishery Cruiser, for she would be open to the public, we would be going down into 'Furrin Pairts' (namely England) and it would be something completely out of the ordinary. As soon as we were told, I put in hand preparations for making the *Norna* as impeccable as we could make her, and during that spring and summer my officers and men caught the fever of preparation; even the most cynical entered into the spirit of the thing although they would never admit it.

In early summer I took my daughter Esther away for a trip and showed her as many islands and sights as the patrol pattern permitted. I had done this already for David, Joseph, Jenny and Becky on the same trip, and Martin. Only Patricia and Hannah never came away with me. Hannah did not want to come at the time and Patricia thinks I did not take her away because I thought she would run off with a sailor. As a matter of fact it was not convenient at the time for several reasons, and in addition to that, I was indeed afraid she would run off with a sailor. In the end Patricia married a soldier who rose through the ranks to become a Major in the Royal Artillery, and I think of him as a son.

THE RESCUE OF THE CREW OF *AURELIA*

On the trip during which we were programmed to visit Portsmouth for the Festival, the weather permitted a long sortie out to Rockall and the outer banks, and while running in from there, having not seen very much, I took the *Norna* across the Anton Dohrn Seamount for we had sometimes been successful in capturing offending vessels on that fishing ground. It was while patrolling the bank that the following report was generated on 13 August 2001:

FROM COMMANDING OFFICER FPV Norna

13th AUGUST 2001

RESCUE OF CREW OF AURELIA

At 2330 BST on the night of Sunday 12th August 2001 the Norna was patrolling the area of the Anton Dohrn Seamount when a DSC alert [This is an electronic system which allows alerts of various kinds to be broadcast for a casualty] was received indicating that a vessel was flooding in position 57 degrees 53 minutes North, 011 degrees 04 minutes West. The Officer of the watch immediately informed me and calculated the distance and course to the casualty. I turned the Norna in that direction and arranged to proceed at full speed, informing Stornoway Coastguard of our ETA of 0125BST. Shortly after this we heard the research vessel James Clark Ross also offer her assistance, and noted her begin to take up station about 7 miles on our port quarter, proceeding at best speed of 15.5 knots.

Stornoway Coastguard advised that the vessel in distress was the Scottish fishing vessel Aurelia BF.15, with 5 men on board. Numerous attempts were made to hail the Aurelia, which was finally contacted at 0010BST. The Skipper informed me that two of his crew had already repaired to the life-raft and were alongside whilst three others including himself were still aboard.

Over the next half hour I spoke with the Skipper of the Aurelia on several occasions to reassure him of our utmost dispatch and to remind him of equipment he might want to take with him should he abandon ship.

At 0043BST a Seaman sighted a light in the general vicinity of the casualty and I confirmed that the Aurelia was still showing emergency lighting. Course was adjusted towards the light and at the same time a target began to paint on the radar in position 57 degrees 52.9 minutes North 011 degrees 01.82 minutes West.

At 0103BST the radar target was seen to disappear and we correctly assumed the vessel had sunk. There was no further response to our VHF calls to the Aurelia but shortly after this at 0110BST we heard the rescue helicopter Mike Uniform hailing us and giving his ETA as 0130BST. He could not hear the Norna at this time.

All this time we continued to approach the casualty, the visibility was good and lights could be seen where the Aurelia had been. We rightly judged these to be the life-raft. This was confirmed at 0114BST when a red flare was seen dead ahead.

At 0121BST we were on scene. I deployed the Norna's sea-boat to pick up survivors. This they did in full darkness with rapidly deteriorating visibility, negotiating large amounts of flotsam. They were recovered with the five man crew of the Aurelia at 0138BST, by Caley Davit in one lift.

The crew were tended briefly by the Chief Steward and the Deck Officers, who coordinated and organised the practical arrangements of transferring the survivors to the helicopter which was now hovering over the Norna, from 0147BST to 0200BST. The transfer was carried out without a hitch.

The Norna then hove to for the night, for the fog had set in thickly and we had *not managed to retrieve the life-raft or the EPIRB [electronic position indicator responder beacon.]*

We searched for the life-raft from dawn and at 0930BST sighted two rafts which we recovered by 1004BST. I still have an infra-red video clip which I obtained from the helicopter crew and it is interesting to see the ghostly figures of the men on the after deck of the *Norna*.

Uncharacteristically, our Superintendent wrote to me: *Thanks for the report on the rescue. A good job very well done. I have forwarded your report to Press Office.*

In due time the rescue was reported in the *Press and Journal* and one of the tabloids, but as usual the facts were not correct. The *Norna* had turned into a fishing boat which was three miles away and sent 'launches' to the rescue. They cannot even report accurately with the report sitting in front of them. Small wonder I do not read newspapers.

THE INTERNATIONAL FESTIVAL OF THE SEA 23-26 AUGUST 2001

The rescue of the crew of the *Aurelia* provided an excellent morale boost for the trip down to Portsmouth, and the preparations which we had been slowly making over the weeks before the festival were coming together. In addition to cleaning the ship (internally and externally) and arranging special food for VIPs, special flag arrangements and notices for explaining the equipment on the bridge and in the engine-room had to be designed and produced. Routes for the safe management of crowds and methods of roping off and guiding people had to be worked out, along with extra gangway arrangements. Risk assessments had to be worked up and all this in the middle of a normal patrol. I am so thankful that I had a tremendous crew and could not have asked for better support.

In due time we made our way southwards towards England via the Irish Sea. It was most enjoyable to go into 'strange' waters, and as we passed the Isle of Man, which we never normally sighted, it began to feel like an adventure. My great grandfather James Quirk had come from the Isle on Man and his marriage certificate describes him as a 'Master Mariner'. I wish I could have met him. In some ways that is why I am making this account, so that my descendants will have a notion of who I was and what it was like.

Our first task would be to pick up the Chief Executive from the Barbican in Plymouth, and so I arranged to arrive there a day early and anchor in Jennycliffe Bay to complete painting the hull so that the *Norna* would be immaculate. As we lay at anchor awaiting the arrival of the Boss, my mind wandered back in time and mulled over the ships and men, including my own relations, who had sailed out of this harbour and into the Channel and beyond. I could see the harbour in sepia and imagined the old minesweepers going about their daily task of ensuring the seaways were clear of murderous mines. My grandfather James Richie had command of one of those minesweepers in the First World War, and I have mounted his Commission papers in a frame. I am proud of him.

By the end of that full day's work at anchor the men had her sparkling and I could have asked no more. We picked up the Boss by sea-boat and brought him aboard and he brought his usual quiet confident air and pleasant refined leadership with him. I think we all liked him because he understood what it was like to be a seaman and was happy to preside over the most efficient Fishery Protection Service in Europe and beyond. He did a tremendous amount of good work to raise the profile of the Service and win us friends in important places. He was a safe pair of hands.

A slow overnight steam from Plymouth brought us to the Needles at exactly the right time on a hazy day which promised warm sunshine. The Solent was heaving with vessels of all sorts which for the most part, thankfully, were keeping out of the shipping lanes. It was better not to look at the radar for the screen was covered with targets.

The entrance to Portsmouth harbour is flanked by massive round castles (I am sure they are called castles) built to defend the harbour during the Napoleonic Wars. This day, after we had picked up our pilot and were heading up between them, they were thronged with tourists and pleasure makers, bent on watching the arrival of the ships participating in the Festival. It was at this point that I wanted to make a great show for I had arranged the purchase of the biggest Lion Rampant and St Andrew's Saltire flags I could obtain. A Lion Rampant on the Jack staff, one on the port yardarm and a Saltire   on   the gaff. Of course, we carried our Fisheries Blue Ensign at the stern. As we approached the castles, at the right psychological moment, I gave the signal and our huge flags were unfurled and blossomed in the sunshiney breeze, as the Chief struck up 'Scotland the Brave' on the pipes and we passed between the castles. It was a fine sight and we received plenty of reaction from the crowds. I think the Boss was pleased.

We berthed in a discreet inner harbour within the vast complex of Portsmouth, which was full of vessels to do with fishing and fishery protection down through the years. I was required to lay the *Norna* alongside the Irish Naval Ship *Aisling*, which did a job similar to ours with the added duties of coastguard and home defence. She was considerably smaller than the *Norna* and I had to be very careful when coming alongside her, but the *Norna* was so handy that she would not have cracked an egg as she rested on the *Aisling's* fenders. Our duties would commence in earnest next day when we would be open to the public, so that evening the Boss and I strolled around the harbour viewing craft which had assembled from all over the world. It was like the Mediterranean, warm and pleasant. As it began to darken we found ourselves at the ' Kronenbourg 1664' beer tent. We ordered up a couple of pints and sat down on the chairs at the quayside. There was a white-hulled Mexican three-masted ship dressed overall with fairy lights, having a party on deck, complete with a mariachi band trumpeting out happy Mexican music into the dusky evening. A steady stream of lovely girls, beautifully turned out, under escort, promenaded before us as they made their way to the ship's gangway to be met by the quartermaster. The Boss and I were, for a brief moment, perfectly at peace and content: two middle aged mariners remembering days long gone and savouring the satisfying cold bite of the lager and the spectacle of happy revellers. We never forgot that evening and afterwards, whenever he came on my ship for some junket or other, I arranged for the 1664 to be on hand. Simple pleasures for simple sailors.

We were open to the public from morning to late afternoon, but the *Norna* being second off to the *Aisling* it meant that the Irish crew intercepted most of the visitors and only the really dedicated came onto us. This was fine because, in the main, the people we dealt with were interested, which made showing them round more enjoyable for us. The Chief Executive left us that day but we had a steady stream of his old cronies from the Navy and business associates to do with ship design and so on who wanted a look at the ship. It fairly passed the time till evening, when a truly carnival atmosphere descended and enveloped the harbour, which felt more like New Orleans, with the humid atmosphere and the happy noise of jazz bands and folk groups. It was very jolly, but the *Norna* was like an oven and sleep was uncomfortable, for we had no air conditioning. It made me think back to Chittagong and Chalna, so long ago and far away. My daughter Patricia visited the next day for she was staying at Larkhill on Salisbury Plain with her husband Mark. Just as well she did, for we were entertaining the officers off the *Aisling* at midday, and the cook had succumbed to the temptations of Irish Guinness of which there was no shortage on the *Aisling*. Patricia stood in the breach and saved her father's blushes by organising and serving the snacks and nibbles. The cook eventually was sacked.

We sailed on 26 August, and I for one was glad to be going home. It had been an interesting few days but I was already missing our fresh Atlantic breezes and was ready for the return journey. Not only that; one of the sailors, who up until Portsmouth had been an outstanding fellow, also fell by the wayside having quaffed too much Guinness and started to have a go at my new First Officer (Executive), which was strange for a nicer fellow you could not meet. Mind you, I have seen it so often before. You have a good seaman in all respects until he takes strong drink, and the next salute he is offering to knock someone's head off. Man's frailty is past understanding. On balance, everyone enjoyed something about the visit, and the Chief Executive was very pleased with his flagship. He sent us a lovely letter of thanks. This was his way, for he was in all respects a gentleman.

So we made our weary way home, tired but very satisfied with our results. As we sailed close past a large Royal Navy ship on our way out of Portsmouth Harbour, a young matelot who saw us coming stopped, came smartly to attention and saluted us. I had the feeling he was Scots.

THE ASSISTANCE RENDERED TO *STEADSFAST* FR.443

Autumn was coming on when our crew sailed again and we did not have long to wait until our next action, for between 30 September and 1 October, I had to report as follows.

At 1606 on Sunday 30th September 2001 a PAN PAN [Urgency message] was heard on 2182 [Safety frequency] and VHF DSC in respect of the Scottish fishing vessel Steadfast FR.443 The vessel had fouled her propeller with the fishing net and was disabled in position 31 miles North north west of Noup Head in the Orkneys. At this time the Norna was at anchor in Pierowall Roads avoiding a south-easterly gale. At 1615 I offered the Norna's services believing no other vessels to be in the vicinity, and immediately started shortening cable. At 1635 engines and auxiliary power were available and anchor aweigh. Best possible sustainable speed was maintained giving an ETA of around 1930.

Passage to the casualty was uneventful and by 1940 the Norna was approaching to close the Steadfast on a north-westerly course running before the sea and swell. The Steadfast was lying with her head to the east-north-east. On the passage the tow-rope had been prepared of sufficient length for just under three cables, and at the same time the fishing vessel had made her own arrangements on board with a 50 metre nylon hawser onto a chain bridle and two tyres, giving over 3 cables of hawser [3 tenths of a mile], which was adequate given the conditions. Approach to the Steadfast was necessarily sedate, however a heaving line was able to be thrown and connection made at the first pass at 2005. Passage was then commenced very slowly, gradually building to 4.5 knots. This pedestrian speed was sustained for the whole passage in order to prevent the tow parting and to give the Steadfast as safe a journey as possible. Conditions providentially moderated shortly after connection to southeast 30 knots, but the swell remained troublesome and precluded sleep for all but the brain-dead.

By 0600 we had reached the mouth of the Westray Firth and I informed the Skipper that I intended to shorten and disconnect tow, out of the tide in Veantrow Bay at around 0730 prior to lashing him alongside for the remainder of the journey which would be carried out in small water.

At 0705 in a position 1.4 miles north of Greenholm Islet with the tide setting south at 4 knots, the tow parted at the Steadfast's tyres. Thankfully our men were on the job immediately and were able to recover the whole 3 cables of hawser in rapid time whilst I deployed the Norna to come close to the fishing vessel to lash her alongside. I am profoundly grateful to my Executive Officer and his men who achieved these evolutions so quickly, as we were 3.3 cables off Greenholm when I managed to make distance against the 4 knot tide. At 0728 we resumed passage to Kirkwall via the buoyed channel to the northwest of Shapinsay.

At 0902 I laid the Steadfast alongside the east end of the north face of the pier at Kirkwall and at 0920 secured the Norna on the same pier just astern of her.

I must record that all my officers and men behaved in a most professional and supportive fashion.

The skipper of the Steadfast visited the Norna at 1100 to convey his heartfelt thanks.

The Assistant to the Marine Superintendent wrote:

David,
Read with interest your report on the above. It must have concentrated the mind when the tow parted! Obviously another tow job well done. Bottle of Grecian 2000 to follow by post.

Note: Not much need for Grecian 2000 these days – no hair!

COMMISSION REGULATION 2056-2001

The end of 2001 saw the publication of Commission Regulation 2056/2001, which was so bewildering in its complexity that I felt obliged to convey my difficulties and misgivings to the Senior Management Board with a plea to examine these difficulties, which I was by no means alone in experiencing, at the next Commanding Officers' Conference. They took me very seriously and arranged for someone to come and attempt to explain it. But that would be later. In the meantime I sat down one day with my current Deck Officers and got to work on rationalising the problems.

The great difficulty was blending the new rules with the existing ones, but that afternoon we produced a document which my 1/O/E printed out in commendable style, and which became the guidelines used not only by our fleet, but also by the Ministry of Agriculture and Fisheries in England. It was pleasantly surprising to see our plagiarised guidelines professionally printed by MAFF!

FIRE!

2001 had been an eventful year one way and another, and as it came to an end it refused to pass out quietly. On 16 November the fire alarm bells started ringing just on lunchtime. Of all the ills that can befall the mariner, fire is probably the worst simply because once it gets a hold, not only is it difficult to extinguish, but there is nowhere to go if you fail, except the life-rafts. The event produced this report:

Shortly before 1200 today, whilst carrying out a FISHREP [a fisheries report] on the Irish crabber PEADAR ELAINE southwest of the Blackstones Bank, a FIRE ALARM sounded in Zone 7 (Engine room, Engine casing and Engineers Workshop). I noted a change of beat in the port engine and saw the power gauge fluctuating. I immediately brought back the pitch on the port engine to zero and de-clutched, whilst turning the Norna away from the crabber. I simultaneously reduced pitch on the starboard engine to reduce the load which was brought about by de-clutching the port engine. I then attempted to shut down the port engine as smoke was reported issuing from the port funnel, but the running light remained on. I then tried to stop the port engine again at the port consul but the running light remained on. I told my officers to repair to Emergency Stations and prepare for fire, which they did, forming Emergency Parties. By this time the Norna was making distance from the crabber. I reduced pitch on the starboard engine, de-clutched and awaited reports from the Chief Engineer. Shortly after this, the Norna blacked out, the Chief having opened the trip switches to the shaft alternators, then having obtained my permission, he shut down the propulsion and the Norna lay stopped in the water. The Fire Alarm was investigated immediately by the Chief Engineer and the Third Engineer, and all hands mustered at Emergency Stations by 1203.

This rapid muster took place because the Third Engineer had been forced to exit the Engine Room via the escape trunk by the Workshop and had spread the word before the sensors had picked up the smoke in the Engine Room. A head count was taken at this time and all hands accounted for, the Chief Engineer and Third Engineer being in contact with the Bridge by radio. By 1206 two sets of two Breathing Apparatus Parties were ready and on Stand By. At 1210 the Chief Engineer called the Bridge to say there was no fire, only smoke, and that he wished to start the fans to clear the space. I concurred with this. At 1210 the Chief again called to inform me that the Engine Room was clearing well and there was no fire. He reported that water had sprayed onto the port shaft alternator and this had occasioned the short circuit flash- over which had driven the Third Engineer from the vicinity of the alternator.

At 1220 the Chief informed me that I could re-engage the starboard engine which he had re-started. The Emergency Parties were stood down at 1230. Around this time the Chief explained that he was concerned that the Starboard Shaft Alternator might also have been exposed to water and was keen to open it up for inspection and remedial drying. We discussed the option of going to anchor in Islay for investigations but ruled it out because of the strong tides running round the Rhinns and the need to close up the land. We decided to press on for the Clyde and maintain sea-watches in the Engine Room to watch the Starboard Shaft Alternator. In the meantime the engineers would de-couple the Shaft Alternator from the Port Engine so that it could become the motive power and allow us to stop the Starboard Main Engine, thereby allowing investigation of the starboard shaft alternator. This would mean that all electrical load would be taken by the Auxiliary Generator.

HQ were informed of our problems via one of the officers in Operations, and the Assistant to the Marine Superintendent in turn undertook to pass the news on to Superintendents and Management, and to make arrangements for our berth in Greenock and the supply of tugs. He also arranged, at my request, for the Vigilant, which was departing the Clyde, to be in attendance at her earliest convenience. I later spoke with the Captain of the Vigilant about 1330 and confirmed we should meet around 1900 tonight when he could escort us.

We arrived safely into Greenock without further incident, fully aware that things could have been much worse. You may rest assured that I prayed to the Lord about my concerns, and as always He gave me calmness, intelligence and courage; and really good men as my crew.

CROIX MORAND CC.623126

I thought we had used up our full measure of excitement for 2001 with the fire in the shaft alternator, and was looking forward to that time of year when everything slows up for the Christmas holidays. We were due to be away from home this year and I had arranged a berth in Stornoway. I wanted the crew to enjoy the festivities in a relaxed and moderate fashion and had the Mates purchase Christmas trees, fairy lights, and decorations for both Messes, giving the Chief Steward his head to buy nice food for the feast. It was in this frame of mind that on 16 December we came on the French trawler *Croix Morand CC-623126* working on the Hundred Fathom Line to the west of the Uists. The weather was reasonable so I got my officers to suit up and pay him a visit. Away they went at the back of nine o'clock and I settled down as usual to match the course and speed of the Frenchman and watch the sea-boat and my Mates on deck.

I have mentioned the new legislation which was coming in, and one of the measures to assist the recovery of Hake was that they were no longer to be intermingled with other species. Before long, the 1/O/E came on and reported that not only were the Hake being mixed with other fish, he was suspicious of the amounts the Skipper was recording in the bins. The deception was that Skippers would under declare the amount of fish in the bins in order to keep fishing long after their quota had run out. At that time the controls on what was being declared as going into the back of the lorries could not be monitored in all cases, so there was huge scope for fraud. The French at that time were famous for using up their quota exactly at midnight on the day it was supposed to finish. A truly miraculous feat of management!

So I told the Mate to weigh the fish in one of the bins, and sure enough he soon reported that there was about twice as much fish in the bin as the skipper had logged. I asked him to weigh another bin, with similar results. Incidentally it is not easy to weigh a third of a tonne of fish on a smallish trawler rolling on the Atlantic swell. Once I had communicated this information to the Duty Officer we arrested the vessel and escorted him to Lochinver for a court case which was held in Tain. I think I must have presented cases in every Sheriff Court in Scotland with a jurisdiction connected with the sea. He received a fine of £3500 and the Chief Executive informed the Minister for Environment and Rural Development. It made a great end to a busy year.

That was a lovely Christmas alongside. I remember we had to rig up a special aerial, for the berth we were on had no television picture because the big Caledonian MacBrayne ferry the *Isle of Lewis* blanked the signal. So the Chief made up a clamp for the aerial we bought, and I fixed it to the top of the mast with my own hands. The picture was excellent. Everyone behaved in exemplary fashion and we were fine and cosy in our berth, although it blew hard on Boxing Day as I recall, so we could not sail. I was not sorry, and neither were my men. I have a photograph of the officers sitting at the Christmas dinner and it records a happy time. So ended 2001

2002

The year 2002 was a year in which not very much happened at sea at all. We caught only two vessels breaking the rules and both of these were Scottish. The first was a small trawler called the *Diamond SY.804* which we boarded in the Skelmorlie Channel in the upper reaches of the Clyde. I am almost ashamed to mention it, for it was supposed to be time filler prior to going into Greenock but my officers went on board and the Skipper hove up his gear and revealed that he was using an undersized net. This was the last thing we wanted to find on the last day of the trip, but we submitted a report anyway. I do not know if it even went to court. I hope not. The other craft was also a Scottish trawler, but he was boarded in the North Minch on 30 November. The vessel the *Harvest Reaper TT.177* (not to be confused with the other vessel of the same name which we assisted), had been 'boasting' to other fishing vessels in the Minch that he was openly flaunting the law which stated that vessels employing a rig involving more than one net being towed simultaneously were not permitted to have nets less than 100 millimetres mesh size.

I was obliged by worsening weather conditions to ask him to haul an hour early, at three o'clock instead of four in the afternoon. The sky was lowering and the wind gradually increasing so that I was becoming concerned for the boarding officers. They duly measured the nets and found that on average the mesh was about 82 millimetres, significantly less than one hundred. We therefore escorted him to Stornoway where we would have facilities to measure the nets properly, arriving at ten to eight in the evening. We immediately set about seizing all offending articles of gear for secure storage until the case could be heard in court. A sample of the catch was also seized and placed in the Fishery Office freezer. After this, the *Harvest Reaper* set off for the other side of the Minch as a gale was now forecast. I then forgot about the *Harvest Reaper* for she was 'small beer' until called to give evidence about six months later.

By this time, some of my officers had been sent to other ships and we all had to meet in the hotel in Stornoway which the Agency had booked us into for the court case. We spent one night there and were sent home next day as the Skipper, for some reason, was not able to attend. I remember we enjoyed an enormous bucket of mussels each which were absolutely delicious. So another six months went by and we all met again, although this time I think I took the *Norna* into Stornoway. The court case was heard and all our witnesses were given a serious grilling by the defence agent. Such cross examination after a year is always difficult but they stuck to their guns pretty well. I was in the witness box for about two hours. However, we found out when we arrived in Stornoway, that the nets and all the gear we had seized, which were supposedly secured in a lock-fast, had been stolen over the Christmas and New Year period! Because of this the Sheriff decided that, since we could not produce 'best evidence', the case could not be proven. So the message is, if you want to get away with a crime, just arrange to steal the evidential productions! What this ruling in effect meant was that our veracity as law enforcement agents was of no value. I think it is stretching the bounds of credulity too far to believe that an interested party was not involved in the theft but of course one cannot say so for certain. We were made to look foolish by this loss of evidence and that annoyed me. I do not know what became of the vessel, nor do I care, but I do not think we came across it again.

Lack of results at sea from a law enforcement point of view did not mean we were not busy, for the Agency like all ship owners had to implement the International Safety Management system or ISM as it was called. This occupied our attention not only during 2002 but right up until I retired. I think it is true to say that, from that year onwards, we never came back to the ship without some change or another in the safety and operational regime having been being enacted. There are certain characters who revel in this type of bureaucracy but I am not one of them, although I was obliged to 'bite the bullet' and embrace the concept. Of course, it was introduced for the very best reasons, but by the time I left the tail was definitely wagging the dog, and we seemed to exist to jump through ever more involved and ludicrous hoops. As I read the *Norna* NEWS for this period, it is awash with little articles about this safety regime. In fact the only thing worth reading is the 'Thought for the Day'. Here is one from 22 July 2002:

Ever since man made a dugout canoe it has happened that, as soon as he made it big enough for two people, he started having crew problems.

That about sums it up.

2003

Our Chief Executive was always keen to show the Agency off in order to raise awareness of our work and organisation, and the *Norna* frequently found herself being used as the PR platform for these exposés. I thoroughly enjoyed these opportunities and always threw myself and my crew into doing the best we could to show off our ship and the Agency. I think that is why the CEO used us so often; quite apart from the fact we were the 'flagship'. So in February we took the Chief Executive of a Fish Producer Organisation, a lawyer by whom I had been cross examined more than once, for a brief trip round the lower reaches of the Clyde. We managed to put him and the Boss onto several fishing vessels to give him a feel of what it was like at the business end of the fishing industry, and in addition allowed him, representing fishermen, to see that we were scrupulous in our even-handed approach to enforcement. I recall on that particular trip we landed them on Ailsa Craig for light relief and they came back with a piece of granite which had been bored to remove a curling stone. I still have it in the garden.

Later on that month we had to carry with us two EU inspectors who had to monitor our implementation of several pieces of EU legislation. We picked them up in Lochinver and they remained with us until the end of the month. They went everywhere we went, naturally, and were always around whenever there was any action. I think we patrolled all over our patch from Muckle Flugga to the Irish Grey Zone and in the end a synopsis of the activities and assessments of the EU inspectors produced by our Headquarters stated:

They were impressed by the professionalism of staff and noted the excellent safety standards on board the FPV. In fact they commented that this was the best FPV they had been on board in the whole of the EU fleets.

They were full of praise for the vessel and noted the difficulties faced by officers during inspections. One boarding was particularly difficult because of stalling tactics employed by the master of the fishing vessel.

It was good for outsiders to make comments like that, for we were very much alone as an enforcement unit and the positive feedback was most welcome so that we could measure ourselves.

During that patrol with the inspectors we were asked by the missile firing range at Benbecula to clear the firing range of all vessels. So we spent the day doing that and received a nice letter of thanks from the Commanding Officer of that facility.

THE ASSISTANCE TO YACHT *CLIONE*

You will notice we had not assisted anyone for some time. However, that was all to change on the night of the 7 May 2003, when the following report was generated:

At 2330BST whilst sheltering in Loch Snizort from a south-easterly gale, the Norna's Officer of the Watch overheard Stornoway Coastguard passing a message about a yacht which was overdue on passage from Strollamus Yard in Skye to Dunvegan in Skye.

I immediately contacted the Coastguard to offer the Norna's services, as it appeared that they were scrambling the helicopter and Portree lifeboat to search the area of the Ascrib Islands in Loch Snizort. Search was immediately commenced but at 2350BST the search units were stood down as the yacht Clione reported she was making her way into Loch Dunvegan.

At 0030BST the First Officer Safety, called me to say that Stornoway Coastguard had issued a Mayday to the effect that the yacht had gone ashore in Loch Dunvegan and required assistance. I immediately arranged for the Norna to proceed at full speed whilst Portree lifeboat and the rescue helicopter Mike Uniform were also re-scrambled.

By 0122BST the Norna was rounding Waternish Point at 14 knots into a south westerly gale but by about 0150BST she had entered the mouth of the Loch and was coming into smaller water, when a light was sighted on the east shore of the Loch. Around the same time the helicopter arrived and started to search, but could not locate the yacht. At 0200BST however, the Norna's people were able to sight the yacht's lights again and then point the Norna's searchlight at the casualty. After some time the helicopter also sighted the yacht but was unable to effect a rescue due to the back-draught of the cliffs which held the yacht.

The Norna's crew immediately made ready the sea-boat and prepared to launch to rescue the yachtsman. At 0214BST the Arctic was launched, and providentially the wind dropped to about 25/30 knots from the West, although in the black dark and the onshore wind the job was still pretty awkward. The searchlight was trained all the time by the Second Officer, as the Arctic ran before the wind to the yacht. They made brisk progress to the casualty, and by 0222BST the coxswain manoeuvred the boat to allow rescue of the yachtsman, who was in good condition. The Arctic was recovered at 0230BST, and after Mr John Whittaker (the yachtsman) had had a quick brew, I made arrangements for the life-boat which had just arrived on the scene to take him to Dunvegan. He transferred to the life-boat at 0247BST and arrived in Dunvegan shortly after 0300BST.

I was asked by Stornoway Coastguard to remain in the vicinity to ascertain the condition of the yacht and the quantity of oil pollution in the morning. I agreed to do this as long as the wind did not haul into the nor-west.

The Norna was able to remain on scene till now (0730BST) to report that the yacht was out of the water in a tiny cove and appeared to be whole and intact. There was no sign of oil pollution from the five gallons of fuel stated to be on board. The Norna could not effect salvage at this time as the wind had hauled to the west-nor-west and was kicking up a sea at the mouth of the little cove, and also on account of lack of water due to low tide.

Captain David L Beveridge
Commanding Officer FPV Norna

The Director of Operations sent me a signal that afternoon:

All of this activity is a credit to the Marine Service in the best traditions of which, whatever happens, will endure to the end of time. A 'Well done' to all who acted so positively and with such good effect. Best personal regards.

It was not like the Director to be so prosy and I think he was genuinely very cheerful about this service. I was always a bit confused by his 'whatever happens' but I think he was exercised at the time by yet more hostile attacks on the Agency.

SKERRYVORE

People take lighthouses for granted, and it is only in recent times that programmes have started to appear on television which tell the story of the great lights and the men who built them. It is a great saga and of course the

Stevenson family, over several generations, were by far the quintessential creators of these structures. Now, it so happened that Rob Anderson, my dear old friend (he was in his late eighties at the time), gave me a book of prayers written by Robert Louis Stevenson while he was out in the South Seas.

(That is, Robert Louis was out in the South Seas. As far as I know, Rob was never in the South Seas, although he once did a world tour when he was Head Designer for Templetons Carpets in Glasgow. Rob had designed a wonderful range of patterns which were incredibly popular and apparently were easy to change the colour-ways on. It seems this is very handy if you are weaving carpets for different tastes. Anyway, one day the owner, Mr. Templeton I presume, came in and said to Rob 'You've been working very hard Rob and you've done a great job with this design so it's time you took a break and went round the world. Just talk to people and get the feel for the next big idea.' You see, that is what entrepreneurs and great employers were like in days gone by. So Rob went on a world tour and had a great time and got some more ideas: I expect that many of us are still walking about on some of Rob's designs, and we do not even know it).

To return to the book of prayers, it was beautifully produced and I think it was quite valuable, but to be honest I did not have a great use for it beyond possessing it. Judge my surprise, therefore, when the Chief Executive told me one day that he wanted to take some the descendants of the Stevenson family out to Skerryvore Lighthouse. Now the Boss never did anything on a whim and I am sure he had a good reason for this trip but I was never sure what it was, beyond providing an excellent opportunity for sightseeing. So as always I threw the *Norna*'s resources into it, and started thinking about what we would do when our guests came. It was then that I decided that it would be a nice touch to pass the book of prayers on to a descendent of RLS.

The Chief Executive had mapped out a programme for the short visit, which went along the lines that we would pick him and a colleague up in Stornoway on 8 August, and then sail via Kyleakin and Kyle Rhea for Tiree, where we would embark three others from Scarnish in Tiree. The evening we passed through the Kyles was quite magical for we had been able to lay on a special dinner which included red crab, gifted by a law abiding Anglo-Spaniard on the Rosemary Bank. Not many people have tasted Red Crab but it is quite special. It's funny the ways things come together. The crab, plus some 1664 beer and a couple of sets on the pipes from the Chief and me, and one could not ask for much more. Next morning when we picked up the other three guests the wind had shifted into the south-east blowing into the bay at Scarnish. Our guests were soaked on the way out to the ship, and one in particular required a pair of my jogger bottoms and a pair of socks, for which she was very grateful; the garments imparting a cosy, if slightly voluminous, Wee Willie Winkie look. South east was the least favourable wind for our purposes, but I was determined to let them see the lighthouse at close quarters.

So when we arrived at the rock, about which we had obtained detailed information from the Northern Lights ship the *Pharos* when we shared an anchorage at St. Kilda earlier in the trip, the guests were able to sail round the rock in the Arctic seaboat, which they found thrilling, taking plenty of photographs. When they had finished and were back on board I presented them all with a memento of their trip and the book to the senior family member. They were very touched; they in turn presented us with a lovely etching of Skerryvore, which I have recently rescued from the Fishery Cruiser Store where it landed after the *Norna* was decommissioned. We took them back to Scarnish, then went up to Oban and dropped off the Chief Executive. He was very pleased and he and all his guests wrote nice letters to us.

Prior to carrying out this task, I did some research about Skerryvore and wrote a little article for the *Norna* NEWS to let the lads know what it was about. It went like this:

If we get half a chance with the weather, we will try to have a fairly close encounter with Skerryvore Lighthouse. The name is Gaelic/Norse of course and would appear to mean 'The big Skerry'. It forms the largest and most impressive part of a huge reef system which extends southwards and southwesterly for about 12 miles from the south end of Tiree. For hundreds of years the reefs proved a formidable and terrifying obstacle to the safe passage of shipping, with huge numbers of craft disappearing without trace, every year. It was not until 1836 that Alan Stephenson, who was Clerk of Works to the Northern Lighthouse Board, after a considerable amount of persuasive argument on his part, was commissioned to build a lighthouse. Alan Stephenson, you will remember, belonged to that family who counted an extraordinarily large number of highly talented engineers, not to mention the famous author Robert Louis amongst their number. To that family, uniquely, we owe almost every one of the 90 or so major lights round the coast of Scotland. It is a debt which we as mariners could never repay.

The construction of the lighthouse must rank amongst the greatest engineering feats ever, even without taking into account the technology of the period in which it was undertaken. The whole project, which employed about 150 men, took about 6 consecutive years to complete, with the work being undertaken each year in the brief weather window between June and September. Whilst simultaneously constructing a pier at Hynish in Tiree, it took two seasons for them to build a suitable 'barracks' beside the footings of the lighthouse, to allow them to work with some continuity, the first attempt being swept away in a November gale. The 'barracks' incidentally were no small feat in themselves, being in the form of a stout wooden 'rocket' shape at the top of six mighty wooden legs fixed in the solid rock. Conditions in the accommodation must have been excruciating, particularly when the men were beset by 'summer gales'. On one occasion they were marooned for a fortnight. One can only guess at the constant dampness, the cramped conditions and the gnawing fear that the whole edifice might carry away.

Cutting the huge base of the foundation into the living rock, undertaken largely by picks which blunted after three strikes, was an outstanding achievement of masonry, of such exactitude that it permitted an accuracy, after the construction of the mighty tower, of within one sixteenth of an inch! The tower virtually grows out of the rock. The bottom four courses of the tower are Tiree black gneiss, whilst the remainder is of pink Mull granite, every block of which had to be hewn and fashioned with the most prodigious accuracy. The blocks weigh up to two and a half tons. Bear in mind this work was carried out with rowing boats and shear legs and a couple of steam donkey cranes, in the Atlantic which we know and love.

The weight of the lighthouse is 58,580 tons and it stands 137 feet high. It is twice the weight of the Bell Rock and over four times the weight of the Eddystone Light. Despite the ever present danger of all kinds during the entire operation, there were very few injuries (figures not available) and no fatalities. Not a Risk Assessment or Permit to Work in sight!

The Stephensons went on to build many more lights, amongst them Dubh Artach and Hyskeir, not to mention Barra Head, Muckle Flugga, and the Cape, but that's another story.

I forget where I obtained this information, maybe it was Wikipedia, so I have no doubt that much of the phrasing owes its origin to whoever wrote the pieces in that worthy source of knowledge. I simply include it because it is good to remember that great building achievement.

BRUIX

As 2003 progressed, I became increasingly aware that opportunities for capturing offenders were diminishing. This was brought about for several reasons, but primarily it came down to two elements. Firstly, the law was changing in ways which made it much more difficult for officers to detect offences, and indeed many of the offences had disappeared due to the redrafting of legislation. Secondly, we were becoming victims of our own success, for whereas in the past Spanish vessels in particular would be either ignorant or dismissive of the rules, they were now far better informed as indeed were all nationalities. Our continuing fight against 'black landings' of our own fleet could not really be dealt with at sea for it was essentially an in-port offence; all we could do at sea was ensure that they completed their logbooks correctly and reduce the opportunities for misrecording. The relationship we had with our own boats was poor during this period for they felt they were being hounded and forced to break the law. In circumventing the normal procedures and arrangements for landing fish, they undermined their own market, and this issue would not be solved for several years, until the advent of electronic logbooks and stricter controls on the hauliers. These measures, combined with a reduction of fishing effort, with 'Days at Sea' legislation reducing the number of days vessels could work offshore, and with the 'Decommissioning' programme which saw many fine vessels being destroyed, have brought about a more stable if greatly reduced Scottish fishing fleet.

When one visits Scottish fishing ports now they are but shadows of what they were in the past. It is very sad and in my view our fishing industry was the victim of our membership of the European Union. Had we been able to protect our waters the way I envisaged, it would be a different story today.

Also around this time, I became aware of attitudes being formed by Operations room staff that the fleet were not really trying, despite the good reports we had whenever inspectors came away with us. For this reason, at one Commanding Officers' Conference I suggested that some of the more vociferous of our critics come away with us and experience our lives at sea, not in the height of summer but rather in December. I am very glad to say that one critic, a fine ambitious young man, rose to the challenge and joined us for the December trip of 2003.

Prior to this officer joining, we had become aware that a certain big French ex-stern trawler, the *Bruix*, was fishing in a closed area at the south end of the Rockall Bank. This area was protected to encourage Cod recovery, as I recall. The Frenchman had ceased to fish with trawling gear and had been converted to fishing with gill nets. We could easily monitor his flaunting of the exclusion zone, for by this time every vessel over a certain size was fitted with a satellite transponder beacon which sent out the position of the vessel at required intervals. So we set off from Greenock with our observer from the Operations Room aboard quite early in December and had to go to Stornoway first for the court case I told you about with the *Harvest Reaper*. By the time that case was lost, the weather had moderated sufficiently to make a trip to Rockall worthwhile. I was constantly at pains during this period to bring our observer's attention to the disparity between the BBC weather forecast and the reality of what was happening just outside the bridge windows. He soon began to realise that theory was seldom close to practice. However, I did identify an improvement in the weather forming and we duly set off for the Rock.

We made good passage in the decaying seas and the wind fell away so that fog began to form by the time we reached the Rockall Bank. This was perfect. I knew exactly where the *Bruix* was fishing, but was concerned that he would realise we were a Fishery Protection Vessel and make a bolt for it. So, as we arrived at the Bank and before we came into radar contact, I began to make the *Norna* look on radar like a regular transatlantic commercial ship just crossing the tail of the Bank. I made sure our course could not be construed as making for the *Bruix* and pressed on as if we were simply ploughing through the fog, making for Canada. As we swept past the closest point of approach unseen, I suddenly put her about and made for the *Bruix*. There was no sign of movement on screen so my ruse had worked.

We soon drew to within about half a mile and I announced who we were and that I was sending a boarding party across immediately. As soon as I slowed down the engines, we could hear the clanking of her gear and the shouts of the French crew as they worked the gill nets. We could not see her even at two cables, or twelve hundred feet. Our observer had been watching this very closely and was now changed and ready, like the rest of the boarding party, to proceed to the *Bruix*. Of course, they caught him red handed and we were soon escorting him to Lochinver, where we berthed. I cannot remember where we had the court but it could have been Dingwall. He was found guilty and fined £5000, and his entire catch confiscated. The value of the fish on our market would have been £90,000 but the agent for the fishing company, a very experienced elderly Greek gentleman, was threatening to leave the fish which would have been an embarrassment for our market. So we did a bit of horse trading and he bought it back for £20,000. I was not really concerned about numbers, simply a successful outcome. The levying of fines was not my province.

Our observer stayed with us for the remainder of the patrol and was the first one ever to do so. I am just remembering we had had a false start that trip for we had to return to Greenock early on to have the steering gear fixed. It was good for him to see the frustrations of the job and the reality of the weather. Capturing the Frenchman had been more than I could have hoped for. Following that patrol, our observer made out a report of his trip which cast us in an extremely favourable light and was most satisfactory.

CHAPTER THIRTY-NINE
A MIXTURE OF TOPICS

RECOVERING JUNK

I should tell you that we often had to recover objects from the water which might be construed as hazards to navigation. These frequently took the form of buoys which had broken adrift, usually over in Canada, due to the movement of ice or to violent weather, and the buoys would then drift across the Atlantic till they arrived in our waters. I recall one of these buoys which was really huge, and to tell the truth I cannot remember if it was whilst I was on the *Norna* or the *Vigilant,* but we were contacted by Stornoway Coastguard because several ships had reported it. Thankfully the positions they gave were fairly accurate so after a bit of searching we finally caught up with this thing off the Butt of Lewis. It stood about ten feet out of the water but, like an iceberg, most of its bulk was submerged and it sported a huge counter-weight and a length of heavy anchor cable. When we came on it the weather was good so I put the boat over the side and the lads went away to secure it. They had a bit of fun doing that for one of them had to jump onto it as it bobbed up and down in the swell to secure it to our towing hawser, and each time it rose and fell in the swell it gave out a raucous bellow like an angry bull. This was its self-generating fog signal. Anyway we made it fast and having recovered the boat, set off for Stornoway. We towed it down the coast of Lewis, and I arranged with the Coastguard for their rescue tug to come and take it off us in Stornoway Bight; for the tug, I think it was *Anglian Prince,* was an anchor handler. They had to work to get it on board but her mighty winches were soon heaving it up the stern ramp. It went on and on and I cannot tell you how much chain there was. They carried it into the harbour and secured it to the end of Number One Pier, where it lay until the first gale of southerly wind when, as the swell made its way into the harbour, the big buoy started to rise and fall as if at sea. Of course, it immediately started to do what it was built for and began roaring out warnings to the sleeping inhabitants of Stornoway. It did not remain long at the end of the pier!

On another occasion, in August 2004, we were in Stornoway waiting for a relief seaman to join, when the Coastguard called to say that an adrift lifeboat had been reported by a commercial ship, the *Nordica Svenita,* whilst on passage off Lewis. The Coastguard had already had the rescue helicopter confirm the position and that there was no sign of life.

So...

Having consulted with the Operations Room, I arranged to depart Stornoway at 1400 on the 5th. When the replacement seaman had joined, we made passage directly to the given position. The Norna arrived on scene at 1800 and commenced search. Conditions were halcyon and so at 1940 the craft was sighted, in position 58 34.8 North 06 58.18 West. The Arctic sea-boat was launched at 2000 and by 2010 the tow-line was connected, the Arctic recovered and the tow commenced at 2015. The Norna entered East Loch Roag at 0100 this morning (6th). At 0128 the Arctic was again launched to disconnect the tow. By 0132 the tow-line was recovered and by 0140 the lifeboat laid alongside the Norna's port side, where she was secured fore and aft. The sea-boat was then recovered and passage continued to the anchorage, where anchor was cast at 0225, and the vessel brought up by 0230.

Next morning we towed the lifeboat to the pier at Breasclete where it was met by Coastguard officers. Strangely there were no markings on the lifeboat to identify the ship from which it had come, and even more strangely it had a huge bite out of the gunwale and bilge as if it had been attacked by an enormous creature...

DIGITAL CAMERAS, NEAFC, ISLAND HOPPING

This rather unwieldy title is held together by the idea of recording events and using that record to some end.

It did not take the highly intelligent officers in the Fishery Protection Fleet long to realise the potential of the digital camera, and before long the cameras were being used for everything from evidential recording in fisheries cases to informing HQ of technical problems or simply recording things that happened. We soon amassed very large numbers of images which formed an excellent library of what we had been about over any period, so it occurred to me that we might be able to produce a record of our year's work by putting it into some kind of collage. I resolved therefore to engage some of the prodigious talent which was operating on the ship in the form of my First Officer (Executive) and my First Officer (Safety). The Mate was particularly skilled with graphics and images and had been the one to produce the spreadsheet which was plagiarised by MAFF. For him, producing a collage was relatively simple and before long he had come up with an A3 plasticised sheet of photos with catchy titles to describe them, which achieved exactly what I wanted. I was delighted with this and still possess all the sheets which were made up over ensuing years. Without them I would have missed much of 2004, for I have none of the statements of the vessels we detected. However, I see from the collage that between the two crews we reported nine vessels; all, I think for boarding ladder offences.

This was the year we really went to town on vessels which did not provide a safe boarding ladder, for up until that time the legislation had not been rigorously enforced, but our officers were frequently in harm's way because of dangerous ladders. Sometimes a ladder looked sound enough but had been allowed to rot on board the fishing boat without ever being looked at, so that as soon as any weight was applied it collapsed. This could easily end in an injury or fatality. Thankfully no one was ever killed in my time, but plenty of men and women were hurt when a ladder parted, quite apart from being scared witless. As I look at the detections for 2004, I note that we were no longer bringing in foreign vessels from the 'frontier' and the light was beginning to go out of the job for me.

This did not mean, however, that we were not going out there, for we started to carry out NEAFC or North East Atlantic Fisheries Commission patrols, not only to the Rockall-generated limits but beyond to the Hatton Bank, more than twenty degrees west. I was one of a small party of our people who had to attend a meeting in London with the NEAFC Secretary and it became clear at that meeting that we were a long way from really enforcing a fisheries regime in International Waters, for the sanctions which could be imposed were fairly toothless. Nevertheless we took it very seriously, and when we were sent out on 18 May 2004 we produced a report of our three-day patrol into the old Rockall-generated limits which we had not patrolled for a long time. Most of our contacts were Russian stern trawlers, factory ships fishing with forty millimetre nets! The slaughter of immature fish was apocalyptic. I made recommendations in that report and in subsequent reports, my observations being proved by the strong photographic evidence which the officers were obtaining, and of course the reports themselves were extremely well put together, with graphs and charts and so on, by this talented crew of mine.

NEAFC patrols would become a regular occurrence in the years following, and it is to be hoped that the information we produced will someday bring about a more rigorous enforcement regime, but I have my doubts.

ISLAND HOPPING

I have always been a tourist. I hesitate to accord myself the more grandiloquent title of 'explorer' although the two activities are not disconnected. I think our family motto should have been 'I wonder what's over the next hill', or in my case the next horizon. Allied to this, and issuing from it, is my love of islands, the 'exploration' of which has been one of my great joys since I joined the Fisheries. It is difficult to describe landing on a desolate uninhabited islet or skerry in general terms, for they are all unique, but it is a little like tramping over new snow. One is aware people have been there before but for now, for this brief moment, the place is yours. You possess it like a conquistador and in some strange way you own the memory and therefore part of the soul of the place. Since I became a commander I have made a point of trying to get my men used to effecting landings on these islands, so that should they have to do it 'in anger', as was the case when we rescued the skipper of the yacht *Clione*, they would be prepared. In addition, I could indulge my little idiosyncrasy. So I and members of my numerous crews have landed on St. Kilda, The Flannan Isles, Sule Skerry, Rona, The Shiants, Staffa, Fladda-chuin, the Fair Isle, Foula, and others which I cannot remember just now. Occasionally these visits coincided with my children being on the ship, and increasingly with the Chief Executive, who would from time to time come away on the flagship to show off our organisation, for public relations purposes. Being well trained by Patsy, my wife, I always tried to obtain some record of these trips, or charged one of the shore party with the admonition 'Take photos and some film!', as part of the brief we always had before any landings were attempted. These were not simply 'jollies'; they were genuine opportunities to train the men and I considered them essential. So did the CEO, as a matter of fact. And they were great fun as well.

My interest in the video camera actually began away back on the *Westra*, when I was her Captain. The Department, as it was at the time, possessed a video camera which was in many respects similar to the type one sees BBC cameramen using in Afghanistan and places like that. This one, however, was powered by enormous batteries which were carried in a belt worn like a deep sea diver, round the waist. The camera itself weighed about twenty pounds or more and so filming at sea was quite gymnastic and muscular. I recall once filming a big French stern trawler north of Muckle Flugga in a heavy swell with hardly any wind, to show HQ why, although the forecast can correctly give light winds, the swell can be huge. This was the case on this day as the Frenchman rose on the swell then disappeared in the trough, and these were big ships of about 500 tons. As I attempted to balance this camera on my shoulder, maintain equilibrium with my diver's belt round my waist and counter the swell as we rolled, you can imagine the filming was not BBC standard, and in fact as I concentrated on obtaining a steady image I forgot about my counter-balance routine and went hurtling towards the bridge wing taffrail. Only superb muscle control and a finely honed set of abdominals (if only) prevented me from plummeting meteor-like into the Atlantic. I was glad when camcorders were invented.

After this I began to see the value of video cameras in the context of demonstrating an actual capture, to show a Sheriff what happened. I persuaded HQ of the value of this and we were supplied with cameras; although we filmed many vessels, to act as an, aide-mémoire, these were never presented as evidence. There were problems with continuity of evidence, but I had never intended the film to be a substitute for good evidence gathering. I made several training movies for new entrants, but they never caught on, although the latest Marine Superintendent remarked one day (when he came on them while throwing stuff out of Pentland House) that they were 'quite good'. By that time my enthusiasm had long since waned, and I was deeply engrossed in learning to play the Great Highland Bagpipe.

LEARNING THE GREAT HIGHLAND BAGPIPE

I regard my sailing with my bagpipe playing Chief Engineer as exceedingly Providential.

Engineers hate Captains referring to 'My Chief Engineer' as if he was a sort of large Jack Russel, but that is not what is in my mind when I use the phrase. I mean it to convey the deepest respect, reliance and trust on my part;

for, as my father, (a Marine Engineer) used to say, 'You won't get far without us'. Never a truer word was spoken. I cannot tell you how often I have thanked God for these clever, gifted men and their great commitment to the good of the ships they sail on. It was a privilege to sail with them all. This Chief was right up there with the best of them and I have already mentioned how willingly and skilfully he realised my alterations to the *Norna's* boat launching arrangements. In 2002 I had spoken to him about teaching me to play and he kindly agreed.

So, armed with a new practice chanter and the College of Piping Tutor One, I would present myself at the door of his cabin, which was adjacent to mine, like a schoolboy, every day in life. I cannot tell you how patient he was with my poor ability, but before too long I was able to make attempts at the simpler tunes, and after about year, I was introduced to the Great Pipe and have been fairly obsessed by the instrument ever since. There is only one way to learn the pipe and that is wholeheartedly. No matter how gifted one is, it requires huge amounts of practice and even now, after ten years of continuous labour, I do not rate myself much of a piper (and neither does anyone else for that matter). The Chief never let me away with anything and always politely and patiently informed me when I was playing rubbish. Soon I joined St. Francis Pipe Band in the Gorbals, which my children Jenny, Martin and Esther had been members of for years. After a couple of years, I was allowed to march round the street with only the drones going, to get the feel of it, then to play properly as my mistakes became less noticeable and outrageous. I have been a playing member since around 2005, and have now carved out a niche for myself as the chap who fixes the pipes. This was bound to happen because I have good skill with my hands and, having gone round several factories and workshops to learn the mysteries of the instrument more intimately, I have become a sort of repair guru. In 2010 I sat the College of Piping exam Grade Four without doing the previous examinations, and am currently studying for the Grade Five. I doubt I could ever progress to Grade Eight but you never know. In 2009 I started a class in my church to teach the chanter and this has carried on ever since with the splendid help I am afforded by John Paton, Kenny Pullins and Dennis Millar, who are all excellent pipers; John and Dennis are Grade One pipers which is the highest band-playing standard. Dennis brings his two sons to learn. I do not know how it was these chaps appeared but they come every week and I am thankful for them, and the class is thriving. I must not forget

317

John MacFarlane who is my right hand man in the running of this class and he is also learning.

I realise I have digressed somewhat for the last couple of pages but we must return to sea to complete my time on the *Norna* and progress to my final ship. Before we do, there are two events worth recalling. The first took place on 2 July 2004, on a very pleasant afternoon, in the North Minch about twelve miles to the east of Stornoway Bight. I forget why we were there on a nice day when we might just as easily have been on the Hundred Fathom Line, but there we were, when the VHF suddenly leapt into life with the usual PAN PANPAN, referring to a yacht called the *Calema*, which had suffered an engine explosion. Thankfully no one was reported as hurt, but they needed assistance so we obtained the position and set off hot foot. I think I will let the skipper of the yacht relate the tale, for he sent me this nice letter about a week later. His name was Professor John H. Knox, FRS, FRSE

Dear Captain Beveridge,

I am writing to express the warmest thanks of myself and the other two crew members of my yacht CALEMA for the assistance you gave us when our engine broke down some 12 miles from Stornoway on Friday 2 July.

It was most kind of you to come to our assistance so soon after you had just left Stornoway. Although the conditions were calm at the time, there was so little wind that it would have taken us five to seven hours to reach Stornoway under sail and maybe even longer. We particularly appreciated the skill with which your crew handled the attachment of the tow, their friendliness, and the great care with which you towed us at 6knots. We were also most appreciative of the final tow by your RIB into Stornoway Harbour to lay us alongside the quay. The whole job was carried out with true professionalism.

When we arrived we were met by two members of the Coastguard who immediately put us in touch with an engineer who was able to come down to our yacht that evening. It was quickly apparent that the engine, as he put it, 'was terminal'. In fact the explosion which had occurred in the engine casing had fractured the casing, causing a major oil leak, which made it unserviceable. It had also damaged the bearings. A new engine is now on order and hopefully can be installed over the next week or two. We then look forward to a safe return to our mooring in Loch Crearan.

I hope it is acceptable to send you a token of our appreciation in the form of a cheque for £100 on our behalf. We would like you to use it either as a small treat for the crew of the Norna or as a gift to a charity of your choice.

We are deeply grateful for your timely and efficient help in an emergency, and wish you all success in the Fishery Protection business.

Yours sincerely,

John H. Knox (Skipper of CALEMA)

So now, after reading that letter, I realise we were leaving Stornoway to head out to the Atlantic. We gave the money to the Sick Children's Hospital in Glasgow, but we drank the box of Kumala wine they gave us. The three men on the yacht were all over seventy. I later wrote an article for our Agency Newsletter about this service, for they were always after contributions. People were always impressed by our professionalism but it was only to be expected, for we practised often, and boat-work was how we made a living.

JOE BORG – EUROPEAN FISHERIES COMMISSIONER

When new European Fisheries Commissioners take up their position, if they have any sense, they like to get around their parish, as it were, and get the feel of what they have let themselves in for. Commissioner Joe Borg was certainly of this type, and our Chief Executive was just the man to make facilities available to let him see what life was like in Scotland. Accordingly, at the end January 2005, he orchestrated a visit by the Commissioner and his entourage to Peterhead, with the *Norna* there to host the refreshments. The CEO knew I would be up for this and would get my men into a frame of mind for putting on a good show; for successful events do not just happen, they are 'created'. The Cook and Chief Steward are probably more important than anyone in these affairs and if they are onside then life is infinitely more straightforward. I was very fortunate in the people I had and I gave them licence to 'show off'; however everyone on board has to be prepared to make an extra effort. I am very thankful that, as always, the crew of the *Norna* rose to the occasion, but we were completely unprepared for the inundation of bodies which arrived with Commissioner Borg, his party, and our own Minister, Ross Finnie, replete with a bevy of assistants, advisers and a platoon of press men and photographers. I do not know how many we had in the Officers' Lounge but it was heaving. As I made my way through the crowd,' managing' the business, I was aware of how my lads were rising to the occasion and was very proud of them. At one point Ross Finnie and I ended up beside each other while he was filling his plate, from a table groaning with good things from poached salmon to chicken piri piri. I suddenly remembered he had recently suffered a heart attack and opened with 'Aye, you have to watch what you eat right enough. How are you feeling now?' I could see that he was glad to make contact with a human who was genuinely interested in how he was feeling and we spent some time talking about health in general, and him in particular, then we had to put on our official hats, and become the Fisheries Minister and the Captain of the *Norna* again.

I then had to take Commissioner Borg and his staff, which I recall was comprised mostly of career women, who were all attractive and very excited about being on a ship, up to the bridge to explain our work in five minutes. I think it went down well and nothing would do but these women must have their photographs taken with the Captain. Mr. Borg was allowed in too, but in the background. It was a cold day so the females had to cuddle up very close.

It's the uniform that does it, I think, but sometimes you just have to take one for the team.

It really was a success and both the Chief Executive and the Minister were pleased, and both wrote to thank us.

For my crew, 2005 was not particularly memorable, although our colleagues on the other crew had a couple of highlights, not the least of which was being alongside in Stornoway when a hurricane hit the Hebrides. They put in a very anxious night which they had the good sense to film in part, and I think someone put the clip on YouTube. Big waves can be seen crashing over the breakwater and onto the Caledonian Hotel. That night a whole family was swept into the sea off the Uists and lost. It was very sad.

The other event they had was to do as we had done, and take the *Norna* to another International Festival of the Sea, in Portsmouth, and they did an excellent job. To be frank I was glad I missed it, for it was really quite stressful and the doctor was beginning to insist that I take medication for hypertension. I ended up on Atenolol, after I had a pre-syncopal episode while navigating the *Norna* past Greenholm in the *Westray* Firth. Funnily enough, after I started the pills, one of the men remarked that the Old Man was pretty laid back these days!

RUSSA TAIGN

I had been wondering how long things would carry on without much action as 2005 progressed, and fisheries cases were becoming fewer and fewer as opportunities diminished. The only cases which seemed to be reported in those days were boarding ladder offences which were less than exciting. So it was with a little increase in the heart rate (not too great an increase, thanks to the Atenolol) that:

[at]0846 on Tuesday 12ᵗʰ July 2005, I heard Stornoway Coastguard transmitting a PAN PAN message in respect of the Scottish fishing vessel Russa Taign which was broken down in position 57 53 North 11 31 West, some 30 miles NNW of the Anton Dohrn Seamount. I immediately called Stornoway Coastguard on Sat B telephone to obtain more details and was informed that the vessel had no hope of a tow until Sunday, there being no other vessels in her vicinity. At this time the Norna was in position 56 25 North 09 22 West, working the Hundred Fathom Line in the vicinity of the Irish Grey Zone, about 120 miles SE of the Russa Taign. Permission was immediately sought from HQOPS and Marine Superintendent, to proceed to help, and this was granted very quickly, so that by 0900 the Norna was heading at best speed to the fishing vessel, with an ETA of 1630. It was explained to the master of the Russa Taign that the Norna would assist her until relieved by either a commercial towing vessel or another fishing vessel. Passage to Russa Taign was speedy and uneventful and a tow-line connected at 1655, and all set by 1730, when tow speed was gradually increased to about 5 knots. [The Russa Taign is about 530 tons gross and the Norna, while very powerful, possesses only primitive towing equipment.]

14ᵗʰ July
The towage towards the Butt of Lewis was uneventful and took all of the 13ᵗʰ with the Norna and the Russa Taign rounding the Butt of Lewis at 0100 on the 14ᵗʰ to rendezvous with the fishing vessel KEILA in the lee of Lewis. The tow line was disconnected at 0140 and recovered. In the meantime the KEILA passed her towing hawser to the Russa Taign and started to tow towards Cape Wrath at 0210. Stornoway Coastguard was informed as soon as the exchange had been effected. The Norna then resumed patrol duties.

This tow was carried out for the most part in benign conditions, with following winds never more than force 6. The distance of the tow was about 180 miles at a speed of just over 5 knots.

Captain D L Beveridge
Commanding Officer FPV Norna
14th July 2005

The *Russa Taign* was a fairly a big ship for us to tow and the distance was quite far, because it meant us coming off patrol for a couple of days, which is why I had to clear it with HQ. My Second Officer filmed the tow connection for me, and I now have it to remind myself that I used to pull big boats in from the North Atlantic.

This Second Officer was a good chum, who had been in command and had had an interesting life before he came to Fisheries. He and I could yarn away for hours and, after he retired, I could vicariously enjoy the lovely places he visited and the holidays he arranged for himself, for he would send me pictures and e-mails. We still exchange Christmas cards.

CHAPTER FORTY
THE NEW *JURA* 2005 – 2007

Towards the end of 2005 it came time to move on again, and I received orders to hand over the *Norna* to another commander, and proceed to Port Glasgow where the new *Jura* was being built by Fergusons Shipyard. She was going to be another level of complexity and development beyond anything we had seen before. She weighed in at over 2,200 tons and was over 80 metres in length. My friend and namesake who had stood by the building of the *Minna* from 2002 to 2004 had also stood by the building of the *Jura*, so I knew that she was going to have some good practical features in areas which he was able to influence. I was not disappointed when I arrived there and it was obvious that both he and his opposite engineering number had worked extremely hard to do an outstanding job. There were signs of logical and practical input everywhere.

I immediately loved the *Jura* because I wanted to, for it had been her predecessor which had brought me into fisheries. I had been the last Commander of the old *Jura* and now I would be the first Commander of the new one, an honour I shared with my old colleague and chum who was six years my junior as a substantive commander, although he came into the fisheries not long after me. There would be two separate crews to permit trip on trip off working, and whilst this was a lovely way to go to sea, I always missed the autonomy of having my own, unique, command. However, my partner was a good man to work with and we jointly set up our operations centre in an old set of offices in the shipyard complex. It was pretty primitive but we soon scrounged, purchased and installed bits of equipment and facilities which made it more pleasant. There can be fewer more depressing places than a Clydeside ship-building yard in November, in lashing rain with muddy puddles, but we had some of our officers with us and soon had them installing planning boards, ship's plans, leave rotas, check lists and all the other tools of management we required, and of course computers.

I was very pleased with the *Jura*. Inevitably there had been some disagreement between the shipyard and our management but I felt that between them they had managed to build something which was very worthwhile. I tended to walk about with a smile on my face and the tradesmen noticed it. I unashamedly told them I thought they were building an excellent ship, and I for one could not wait to take her to sea. This seemed to cheer some of them up, for they were oft-times quite glum, aware of the tension between owner and shipbuilder, perhaps.

We started gathering as crews when the building process was coming to an end and it would soon be time for sea trials, firstly the builder's trials then owner's trials; so in late December 2005 and January 2006 we started to find out what the *Jura* was made of. Of course there were problems to overcome, but in the main I could see she was going to be a great ship.

From a manoeuvring point of view we could not have asked for more; with a Becker rudder on a single propeller, an omnidirectional forward thruster which, when set to drive forward could actually propel the ship at about three knots, and a stern thruster, we were very adequately served. What I was less impressed by was the absence of stabilising fins, for she relied on stability tanks, and the size of the anchors and both of these areas would prove problematical in the future. For carrying out boardings we had two magnificent twenty four foot Pacific boats, one on each side of the ship, launched from Neddeck davits which were a further development of the Caley Davit principle. When I thought back to the days of the old *Norna*, we had come a long way.

I have retained many of my voyage notes for the first year, giving a day by day account of my experience of the *Jura*, and I can see that at one point I had to adopt the same mental attitude I had on the *Morven*, as we lurched from one problem to another. We were constantly trying to become familiar with her and build up a working knowledge and understanding of her; and some of this learning process could be quite challenging, involving blackouts, when we lost all power, or failure of different parts of the plant. One day, I forget when, but I remember there was a strong Northerly breeze blowing off the Cock of Arran as we cruised round the top of that island, we were left without power. We were a few miles off the Cock but the *Jura* carried a lot of windage and started to set very quickly onto the land. I phoned down to the Chief Engineer and asked him for the forward thruster. This Chief was one of the smartest fellows you could meet and a brilliant diagnostic engineer so it did not take him long to work out a means of getting power to the big thruster. He got it going and I deployed it none too soon, for the land was becoming much too clear in the bright sunshine. Sure enough, I was able to bring her head to wind then start to make way through the water till we got up to Ardlamont Shelf, where we dropped the anchor. Manoeuvring was easy with the two thrusters and I began to realise the potential of this gear. We could not get main propulsion, so we hove up the anchor, and I took her up the Clyde on the thruster alone. It was no problem. We anchored at the Tail of the Bank and I think Rolls Royce came out to the ship to repair the control system. That was the problem with complex computer controlled equipment, something very small could affect the whole installation.

What comes out loud and clear during this first year is, we were focussing on working the *Jura* up into an efficient unit, and the fisheries had to take a back seat. We had so many areas which required attention at once, that every minute of the day was filled and there was always something else importuning us with pressing need. Sometimes we were glad to get back home in one piece for the constant need for vigilance was very wearing, and one never came back to the ship as one left it. Change was incessant and demands came thick and fast from all directions, with all the new initiatives which seemed to fill the airwaves and demand our attention. I would find myself thinking back to the days before computers, when we went to sea with a few foolscap notebooks to manage the ship, and sailed away to patrol the frontiers; life was simpler then, and much more exciting, from the point of view of catching offenders. You see, when the satellite monitoring came in, we knew what was at sea and exactly where they were, and the element of surprise and interest as we hove over the horizon was removed. We could 'target' vessels, or rather the Operations Room could, and that was an element which I could see would develop at the expense of our autonomy as commanders. I began to think about retiring.

The Chief Executive was keen to show off his new ship, and gave us several opportunities to do just that. One of the earliest ones saw us finishing up in Scrabster after a short cruise with a few people on board with his opposite number from England, I think. I was just berthing her on the quay when there was a puff of smoke from the forward ventilators and the fire alarms and bridge alarms all started sounding at once. I put on my best 'this sort of thing happens all the time face' and set about trying to berth her without the forward thruster, while being assailed by all the alarms and simultaneously organising fire control. I got her alongside by reverting to 'old style' manoeuvring and the Mate reported no fire, only lots of expensive smoke coming from our lovely big thruster. Shortly after this the Boss and his colleagues disappeared up the road to a hotel and the Chief reported that the motor of the thruster looked as if it was ruined. Some water had leaked into the motor housing from 'an impossible source' and wiped it out. So we went home without it and went back to basics.

As the first year melded into the next, I began to report to the Superintendent some of the issues which were increasingly exercising me, speaking with some real experience instead of just a 'notion'. One of my major concerns was the size of the anchors which, as far as I was concerned, were too light by about a ton. Also, I was unhappy about the length of anchor chain we had on each anchor, reckoning it should be ten or eleven shackles instead eight. This was based on my observations during the last year as I had attempted to anchor unsuccessfully in several tried and tested anchorages where we had anchored from ancient days. Once, we ended up 'dodging' in Kirkwall Bay all night in sixty knots of wind because she dragged. I had never experienced this in twenty eight years in the fisheries and was most disenchanted, and wrote about it. I thought I had been ignored, but I hear that a couple of extra shackles were added to each anchor, and Lloyds and other experts were consulted.

The other issue was the tendency she had to roll, sometimes violently. I and my opposite number on his patrols, did many experiments to see if we could alleviate this, taking experts away with us and changing ballast all over the ship. In the end we found that the stability tanks could not respond quickly enough to her rolling period and were actually contributing to the roll instead of reducing it! After I left, huge bilge keels were fitted which apparently improved the situation markedly, for they slowed the roll and allowed the tanks time to work.

A MISSION TO DENMARK

I said before that fishery cruisers seldom 'went foreign' and that was the case for most of my career, but developing relationships with our friends on the other side of the North Sea brought about new opportunities for working with other nationalities, and in March 2007 the *Jura* was required to cross into Danish waters and carry out enforcement exercises in combination with the Danish authorities. This was a tremendous opportunity for the *Jura* to spread her wings and we all rose to the occasion with enthusiasm. We had to learn new protocols and communication arrangements and start to think about operating in areas new to us. It was most exhilarating, and with the prospect of a night alongside in Esbjerg who could ask for more?

Of course, the trouble with all sea-orientated operations is they are always at the mercy of the weather and this trip to Danish waters was no exception. March that year adopted the persona of lion rather than lamb, and our wings were commensurately clipped. However, as always, we did our best and achieved a few inspections but nothing like we had hoped for. Our night in Esbjerg was beginning to evaporate under the pressure of unfulfilled aspirations when one of my seamen fell on deck and damaged his hand, requiring immediate medical treatment. Of course, one had to do one's best for the man and so I arranged to take the *Jura* into port. Once alongside, the weather began to deteriorate further and I decided to remain alongside for the night. It was a long way to come and not have a look at the place. I actually managed to go ashore alone and caught the ferry to the island of Fano, which lies close to Esbjerg. It is a lovely quaint little fishing island and I felt very at home there. With its low-lying thatched cottages and houses mostly painted a russet brown, narrow streets and quiet ambience, even during the Easter holidays, it was a place I could take to. As I wondered around absorbing the 'feel' of the place, I mused on how pleasant it would be to be a permanent tourist, and I began to think about my own life and the resolve to retire became fixed.

We sailed next day after our seaman had received treatment and got back to work, but the weather prevented us carrying out our mission and so we returned home.

VISITORS AND JUNKETS

The Atlantic Salmon Trust is an organisation which is of course interested in our work and our ability monitor all aspects of fishery protection, including 'redfish'. Accordingly, at the end of May 2007, the CEO arranged for Brigadier General Seymour Monro (son of dear old Sir Hector Monro who was so kind to me when my father died) and Dr. Richard Sheldon, both key players at that time in the Trust, to join us for the day. Interestingly, Dick Sheldon had been shipmates with my First Officer (Executive) on the old *Scotia,* when they did a salmon survey in Faroese waters years ago. Anyway, they came away with us for the day round the Forth and were persuaded that the *Jura* was able in all respects to protect anything that needed protecting. I piped the two of them off the ship when we berthed in Leith, in memory of old Sir Hector.   This provided a good test of our facilities for looking after guests, prior to the next and my last 'junket' before retiring. We were to convey a new Minister, a Cabinet Secretary and another Civil Servant to St. Kilda as part of a brief familiarisation tour on taking up their new posts. These tours were important to enable such people to appreciate the true nature of the brief they had been given, and I was all for it. After all, we would have been out there anyway and they were only observing what we did as a matter of course. We did, however, want to impress them so we 'put our best foot forward', as the Boss described it in his thank-you letter to us, and ensured that their visit was not only informative but also enjoyable. The climax of their trip was when we anchored in Village Bay, St Kilda, and sent them ashore with their own little rucksacks, compasses, maps and a nice picnic. They came back wiser and better men for the fog came down as it often does out there in summer and they briefly had to navigate back down from the from the top of Hirta, the highest point. That night I suggested to the Chief Executive that Hirta was a splendid name for the new ship we were having built in Poland, and in his non-committal way he processed the idea.

The new ship was called the *Hirta*.

Incidentally, when we were discussing the name for the *Jura*, I and quite a few others were keen on that name, for the old *Jura* was a well loved ship. 'Jura' is Norse for 'Deer' - fleet of foot, strong in heart, proud in countenance. That was how I saw her.

The last guest I carried was the marine artist, illustrator and author Michael Leek, who came to sea with us to take photographs and make sketches. Michael has written a book about marine art down through the ages, of which he kindly gifted me a copy. It is a splendid piece of work and he is an outstanding artist in his own right. He sent us CDs of all his photographs and they are of excellent quality. One of the photos he took was of the whole crew and myself, posed on the after deck, and he put it in a nice setting with two photos of the *Jura* below. I had it mounted along with some other mementoes.

And that was that. I never carried any more interesting guests on my ship for I had requested early retirement, which had kindly been granted.

Once I had made the decision to retire, I began to become very cautious about everything, erring excessively on the side of safety, partially because we were being pushed into that mindset by the avalanche of safety-orientated initiatives and regulations, but mostly because I did not want to falter at the last after forty years without a blemish on the old escutcheon. Now, anyone with even a rudimentary knowledge of the Bible will tell you that when you see the number forty you should look out, because stuff is going to happen. Usually unpleasant stuff like lots of rain and so on, as was the case with Noah. When I sent men away in the boat, I worried for their safety. When I manoeuvred the ship, I was ultra canny. When the men were on deck tying up I watched them like a hawk, until one day I realised that the Good Lord who had taken me all these miles and through all these incidents and to all these places was not about to desert me at the last. He is the same yesterday, today and forever and He does not forget His covenant. And with that I got a grip of myself, which was just as well because towards the end of 2006 we experienced some truly violent weather which culminated in us remaining alongside in Aberdeen for three days of violent storms. I retained the barograph chart of these storms to remind myself, when I had my feet up at the fireside!

RETURN TO THE CLYDE

In the late summer of 2007 I took the *Jura* up the Upper Clyde to be a feature in the Glasgow River Festival. I had last sailed out of the Clyde forty one years previously as an apprentice on the old *Mangla*, and now I was returning on my own ship the Jura. Once there had been shipyard after shipyard, building mighty vessels, with dirty, bustling, noisy industry and brown, filthy water swirling past endless slipways; now there were trees everywhere, and they tell me salmon are caught in the Clyde. There are not many cranes now, and little to remind us that this was once one of the greatest rivers in the world.

For me there was a strange cyclic element to this and it caused me to consider yet again the marvellous Providence which had ordered my goings out and comings in. By this time I had grown out of my vexatious forebodings but I still kept a wary eye on things, alert to the unexpected.

LAST PATROL

On my last patrol, in October 2007, we were dodging up in the Shetlands in yet another severe gale and I suddenly had the same feeling I experienced all those years ago in Lamlash harbour, on the *Morven*. A sense that something was about to happen. I had hardly formed the thought when PAN PAN, PAN PAN, PAN PAN burst over the airwaves. A fishing vessel had broken down on the way to the Yell Sound in the north westerly gale we were sheltering from and was being blown towards the land. I could not believe it! However, I called the Coastguard offering our services, and was asked to proceed. I passed the word that we were in action and prepared to build up to maximum speed. We raced towards the southern entrance to the Yell Sound and as we made the approach to the navigational channel the VHF broke into life again. '*Jura Jura Jura*, this is Shetland Coastguard, we have the Coastguard tug, which is closer than you, proceeding to the casualty. You will not be required, Captain.' So I said 'Thanks very much' and that was that. To be frank, I was relieved, but in my mind I thought, 'Sometimes you just have to be willing; you do not always have to do it'. Or more succinctly in the Doric 'Ye needna ride gin yi saddle'.

When the weather faired a bit, I started to point the *Jura* southwards for the Orkneys with the intention of anchoring in Pierowall Roads, in the North Sound. It was one of my favourite anchorages and it would be just about the last time I would anchor in my career. We dropped anchor in time for tea, then my First Officer (Executive) said that the men wanted to see me down in the Crew's Mess, and that I should wear a tie. I duly arrived at the allotted time and they had the place all set with a lovely buffet and what have you, and some strong drink including red wine, which they invited me to sample. They were all smiling and happy and the Mate, who has a strong sense of theatre, made a special presentation. They had commissioned a Strathspey for the pipes written by a Shetland composer called Peter Woods. They had the music mounted in a frame with pictures of the old *Jura* and the new *Jura*. I was extremely touched and absolutely delighted. I was so proud of them all. I will treasure that gift always, and it is a splendid little tune. It is called 'Farewell to the Sea' or 'Soraidh Slan Leis a Chuan' in the Gaelic. The Gaelic translation was provided by one of my excellent seamen who hailed from Benbecula. Sometime after I had retired I was told he had taken his own life on his boat on which he lived. I represented the Agency at the funeral in Benbecula and played the pipes as we carried his body down to lay him in the sand of the machair overlooking a stormy Atlantic on which we had spent so many years. I spoke at the funeral to a packed congregation to let them know how much I valued him as a seaman and as a man. I had to tell them that he had just run into a storm in his mind and had not been able either to heave to or to put about and run before it. They were mostly seamen and understood me fine. His people were the kindest folk imaginable. They presented me with his fob watch as a memento, and offered me their hospitality - always. Maybe someday I will return to the Hebrides.

From the anchorage in Orkney we set off south for home, for the last time stopping briefly, I think, at Gardenstown where my mother lived, then on to the Forth. I think we anchored that night for old times' sake, and I mulled over the fact that this would be the last time I would take a ship into Leith, wondering how it would go on the morrow.

The day dawned bright and not too breezy and we embarked the pilot as arranged. Now, I did not want or need a pilot, but every ship over 80 metres was required by the port regulations to take one or the master had to sit his pilot's licence, which I had neither time nor inclination for. I wondered how many times I had taken ships in and out of Leith without pilots, in all weathers including storms. I had the steward give the pilot a cup of coffee and asked him to have a seat while I berthed my ship. It was an absurd rule for us to follow, but it was par for the course in this crazy rule-ridden world. I knew I would not miss that aspect of life at sea. I lined the *Jura* up for the leading lights, carefully gauging the effect of wind and tide, and started down the fairway for the last time. I tried to start the forward bow thruster, and nothing happened! So she was going to try me to the last. I mentally readjusted my plan and pressed on for the locks. We slipped in past the big circular fender at just the right distance and speed, sedately making our way up the lock till I laid her gently alongside. That was the easy bit, for there was a westerly breeze holding her on to the lock wall, and she carried a lot of windage not unlike the first time I took the *Westra* to sea. Getting off would be the challenge. Of course, I had told the Chief as soon as the defect was discovered and he was racing about trying to repair it. I stood on the bridge wing and watched the level change in the dock, wondering if my last berthing was going to go badly, and silently asking God to help the Chief. I think the Chief and I simultaneously remembered that the Second Engineer had changed the bulbs on the buttons before arrival. He checked the STOP button and sure enough one edge had jammed down under the casing, thereby making a start impossible. He started up the thruster; the lock gates opened and I was able to berth her with all the facilities available, at Ocean Terminal, just ahead of the Royal Yacht *Britannia*. It was 4 October 2007. I rang the Finished With Engines button for the last time, and brought to an end forty one years of seafaring.

Patsy, my lovely, faithful wife came down to collect me and all my gear which filled a cubic metre stores crate! I do not know how I managed to accumulate all that stuff but I always made my ships a home from home, so maybe that was it. Added to this were the many presents which my crew had generously given me. Books, an engraved compass from my Second Officer, videos, DVDs and many other kind tokens of friendship, and of course my framed Strathspey.

I then handed over to my fellow Captain for the last time.

As I stood hanging around on the bridge talking to him I happened to look down onto the quay in time to see some of my family slinking along, trying to keep out of sight. Patsy had organised all the available children to attend! Esther, Hannah, Becky, Jenny, Joe and David. Martin was not able to get away from his work and Patricia had to look after her children. It was most unexpected and delightful to have them there to share the moment, and prevented me from becoming maudlin.

We then set off for home, where Patsy had organised a family welcome party with photos of all my old ships up on the walls. The pièce de résistance was when she presented me with our air tickets for a trip to Rome. We had promised ourselves this trip all our married life and now we were going. It was a truly wonderful home-coming.

Our trip to Rome surpassed all my expectations and we saw and did things we had only dreamt of. It was such a kind thing for her to arrange, and we will never forget it.

We were not quite finished with the Scottish Fisheries. We were invited to attend a retirement party in my honour on 25 October 2007 on board the *Jura*. Again as many of my family as could manage attended, with Jenny, Becky and Peter my son in law, Hannah, Martin, Joe and David being able to be present. So many old colleagues from sea and the office attended, I felt very honoured. I was presented with an engraved barometer from the Agency and there was still over three hundred pounds left over for a cheque with which I would buy a reclining chair.

There is something really satisfying about retirement parties if you have enjoyed a happy employment. People say nice things about you, so much so that it is like attending your own funeral. I thoroughly enjoyed it. The Boss made a lovely speech and sent me a letter which I am re-producing now:

I am writing to thank you for your exceptional contribution to the operation of the Scottish Fisheries Protection Agency and indeed to the fleet's activities when under the auspices of DAFS.

The manner in which you hosted many events and functions on behalf of the SFPA on your ships, from the old Jura to the new and all in between was invariably exemplary. For me personally it was always a great pleasure to witness your unique style at first hand when I accompanied you on these occasions.

Your efforts have undoubtedly raised the profile of the Agency since its inception and played a major role in its development to its present state of vastly improved efficiency and effectiveness.

You have always placed great store in looking after the interests of those under your command.

You made the difference when needed and many people both afloat and ashore have progressed and prospered in the wake of your tutelage.

After forty one years at sea, of which twenty one were in command, your wish to retire was well understood. However I suspect prospects of a 'well earned rest' as such are slight given your many and varied interests, not least those involving your lovely family.

Many on the marine side have commented that your retirement marks the end of an era, which is a sure indication of the esteem in which you are held.

On behalf of everyone in the Agency I wish you and your family well for your retirement and look forward to seeing you again in the not too distant future, hopefully at the commissioning of the Hirta when she enters service next year.

Chief Executive.

There were kind wishes and meaningful messages from other colleagues from the office, away at sea or building the new ship in Poland. Good friends one and all, with whom I had shared so many experiences. I felt and feel very close to them all.

333

The last word however must go to our raconteur Chief Steward. I mentioned his ability to write humorously: here is what he wrote;

The SFPA will be a blander place after today, as one of our genuinely colourful characters retires. No more will the skirl of the pipes be heard resonating from the bridge, like a vacuum cleaner being skinned alive, scaring the wits out of every seagull in the North Sea. The dumbbells in the gym will have a well-deserved rest from their gruelling afternoon workout, and the 'Bing Bong' will fall silent, leaving the crew rudderless without their daily bulletin and weather forecast. People looked forward to these broadcasts with as much excitement as they tune into Radio 4 for The Archers.
A natural leader, you always steered a true course and ran a tight ship! (Not so tight after the drink and drug policy was introduced). Always cheery with a friendly smile for all, your great enthusiasm will be missed, and your innovations, like the tartan carpet you procured for the Norna saloon, which was such a conversation piece! Second Mates will have to give up carpentry, plumbing and tiling, and return to the 12/4 watch and boring old navigation. There were no idle hands for the devil to employ when he was on the bridge! Everyone was encouraged to take up a second career option. I personally had the pleasure of sailing with you on three occasions, the first time on the ill fated Switha, when we were young and fit and had things like hair and teeth. Later we sailed together on the Jura, more mature then, but still pretty lively; and finally our paths crossed on the Norna, when we were both clapped out. On every encounter you were never anything less than a gentleman, and always more than just a Captain.
It is a sad day indeed when someone as large as Captain David Beveridge, affectionately known to all and sundry as DLB, retires. The Fisheries will be poorer for his departure, but I am sure he won't be sitting on his laurels; you can't keep a good man down, and with your love of your family and church I'm sure you will be kept very busy. If you ever find yourself at a loose end, just remember there is a new career waiting for you at B&Q, and with your bus pass in your pocket the world is your lobster! On behalf of the Captain and his crew on the Minna, we would like to take this opportunity to wish you a long and happy retirement. Lang may yer lum reek!

I think this tribute was amongst my favourites and was glad that he felt moved to apply his wit to my departure.

So here I am putting the final touches to this account after five years of retirement. It has only taken me about six months to write it and it has flowed easily enough. In some ways I think I have been writing it all my life. My next task is to write an account of our family starting in the present and working back in time, as far as I can, but that will be an altogether more difficult task.

I have no idea how I ever found time to go to sea. Life is so busy. So much has happened since the retirement, not the least of which has been the birth of another five wonderful grandchildren, to bring the current total to eight (with another on the way). I cannot recount all the blessings we enjoy as a family, for they are beyond number. I will forever bless the day I threw my lot in with the Lord Jesus Christ and trusted in Him, and I will give Him the glory for any good that I ever did.

I am glad to say I did manage to keep sufficient water under the keel!

Captain David Littlejohn Beveridge
Gardenstown, Aberdeenshire and Glasgow,
September 2012

GLOSSARY

Ballast – Weight added, usually to the bottom of a ship to increase stability by lowering the Centre of Gravity. Ballast can be either solid of liquid. It can take the form of e.g. concrete, pig iron or stones, or more commonly in modern ships, water, either salt or fresh.

Barque – A sailing vessel rigged with three or more masts the aftermost one of which is rigged with fore and aft sails, all other sails being square sails. It was regarded in the days of the 'windjammers' as the best compromise sail plan, as fewer crew were required than on fully rigged ships, where all the sails were square sails with the exception of the 'spanker'.

Bilge – The area of the ship or boat where the sides curve into the bottom. Bilges are usually rounded like a radius on ocean going ships but there are many examples of bilges which are simply formed by welding or riveting the side to the bottom with no attempt to 'fashion' the plating. Even in wooden, fibre glass or concrete construction the bilge can be 'unfashioned' and little attempt made to give the bilge a pleasing form. The term is also used to describe the inside compartments of the bottom of the ship where the sides meet the bottom. These areas are called the 'bilges' where water and other liquids collect, necessitating pumping out.

Bitts– Two very strong posts usually formed as a pair either by casting or welding to provide a means to secure ropes and wires for mooring the vessel and other securing purposes.

Bosun– A contraction of 'Boat Swain'. The Bosun is the petty officer in charge of organising the deck crew under the Mate (Chief Officer).

Breasthook – A triangular piece of wood or metal which is inserted at the bow, to provide strength in the area where the two sides of the vessel are joined.

Bulkhead - A transverse wall inside a ship or boat. It can be watertight or otherwise.

Clinker-built– A type of wooden construction in boat building whereby the edge of the upper plank overlaps the lower giving the hull a 'ridged' appearance. The other common method of construction is 'carvel' wherein the planks are laid edge to edge with no overlap and so a smooth finish is achieved.

Derrick–A guyed spar which is used as a lifting device. The 'derrick head' is supported by a 'topping lift' which is a wire used to raise the derrick head. This wire is led through a block mounted at the top of the 'derrick post' or other strong point to provide a lifting point for the derrick head. This wire is usually hauled by a winch then 'made fast' on a 'cleat' or set of bitts. The 'runner' is a wire which passes through a pulley block mounted on the underside of the derrick head and led through another block or pulley at the 'foot' of the derrick. This is also controlled by a winch. The derrick itself can swing on the pivot point at its foot called the 'gooseneck'. The guys are usually comprised of a wire 'pennant' and a tackle for adjusting the position of the derrick head. There are many ways to rig a derrick to enhance its lifting capacity.

Downhaul– A rope or set of ropes for hauling down or securing a sail or spar.

Focsle – A contraction of the descriptive phrase 'Forward Castle'. In early sailing vessels the ends of the vessel were raised as 'castles' to permit fighting. There is no 'after castle' today as after end of the ship is called the 'Poop' on British ships.

Gantline– A manila rope of about 2.5 inch circumference used in rigging a 'Bosun's Chair' or 'Stage' for working aloft singly, in the case of the chair or in pairs with a stage.

Halyard – A lightweight piece of cordage usually referring to the ropes to which flags are attached for raising and lowering. The halyard is 'rove' or 'riven' through a halyard block or pulley attached to the top of the mast.

Hawser – A term usually applied to a mooring rope or heavy pulling rope, such as a 'Towing Hawser'.

Lugsail – A 'free footed' sail of trapezoidal shape usually fitted to smaller sailing craft such as fishing vessels like 'Zulus' 'Fifies' and 'Scaffies'in Scotland and ships lifeboats. At one time it was very common in European waters. It took several forms such as the 'Standing lugsail' the position of which was not altered from one 'tack' to the other, or the 'Dipping lugsail' in which the yard of the sail was 'dipped' onto the other side of the mast with a change of 'tack'.

Sextant – A nautical instrument used to measure angles either of the angular altitude of heavenly bodies or objects above the horizon, or angles between objects such as lighthouses. Its arc is a sixth part of a circle hence 'sextant'.

Wheelhouse – Descriptive term for the place where the ship's steering wheel is mounted. At one time the wheelhouse was separate from the 'Chartroom' and the 'Bridge-wings' but in modern vessels they tend to be incorporated into one large space. The whole is now referred to as the 'Bridge', although bridge-wings are still common today.

Ship	Type	Built	Company	Rank
Mangla	Cargo Liner	1959 Port Glasgow	T&J Brocklebank	Apprentice
Maturata	Cargo Liner	1955 Port Glasgow	T&J Brocklebank	Apprentice
Lucellum	Tanker (Products)	1958	H.E.Moss & Co	Apprentice
Lucigen	Tanker (Products)	1962	H.E.Moss & Co	Apprentice
Mahronda	Cargo Liner	1947	T&J Brocklebank	Third Mate
Mahronda	Tanker (Products)	1947	T&J Brocklebank	Third Mate
Luxor	Cargo Liner	1960	H.E.Moss & Co	Third Mate
Port Victor	Cargo Liner		Port Line	Third Mate
Lucigen	Tanker (Products)	1943 Clydebank	H.E.Moss & Co	Third Mate
Luxor	Tanker (Products)	1962	H.E.Moss & Co	Chief Mate
Lustrous	Tanker (Products)	1960	H.E.Moss & Co	Chief Mate
Lumen	Tanker (Products)	1968 Sweden	H.E.Moss & Co	Chief Mate
Lumiere	Tanker (Products)	1971 Sweden	H.E.Moss & Co	Chief Mate
Lustrous	Tanker (Products)	1972 Sweden	H.E.Moss & Co	Chief Mate
Luminous	Tanker (Products)	1968 Sweden	H.E.Moss & Co	Chief Mate
Lucellum	Tanker (Products and crude)	1968 Sweden	H.E.Moss & Co	Chief Mate
ACT3	Container Ship	1975 Luzon Canada	ACT (Cunard)	Chief Mate
ACT6	Container Ship	1971 Vegesak Germany	ACT (Cunard)	Chief Mate
ACT2	Container Ship	1972 Vegesak Germany	ACT (Cunard)	Chief Mate
Vigilant	Fishery Protection	1935 Dumbarton	DAFS	Second Officer
Switha	Fishery Protection	1948 Selby	DAFS	Second Officer
Westra	Fishery Protection	1975 Aberdeen	DAFS	Second Officer
Jura	Fishery Protection	1973 Aberdeen	DAFS	First Officer
Scotia	Research Stern Trawler	1971 Port Glasgow	DAFS	Second Officer
Westra	Fishery Protection	1975 Aberdeen	DAFS	First Officer
Scotia	Research Vessel	1971 Port Glasgow	DAFS	Junior First Officer
Westra	Fishery Protection	1975 Aberdeen	DAFS	Skipper (First Officer)
Morven	Fishery Protection	1983 Isle of Wight	DAFS	Junior First Officer
Jura	Fishery Protection	1973 Aberdeen	DAFS	Officer in Charge
Scotia	Research Stern Trawler	1971 Port Glasgow	DAFS	Junior First Officer
Jura	Fishery Protection	1973 Aberdeen	DAFS	Senior First Officer
Vigilant	Fishery Protection	1982 Port Glasgow	DAFS	Commander
Norna	Fishery Protection	1959 Dumbarton	DAFS	Commander
Jura	Fishery Protection	1973 Aberdeen	DAFS	Commander
Sulisker	Research Stern Trawler	1981 Port Glasgow	DAFS	Commander
Scotia	Fishery Protection	1971 Port Glasgow	DAFS	Commander
Norna	Fishery Protection	1988 Lowestoft	DAFS	Commander
Vigilant	Fishery Protection	1982 Port Glasgow	DAFS	Commander
Westra	Fishery Protection	1975 Aberdeen	DAFS/SFPA	Commander
Vigilant	Fishery Protection	1982 Port Glasgow	SFPA	Commander
Norna	Fishery Protection	1988 Lowestoft	SFPA	Commander
Jura	Fishery Protection	2005 Port Glasgow	SFPA	Commander

45. Norna west of Shetland (SFPA Aircraft Crew)

46. Harvest Reaper aground (Rescue Helicopter Crew)

47. Norna about to tow Harvest Reaper (Rescue Helicopter Crew)

48. Norna passing towline to Harvest Reaper (Rescue Helicopter Crew)

49. New Jura at Sea (Michael Leek)

50. New Jura at Sea (Michael Leek)

51. Pacific 24 (Michael Leek)

52. DLB - scaring the seagulls (Michael Leek)

53. Time to retire (Michael Leek)

54. DLB's Crew on the new Jura (Michael Leek)

55. Houses in Fano Island, Denmark (DLB)

56. Houses in Fano Island, Denmark (DLB)

57. Our children Left to right
Jenny,Tisha,Joe,Martin,David,Hannah,Esther,Becky. (Patsy
Beveridge)

58. DLB on Fair Isle (Mark Lockwood – Jura collection)

59. Heading for St. Kilda (Michael Leek 2007)

60. Stac Lee – St. Kilda (Michael Leek 2007)

61. Approaching St. Kilda (Michael Leek 2007)

62. Jura in Village Bay St. Kilda (Michael Leek 2007)

63. Fulmar Petrel (Michael Leek 2007)

64. Jura dead calm North Atlantic (Michael Leek 2007)

65. Boarding a Dutch super trawler (Michael Leek 2007)

66. Returning to Jura (Michael Leek 2007)

67. Launching Pacific 24 (Michael Leek 2007)

68. Pacific 24 housed in telehead (Michael Leek 2007)

69. Pacific 24 being recovered (Michael Leek 2007)

70. Sula Sgeir (Michael Leek 2007)

71. Jura's focsle at St. Kilda (Michael Leek 2007)

72. Jura alongside in Stornoway (Michael Leek 2007)

73. Sunset beams North Atlantic (Michael Leek 2007)

74. St Kilda (Michael Leek 2007)

75. Sula Sgeir – crabber ' Boy Shane' (Michael Leek 2007)

76. Bringing the boat back (Michael Leek 2007)

77. Jura in Fair Isle Channel with SFPA plane (2006 Vigilant collection)

78. Vigilant in Fair Isle Channel (2006 Jura collection)

79. Vigilant in Fair Isle Channel with SFPA plane (2006 Jura collection)

80. Jura in Fair Isle Channel with SPFA plane (2006 Vigilant collection)

81. Norna 2004 from SFPA plane (SFPA aircraft observer)

82. Fladdens Lighthouse 2003 (Norna collection)

83. Norna at the Fladdens 2003 (Norna collection)

84. David and Patsy